WITHDRAWN

HISTORY AND STRATEGY

ADVANCES IN STRATEGIC MANAGEMENT

Series Editor: Brian S. Silverman

Recent Volumes:

ADVANCES IN STRATEGIC MANAGEMENT   VOLUME 29

HISTORY AND STRATEGY

EDITED BY

STEVEN J. KAHL
*Tuck School of Business, Dartmouth College,
New Hampshire, USA*

BRIAN S. SILVERMAN
*Rotman School of Management,
University of Toronto, Canada*

MICHAEL A. CUSUMANO
*Massachusetts Institute of Technology,
Sloan School of Management, USA*

Emerald

United Kingdom – North America – Japan
India – Malaysia – China

Emerald Group Publishing Limited
Howard House, Wagon Lane, Bingley BD16 1WA, UK

First edition 2012

British Library Cataloguing in Publication Data
A catalogue record for this book is available from the British Library

ISBN: 978-1-78190-024-6
ISSN: 0742-3322 (Series)

ISOQAR certified
Management Systems,
awarded to Emerald for
adherence to Quality
and Environmental
standards ISO 9001:2008
and 14001:2004,
respectively

ISOQAR
REGISTERED

UKAS
MANAGEMENT
SYSTEMS

0026

Certificate Number 1985
ISO 9001
ISO 14001

INVESTOR IN PEOPLE

CONTENTS

**PART III: ANALYTIC NARRATIVES:
HISTORICAL NARRATIVE MEETS ECONOMIC
AND SOCIOLOGICAL THEORY**

LIST OF CONTRIBUTORS

Michael A. Cusumano	Sloan School of Management, Massachusetts Institute of Technology, Cambridge, MA, USA
Shane Greenstein	Kellogg School of Management, Northwestern University, Evanston, IL, USA
Paul Ingram	Columbia Business School, Columbia University, New York, NY, USA
Steven J. Kahl	Tuck School of Business, Dartmouth College, Hanover, NH, USA
Matthias Kipping	Schulich School of Business, York University, Toronto, ON, Canada
Ryan Lampe	Department of Economics, DePaul University, Chicago, IL, USA
Huseyin Leblebici	College of Business, University of Illinois at Urbana-Champaign, Champaign, IL, USA
Gregory J. Liegel	Department of Sociology, The University of Chicago, Chicago, IL, USA
Christopher McKenna	Said Business School, University of Oxford, Oxford, UK
Petra Moser	Department of Economics, Stanford University, Stanford, CA, USA
Johann Peter Murmann	Australian School of Business, University of New South Wales, Sydney, NSW, Australia; Wharton School, University of Pennsylvania, Philadelphia, PA, USA
Damon J. Phillips	Columbia Business School, Columbia University, New York, NY, USA

Hayagreeva Rao	Graduate School of Business, Stanford University, Stanford, CA, USA
Brian S. Silverman	Rotman School of Management, University of Toronto, Toronto, ON, Canada
Gerarda Westerhuis	Research Institute for History and Culture, Utrecht University, Utrecht, Netherlands
JoAnne Yates	Sloan School of Management, Massachusetts Institute of Technology, Cambridge, MA, USA

THE INTEGRATION OF HISTORY AND STRATEGY RESEARCH

Historical research has played a prominent role in the evolution of the strategy literature. Alfred Chandler's history of the development of new administrative forms and the ensuing argument that structure follows strategy has played a central role in the development of strategy as a field. His 1962 book, *Strategy and Structure*, remains one of the most cited manuscripts within strategy. Detailed histories of technology evolution, dating as far back as Gilfillan's (1935) study of the introduction of steamships, have helped form theories of technological strategy and industry evolution. However, while historical work often is cited within strategy research, historical articles themselves remain underrepresented in contemporary strategy journals.

There may be several reasons for this. While there may be general agreement that good theory embodies generality, parsimony, precision, and explanatory power, historians and strategists tend to favor different aspects. Historians place more weight on explanatory power and details, but strategists tend to favor generality and different types of evidence. Moreover, the craft of doing historical research is different from common forms of quantitative and qualitative strategy research. Historians tend to write books, not journal-length articles. This work, in turn, evokes different norms of evaluation. Historians base their insights on interpretation of deep archival or interview research as opposed to showing their raw data for evaluation from others, as is the norm in social sciences. However, historical analysis has thrived within other disciplines that play a prominent role in strategic research, such as economics and sociology. This is even more puzzling considering that economics and sociology share some of the same conventions as strategy research.

In this volume, we explore the linkages between historical analysis and strategy research. In the introduction, we begin to postulate how history and strategy research can inform each other. The chapters in this volume illustrate how historical analysis can be done within the field of strategy.

WHAT IS HISTORICAL RESEARCH?

Historical analysis is more than just recognition that it is important to understand the context of the phenomenon being studied or the process of change and institutional development. Rather, historical analysis is a research discipline in its own right, with some theoretical aspirations and assumptions built in. Typically, the historical method involves a deep dive into a small number of cases or phenomena and their evolution over a period of time. Data come from archival research focusing on written artifacts (published and unpublished documents of some kind), possibly supplemented by interviews if the topic is recent enough. The goal is usually to be inductive, not deductive – that is, to have some general idea of what to study but then to let the "facts" or "data" speak, rather than use facts, data, or case examples to illustrate a particular theory. It follows that the practice of doing historical research is based more in the narrative tradition – telling "his story" – in the sense that it uses this data as input to explain what happened, and how and why it happened, as opposed to analyzing data to unearth general principles that explain strategic behavior. To the extent that historians do make more general claims, they use multiple case studies or large sets of descriptive data.

Chandler again provides a useful model for understanding the variety possible in historical research topics and methods as well as the contributions to strategy. His first book, *Strategy and Structure*, involves a detailed analysis and comparison of four companies, du Pont, General Motors, Standard Oil (current Exxon-Mobil), and Sears, followed by a broader analysis of the diffusion of this new structure. His 1977 book, *The Visible Hand*, which won the Pulitzer Prize, focuses not on case studies but more on broad themes in the evolution of modern management practice since the mid-19th century, such as the revolutions in transportation and communication, and in mass production and mass distribution. Chandler's (1994) book, *Scale and Scope*, is at yet another level of analysis, using nation-level statistics and case studies to illustrate how scale and scope (the size and breadth of firms) played different roles in the evolution of capitalism and multinational firms in the United States compared to Great Britain and Germany.

Like many fields, history has a variety of units of analysis – people, countries, and time periods. Those most common to strategy research include firms, industries, and technologies in which historians seek to explain such things as emergence or decay, success or failure, and diffusion or rejection of particular practices or philosophies of management and competition. More

Table 1. Examples of Historical Research for Prevalent Strategic Topics.

Strategy Topic	Historical Examples
Strategy and structure	Chandler (1962, 1994)
Resource-based view	Chandler (1962)
Dynamic capabilities	Cusumano, Mylonadis, & Rosenbloom (1992)
Industry evolution	Jones (2010), Khaire (forthcoming), Kipping and Engwell (2002), McKenna (2006), Murmann (2003)
Technology strategy	Cusumano and Selby (1995), David (1985), Gilfillan (1935), Hughes (1983), Moser (2005), Mowery (1984), Nicholas (2003)
Diffusion	Fischer (1994), Kirsch (2002), Yates (2005)
Behavioral strategy	Bingham and Kahl (forthcoming)
Strategic process	Chandler (1962)
Strategic leadership	Tedlow (2010)

recently, this list has expanded to include emerging strategic topics in psychology and behavior. For instance, Bingham and Kahl (forthcoming) analyze how the insurance industry's cognitive schema of the computer emerged. Table 1 identifies examples of historical research for prevalent strategic topics. While certainly not exhaustive, this table is revealing in the sense that, while there is a concentration of historical research in technology and industry evolution, other core strategic topics such as the resource-based view of the firm and dynamic capabilities, or the strategy decision-making process, do not seem to have attracted a commensurate level of historical research. Or, at least, not many historians come readily to mind who are working in these areas.

HOW CAN HISTORICAL ANALYSIS AND STRATEGY RESEARCH INFORM EACH OTHER?

While historians themselves may strive to be atheoretical, one important way historical analysis informs strategy research is in the development of theory. While the small N and the context dependent nature of history limits its ability to produce generalizable principles, history can leverage this characteristic to help extend or test existing theory. In particular, historical analysis can identify anomalies to existing theory which help identify existing limitations and boundaries. For example, Paul David (1985) challenged existing stochastic and economic theories of technological competition through his analysis of the adoption of the QWERTY keyboard configuration. He concluded, "I believe there are many more QWERTY worlds out there in the past, on the very edges of the modern economic analyst's tidy universe; worlds we do not yet fully perceive or understand, but whose influence, like that of dark stars, extends nonetheless to shape the visible orbits of our contemporary economic affairs" (David, 1985, p. 336).

Historical analysis also highlights the role of temporality and context. While much research in strategy is longitudinal in design, most studies simply factor time and change into their analysis. In contrast, history places how the process unfolds front and center in its analysis, which can add insight into how the patterns of change and underlying mechanisms influence strategic outcomes. This more nuanced treatment of time and sequence of events is particularly important as strategy research moves toward more dynamic models of strategic behavior. For example, dynamic capabilities have recently emerged as a framework to explain a firm's competitive advantage. Central to this view is the notion of patterned activity within firms and change (hence the term, "dynamic"). Much of the strategy research simply identifies different kinds of capabilities and then focuses on the strategic effects of these capabilities. In this case, historical analysis would be helpful not only to explain where these capabilities come from, but also to address how the temporal sequences and the setting of patterns influence these outcomes as well.

Finally, historical analysis can provide insights into the paths not taken. Performance is a common dependent variable within much of strategy research, which requires having some variation in performance outcomes. However, most studies focus on explaining success such that the common statistical models explaining variation implicitly assume the factors that explain higher performance outcomes also explain poorer outcomes. With the notable exception of innovation studies, failure is rarely isolated and explored. One of the values of historical analysis is that it also addresses what could have happened and does not presume that what explains what did happen also explains what did not happen.[1]

In return, the field of strategy is rich in different theories of competitive advantage that isolate different kinds of explanatory variables, ranging from environmental conditions to firm-level resources and capabilities to strategic implementation. The variables, in turn, can help historians make their historical analysis be more theoretically informed. A great example of this kind of approach is Padgett and Ansell's (1993) historical analysis of the Medici family's rise to power in Italy. This analysis draws from social network theory to inform how it unearths data and develops its explanation of this historical event.

Methodologically, strategy also offers more quantitative techniques that can be applied to historical research. Just because history embraces the narrative tradition does not mean that it cannot incorporate quantitative analysis. Quantitative analysis, ranging from descriptive statistics of key explanatory variables to regression analysis, can provide additional evidence for an historical explanation as well as sharpen its precision. This quantitative approach is more prevalent in economic historical analysis (e.g., see Nicholas, 2003), but it could be applied to a wider variety of historical analysis. In this volume, Kahl, Liegel, and Yates (2012) use frequency counts to demonstrate the differences in interpretation of the computer between the insurance industry and manufacturing. Phillips (2012) uses historically informed regression analysis in his study of the long-term success of "orphaned" jazz music.

STRUCTURE OF THIS VOLUME

This volume presents work at the intersection of history and strategy. The studies cover a wide range of phenomena, from the cultural longevity of pre-Depression jazz songs to the propagation of wireless technology in the early 21st century. The studies apply a wide range of theoretical lenses to phenomena, including institutional entrepreneurship, industrial organization, political theory, and nascent approaches to business models. The studies also exploit a wide range of empirical methods, from single-case study through large-sample statistical estimation, as well as offering varied views on roadmaps for conducting and facilitating research in history and strategy. We believe that this broad spectrum of studies serves to indicate the plethora of opportunities to integrate historical and strategy methods.

Part I: History, Strategy, and Innovation

Greenstein (2012) studies the recent development of Wi-Fi technology in the United States. He describes how the rapid development of Wi-Fi was driven in "bottom-up" fashion; after basic performance standards were set by technical committees, numerous firms conducted economic experiments to determine what types of wireless-related products would be demanded by the market, and at what prices. Of particular interest, he notes that the Federal Communications Commission rarely allows for such bottom-up development of communications technologies that require spectrum. The wireless case appears to have inadvertently resulted from a surprising convergence of disparate ideologies among various FCC commissioners and a uniform belief that the frequencies used by today's wireless devices were "garbage spectrum," useful only for garage doors, baby monitors, and the like. Greenstein's analysis highlights the importance of providing "regulatory space" – that is, of not trying to impose overly restrictive regulatory rules – to allow for the institutional entrepreneurship and economic experiments that can discover new, valuable products and services. He links this both to the general sweep of history – Rosenberg's (1992) argument that decentralized economies are better able to produce innovation than centralized economies because they allow experimentation – and to specific arguments about the appropriate role of regulators in technology-intensive sectors of the economy.

In Cusumano's (2012) view, Wi-Fi would be an example of an industry platform, defined as "a foundation or core technology ... in a 'system-like' offering that increases significantly in value to users with the addition of complementary products and services" (p. 37). Cusumano explores the strategic choices available to firms that aspire to build industry platforms to create and capture value. He compares cases of successful and less-successful platform strategies in the personal computer, videocassette recorder, and consumer internet-based (e.g., iTunes) industries, and uses these to draw general lessons for development of such strategies. A key point is that although it is often beneficial to pursue a platform strategy rather than a product strategy in technology-based industries, such strategies require significant changes in mindset regarding issues such as openness of systems and the degree to which a firm cooperates rather than competes with others in its ecosystem.

Lampe and Moser (2012) study a different mechanism for cooperation versus competition in technology-based industries: "patent pools," in which member firms combine patents and collectively license them to non-members. Theoretical research on patent pools suggests that they can enhance welfare by reducing licensing-related transaction costs in industries where ownership of key technologies is distributed across numerous firms. This research also indicates that patent pool members, if left to their own devices, will prefer not to license to non-members, thus raising their private gains while reducing welfare. Yet this is difficult to study empirically because antitrust authorities have generally compelled patent pools to license. Lampe and Moser study the behavior of 20 US patent pools during a New Deal-era relaxation of compulsory licensing rules. They find that nearly 3/4 of these pools do indeed restrict licensing, thus confirming the insight of the dominant theoretical models. At the same time, they find that a nontrivial minority of pools choose to license freely during this period. Upon closer inspection, they find that pools in this minority appear to license in order to limit competition with substitute technologies. Although the licensing literature has identified this motivation before (e.g., Gallini 1984), it has rarely been extended to patent pools in the extant literature.

Together, these studies paint a vibrant picture of the utility of a combined history/strategy lens for understanding innovation. By marrying historical example and historical research methods with theoretical lenses from strategy, the chapters both inform our understanding of their specific contexts and offer potentially generalizable principles for strategy formulation, policy guidelines, and the interaction between the two.

Part II: History and Industry Evolution: Convergence, Divergence, and Institutional Background

Murmann (2012) provides an impassioned call for the marriage of history and strategy research, and proposes the establishment of a supporting institution to accomplish this. Noting fundamental differences in the "ideology" of history and strategy research – notably, strategy's search for universal laws versus history's emphasis on the importance of local context – he begins by providing some personal history as he recounts the steps by which he came to recognize the value of the historical approach. (We suspect that much of this recounting will resonate with readers' own experiences.) Murmann then lays out a compelling view of the benefits that a comparative-historical lens can bring to the study of strategy, illustrating this with examples from a cross-national comparison of the synthetic dye industry over a 60-year period. After making the case for such research, he then outlines an approach by which numerous scholars working collaboratively could facilitate such research by developing a data repository specifically designed to support longitudinal, cross-national (or cross-regional) studies of specific industries. We hope that this approach will reach fruition, and we look forward to the insights that will be generated by understanding convergence and divergence across industries and nations.

Divergence does not occur only at the industry or nation/region level. In his study of the development of the credit card industry, Leblebici (2012) explores within-industry divergence at the level of the business model. Leblebici describes how the first wave of credit card providers, beginning with Diners Club and including American Express, relied on a "closed" business model in which all activities (billing, payment, authorization, settlement, marketing, etc.) were handled by a single nonbank firm. As regulatory restrictions on banks loosened and as information technology facilitated communication across firms, new entrants Visa and MasterCard introduced a new "open" business model in which these activities were divided among firms that were joined together through a network. (This model was itself the result of a great deal of economic experimentation, some of which proved quite costly to the experimenters!) Leblebici argues that the open model was structurally superior to the closed model due to its ability to distribute incentives and firms' attention in particularly appropriate ways, and he demonstrates that the open model appears to have won the battle for market share in the United States. More generally, Leblebici frames his analysis as an explication of a broad framework for combining historical narrative and strategy theory, as well as an approach that may help operationalize the concept of the business model.

Although Murmann and Leblebici tend to emphasize divergent processes, and indeed much of strategy research focuses on the impulse to differentiate, alternate theoretical approaches such as institutional theory highlight forces that encourage convergence. One source of convergence is the consulting industry; consulting firms encourage mimetic or normative isomorphism by offering similar advice to multiple firms – in fact, one of the most profitable activities for a consulting firm is to get paid to give the same advice to client after client.[2] McKenna (2012) and Kipping and Westerhuis (2012) both explore this general issue, but with fascinating twists.

McKenna (2012) traces the evolution of management consulting services from the 1930s through the end of the 20th century. He classifies the services as falling into waves: organizational design advice, including multi-divisionalization efforts (1940s–1960s), strategic advice (1970s–1990s), and advice-as-legitimation (1990s onward). McKenna describes how each new wave was precipitated by a combination of stagnant demand for the existing services, changes to the institutional environment that opened up new opportunities, and a jockeying for position among the major firms. Thus, McKenna proposes that consulting firms both encourage isomorphic behavior among firms *and* serve as "institutional entrepreneurs" who devise new types of advice and thus spur change in clients' organization or strategy (which then becomes the new "equilibrium" to which most large firms converge).

Kipping and Westerhuis (2012) explore deeply two cases in which American consulting firms brought the multidivisional form to Dutch banks. On the surface, this appears to be a classic example of isomorphic behavior: both banks adopted the multidivisional form. However, although the two banks were similar in many respects, they adopted the multidivisional form at different times and to substantially different degrees. By comparing the archived records of these banks, including internal reports and the minutes of meetings, Kipping and Westerhuis are able to explore why the banks diverged in timing and degree of multidivisionalization even as they ostensibly succumbed to the isomorphic pressure to divisionalize. Whereas the bulk of literature on M-form adoption has focused on economic incentives or institutional isomorphism, Kipping and Westerhuis find evidence that the extent and timing of multidivisionalization was driven largely by political considerations within the banks – considerations that had little apparent connection to divisionalization. Thus they extend the extant literature, both by introducing an alternative factor that can affect the spread of organizational form and by demonstrating the importance of exploring the depth of an organizational change rather than simply whether such organizational change occurs.

Overall, these studies offer a range of approaches to considering convergence and divergence in strategy, organization, and industry evolution. They also demonstrate how strategy scholars can open significant new vistas for research by taking seriously the deviations from "average" industry effects, be they deviations in industry patterns across nations, deviations in business models within an industry, deviations in products/ services offered over time, or deviations in the degree to which firms adopt organizational innovations.

Part III: Analytic Narratives: Historical Narrative Meets Economic and Sociological Theory

Ingram, Rao, and Silverman (2012) offer a roadmap for increasing the integration of historical approaches into strategy research projects. They begin with a discussion of "what is history," comparing the research impulses of historians to those of strategy scholars to generate a typology of research approaches that situates historical research as highly complementary to "conventional" strategy research. They then ask "why do history?"

and offer examples of the benefits that come from applying a historical approach to research questions in strategy. Notably, history can provide exogenous variation and instances of change that allow tight testing and extension of strategy theory, and the historical approach to detail and inference can support the development of strong causal explanations. Finally, they discuss "how to do history." Drawing on the analytic narratives approach from economic history (Bates, Greif, Levi, Rosenthal, & Weingast, 1998), they develop a five-step roadmap for conducting research at the intersection of history and strategy. They illustrate this with a discussion of an in-process study of asset ownership and incentives in the Liverpool transatlantic shipping industry in the 18th century.

Kahl et al. (2012) employ an analytic narrative approach in their study of the mid-20th-century efforts of Edmund Berkeley to propagate the analogy of newly developed business computers as "giant brains." Berkeley was a prominent executive in the insurance industry and an early computer expert/evangelist. He undertook enormous efforts to promote the "computer as brain" metaphor. This analogy became widely accepted in the general manufacturing sector. However, despite his central role in the insurance industry, the analogy failed to take hold in that industry. Kahl et al. demonstrate that differences in the hierarchical structure of the audience – notably, the centralized structure of actuaries, accountants, and administrators in the insurance industry, versus the more decentralized structure in manufacturing – appear to explain the mixed results in analogy diffusion. More generally, their contrast of a successful and a "failed" case of institutional entrepreneurship demonstrates the power of a comparative-historical approach to advance institutional theory.

Phillips (2012) studies the success of "orphaned" products – products from startups that fail soon after production. A longstanding debate in strategy research centers on the extent to which managerial decisions affect the success of a firm or its products. Phillips exploits a historical setting to take this debate to its logical extreme: if the firm that generated a product no longer exists, then by definition its managers' postproduction actions can no longer be a factor in that product's success. Specifically, he studies the success of jazz tunes recorded during the Great Depression by start-up record companies that fail shortly after production, where success is measured by the number of cover versions subsequently recorded through the rest of the 20th century. He finds evidence (perhaps not surprisingly) that changing tastes play a key role in the long-term appeal of jazz tunes. In addition, he finds that a soon-to-be-defunct record company's decision-makers were able to influence the long-run appeal of tunes by their choice of artist and by their early marketing efforts. Overall, Phillips's study demonstrates "how strategy, history, and sociology might combine to further scholarship on the management of organizations" (p. 316).

Together, these studies demonstrate the potential power of analytic narrative, comparative-historical approaches. Theoretically, these studies show how historical research can test and extend economic, sociological, and management theory. Empirically, the examples in Ingram et al. and the methodology sections in Kahl et al. and Phillips jointly provide guideposts for scholars who are eager to incorporate analytic narrative approaches into their research.

The works in this volume provide examples of the intersection between historical analysis and strategy research. While each chapter stands on its own merits, collectively they are meant to encourage further exploration of this intersection at the methodological, theoretical, and empirical levels. Hopefully, this will lead to further integration between the disciplines and help advance both historical and strategy research agendas.

Steven J. Kahl
Brian S. Silverman
Michael A. Cusumano
Editors

NOTES

1. In a recent article in *Strategic Management Journal*, Durand and Vaara (2009) explore the potential use of counterfactuals in strategy research.

2. One of us worked for a consulting firm before earning his Ph.D. He worked for a firm that went up and down the east coast of the United States, selling the same strategy-improving project to each major port. The work was intensely boring after the first project ... but it was also immensely profitable for the firm.

REFERENCES

Bates, R. H., Greif, A., Levi, M., Rosenthal, J.-L., & Weingast, B. R. (1998). *Analytic narratives*. Princeton, NJ: Princeton University Press.

Bingham, C., & Kahl, S. (forthcoming). The process of schema emergence: Assimilation, deconstruction, unitization and the plurality of analogies. *Academy of Management Journal*.

Chandler, A. D. (1962). *Strategy and structure*. Cambridge, MA: MIT Press.

Chandler, A. D. (1977). *The visible hand*. Cambridge, MA: Harvard Press.

Chandler, A. D. (1994). *Scale and scope*. Cambridge, MA: Harvard Press.

Cusumano, M. A. (2012). Platforms versus products: Observations from the literature and history. In S. J. Kahl, B. S. Silverman & M. A. Cusumano (Eds.), *Advances in strategic management* (Vol. 29, pp. 35–67). Bingley, UK: Emerald Group.

Cusumano, M. A., Mylonadis, Y., & Rosenbloom, R. (1992). Strategic maneuvering and mass-market dynamics: The triumph of VHS over Beta. *Business History Review*, *66*, 51–94.

Cusumano, M. A., & Selby, R. W. (1995). *Microsoft secrets*. New York, NY: First Touchstone.

David, P. (1985). Clio and the economics of QWERTY. *American Economic Review*, *75*(2), 332–337.

Durand, R., & Vaara, E. (2009). Causation, counterfactuals, and competitive advantage. *Strategic Management Journal*, *30*, 1245–1264.

Fischer, C. S. (1994). *America calling: A social history of the telephone to 1940*. Berkeley, CA: University of California Press.

Gallini, N. (1984). Deterrence by market sharing: A strategic incentive for licensing. *American Economic Review*, *74*(5), 931–941.

Gilfillan, S. C. (1935). *Inventing the ship*. Chicago, IL: Follett.

Greenstein, S. (2012). Economic experiments and the development of Wi-Fi. In S. J. Kahl, B. S. Silverman & M. A. Cusumano (Eds.), *Advances in strategic management* (Vol. 29, pp. 3–33). Bingley, UK: Emerald Group.

Hughes, T. P. (1983). *Networks of power: Electrification in western society, 1880–1930*. Baltimore, MD: John Hopkins University Press.

Ingram, P., Rao, H., & Silverman, B. S. (2012). History in strategy research: What, why, and how? In S. J. Kahl, B. S. Silverman & M. A. Cusumano (Eds.), *Advances in strategic management* (Vol. 29, pp. 241–273). Bingley, UK: Emerald Group.

Jones, G. (2010). *Beauty imagined: A history of the global beauty industry*. Oxford, UK: Oxford University Press.

Kahl, S. J., Liegel, G. J., & Yates, J. (2012). Audience structure and the failure of institutional entrepreneurship. In S. J. Kahl, B. S. Silverman & M. A. Cusumano (Eds.), *Advances in strategic management* (Vol. 29, pp. 275–313). Bingley, UK: Emerald Group.

Khaire, M. (forthcoming). Context, agency, and identity: The Indian fashion industry and traditional Indian crafts. *Business History Review*.

Kipping, M., & Engwell, L. (2002). *Management consulting: Emergence and dynamics of a knowledge industry*. Oxford, UK: Oxford University Press.

Kipping, M., & Westerhuis, G. (2012). Strategy, ideology and structure: The political processes of introducing the M-form in two Dutch banks. In S. J. Kahl, B. S. Silverman & M. A. Cusumano (Eds.), *Advances in strategic management* (Vol. 29, pp. 187–237). Bingley, UK: Emerald Group.

Kirsch, D. (2002). *The electric vehicle and the burden of history*. New Brunswick, NJ: Rutgers University Press.

Lampe, R., & Moser, P. (2012). Patent pools: Licensing strategies in the absence of regulation. In S. J. Kahl, B. S. Silverman & M. A. Cusumano (Eds.), *Advances in strategic management* (Vol. 29, pp. 69–86). Bingley, UK: Emerald Group.

Leblebici, H. (2012). The evolution of alternative business models and the legitimization of universal credit card industry: Exploring the contested terrain where history and strategy meet. In S. J. Kahl, B. S. Silverman & M. A. Cusumano (Eds.), *Advances in strategic management* (Vol. 29, pp. 117–151). Bingley, UK: Emerald Group.

McKenna, C. D. (2006). *The world's newest profession: Management consulting in the twentieth century*. Cambridge: Cambridge University Press.

McKenna, C. (2012). Strategy followed structure: Management consulting and the creation of a market for "strategy," 1950–2000. In S. J. Kahl, B. S. Silverman & M. A. Cusumano (Eds.), *Advances in strategic management* (Vol. 29, pp. 153–186). Bingley, UK: Emerald Group.

Moser, P. (2005). How do patent laws influence innovation? Evidence from nineteenth-century world fairs. *American Economic Review*, *95*(4), 1214–1236.

Mowery, D. C. (1984). Firm structure, government policy, and the organization of industrial research: Great Britain and the United States, 1900–1950. *Business History Review*, *58*, 504–531.

Murmann, J. P. (2003). Knowledge and competitive advantage: The coevolution of firms, technology, and national institutions. Cambridge, UK: Cambridge University Press.

Murmann, J. P. (2012). Marrying history and social science in strategy research. In S. J. Kahl, B. S. Silverman & M. A. Cusumano (Eds.), *Advances in strategic management* (Vol. 29, pp. 89–115). Bingley, UK: Emerald Group.

Nicholas, T. (2003). Why Schumpeter was right: Innovation, market power and creative destruction in 1920s America. *Journal of Economic History*, *63*(4), 1023–1058.

Padgett, J., & Ansell, C. K. (1993). Robust action and the rise of the Medici, 1400–1434. *American Journal of Sociology*, *98*(6), 1259–1319.

Phillips, D. J. (2012). Orphaned jazz: Short-lived start-ups and the long-run success of depression-era cultural products. In S. J. Kahl, B. S. Silverman & M. A. Cusumano (Eds.), *Advances in strategic management* (Vol. 29, pp. 315–350). Bingley, UK: Emerald Group.

Rosenberg, N. R. (1992). Economic experiments. *Industrial and Corporate Change*, *1*(1), 181–203.

Tedlow, R. S. (2010). *Denial: Why business leaders fail to look facts in the face – And what to do about it*. New York, NY: Penguin Group.

Yates, J. (2005). *Structuring the information age: Life insurance and technology in the 20th century*. Baltimore, MD: John Hopkins University Press.

PART I
HISTORY, STRATEGY, AND INNOVATION

ECONOMIC EXPERIMENTS AND THE DEVELOPMENT OF WI-FI

Shane Greenstein

ABSTRACT

Purpose – *What role did economic experiments play in creating value in the commercial market for wireless Internet access? Rosenberg (1992, p. 181) defines such experiments broadly, "to include experimentation with new forms of economic organization as well as the better-known historical experiments that have been responsible for new products and new manufacturing technologies."*

Design/methodology/approach – *The chapter provides an overview of the experience of a number of firms, focusing on the period between the late 1990s and early part of the 21st century, when the technology first blossomed in commercial markets. The chapter uses the experience of Lucent and Intel as primary illustrations of key concepts, and the chapter discusses how the framework generalizes beyond the experience of these two firms.*

Findings – *The distinction between directed and undirected experiments helps understand events in the evolution of Wi-Fi's value. They also bring new perspective to an extensive debate in communications policy about the best way to assign and allocate spectrum, focusing on the importance of the regulatory decision to provide space in which experiments can take place.*

History and Strategy
Advances in Strategic Management, Volume 29, 3–33
Copyright © 2012 by Emerald Group Publishing Limited
All rights of reproduction in any form reserved
ISSN: 0742-3322/doi:10.1108/S0742-3322(2012)0000029005

Originality/value – *This framework has value for business history of the commercial Internet. This lens stresses the importance of preserving discretion to move business away from applications with low value, namely, away from allocations that used a conceptualization of the technology founded on a poor-use case, which later lessons showed had lower value than alternatives.*

Keywords: Wi-Fi; IEEE Committee 802; wireless; spectrum; communications equipment, Federal Communications Commission

What role did *economic experiments* play in creating value in the commercial market for wireless Internet access? Rosenberg (1992, p. 181) defines such experiments broadly, "to include experimentation with new forms of economic organization as well as the better-known historical experiments that have been responsible for new products and new manufacturing technologies." These lessons may be learned through experience in a market, because participants have limited ability to use alternatives to learn the determinants of market value – that is, to learn operational details and demand levels at previously untested volume and price levels. A laboratory test or customer survey cannot yield equivalent lessons as easily or cheaply as market experience. Scientists, engineers, or marketing executives cannot distill equivalent lessons at similar cost from building a prototype or interviewing potential customers (Stern, 2005).

How does a framework of economic experiments analyze the evolution of wireless Internet access, namely, the equipment and services built around Institute of Electrical and Electronics Engineers (IEEE) Standard 802.11, a.k.a. Wi-Fi? The chapter provides an overview of the experience of a number of firms, focusing on the period between the late 1990s and early part of the 21st century, when the technology first blossomed in commercial markets. The chapter uses the experience of Lucent and Intel as primary illustrations of key concepts, and the chapter discusses how the framework generalizes beyond the experience of these two firms.

As in prior studies of economic experiments (Greenstein, 2008), this study distinguishes between directed and indirect experiments. A firm conducts a directed experiment when it invests in actions designed to help it learn about unknown factors shaping value, such as market demand, operational costs, or optimal combinations of organizational forms, operational processes, and customer behavior. A firm engages in indirect experiments when it learns lessons from observing other firms' actions, usually as a by-product of participating in market competition.

The distinction helps understand events in the evolution of Wi-Fi's value. Futurists had predicted the rise of mobile computing even before the rise of the commercial Internet. Most of the predictions turned out to be correct in a broad sense – that is, a substantial demand for wireless data communication did eventually emerge. Yet, in a very specific sense, most futurists did not, and could not have, forecast what implementation would satisfy the nascent demand, in part due to what was learned from directed and indirect experiments. The accumulated lessons revealed what no market actor could have forecast, namely, the combination of product traits, cost factors, and operational norms that emerged for delivering profitable services.

The lens brings new perspective to an extensive debate in communications policy about the best way to assign and allocate spectrum.[1] Wi-Fi is but one of several examples in the modern policy debate. The chapter develops several insights about this example, namely, about which aspects of the spectrum rules for Wi-Fi did and did not play a significant role in shaping exploratory activity. The chapter stresses how and why it was important that the rules did not limit user and supplier discretion to alter the application of technology in response to lessons learned through economic experiments – that is, the rules did *not* fix the application at an early moment, such as the time of allocation of spectrum. Preserving such discretion retained the potential to move business away from applications with low value, namely, away from allocations that used a conceptualization of the technology founded on a poor-use case, which later lessons showed had lower value than alternatives.

This analysis also addresses one of the perennial points of this debate, regarding which aspects of Wi-Fi market experience resulted from deliberate policy choice and which were unplanned by-products of chance events. The chapter argues that many pieces of its infrastructure and commercially viable products could not have emerged without considerable and extensive planning. That planning is evident in the allocation of unlicensed spectrum, in the IEEE Standard for interoperability, 802.11b, and in the design of several catalytic products, such as the Apple Airport, or the Intel Centrino design. At the same time, important features of the market experience also were unforeseen, and emerged in response to economic experiments. This is especially apparent in the standard use cases for applications of wireless Internet access. For example, the government agency that released the spectrum did so under the general presumption that it was "garbage spectrum," useful for low-value activities such as baby monitors, garage door openers, and mobile handsets that communicated with receivers at short range inside residences. The design that initially emerged from Committee 802.11 made references to a series of more advanced use cases, such as wireless retailing, and data-transfer in warehouses. Some of these applications did, in fact have value, but other later and valuables uses of the technology were quite different. For example, later wireless Internet access became pervasive in many settings – residences, businesses, or third-party public spaces, either for unrestricted use or allocated through the use of paywalls.

Economic experiments have been the focus of scholarly interest, and this chapter overlaps with several different strands of the literature. For example, Thomke (2003a, 2003b) investigates a range of experimentation behavior in retail banking, as well as other settings such as integrated circuits. Using these examples as references, he provides systematic approaches for understanding how managers can conduct a directed economic experiment, with an eye toward designing the experiment to enable assessing their results (see, especially, Thomke, 2003a). While that conceptual approach is similar to a directed economic experiment, as discussed in this chapter, Thomke's research focuses on measurement and control of the design for assessment, which makes it a quite distinct framework. The framework presumes that managers control many dimensions of the experiment, or many aspects of the situation that generates data.

In this chapter, in contrast, the participants controlled some aspects of experiment design (in a directed experiment), but the situation was often less than ideal. The market environment changed too quickly to enable any firm to control all aspects of an experiment, or did not allow for experiments that yielded the most desirable information. In addition, from participating in market events, or undertaking studies of outcomes, firms inferred lessons based on the actions that others had taken. This still involved learning from economic experiments – albeit, it is an indirect experiment – but it did not allow for certainty in conclusions about causal inference or an ideal measurement approach.

This chapter's approach also comes close to studies of technological pioneering, which have analyzed behavior that resembles directed economic experiments in less than ideal market settings. For example, in their study of the VCR, Rosenbloom and Cusumano (1987) stated that technological pioneering involves a series of managerial choices over "the timing of market entry (first mover, follower), product positioning (segmentation, pricing, etc.), and the organization of production and distribution (make or buy, channels, etc.)." In their setting the successful designs "… emerged from an iterative process by which the pioneers came to understand not only the full range of capabilities inherent in the new technical synthesis, but also how to realize those capabilities in commercial-scale production and what value the market would place on them once achieved. Each successful organization learned these lessons largely by experience, that is, by offering products to users, studying the responses, and trying again until they got it right – in effect, 'learning by trying'." This conceptualization closely resembles what this chapter calls a directed economic experiment. This chapter pursues an additional and related insight – about how firms learn from accumulated lessons in a market, and how accumulation shapes the evolution of market outcomes.

The chapter also resembles Rosenbloom and Cusumano in another respect, in placing emphasis on experimentation in the design of the product, rather than placing emphasis on the choice of price or the design of the business. To be sure, experimentation with pricing does play a role in explaining the experience in Wi-Fi, but many of the insights from that observation merely echo observations made in Greenstein's (2007) study of experimentation in Internet access. Moreover, Leblebici's (2012) study of credit card pricing also illustrates a number of new themes about the interplay of pricing experiments from several firms, and the novel differences should be highlighted. The interested reader should go to those papers for them.[2]

This framework also has value for business history of the commercial Internet, as a scholarly activity in its own right. While the factors shaping the invention of the core technologies behind the Internet have received attention (e.g., Abbate, 1999), there is considerably less analysis about the evolution of the technology after commercialization began to shape the Internet. This chapter provides a framework that delineates the durable from the detail, in particular, reducing the extent of "Internet exceptionalism" in the explanation for events. That is, the chapter does not argue that aspects of the commercial Internet followed its own unique set of economic and business rules. Instead, it stresses a general framework with durable lessons for economic and strategic analysis of exploratory activity. Events within Wi-Fi are but one application of that framework.

This lens shifts emphasis in analyzing the creation and development of the commercial Internet. While many aspects of its technical development have received careful attention, the lens of economic experiments focuses the analysis on the interplay of technical decisions and exploratory activity that create value. While this lens is consistent with standard diffusion frameworks, such as an s-curve,[3] this lens stresses additional factors, such as how lessons emerged, and how these changed key aspects of the final product and service, and changed operational practices and organizational forms for supporting those changes. This lens is more in keeping with the emphasis in Ingram, Rao, and Silverman (2012), which develops a detailed study that focuses on building causal generalizations by contrasting events that did and did not happen.

IT STARTED WITH SPECTRUM POLICY

The United States government has a very restrictive spectrum system. Governed by the 1934 Communication Act, the law gives the Federal Communications Commission (FCC) authority to license or bar companies from using spectrum. Known as allocation through "command and control," this system was first adopted in order to minimize one user interfering with another. At one time it was thought that interference was a primary concern in all uses of spectrum. Hence, a central government administration could allocate rights to use spectrum, as well as determine other technical details, such as power over frequencies, which prevented one user's activity from stepping on top of another.

Until the 1990s all spectrum was allocated by FCC staff, and only after considerable planning. After long deliberations spectrum was given to specific firms and for very circumscribed purposes. To put it in very human terms, the owner and the purpose for the spectrum were determined far in advance by expert committees comprised of engineers, whose deliberations were approved of by the FCC. The choices made by committees were rarely reversed, arising only in exceptional circumstances.[4]

Command and control eliminated economic experimentation, or severely circumscribed its scope, at best, to learning by doing, namely, the reduction of costs in a well-specified activity. Circumscribing use eliminated many economic experiments before any ever got started, because it eliminated attempts to experiments to find applications other than those permitted at the outset, or refine uses in response to new information about the value of different applications. For many years that begged a question: If market participants had had the ability to decide how to employ the spectrum for a range of economic experiments, would they come to a different conclusion about how to deploy it?

In the early 1980s, one employee at the FCC, Michael Marcus, asked this question about spectrum for short-range uses (Marcus, 2009). The question was particularly pointed, because the justification for command and control was much weaker when it came to short-range use of spectrum. Any application in a short range – for example, garage door openers, or baby monitors, or wireless handsets – were activities where one household's use was less likely to interfere with another's, especially if the devices using the spectrum only worked at short range (e.g., with low power). Engineers could potentially design rules for devices so a small number of multiple users could employ the same spectrum. Why would the FCC have to worry about interference if a user could not transmit a signal more than one hundred feet? Perhaps neighbors could work out the issues themselves, or perhaps simple technical solutions could be found (such as automated selection among multiple channels), and the FCC could just leave market participants to find those solutions.

The use case for short-range spectrum, for example, mobile handsets inside homes, also suggested that a lighter hand for regulation might make work in practice. Why would the FCC have to designate the licensee, namely, an owner and designer, when plenty of firms could make such equipment? More to the point, why would the FCC want the administrative burden of licensing hundreds of firms who made use of the spectrum in thousands of places?

As is typically the case in Washington, this simple proposal did not get far until sensible voices of all ideological stripes saw the wisdom in it, albeit each saw something different in it. Indeed, the policy did not come to fruition until both parties signed on to it, which took more than a decade.

Initially Marcus received a warm reception from those who had sympathy with free-market ideology saw an opportunity to nurture markets. The recent election of the Reagan administration had installed many commissioners with such sympathies. A task force was appointed, and began to consider how such a system would work.

But the initiative did not make it from blackboard to implementation at any point in the 1980s. Adherents to the established system raised many questions, and momentum stalled. After many years another set of commissioners determined the priorities in the agency. Eventually backlash inside the FCC bureaucracy became powerful again, especially among those who did not see any merit to departing from command and control mechanisms. Marcus then became a target for deliberate efforts aimed to make him leave the FCC. Marcus (2009) received terrible employee reviews, and was hounded out of his job.

After the 1992 election the Clinton administration installed commissioners who had a taste for reform. Giving spectrum to users appealed to a
Democratic administration that wanted to experiment with new forms of
government, diffusing discretion to users and small manufacturers. It also
foresaw information and communication technologies as a bridge toward
a revolution in new services and productivity growth. Reed Hundt (2000),
the new chair of the FCC, felt he had a mandate for action, and he took it in
many different areas.

The FCC took up the descendent of Marcus' proposal again, and this
time pushed it through. By late April of 1996 the FCC took the last legal
step. The FCC initiated a "Notice for Proposed Rule Making" to make
available a small amount of unlicensed spectrum for what became known
as Unlicensed National Information Infrastructure (U-NII) devices. It
was understood from the FCC's order that the commission anticipated
"short range, high-speed wireless digital communications" and devices that
supported "the creation of new wireless local area networks ("LANs")
and ... facilitate wireless access to the National Information Infrastructure
("NII").[5] Beyond that, however, little else was specified about the design
or application of the spectrum. The lack of such specifications was, in fact,
the key administrative innovation. After deliberating over that summer, the
commission made spectrum available. The order that emerged on January 9,
1997, stated "we are adopting the minimum technical rules necessary to
prevent interference to other services and to ensure that the spectrum is used
efficiently."[6]

Known as the Part 15 rules, the allocation was regarded by traditional
defenders of command and control as "garbage spectrum," a throwaway to
uses with low value, and a symbolic salvo in an ideological battle. The
standard use cases used for reference – as mentioned, garage door openers,
wireless handsets, and baby monitors – were also thought to be low value in
total.[7] More to the point, forecasts about mass-market wireless access to
Internet data services did not play a central role in the design of these rules,
or tip sides in the ideological fights in favor or against aspects of these rules.
At most, these rules issued just as the commercial Internet was getting off
the ground, and connection between these commercial events was distant.
Use of euphemisms like the "NII" was symptomatic of that distance.

Something key was embedded in Part 15 rules, and it is worth noting.
Consistent with Mike Marcus's original proposals, the spectrum did not
have tight restrictions on its purpose – that is, the FCC did not control the
applications to which the applications were targeted, as long as the purpose
did not interfere with other activities outside the band. Equipment makers

were free to design their products in response to what they learned about its value from experimenting with its use. The spectrum was released with a few minor usage cases in mind, but the rules were made flexible enough to accommodate additional uses in the event of their invention.

In light of these events, it is interesting to recall that Rosenberg (1992) highlighted the freedom to experiment as a key difference between capitalist and Russian-style socialist systems. Lack of freedom in the latter system led to (a) lack of high-powered incentives for success; (b) lack of competition; (c) lack of downside to not innovating; and (d) preference for the status quo. Regulated spheres with Congressional oversight tend to naturally contain all four of these. Hence, it is not natural for policy makers to allow for experiments at all times, and, as such, the FCC's ability in this instance stands as an interesting exception to the prevailing norm.

In retrospect, it is also tempting to label Marcus as an administrative entrepreneur for pursuing a new procedure, namely, for doggedly pursing a new course of action laden with uncertain payoff. It would be appropriate to also apply that label to later actors, such as Reed Hundt, who saw the proposal through to the end, implementing it. More generally, this experience is consistent with the hypothesis advanced by Kahl, Liegel, and Yates (2012) that proposed institutional changes must more directly fit in with centralized audience structures. The FCC's centralized structure worked against Marcus' proposal at one time, but helped advance it with leaders who found it easy to assimilate.[8]

STANDARD COMMITTEES AND THEIR DESIGNS

The IEEE sponsors many committees that write standards in advance of products. In the best cases these committees endorse standards for products that need to interoperate, helping to coordinate designs from multiple suppliers. Any standard emerging from these discussions were not legally binding on industry participants, but the committee was formed with the hope that such a design could act as focal point for an interoperable design. In the best case, firms would embed the design in their products, such as routers and receivers, and these would become interoperable as result. Firms could differentiate along other dimensions if they so choose to do so.

Committee 802 was formed in the early 1980s, before the privatization of the Internet was ever proposed. By the late 1980s the committee was well known among computing and electronics engineers because it had helped design and diffuse the Ethernet standard for local area networks.[9]

By the late 1980s Committee 802 had become a victim of its success. It had grown larger, establishing subcommittees for many areas, ostensibly to extend the range of uses for Ethernet. A close look at the engineering suggested that sometimes this label was mere window-dressing for otherwise complex deliberations. For example, while "wireless local area networking" accurately described the aspirations for users, for suppliers the application hardly had any connection to existing local area networking. Due to the very different error-correction issues, the software for a wireless local area network would end up bearing only a slight resemblance to that for a wired local area network, and contained many important technical differences.[10]

More to the point, the original charter and motivation for this subcommittee was not focused on what eventually became a large market in the home, hotels, airports, and coffee shops. Subcommittee 802.11 was established in 1990. Like all subcommittees of this broad family of committees, it concerned itself with a specific topic, in this case, designs for interoperability standards to enable wireless data traffic over short ranges – ostensibly doing with wireless technology what a local area network did with wires.

At first the committee did not get very far, lacking any clear direction. But then a new chair was appointed, Vic Hayes. Hayes was a technologist with a visionary outlook, a cheerful demeanor, and, more importantly, the patience to see his vision to realization. Hayes first developed wireless technologies for National Cash Register, or NCR. At the time it was a sub-division of AT&T, which would later become Lucent (and today it is a division of Agere Systems). In that capacity Hayes first developed prototypes for wireless terminals for stockbrokers. Other applications for the technology were forecast, such as easy rearrangement of retail space (see Kharif, 2003). From this experience he had a firm vision of the value of a standard that many component vendors could use to make interoperable equipment.

Other potential applications for this standard came up in the earliest meetings. One of the earliest prototypes had been a wireless local area network for a university campus.[11] Another was short-range wireless Ethernet in warehouses with complex logistical operations. Several firms had built expensive prototypes of these devices, but had not found many buyers, or otherwise experienced very limited commercial response. Indeed, throughout the first half of the 1990s, as Committee 802.11 met and continued to do its work, pioneering firms continued their experiments, and continued to generate almost no interest among users.[12]

As with most such committees, Hayes tried to involve members who brought appropriate technical expertise and who represented the views of most of the major suppliers of equipment in which this standard would be embedded. At first, therefore, the group was comprised of enthusiastic designers focused on the needs of big users (e.g., FedEx, United Parcel Service, Wal-Mart, Sears, and Boeing), where the value of the application seemed most transparent. It almost goes without saying though it is obvious in retrospect, notably absence from the earliest meetings were representatives of many of the suppliers of valuable equipment a decade later, such as firms from electronics and computing.

To be fair to some of these firms, the potential demand for wireless local area network was becoming apparent to others as well. Specifically, several related efforts arose, such as HomeRF and Bluetooth. Both were founded in 1998. The former was organized by firms such as Motorola and Siemens, and at its peak involved over a hundred companies before it disbanded.[13] The latter was established by Ericsson, Sony-Ericsson, IBM (International Business Machines), Intel, Toshiba, and Nokia, and currently still exists, and today it involves thousands of firms. It focused on very short-range uses, and, as such, tended to have a set of applications distinct from Wi-Fi.

Subsequent events would change the predominant use case, as economic experiments showed participants that high market value lay in a different configuration of technology, operations, and pricing than had originally been envisioned. In a later chapter Rosenberg (1996) would discuss the ways in which unanticipated learning altered the value of technologies. In this instance, what happened in Wi-Fi fit a category of unanticipated learning that Rosenberg (1996) labels (and I paraphrase here) "an invention motivated by a specific application that unexpectedly finds broader use."

EMBEDDING THE DESIGN IN PRODUCTS

Wi-Fi did not emerge through a linear development path, namely, evolution along a set of prespecified and classified stages. Economic experiments played a role in shaping that path, as pioneering firms took actions in response to the actions of the standard committee. The market experience of the prior to 1997 had generated many designs, but no mass-market demand had emerged for any of them.[14] The design from IEEE Committee 802.11 would change that.

Subcommittee 802.11 first proposed a standard in 1997 that received many beta uses, but also failed to resolve many interoperability issues (among many issues). Learning from this experience, the committee rewrote the standard over the next two years. What came to be known as 802.11a was ratified in early 2000. Just prior to that in late 1999, the committee published Standard 802.11b, which altered some features (changing the frequency of spectrum it used, among other things). It was given the label "b" in anticipation that "a" would emerge soon as well. The draft of 802.11b eventually caught on widely, partly because it was licensed for usage in Europe and Asia as well as North America, while for some time 802.11a was only licensed in North America (Liu, 2001; Kharif, 2003).

It also caught on due to actions taken by Steve Jobs and Apple. Jobs had just returned as Apple's CEO in 1997. This was a point in time where many industry developers were still unsure whether the IEEE design ever would become embedded in a mass-market product. This moment arose just after IEEE Standard 802.11 had initially been published, but before it was revised as both 802.11a and 802.11b.

Apple initiated a meeting with Lucent, who had supplied many key engineers to Committee 802.11, including its leader, Vic Hayes. Lucent's wireless LAN management responded with ambitions to bargain hard to become the dominant equipment supplier of wireless LANs. Apple was still a fraction of Lucent's size, though, as it happened, one would never have known it from the way Jobs behaved when the meeting actually took place.

Cees Links, from Lucent, attended the meeting and he describes how it began awkwardly (Lemstra, Hayes, & Groenewege, 2011, Chap. 4, pp. 129–131). Jobs was late, and one side showed up in suits and ties while the other did not. Jobs finally walked in and the conversation started, with Jobs doing a majority of the talking at the outset. Then Links describes the following exchange:

> Then Steve asked, "Are there any questions?" I tried to show a few slides: key wins, market positioning, product offering, value creation, etc. Presenting slides with Steve Jobs is actually quite easy: you put up the slide, and he will do the talking, not necessarily related to the slide: then he asks for the next slides.

Links goes on to describe a short dialogue between Jobs and the senior management team from Lucent. His description of the end of the meeting is the most revealing.

> Turning the conversation back to wireless LANs, [Jobs declares,] "We need the radio card for $50 and I want to sell at $99." Then Steve apologized; he had to leave. Standing up, he said "Hi!" and went. The room fell silent.

None of the wireless local area networking producers until then had ever achieved that price point. This price level was regarded as quite an ambitious target.[15] NCR/Lucent eventually achieved that price point, albeit only after negotiations continued with Apple throughout production, as Apple changed the product requirements.[16] That is how the Apple Airport – the first mass-market Wi-Fi product – emerged. There was nothing technically new about it; it embedded the 802.11b design in a functioning product that Apple sold. However, it was commercially viable for the mass market, including a branded version from Apple, which Apple distributed as part of a system that Apple endorsed.

That still left a large part of the PC industry uncovered, as the design for Apple was not compatible with any PCs with a Windows operating system from Microsoft. That segment of the market was the largest segment, and it became first addressed at Dell Computer.[17] Michael Dell, founder and CEO of Dell Computer, by then one of the largest PC providers in the world, heard about the announcement of the Apple Airport and called Lucent. According to the account from Cees Links, Dell was "furious" because Dell was not first to experiment with a product release (Lemstra et al., 2011, Chap. 4, p. 131).[18] Lucent executives had to remind Dell that he had an opportunity to be in on discussions as early as 1992, but Dell has decided in 1993 that no market for the technology existed (Lemstra et al., 2011, Chap. 4, p. 131). They subsequently came to a deal. Making a version for Dell became a priority thereafter, and making it compatible with Windows XP was the main challenge for the team at Lucent. Eventually Lucent would succeed at that as well. To do that Lucent and Microsoft cooperated in changing the design of Windows XP, and a new version was released in 2001 that supported 802.11b in all Windows-based systems.

Those first two projects pioneered the mass market for laptop use, pioneering the technical issues affiliated with the challenges of the Apple and Windows operating systems, as well as the hardware. Both were directed economic experiments, investments in product designs embedding 802.11b, aimed at fostering sales as part of either Apple's or Dell's portfolio of products. In both examples, one pioneering firm, Lucent, would gain considerable sales from its position, and (in retrospect) would retain the position as a leading provider of equipment for several years.

The importance of those two experiments for the market's development is more readily apparent in retrospect than it was at the time. After those two projects, the consumer-oriented mass market took off, with a large number of other firms also entering into production. Those two projects served as the bridge between years of experimentation and mass markets, showing other equipment firms that real money could be made if oriented toward the demand perceived by the pioneering key firms.

As it turned out, these events also generated a response from many users, who quickly began using this equipment in a variety of settings, campuses, buildings, public parks, and coffee shops. Unsurprisingly, other vendors tried to meet this demand as well. Around the same time as the publication of 802.11b, firms that had helped pioneer the standard – including 3Com, Aironet (now a division of Cisco), Harris Semiconductor (now Intersil), Lucent (now Agere), Nokia, and Symbol Technologies – formed the Wireless Ethernet Compatibility Alliance (WECA). WECA branded the new technology Wi-Fi, which was a marketing ploy for the mass market, since WECA's members believed that "802.11b" was a much less appealing label.[19] The aim was clear: nurture what enthusiasts were doing and broaden it into sales to a broader base of users.

WECA also arranged to perform testing for conformance to the standard, such as certifying interoperability of antennae and receivers made by different firms. This is valuable when the set of vendors becomes large and heterogeneous, as it helps maintain maximum service for users with little effort on their part. In brief, while the IEEE Committee designed the standard, a different body (of similar firms) performed conformance testing.[20]

Events then took on a momentum all of their own. Technical successes became widely publicized. Numerous businesses became users of Wi-Fi, and began directed experiments supporting what became known as *hotspots*, which was an innovative business idea. A hotspot is a data transmission mediated by a third party for local use in a public space or on a retail premises. A hotspot in a public space could be free, it could be installed by a home owner, or it could be maintained by a building association for all building residences. It could be supported by the café or by a restaurant or by a library trying to support its local user base. Or, it could be subscription-based, with short term or long-term contracts between users and providers. The latter became common at Starbucks, for example, which subcontracted with T-mobile to provide the service throughout its cafés.

Hotspots were similar to, but outside of, the original set of use cases for the standard. Since nothing precluded this unanticipated use from growing, grow it did. It grew in business buildings, in homes, in public parks, and in a wide variety of settings, eventually causing the firms behind HomeRF to give up. The growing use of Wi-Fi raised numerous unexpected issues about interference, privacy, and using the signals of neighbors. Nevertheless, these issues did not slow Wi-Fi's growing popularity.[21] Web sites sprouted up to give users, especially travelers, directions to the nearest hotspot. As demand grew, suppliers gladly met it. As in a classic network bandwagon, the growing number of users attracted more suppliers and vice versa.

Economic experiments played an enormous role in this evolution. While several pioneering firms took important steps in initiating market development, no single firm was responsible for all the economic experiments that eventually altered the state of knowledge about how to best operate equipment using IEEE Standard 802.11b. Rather, many firms responded to user demand, demonstrations of new applications, tangible market experience, and other events, and the lessons accumulated.

The last observation resembles analysis of behavior often found in industry-wide platforms. As explained by Cusumano (2012), platforms can operate on industry-wide levels. That occurs when all participants take actions using standards that invite activity from complementary component providers. In this instance of Wi-Fi equipment, the presence of a standard, related institutions for conformance, and the universal participation of virtually all the industry encouraged experiments in antennae and receiver design, as well as in deployment of final equipment in new operational modes (such as a hotspot). In short, because Wi-Fi deployed at an industry-wide level, experimenters could presume (safely) that others would make use of the same design, which led each experiment to specialize on narrow issues and specific issues of interest to the experimenter.

INTERPLAY BETWEEN DIRECTED AND UNDIRECTED EXPERIMENTS

Later events in the development of Wi-Fi illustrate how directed learning can build on an undirected economic experiment. Specifically, reacting to the undirected experiment that generated Wi-Fi, Intel created *Centrino*, a large program that would install wireless capability in its notebook computers. It was officially launched in March 2003, though industry insiders knew about the plans much earlier. Indeed, plans for it began to emerge at Intel partly in response to the events just described.

That said, as with many aspects of growth in wireless access, the Centrino program is easy to misunderstand. It was much less obvious to Intel in advance than it was in retrospect.

At the turn of the millennium Intel's strategic plans were responding to multiple market forces. While demand for desktop and notebook computers had grown along with the Internet in the 1990s, Intel's own marketing department forecast an imminent slowdown in the share of desktop sales, as well as increasing engineering challenges supplying faster chips. More worrisome, Intel had branded itself as a firm that always marketed better and faster microchips, while it was no longer clear that demand for bigger/ faster would arise across all segments of computing. Notebook users valued mobility, for example, and that placed value on distinct attributes, such as longer battery life, less energy-intensive chips, smaller storage, more compact designs, less weight, and less heat. Even by the late 1990s many mobile users had shown a willingness to give up improvements in bigger and faster microprocessors in order to get improvements on these other attributes.

In 2001, in response to a number of initiatives and studies, Intel's management decided it was time to change priorities. Labeling this a "left turn," the company chose to embed a Wi-Fi connection in all notebooks that used Intel microprocessors.[22] This was easier said than done. The choice *not only* involved redesigning the Intel microprocessor, Intel's core product, stressing lower power and lower processing speeds. It also involved redesigning the motherboard for desktop PCs and notebooks, adding antennae and supporting chips. Intel made a number of reference designs and made them widely available at low cost.

Intel's management hoped that its endorsement would increase demand for wireless capabilities within notebooks by, among other things, reducing weight and size while offering users simplicity and technical assurances in a standardized function. The firm also anticipated that its branding would help sell notebooks using Intel chips and motherboard designs instead of using microchips from Advanced Micro Devices (AMD). Furthermore, antenna and router equipment makers anticipated that a standardized format for wireless notebooks might help raise demand for their goods.

The Centrino redesign brought one obvious benefit to users, namely, it eliminated the need for an external card for the notebook, which was usually supplied by a firm other than Intel and installed by users or original equipment manufacturers (OEMs) in an expansion slot. Intel hoped for additional benefits for users, such as more reliability in wireless functionality (as standards diffused), fewer set-up difficulties (as standards diffused), longer-lived batteries (due to less need for heat reduction), and thinner notebook designs (due to smaller cooling units).

Intel's management further worried that the environment would not encourage use of wireless notebooks, so Intel's management considered taking exploratory actions far outside of its core product, microprocessors.

As it would turn out, the actions were not far outside its philosophical approach to managing the demand for microprocessors. Intel long ago made a distinction between managing its first job, making microprocessors, and managing anything that helped it sell more microprocessors, which was often given the label "Job 2" (Gawer & Cusumano, 2002).

For example, the company launched a program to change the environment in which notebooks diffused. Intel certified 15,000 additional hotspots in hotels, airports, and other public places by the time Centrino launched (Burgelman, 2007).

As another example, Intel made motherboard designs available to others. The firm had crept into the motherboard business slowly over the prior decade as it initiated a variety of improvements to the designs of computers using its microprocessors. Years earlier, the firm had designed prototypes of these motherboards and by the time it announced the Centrino program, it was making some motherboards, branding them, and encouraging many of its business partners to make similar designs. The wireless capabilities of a notebook had not been the focus on these earlier programs, so the announcement of the Centrino program represented a shift in strategic aims and direction for the Intel programs affiliated with motherboards. It was not a new program per se.[23]

This latter program illustrates one of the interesting conflicts that emerged in Wi-Fi's development. Intel's motherboard designs could increase the efficiencies of computers, but that benefit was not welcomed by every OEM who assembled PCs or other industry players. Firms such as Texas Instruments and Intersil had lobbied earlier for different designs for the 802.11g upgrade, investing heavily in the efforts at Committee 802.11. Neither of them had intended to help Intel's business, and neither of them wanted to see Intel increase its influence over the designs that were deployed to most users.

Moreover, Intel's design eliminated some differences between OEMs and other component providers. Many of these firms resented both losing control over their designs and losing the ability to strategically differentiate their own designs. At the same time, other OEMs liked the Intel design, since it allowed the firms to concentrate on other facets of their business. That competitive rivalry eventually generated cooperation from every small OEM. Intel found it had to induce cooperation from many big firms with marketing programs.

Intel ran into several crises at first, such as insufficient parts for the preferred design and a trademark dispute over the use of its preferred symbol for the program. However, the biggest and most important resistance came from the largest distributor of PCs, Dell Computer. This firm insisted on selling its own branded Wi-Fi products right next to Intel's, thereby supporting some of the card makers.

Despite Dell's resistance, the cooperation from antenna makers and (importantly) users helped Intel reach its goals. By embedding the standards in its products, Intel made Wi-Fi, or rather Centrino, easy to use, which proved popular with many users.

The Centrino example illustrates the array of deliberate firm activities taken during a short period that built on top of learning from an earlier undirected economic experiment. The activities in IEEE Committee 802.11 ended up affecting the activities of many other firms, such as equipment manufacturers, laptop makers, chip makers, and coffee shops, which then shaped new activities in Committee 802.11 as well.

This example also illustrates that economic experiments can – and do – happen in spite of overt conflict between firms. Those firms may be either direct competitors or participants in a value chain with diverging interests. Conflict arises, as it did here, when all can forecast that the success of one firm's experiment adversely affects the business fortunes of another.

EXPENDITURE ON EXPERIMENTS
AND CREATING VALUE

Firms expend costly resources on economic experiments, for instance, in assets and personnel to either conduct directed economic experiments or to learn from market events. Consider the private costs and benefits from conducting experiments. By helping market participants learn about the nature of demand in quickly evolving environments, companies can effectively position their offerings and pricing structures. Such lessons increase value by:

- generating more revenue through improvement of an existing service;
- enhancing profits from lowering operation costs or avoiding higher investment expenses; or
- enhancing pricing power through targeting services to customers better than rivals do.

In an especially competitive setting, such lessons also can contribute to raising the probability of survival by teaching a firm to avoid outcomes where rivals can out-maneuver them.

In general, many of these benefits cannot be measured. If they can be measured – even partially – the private value of many lessons can be measured in terms of the additional revenue it contributes to a firm's business and/or the additional cost savings it generates. In such a setting, a firm can design an experiment to filter out noise, or to develop a metric singularly associated with benefits, so as to expose the cost/benefit trade-off between different choices.[24]

Revenue might increase through one of several mechanisms. For instance, firms may learn to alter pricing practices, and those changes will alter total revenues. The history of access pricing illustrates several examples. For example, the acceptable pricing norm among most users for hourly limitations changed over time, as ISPs learned about the reaction of different customer segments to distinct menus of choices. Eventually Wi-Fi charges in many hotspots reflected carrier perception about what the market demand could support.

Pricing experiments often coincide with experiments regarding the range of services offered. During the mid to late 1990s, for example, virtually all ISPs experimented with changes to the standard bundle offered, such as default e-mail memory, instant messaging support, and hosting services in which the ISP maintained Web pages for clients. Most Wi-Fi hotspots, in contrast, did not change the standard bundle much. A wide range of regional ISPs experimented with performing services complementary to access, such as hosting services, networking services, and Web design consultations.

Learning oriented toward cost reduction may be difficult to distinguish from learning oriented toward enhanced revenue. For instance, as dial-up ISPs learned from one another about the efficient deployment of 56 K modems, those who deployed it found they could charge a modest price premium for faster service (approximately five dollars), but that that premium disappeared in less than a year, after the modems became more common.[25] Similarly, many hotspot providers initially charged for access, but later found competition reducing their ability to price the service. Instead, Wi-Fi merely became an element of service for a location.

The ambiguities between costs and revenues also could arise with decisions about the scope of the firm. A modest investment could be an investment that leads to greater customer retention. Better customer retention eventually manifests as greater sales values and higher firm prices, but it may be difficult to attribute a specific change in price or volume to only that investment.

Importantly, the lessons learned from an experiment may or may not have *any* comparative value – that is, in altering the value of a firm's service in comparison to rivals. It will have such value, generally speaking, if a firm uniquely learns a lesson and no other rival does. It will not when all firms have it and, therefore, it does not support differentiation. In that case, it becomes a part of generally accepted and industry know-how.

INDUSTRY-WIDE BENEFITS

Two additional factors shape the benefits and costs from economic experiments at the industry-wide level but *do not* shape costs and benefits at the private level. Generally speaking, all of these are hard to measure. This section highlights two themes:

- Consumers reap some benefits from an experiment – in the form of lower prices and new services – and these benefits do not necessarily play any role in the benefits experienced by the firm who conducts a directed economic experiment.
- One firm's experiment shapes the actions of another, an effect that can take many forms, and these do not directly show up in a firm's accounting. These are particularly hard to measure because one firm may benefit while another incurs a substantial fraction of the cost.

Consumer benefits from economic experiments are difficult to measure except when it leads directly to a decline in price for an existing service. In practice, however, that is rare. Consumers may also benefit from higher quality goods, better supply of services that previously did not exist, or thicker supply of products tailored to niche demands, among many benefits for which no price may be recorded.

An especially difficult-to-measure benefit is the consequence from learning that takes place at all market participants. When a new service or improvement is reasonably permanent, the firm who commercializes it may see returns to the investment in the form of increases in final revenue or other strategic advantages. If a new product or service is quickly imitated by all firms, it quickly becomes a standard feature of doing business in a downstream market. The benefits from the new technology are quickly passed onto consumers in the form of lower prices and/or better products. In this case, the benefits to a firm do not appear as an increase in revenues but may not appear as lower prices; but they exist nonetheless, in the form of losses the business avoided, or better quality services, which match the quality found elsewhere.

By traditional economic reasoning, at least two externalities shape the difference between private and industry-wide learning. There is an information externality *between* firms, as when one firm's directed experiment teaches another firm a lesson, or a set of actions interact in an undirected experiment and teach every industry participant a lesson. There is also an information externality *over time*, as when the lessons of prior experiments generate lessons on which further experiments are built. The example of Wi-Fi shows that these two externalities are pervasive, as well as difficult to distinguish from one another.

The positive information externalities between firms take one of two forms. In one case, what worked for one firm becomes known and imitated by others. For example, success from an experiment at one hotspot in one location in 2001 implied it might be profitable in another location with similar features.

Alternatively, what did not work for one firm becomes known and, therefore, avoided. For example, the difficulties with the first design for 802.11 become known from experiences in 1997, leading equipment firms to delay building plans until a more suitable design emerged and with institutional support for enforcing interoperability.

Negative information externalities take a common form. That is, a successful experiment for one firm becomes known and implies a loss for someone else – for example, Intel's Centrino success in 2003 implied a loss at wireless card makers.

Inter-temporal externalities also lead to divergence between private costs and benefits and industry-wide costs and benefits. One party (in a directed economic experiment) or several parties (in an undirected economic experiment) assume the cost of generating lessons while many others gain the benefits later. That is, those who pay for lessons in an early market are not necessarily those who use them most profitably in a later market, and no contract between them governs the early investment.

An important feature of inter-temporal externalities is the asymmetries to the costs and benefits of generating lessons about commercial failure. Lessons about how to avoid commercial failure can be as valuable to observers as those who employ them, but the firm whose failure illustrates the lesson for others rarely, if ever, does so for that purpose, and almost never under contract with the others who (later) gain the benefit of the lessons learned from the failure.

In an extreme case, a firm may learn a lesson, teach others from its failure, but go bankrupt before it is able to use that lesson. Even though the lesson was expensive to the stockholders of the firm that initiated the experiment, it was inexpensive to the survivors.

An additional insight arises from these classifications. User-generated innovations can play an important part in generating inter-temporal externalities.[26] The study of lead users highlights a related observation. That is, a lead user with an unusual enthusiasm or desire to push in a new direction may explore new designs and non-incremental business possibilities, which later grow into wide uses. In this instance, such lead users were hotspot developers of Wi-Fi, and their action yielded a set of new lessons that shaped the general market.

While learning from directed experiments is challenging, learning lessons from market experience is much more challenging. As this example illustrates, no single firm controlled all the key aspects of the market experience, and no firm possessed the ability to rerun market events with one factor changed. At the same time, by merely participating in the market experience, and conducting thoughtful review, a participant could infer many of the key lessons the pioneers were learning. The next section develops this insight more systematically.

SPREADING LESSONS

Do different types of lessons exhibit different patterns of spreading after an experiment? Answering this question provides an important step toward understanding when participating in a market helps teach other firms. It also helps illustrate how private and collective costs and benefits tend to diverge the most and least.

There are four distinct types of lessons. The first are *market lessons*. These pertain to norms and patterns of market-based actions, such as how to write a contract that users find acceptable, and how to price services, and so on. Second, *technical lessons* pertain to the design of a piece of equipment – for example, knowing how to configure Wi-Fi so that it works in the type of space/location at all times that fits the supplier's needs. Third, *heuristic lessons* combine both technical knowledge with either market or operational knowledge about how employees behave in firms and how customers react to firm behavior – for example, knowing how to deploy Wi-Fi for a maximal set of users. Fourth, *complex lessons* are marketing and operational lessons that involve many functions inside an organization – for example, knowing how to integrate the use of Wi-Fi into a wide variety of other offerings.

Private incentives to generate economic experiments will be less than the industry benefits in situations where lessons spread quickly and others benefit, as occurs with technical lessons, market lessons, and some heuristic lessons. Several examples will illustrate.

In 1999 the technical lessons about Wi-Fi were often rather trivial for an ISP to learn. The technical steps between a dial-up ISP and Wi-Fi were relatively incremental – many firms just added a connection. Generally, these technical skills were common among those who operated bulletin boards, computers, ISPs, or related equipment. Most local and national ISPs already had procedures in place to, for example, implement billing, publicize their services to local users, or address user service calls. Doing so for Wi-Fi in a coffee shop or restaurant was easy. Though the market actions changed, these were relatively easy to execute within existing organizational procedures.

Technical lessons tend to spread easily because they tend to become codified quickly.[27] It is almost tautological that such codification leads to easier transmission of the knowledge. For example, lessons about the design for a modem bank, a server, or other modem equipment became codified almost immediately, and for sound economic reasons. Most equipment suppliers in competitive markets would not consider selling equipment if information about it were not codified because most buyers demand it as a condition of purchase. Related, vendors of equipment also would have developed a set of marketing parameters for their buyers, guiding them toward best-practice deployment.

Wi-Fi not only benefited from these factors, but an additional matter helped codify lessons. Committee 802.11 published its designs and made the information available without restriction.

Others lessons pertain to heuristic knowledge about how to operate that equipment efficiently. For example, lessons about how to manage a Wi-Fi router at peak usage levels might not be known initially after a new piece of equipment became available for use, but such lessons would be learned through trial and error. As it turned out, those lessons spread to different coffee shops through a variety of mechanisms – that is, administrators in key locations coordinated it (e.g., at Starbucks), franchises communicated with one another (e.g., at McDonalds), bulletin boards emerged to support different types of user groups, and the Wi-Fi association invested in support activities as well.

Several factors affect the speed at which heuristic lessons spread. On the one hand, some heuristic lessons spread slowly because, as sources of potential competitive advantage, they are guarded by the firms that first discover them. For example, firms guard their strategies for how to deploy equipment efficiently and they may also guard information that indicates details about their future designs.

On the other hand, some firms, such as equipment providers, have strong incentives to spread lessons, since their spread contributes to further sales. Such tension was inherent in the diffusion of Wi-Fi, for example. Intel's program to further fund development of certification of hotspots is another illustration.

To be clear, not all heuristic lessons spread, nor did all designs become codified. While numerous channels opened to provide information to support deployment of frontier applications, some equipment manufacturers guarded the coding that was relevant to the next generation of designs, called "mesh-networks." Despite some initial excitement about mesh-networks, most such experiments did not coalesce and develop into large-scale codified practices.[28]

User and vendor organizations also shape spreading of lessons. Most dial-up ISPs used similar software tools for monitoring users, particularly after these showed up in the discussion boards at an Open Source project, such as Apache, the most popular web server. The community effectively coordinated many innovative efforts for dial-up ISPs in the mid to late 1990s, by sharing multiple upgrades and fixes to the source code among ISPs. Designs embedded in standards in many organizations also contributed to sharing of lessons. Organizations, such as the Internet Engineering Task Force (IETF) and the World Wide Web Consortium (W3C), for instance, also facilitated the movement of lessons. Committee 802.11 was, therefore, not much different.

The variance in idiosyncratic factors also can slow the codification of such heuristic lessons. First, one community of users may differ from another. For example, peak ISP usage occurs around the same time of day in different locations, but the similarities end there. Surfing behavior varies according to gender, family status, age, education, and income of the members of the household, the sum of which varies across cities, and even from one vendor to another within the same city. Such variety interferes with finding commonalities in, for example, marketing strategies (for a new feature) across locations or vendors.

In addition, a heuristic operating rule established to resolve other operational issues might interfere with the functionality of a new lesson. For example, most restaurants wanted a way to limit overuse of capacity, especially when users failed to log off after ceasing or delaying use. Some instituted rules for automating log offs after short periods of nonuse, while others did not because users resented it (and, as a result, would leave for other vendors). Modem capacity usage differed depending on these rules.

Any heuristic lesson about how to operate new equipment at capacity would have to take into account such rules, but such variety interfered with uniform rules for all operators.

Not all lessons can be reduced to simple heuristics – some are complex lessons. These might emerge, for example, from lengthy investigations by firms seeking to lower cost or generate extra revenue. They often are interdependent, where one operational goal reinforces the other, or associated with unique firm features, such as scale. In either case, complex lessons cannot be easily summarized by a simple heuristic rule of thumb or by an answer to a single question. Almost by definition, these lessons resist immediate codification and are the slowest to move from firm to firm.

As with heuristic lessons, users of Wi-Fi hesitate to share complex business lessons. For example, management at one hotel chain would not lightly discuss with other hotel chains which type of customer showed a willingness to pay for it. Firms also hesitate to share information about what sort of costly activities build customer retention most effectively – for example, did users have greater willingness to pay incrementally for access or as a standard part of their contract?

Also as with heuristic lessons, the same factors interfered with codification and the spreading of complex lessons, namely, idiosyncrasies arising from differences across communities and between other operating rules. That does not means complex business lessons never spread. Rather, they spread with more effort and at greater cost. In general, they spread more slowly and to fewer firms at any point in time.

These examples support a modified version of the commonly stated canard that "all ideas become public goods." Rather, *some* ideas become public goods, and, due to the conditions shaping the spread of lessons, some remain privately held for a short period. Even while technical information and market lessons move quickly between locations and firms, the ability of a firm to prevent direct rivals from imitating its business actions immediately slows others. Some complex lessons also do not tend to spread to others, at least for a short time.

These distinctions have important implications for the design of collective institutions to foster economic experiments. All market participants (and especially users) benefit from the spread of lessons. Spreading lessons can facilitate increases in sales, and, in some circumstances pricing authority. It can, therefore, be a viable strategy for a pioneer to grow the size of the market, and gain simply by holding onto a percentage of the total growth.

Such reasoning could rationalize the strategic approach of Lucent in its investment in the IEEE Committee, and it could rationalize the strategic approach of Intel in its investment in Centrino. Both grew the size of the market, and, as major suppliers in each case, both firms benefited from that growth.

SUMMING UP: ECONOMIC EXPERIMENTS IN A COMPLEX WORLD

This chapter has argued that *economic experiments* played an important role in value creation during the first decade of commercial Internet access. It illustrated how the lens of economic experiments helps understand the actions of many firms, and touched on a wide array of actions. In brief, it argued that economic experiments were essential to value creation.

The chapter also illustrates how to move toward a general approach to analyzing economics experiments. The approach resembles analysis found in other settings, such as studies of pioneering. In addition, the chapter stresses how the framework could be useful for guiding policy about spectrum.

It is possible to view economic experiments from two perspectives. It is possible to view them from the perspective of a single firm. That is useful for designing further firm experiments, and for summarizing the lessons for firm investments in operations, product design or organizational architecture. It is also possible to view from the perspective of a market analyst. That is useful for summarizing the accumulated lessons of many firms' actions. Again, that could shape firm investments in operations, product design or organizational architecture. It also could shape assessment of the strategic position of several firms in comparison to one another.

There is an important tension between the two types of perspectives, and that frames several open questions. The tension arises from a fallacy of composition – namely, the whole can be quite different than the sum of its parts. The fallacy arises in economic experiments due to three mismatches – in motive, in investment timing, and in the realization of value.

First, there is a mismatch between a single firm's motive and the outcome at the level of the industry. Firms conduct economic experiments to resolve uncertainty about the underlying determinants of market value. Yet, as it typically turns out, since no firm's experience can be viewed in isolation of others, each firm teaches others lessons, which, in turn, lead to more experiments. The interplay between firms increases the possibility for the emergence of an undirected economic experiment, itself creating another barrier to making any near-term forecast about the creation of value at a specific firm. In total, therefore, while each firm may take action to reduce uncertainty, through their response to one another in market competition, together their actions may lead to more uncertainty, not less.

There is a second mismatch between investment timing and delayed assessment of lessons. This arises because economic experiments yield lessons, some of which are private and some of which become public over time. Public lessons accumulate over time, leading to changes in industry wisdom about how to deploy technology into its most valuable uses. Those lessons, in turn, may support more economic experiments, leading in new directions. If the accumulation becomes substantial, then there is, almost unavoidably, an inherent mismatch between the motivation of earlier experimenters and later users of lessons. Experimenting early is expensive, and the direction of investment is determined by concerns that later users did not – indeed, could not – influence. Only later the most important lessons for value become known, creating the potential for large differences between ex ante and ex post assessment of the valuable lessons, and the best settings in which to have learned them. That raises a simple possibility, namely, that the early generations are not necessarily going to become the ones who use the lessons most profitably.

The third mismatch stresses a related point, about the mismatch between private costs of investments in economic experiments and realized value from using lessons. Firms and users generate lessons, and, generally speaking, do not take actions and make investments for the benefit of others. Yet, without meaning to do so, because information leading to lessons becomes public knowledge, one generation of participants may pay for a lesson that later generations use with little expense. Yet, no accountant would (or could) record the value or the cost in a ledger. No manager or policy maker would (or could) find it feasible to align incremental costs and benefits in such a situation.

The three mismatches arise in settings where the accumulation of private experimentation quickly changes the assessment of the environment. In such settings it may be challenging to make certain inferences about causation, namely, about which operation features and aspects of the final product determine value. It would seem, therefore, that the environments in which economic experiments shape the value of outcomes are among the most challenging environments in which to formulate strategic action.

NOTES

1. This is quite a large debate (see, e.g., Benklar, 2002; Faulhaber & Farber, 2003; Frischmann, 2012).

2. The credit card firms appear to have engaged in several experiments at different points. The first entrant, Diners Club experimented with its revenue model, beginning with merchant fees only and then adding a consumer fee for the card. Several other firms jumped in after observing Diner's Club's success (although they all failed). Later, American Express entered at a different price point. Ultimately, Bank of America and others ran several experiments with their "open-loop" system before converging on the Visa and Mastercard systems.

3. Lemstra et al. (2011) provides the most thorough overview of developments, and from many perspectives. The narrative provided in Chapter 4, in particular, stresses the standard s-curve framework, "Crossing the Chasm."

4. Perhaps the best-known modern exception arose during the design of the broadcasting standard for color television. The Korean War delayed the deployment of the first approved design, and the after the war it was reconsidered, leading to deployment of a technically superior design.

5. See the review of FCC policies found on http://www.cybertelecom.org/broadband/wifi.htm (accessed May 2007), a nonprofit site which links to the original FCC material and summarizes it. Subsequent clarifications and rules emerged several times thereafter, partly to promote equipment export to other parts of the world by aligning spectrum in the United States with similar policies elsewhere.

6. See the review of FCC policies found on http://www.cybertelecom.org/broadband/wifi.htm (accessed May 2007).

7. See, in particular, the discussion in Marcus (2009).

8. Indeed, once the standard was in place, it diffused into a much more decentralized structure, one comprised of industry equipment manufacturers. There it would face far fewer obstructions. This is also consistent with Kahl's analysis.

9. The story of the growth of a local area network market around the activities in committee 802 is well told in Von Burg (2001).

10. See Chapters 2, 3, and 4 of Lemstra et al. (2011).

11. See the description of Hills (2005), who began developing the equivalent of a Wi-Fi network for the Carnegie Mellon campus in Pittsburgh, starting in 1993.

12. Also see Chapters 2, 3, and 4 of Lemstra et al. (2011).

13. HomeRF did not generate the enthusiastic sales that those who designed it predicted – even though the designers considered it technically superior to the alternatives. For speculation about why HomeRF failed, see, e.g., http://www.cazitech.com/HomeRF_Archives.htm

14. This is a necessarily brief synopsis of the account in Lemstra et al. (2011, Chap. 4).

15. A $100 retail price would have been anything from one-fifth to one-tenth the price of equipment in the first half of the decade. A cost of $50 would require economies of scale in production and extensive use of standard components, as the cost of production cost of cards was higher than $100 at the time of the meeting between Apple and Lucent. As described in Lemstra et al. (2011, Chap. 4, p. 131), it required Lucent to put into the initial price some of the

learning curve benefits it anticipated, which was a departure from existing practice.

16. In particular, see Lemstra et al. (2011, Chap. 4, p. 130), which describes changes in product requirements linked to "all-or-nothing type of negotiations."

17. For an account see Lemstra et al. (2011, Chap. 4, pp. 131–32).

18. Links says Michael Dell "was furious about the fact that he had been beaten by Apple ..."

19. The choice of the label "Wi-Fi" resembled "Hi-Fi" or high-fidelity, a term commonly used to describe high quality and expensive musical components. The choice of branding was deliberate, as it signaled high quality transmission. Yet, it was also a clever choice of words, since 802.11b actually has little to do with music or fidelity, and "Wi-Fi" is a made-up phrase. It did not stand for any combination of longer words.

20. This is not particularly novel institutional arrangement. Perhaps the difficulties experienced with incompatible equipment in 1997 had taught participants not to ignore this activity.

21. For example, in high-density settings it was possible for there to be interference among the channels, or interference with other users of the unlicensed spectrum reserved by the FCC, such as cordless telephones. The diffusion of so many devices also raised questions about norms for paying for access in apartment buildings, from neighbors, and others (see Sandvig, 2004).

22. For a full account, see Burgelman (2007).

23. For history and analysis of Intel's investments in different projects, including, but not necessarily *Centrino*, and why its management chose to invest heavily in some complementary technologies and not others (see, e.g., Gawer & Cusumano, 2002; Gawer & Henderson, 2007).

24. See Thomke (2003a) for systematic approaches for designing experiments so they can be measured in settings where firms control many of the key aspects of the experiment.

25. For documentation of this, see Stranger and Greenstein (2007).

26. See Von Hippel (1988) about lead users in general, and Sandvig (2004, 2007) about wireless technology lead users in particular.

27. In this context, "codified" refers to an idea put in a structured format that another technically trained individual can understand without having the author present – for example, words, mathematical formulas, plans, pictures, or professional drawings (see, e.g., the discussion in Nelson, 2007).

28. Sandvig, Young, and Meinrath (2004) document the tension between equipment firms and mesh-network user groups. The firms guarded their code, delaying experimentation at user groups, because the firms were also anticipating that they would deploy such designs in the near future.

ACKNOWLEDGMENTS

I am grateful for comments from seminar audiences, the editors of this volume, and from Robert Cannon, Ben Jones, Brian Kahin, Kristina

McElharen, Paul Ohm, Bill Rogerson, Christian Sandvig, Alicia Shems, Jim Speta, Scott Stern, Phil Weiser, and Joel West. I am responsible for all errors.

REFERENCES

Abbate, J. (1999). *Inventing the internet*. Cambridge, MA: MIT Press.

Benklar, Y. (2002). Some economics of wireless communications. *Harvard Journal of Law & Technology, 16*(1), 25.

Burgelman, R. A. (2007). Intel Centrino in 2007: A new platform strategy for growth. Stanford Case, SM-156. Graduate School of Business, Stanford University, Stanford, CA.

Cusumano, M. A. (2012). Platforms versus products: Observations from the literature and history. In S. J. Kahl, B. S. Silverman & M. A. Cusumano (Eds.), *Advances in strategic management* (Vol. 29, pp. 35–67). Bingley, UK: Emerald Group.

Faulhaber, G., & Farber, D. (2003). Spectrum management: Property rights, markets, and the commons. In L. F. Cranor & S. Wildman (Eds.), *Rethinking rights and regulations*. Cambridge, MA: MIT press.

Frischmann, B. (2012). *Infrastructure, the social value of shared resources*. Oxford, UK: Oxford University Press.

Gawer, A., & Cusumano, M. (2002). *Platform leadership: How Intel, Microsoft and Cisco drive industry innovation*. Boston, MA: Harvard Business School Press.

Gawer, A., & Henderson, R. (2007). Platform owner entry and innovation in complementary markets: Evidence from Intel. *Journal of Economics and Management Strategy, 16*(1), 1–34.

Greenstein, S. (2007). The evolution of market structure for internet access in the United States. In W. Aspray & P. Ceruzzi (Eds.), *The internet and American business*. Cambridge, MA: MIT Press.

Greenstein, S. (2008). Economic experiments and industry know-how in internet access markets. In A. Jaffe, J. Lerner & S. Stern (Eds.), *Innovation, policy and the economy* (Vol. 8, pp. 59–109). Cambridge, MA: MIT Press.

Hills, A. (2005). Smart Wi-Fi. *Scientific American*, October.

Hundt, R. (2000). *You say you want a revolution: A story of information age politics*. New Haven, CT: Yale University Press.

Ingram, P., Rao, H., & Silverman, B. S. (2012). History in strategy research: What, why, and how? In S. J. Kahl, B. S. Silverman & M. A. Cusumano (Eds.), *Advances in strategic management* (Vol. 29, pp. 241–273). Bingley, UK: Emerald Group.

Kahl, S. J., Liegel, G., & Yates, J. (2012). Audience structure and the failure of institutional entrepreneurship. In S. J. Kahl, B. S. Silverman & M. A. Cusumano (Eds.), *Advances in strategic management* (Vol. 29, pp. 275–313). Bingley, UK: Emerald Group.

Kharif, O. (2003). Paving the airwaves for Wi-Fi. *Business Week*, April 1.

Leblebici, H. (2012). The evolution of alternative business models and the legitimization of universal credit card industry: Exploring the contested terrain where history and strategy meet. In S. J. Kahl, B. S. Silverman & M. A. Cusumano (Eds.), *Advances in strategic management* (Vol. 29, pp. 117–151). Bingley, UK: Emerald Group.

Lemstra, W., Hayes, V., & Groenewegen, J. (2011). *The innovation journey of Wi-Fi: The road to global success*. Cambridge, UK: Cambridge University Press.

Liu, B. (2001). *Is new standard for 802.11 out of luck?* InternetNews, November 4, 2001. Retrieved from http://www.internetnews.com/wireless/article.php/10692_923821. Accessed on April 2007.

Marcus, M. (2009). Wi-Fi and bluetooth: The path from Carter and Reagan-era faith in deregulation to widespread products impacting our world. *INFO*, *11*(5), 19–35.

Nelson, R. (2007). *On the evolution of human know-how.* Mimeo. Columbia University.

Rosenberg, N. (1992). Economic experiments. *Industrial and Corporate Change*, *1*(1), 181–203.

Rosenberg, N. (1996). Uncertainty and technology change. In R. Landau, T. Taylor & G. Wright (Eds.), *The Mosiac of economic growth* (pp. 334–356). Stanford, CA: Stanford University Press.

Rosenbloom, R., & Cusumano, M. A. (1987). Technological pioneering and competitive advantage: the birth of the VCR industry. *California Management Review*, *29*(4), 51–76.

Sandvig, C. (2004). An initial assessment of cooperative action in Wi-Fi networking. *Telecommunications Policy*, *28*(7/8), 579–602.

Sandvig, C. (2007). *Wireless play and unexpected innovation.* Working Paper. University of Illinois. Retrieved from http://www.spcomm.uiuc.edu/csandvig/research/

Sandvig, C., Young, D., & Meinrath, S. (2004). Hidden interfaces in ownerless networks. Paper presented to the 32nd Annual Telecommunications Policy Research Conference (TPRC) on Communication, Information and Internet Policy, Arlington, VA. Retrieved from http://www.spcomm.uiuc.edu/csandvig/research/

Stern, S. (2005). Economic experiments: The role of entrepreneurship in economic prosperity. In *Understanding entrepreneurship: A research and policy report.* http://research. kauffman.org/cwp/ShowProperty/web/CacheRepository/Documents/Research_Policy_ Singles.pdf

Stranger, G., & Greenstein, S. (2007). Pricing in the shadow of firm turnover: ISPs in the 1990s. *International Journal of Industrial Organization*, *26*(3), 625–642.

Thomke, S. (2003a). *Experimentation matters: Unlocking the potential of new technologies for innovation.* Boston, MA: Harvard Business School Press.

Thomke, S. (2003b, April). R&D comes to services: Bank of America's pathbreaking experiments. *Harvard Business Review*, *81*(4), 70–79.

Von Burg, Urs. (2001). *The Triumph of ethernet: Technological communities and the battle for the LAN standard.* Palo Alto, CA: Stanford University Press.

Von Hippel, E. (1988). *The sources of innovation.* New York, NY: Oxford University Press.

PLATFORMS VERSUS PRODUCTS: OBSERVATIONS FROM THE LITERATURE AND HISTORY

Michael A. Cusumano

ABSTRACT

Purpose – *This chapter discusses the difference between a product strategy and a platform strategy, relying on examples from the history of Apple and Microsoft in personal computers and other devices as well as Sony and Japan Victor Corporation in videocassette recorders.*

Design/methodology/approach – *The chapter begins with a review of how the term "platform" has been used in the management literature and defines an industry-wide platform (as compared to an in-house company product platform) as a foundation technology (or service) that brings multiple parties in a market together for a common purpose. An industry-wide platform can generate powerful network effects between the platform and complementary products and services that make the platform increasingly valuable. Apple, with the Macintosh computer, and Sony with the Betamax VCR as well as other products, such as the Walkman media player, are examples of firms that developed excellent products but followed a product-first strategy and ended up losing in these markets or becoming niche players. They paid relatively little attention to opening up their technology to outside firms and cultivating an ecosystem of partners.*

History and Strategy
Advances in Strategic Management, Volume 29, 35–67
ISSN: 0742-3322/doi:10.1108/S0742-3322(2012)0000029006

Apple changed in the early 2000s with the iPod and iTunes, and then the iPhone and iPad, and has risen from near bankruptcy to become an enormously valuable and profitable platform leader.

Findings – *Historical examples suggest that, in a platform market, the winner is not the firm with the best product, but rather the firm with the best platform – that is, the foundation technology or service that is most open to outsiders and which stimulates development of the most compelling complements.*

Originality/value – *This result extends the literature's understanding of platform strategy.*

Keywords: Platforms; platform strategy; two-sided markets

INTRODUCTION

This chapter focuses on a relatively new concept in the strategic management literature: the notion of industry-wide as compared to company-specific "platforms" for building related sets of products or services.[1] I begin with a review of how the term platform has been used in the relevant literature, principally in the fields of product development and operations management, economics, and strategy. Then I discuss the historical cases of Apple versus Microsoft in personal computers and Sony versus JVC in video recorders. I conclude with some observations regarding the potential strategic differences and managerial implications of a product-focused strategy versus a platform-focused strategy, and the insights that an historical approach to this topic brings.

USE OF THE TERM "PLATFORM"

The word "platform" seems to have first come into wide usage in the management literature as a term meaning foundation of components around which an organization might create a related but differentiated set of products or services. For example, Toyota's Corolla sedan, Celica sports car, Matrix hatchback, and Rav-4 sports utility vehicle are different products built in separate projects with different customer segment targets. But they share the same underbody platform (Cusumano & Nobeoka,

1998). Since the early 1990s, Microsoft also has built the Office suite (mainly the Word, Excel, and PowerPoint applications) around shared components that we can think of as elements of a desktop productivity platform, such as for text processing, file management, and graphics (Cusumano & Selby, 1995). In the 1990s, many researchers in operations and technology management as well as in strategy and economics popularized the concept of an in-house "product platform" used to create such families of related products, particularly when discussing modular architectures and component reuse.[2]

In my 2002 book with Annabelle Gawer, *Platform Leadership*, and in subsequent chapter, we began to use the term differently, relying heavily on historical cases such as the evolution of the personal computer (Gawer & Cusumano, 2002). We tried to distinguish between an in-house product platform and an "industry platform." In our view, the latter had two essential differences. The first is that an industry platform is a foundation or core technology (it could also be a service) in a "system-like" offering that increases significantly in value to users with the addition of complementary products and services. The platform producer often (but not always, as seen in the case of Microsoft) depends on outside firms to produce these essential complements. The Windows personal computer and a smartphone (a web-enabled cell phone that can handle digital media files as well as run computer-like applications) are just boxes of relatively little value without software applications, digital content, or wireless telephony and Internet services. Cisco has a platform that has evolved since the 1980s and 1990s from a specialized computer system called a router that connects corporate networks with the Internet to a software layer, the Internetworking Operating System (IOS). IOS or even an Internet router have little value by themselves but become much more useful when customers deploy the software or the hardware with a variety of networking equipment, such as different types of routers, computer servers, telecommunications switches, and wireless devices, from Cisco and other vendors, as well as different applications. For these reasons, a potential industry platform should have relatively open interfaces in the sense of being easily accessible technically and with inexpensive or free licensing terms. The goal is to encourage other firms and user communities (such as for the "free" Linux operating system) to adopt the platform technology as their own and contribute complementary innovations. These external innovators form the platform "ecosystem."

The second essential difference between a product and an industry platform, as various researchers have described, is the creation of "network effects." These are positive feedback loops that can increase value at exponentially rising levels as adoption of a platform grows and as more ecosystem partners add complementary innovations. The network effects can be very powerful, especially when they are "direct" or on the "same side" of the market as the platform and the user or the complementor. For example, applications written specifically for Windows PCs can only work on these machines (unless the user has special virtualization software) and users can only exchange applications if they have the same PCs and operating systems. The network effects can also be "indirect," such as when software application distributors decide to stock more Windows applications compared to competing systems such as the Macintosh because they see many more companies licensing the Windows operating system and selling Windows PCs, and more users adopting Windows as their computing platform. Indirect or "cross-side" network effects can be very powerful as well.

Perhaps most important, a network effect means that the more external adopters in the ecosystem that create or use the complementary innovations, the more valuable the platform (and the complements) become. This dynamic, driven by direct or indirect network effects or both, should encourage more users to adopt the platform, more complementors to enter the ecosystem, more users to adopt the platform and the complements, almost ad infinitum.[3]

We have seen many platform-like battles and network effects in the history of technology, mainly in cases where competitions emerge due to incompatible standards and when a product by itself has limited value. Standards by themselves are not platforms; they are rules or protocols specifying how to connect different products or modules and use them together. Prominent past examples of platforms incorporating specific standards include the telegraph (what format or language to use for coding and decoding messages and sending the electrical signals), the telephone (how to do the same thing as the telegraph but with voice signals), electricity (the battle between alternating vs. direct current), radio (struggles over the establishment of AM and FM standards, broadcasting technology, and content), television (what standards to adopt initially, and then the movement from black-and-white to color), magnetic-tape video recording (VHS versus Beta formats and content), and computer operating systems (from IBM mainframes to PCs, the Macintosh, and Linux).

Other recent hardware and software platform battles have emerged over Internet portals, search, and content delivery; online marketplaces; smart-phone operating systems and transmission technologies; video-game consoles and games; electronic payment systems; foreign exchange trading systems; electronic stock brokerage systems; alternative automotive power systems; and social networking sites. Some platforms become relatively open to multiple players. For example, Leblebici's discussion of the credit card industry describes a platform-like battle over payment and credit systems (2012). This is clearly a multi-sided market (users, credit card companies, and retailers) where the credit card serves as a platform to bring these sides together. Unlike in the desktop PC industry, where Microsoft has dominated the software platform and Intel the hardware core, we have multiple winners (Visa, Mastercard, American Express, Diner's Club, etc.), with interoperable and substitutable systems managed through banking networks or the separate firms. The history of Wi-Fi technology as described by Greenstein (2012) represents another relatively open technology that brings many parties together (users, makers of various devices, service providers, application developers, etc.) but without one firm dominating the platform (Greenstein, 2012). Even the human genome database has become an open platform of data and knowledge for researchers and pharmaceutical companies as they compete (and sometimes cooperate) to analyze how genes function and discover new drug products. In fact, the more we look inside modern society and its technological artifacts – the computer, cell phone, media player, home entertainment systems, office equipment, or even the automobile – the more we will see platforms, and platforms within or on top of platforms.

We also can see platform competition and network effects surrounding non-technology products and services – reinforcing the idea that this principle is not simply for high-tech managers. This kind of platform reflects a more general usage of the term as a mechanism simply for bringing multiple parties – usually buyers and sellers – together for a common purpose (Eisenmann, Parker, & Van Alstyne, 2006). Shopping malls, for example, are platform-like networks that bring together buyers and sellers. In addition, Wal-Mart has created a global supply-chain and retail platform to feed its retail stores. Marks & Spencer has done the same thing on a smaller scale while Best Buy is doing the same thing in electronics goods and home appliances retailing. Other examples include CVS and Walgreens, which use their networks of pharmacy-retail stores to offer an increasing variety of customer services from new internal divisions and acquisitions as well as partners. They started with filling prescriptions but now offer photography, flu shots, and basic health care in their retail locations, at people's homes, or in their workplaces. Whether these financial inter-mediaries or supply-chain and retail networks are truly industry platforms in the sense of Gawer and Cusumano (2002) depends on whether they generate at least weak indirect network effects and thus positive feedback loops between the platform and the complements or between users and other participants in the market.

Not surprisingly, we have seen a growing amount of research on industry-level platforms, initially by economists but increasingly by scholars of strategy and innovation.[4] In particular, competition in the consumer electronics and computer industries spurred a great deal of thinking on this topic in the early 1980s, just as the arrival of the World Wide Web did so again in the mid-1990s. Influential early work mostly focused on theory, with few detailed examples and no large-sample studies. But the key concepts are all there and now are familiar to researchers and managers alike: how technical standards and compatibility or user adoption affect the course of platform industries and product designs, the phenomenon of network effects and positive feedback, and the role of switching costs, pricing, and bundling (see, e.g., Arthur, 1989; Bakos & Brynjolfsson, 1999; David, 1985; Farrell & Saloner, 1986; Farrell & Shapiro, 1998; Katz & Shapiro, 1992; Langlois, 1992; Nalebuff, 2004; Shapiro & Varian, 1998). More recent economics work has focused on models that improve our understanding of how "multi-sided" platform markets function (see Rochet & Tirole, 2003; Rochet & Tirole, 2006; also Bresnahan & Greenstein, 1999; Schmalensee, Evans, & Hagiu, 2006).

In the literature connecting strategic management and innovation, recent studies also analyze multi-sided platform competition as well as how to manage complementors, use the ecosystem for generating new products and services, and compete as a complementor (see Adner, 2006; Yoffie & Kwak, 2006). For example, the battle between Netscape and Microsoft in the browser wars illustrated the use of one-sided subsidies. By this term I mean the strategy of "free, but not free" – give one part of the system away, such as the Internet browser, but charge for another part, such as the web application server or the Windows operating system. Adobe has done the same thing by giving away the Acrobat Reader and charging for its servers and editing tools, technical support, and online services. Some firms give one part of the platform system away to some users (students or the general consumer) but charge others (corporate users). Intellectual property also can be "open, but not open" or "closed, but not closed." By these terms I mean that firms can make access to the interfaces easily available but keep critical parts of the technology proprietary or very distinctive. Netscape did this with the Navigator browser and an array of servers, special versions of scripting and programming languages, and intranet and extranet combinations. Microsoft has done this with the entire set of Windows client and server technologies, as well as Office and other Windows applications (Cusumano & Yoffie, 1998). Mobile operating system vendors also have a combination of open but not completely open features and licensing practices (Anvaari & Jansen, 2010). At the broader ecosystem level, other researchers have written about the emergence of "keystone" firms – industry leaders ranging from Wal-Mart to Microsoft and automobile companies that encourage innovation by cultivating networks of firms to make modularized components (Iansiti & Levien, 2004). We also have important work by Eisenmann, Parker, and Van Alstyne on the conditions that make for, and prevent, "winner-take-all" markets (see Eisenmann et al., 2006; also Eisenmann, 2006; Eisenmann, Parker, & Van Alstyne, 2007; Parker & Van Alstyne, 2005).

Given the breadth and growing popularity of platforms as a research topic, it is important to be clear about what an industry platform is not. Although it is not a technological standard, technology-based platforms usually incorporate existing industry standards and help establish new ones. Microsoft and Intel, by promoting certain standards within Windows and the "x86" line of compatible microprocessors, did this with applications programming and connectivity standards for the personal computer, beginning with the first IBM PC. Cisco, by bundling certain protocols within its operating software for routers and other equipment, did this with networking. Many of these technologies are protected by patents or "patent pools" as described by Lampe and Moser are controlled by a small number of firms that may indeed serve as platform leaders (Lampe & Moser, 2012). For the most part, however, platforms become widely adopted due to the power of direct and indirect network effects between the platform and complements.

Nor is an industry platform the same as a "dominant design," though a successful platform is, by definition, widely adopted. James Utterback and the late William Abernathy have defined a dominant design as a particular configuration of a product that wins allegiance from the majority of users and thus influences what subsequent designs look like. The QWERTY keyboard, the Ford Model T, and the IBM PC all have played this role in their industries (Utterback, 1996). But, just as different product designs may compete to become the dominant form, an industry may generate multiple platform candidates that compete for dominance. Some industries never experience a dominant design or a dominant platform. In any case, though, industry platforms differ from dominant designs in that they are part of a system – the platform and the complements – and are not stand-alone products. They also require network effects for the platform to grow in value to users. In addition, the dominant designs of Utterback and Abernathy appear in the latter stage of an industry evolution as part of the maturation process and managerial shift of attention from product design to the production process. It may happen that platforms emerge later in an industry's development. But they can appear early as part of a competition to establish a dominant platform.[5] And some competing platforms may persist for long periods of time without any one leader emerging.

PRODUCT VERSUS PLATFORM: APPLE AND SONY

A product strategy can turn into a platform strategy and a best-selling product is an excellent start to a successful industry platform. But various examples suggest that, in the early stages of competition, a *product* strategy differs from a *platform* strategy, and there are significant consequences for both the innovator and for users. We can learn a lot about the differences and consequences of a product versus a platform strategy simply from observing the historical behavior of Apple and Sony – two accomplished product companies where, the evidence suggests, senior managers have not always thought "platform first."[6]

Apple versus Microsoft

It is generally recognized today that Apple, Inc., founded by Steve Jobs and Steve Wozniak in 1976, ranks as one of the most innovative product companies in history (Yoffie & Kim, 2010). But, I argue in this chapter that, at least prior to the 2000s, Apple focused more on developing great *individual products* rather than trying to create an *industry-wide platform* that was relatively easy for a large number of other companies to adopt for their own complementary products and services. Consequently, Apple missed out on some enormous business opportunities that could have made the Macintosh personal computer the industry's dominant design and standard and, more recently, even further increased or sped up adoption of the iPod and the iPhone products as well as the iTunes digital media service. Instead, the vast majority of personal computer users adopted cheap and powerful but more difficult-to-use DOS computers, which lacked a graphical user interface, and then Windows machines, which generally lagged behind the Macintosh in ease of use until recent versions such as Windows 7, introduced in 2009 (Mossberg, 2009). In the global smartphone market,

Apple in early 2012 also narrowly trailed adopters of Google's Android operating system, despite the remarkable popularity of the iPhone. One reason may be that Apple did not license the iPhone software or handset design, just as it chose, for the most part, not to license the Macintosh operating system technology.

Apple missed an opportunity to dominate the PC market as it was evolving in the 1980s. At least one reason seems to be a narrowly conceived product-focused (not a platform-focused) strategy in the sense that Apple did not license its technology and try to cultivate a broad set of industry partners, like Microsoft and Intel did with their DOS software and microprocessor technologies (Cusumano & Selby, p. 148; Isaacson, 2011). The Macintosh pioneered graphical user interface technology (albeit inspired by Xerox – another great product company that missed an enormous business opportunity) for the mass market. Other landmark Apple products include the first mass-market PC, the Apple II, introduced in 1977; the PowerBook, which in 1991set the design standard for laptops; the unsuccessful though still pioneering Newton PDA, first sold in 1993; and the iMac all-in-one "designer PC," released in 1998. More recently, we have seen the iPod digital media player (2001), the iTunes digital media service (2003), the iPhone (2007), and the iPad (2010). Steve Jobs did not himself design these products. He was absent from the company during 1985–1997 and returned only when Apple acquired one of his less successful ventures, NeXT Computer. But even then, NeXT technology and the UNIX operating system provided the basis for another hit Apple product released in 2001, the Mac OS X operating system. Most importantly, Jobs created the design culture and hired or supervised the people (such as Jonathan Ive, chief designer of the iMac, the iPod, and the iPhone) most responsible for the company's historical legacy and recent revival.[7]

The computer industry probably would have looked very different today if Steve Jobs, earlier in his career, had thought a bit more like his archrival, Bill Gates. Microsoft, founded a year before Apple in 1975, generally has not tried to develop "insanely great" products (Job's goal for the Macintosh) (Levy, 1994). Occasionally, some have been very good – such as BASIC for the Altair PC kit, the early versions of Excel for Windows (1990), Internet Explorer version 4 (1997), and Windows 7 (which, in 2009, finally caught up to the Macintosh, after 25 years). Mostly, Microsoft has tried to produce "good enough" products that could also serve as industry platforms and thereby bring cheap and powerful computing to the masses (and significant profits to Microsoft). DOS, Windows, and Office have done this, in different turns, since 1981.[8]

But it is also true that, unlike Apple, Microsoft has not found great platform success outside of Windows for the desktop and its major complementary application, Office. Together, these two products accounted for 58% of 2011 sales and 77% of operating profits (see Box A1). This observation suggests a potentially limiting side to firms that establish dominant platforms: It is hard to evolve beyond them. Microsoft has extended Windows to enterprise computing and the server market, and introduced online versions of Windows and Office that come under the rubric of "software as a service" or "cloud computing" (Cusumano, 2010a). The Xbox console has done moderately well as an integrated hardware–software platform for video games and some home entertainment. But Microsoft through Windows 7 had minimal presence in the fastest growing market that bridged cell phones and consumer electronics – smartphones and tablets. Windows 8 seemed more promising to make a dent in the smartphone market in future years. Nonetheless, it is hard to argue with the financial results Microsoft continues to generate as a result of its dominance of the Windows platform, for both consumer and enterprise computing, as well as Office, the most important complementary product for Windows (and a platform in its own right in that many companies build additional products that take advantage of accessible features in Office).

Sony versus JVC

Another company that historically seems to have focused more on stand-alone products rather than industry-wide platforms is Sony. This orientation was particularly evident in the competition with Japan Victor Corporation (JVC) to introduce a home videocassette recorder (VCR) (see Cusumano, Mylonadis, & Rosenbloom, 1992; Rosenbloom & Cusumano, 1987). To explain the outcome of this competition, we need to go back to 1969–1971. During this period, Sony engineers had compromised their technology goals when designing an earlier video-recorder device using 3/4-inch wide tape, called the U-Matic. They compromised in order to get the support of other firms in Japan and elsewhere. As a result, the large, bulky, and expensive U-Matic failed to attract home users (Cusumano et al., 1992, p. 60). But institutions such as schools and police stations did purchase the machines. These customers provided Sony as well as JVC and other vendors with the inspiration to continue and enough feedback to design a more successful home product. When Sony introduced their smaller 1/2-inch tape machine in 1975, dubbed the Betamax, company executives again tried to persuade other firms to adopt their technology as the new industry standard. Sony's goal was to replace the 3/4-inch format as well as competing formats under development at several firms. But this time Sony engineers refused to alter the Betamax design to accommodate other firms in Japan or in the United States. General Electric, for example, wanted a much longer recording time for American consumers. The original Betamax recorded for only one hour.

JVC, backed by its giant parent Matsushita Electronics (recently named Panasonic after its US brand name), in fall 1976 came out with its own product, Video Home System (VHS). This offered two hours of recording. Within five months, Sony matched the two-hour time, such as by using thinner tape. Some observers also thought VHS was technically inferior to the Beta machines. This reputation, along with improvements in the recording time, should have provided Sony with more staying power in this market. But JVC and Matsushita continued to match Sony reasonably quickly with new features and longer recording times, and comparable prices. Sony eventually came out with an unmatched 8 hours of recording time in 1982 (see Table 1).

Features and prices ultimately mattered little because the VHS and Betamax machines were very comparable technically and hard for users to differentiate. Simultaneously, however, there were powerful network effects. VHS and Betamax, though both based on the U-Matic, utilized different cassette sizes and incompatible signal-encoding formats. At the time,

Table 1. VHS and Beta Recording-Playing Time Comparison.

Year/Month	Beta	VHS
1975/May	1 hour (Sony)	
1976/October		2 hours (JVC)
1977/March	2 hours (Sony)	
1977/October		4 hours (Matsushita)
1978/October	3 hours (Sony)	
1979/March	4.5 hours (Sony)	
1979/August		6 hours (Matsushita)
		4 hours (JVC)
1979/December		6 hours (JVC)
1982/March	8 hours (Sony)	
1982/September	5 hours (Sony)	

Source: Cusumano et al. (1992, Table 7, p. 77). Reprinted with the permission of Cambridge University Press.

the machines were sufficiently expensive that consumers were unlikely to own more than one format. As discussed earlier in this chapter, the research by Eisenmann, Van Alstyne, and Parker suggests that three factors in combination – (1) little room for platform differentiation, (2) strong network effects between the platform and the complements, and (3) the unlikelihood of users buying more than one platform, which they call "multi-homing" – should lead to a winner-take-all or winner-take-most market. Indeed, a review of the history indicates that this is what happened.

Of equal importance, we can see that the market dynamics here did not simply unfold through some natural or random process. JVC and Matsushita *deliberately* worked to position VHS as a new *industry* standard and worked very hard to make this happen by broadly licensing the technology, cultivating partnerships, and promoting the distribution of VHS-format prerecorded tapes (Cusumano et al., 1992, pp. 65–66). For example, the JVC executives and development team humbly visited competitors and potential partners, asked for feature suggestions, and did their best to accommodate them. JVC and Matsushita also broadly licensed the new technology on inexpensive terms to some 40 firms. They provided essential components (like the helical scanner, which was very difficult to mass produce) until licensees were able to do the manufacturing themselves, with assistance from JVC and Matsushita. In contrast, the Beta group totaled merely 12 firms at its peak, with Sony doing the bulk of the manufacturing (see Table A1).

JVC and Matsushita, with great foresight lacking in Sony at the time, aggressively cultivated a complementary market in prerecorded tapes and retail distribution. Matsushita even used its engineering resources to build machines that replicated tapes at very high speeds for the prerecorded market (Cusumano et al., 1992, p. 86). All of these very deliberate moves – which my coauthors and I in a 1992 article called "strategic maneuvering" – helped establish the VHS technology as a new platform for the consumer electronics industry and "tip" the market toward VHS. The network effects increased in strength as the much larger number of firms licensing VHS brought more production capacity to their standard, which encouraged more tape producers and distributors to make many more prerecorded VHS tapes. Retailers increasingly used their limited shelf space for VHS prerecorded tapes (Cusumano, et al., 1992, p. 57). Users responded and bought more VHS machines, which encouraged more firms to license the VHS standard and then more tape producers, distributors, and consumers to adopt VHS. Betamax went from a 100% share in 1975, the beginning of the market, to zero by the later 1980s (Table A2).

STRATEGIC EVOLUTION: THE TRANSFORMATION OF APPLE

The Macintosh story resembles the Betamax story, but with a critical difference. Apple's product survived, even though it remained for many years only on the periphery of the PC industry in terms of market share – falling to as low as 2% of global PC sales in the early 2000s until the popularity of the iPod and then the iPhone encouraged more customers to try the Macintosh, especially in the United States (Yoffie & Kim, 2010). Poor responses (Cusumano, 2006; Mossberg, 2009) to Microsoft's Windows Vista operating system, introduced in 2006 and then replaced by the much-improved Windows 7 in 2009, also persuaded many users to switch over to Apple. Still, the US market share for the Mac peaked at around 10% during 2008–2011, and seems to have leveled off. The main point is that Apple's strategy never got the Macintosh beyond a few percent of the global personal computer market, compared to 90–95% for Windows PCs (Yoffie & Slind, 2008). Of course, the Mac's innovative software and hardware designs have attained great "mind share" or attention in the industry, and forced responses from Microsoft and PC hardware manufacturers. This competition remains vitally important to stimulating innovation and is the reason we now have Windows 7 and its successor, Windows 8. Nonetheless, there are strategic similarities between Sony and Apple that, at least in retrospect, suggest there were superior strategic approaches.

Like Sony, Apple chose to optimize the Mac's hardware–software system and complete the design on its own as well as control the flow of revenues (and profits) from the product. By contrast, a *platform* strategy would have meant licensing the Macintosh operating system widely and working much more openly and actively with other companies to evolve the platform *together* and create complementary applications. Microsoft and its ecosystem partners have done this for the Windows PC. Apple did not do very much of this platform evangelism and has remained (with a brief exception many years ago) the only producer of the Mac. This product-centric strategy with manufacturing dominated by one firm (Apple), compared to the many producers of Windows PCs, has kept prices relatively higher and diffusion of the Macintosh relatively low (Yoffie & Kim, pp. 2–6). Moreover, the more "closed" and costly Macintosh did not stimulate the enormous mass market in applications that Microsoft and Intel have done for the PC. The Macintosh lived on initially as a minor second standard mainly because it found two niches – desktop publishing and consumers (including institutions such as primary schools) willing to pay more for an easier-to-use and more elegant product.

This brings our story to more recent Apple products that have done much better in the market. They also demonstrated enormous industry-platform potential – which Apple has finally tapped! The iPod, with its unique "click wheel" interface and new touch screen, is the best-selling music player in history, with its own near-monopoly – about a 70% market share. It has attracted complementary hardware innovations that have made it more valuable, such as connectors for a car or home-stereo system, or add-ons that turn the iPod into an FM radio, digital recorder, or camera. Initially, however, Apple introduced the iPod as another "closed" product system that worked only with the proprietary Macintosh computer and the relatively open iTunes music warehouse. It did not support non-Apple music formats or software applications, though any content provider could join iTunes. Eventually, it seems that consumer and market pressure persuaded Apple to open up the interfaces to the iPod software (but not the hardware) so that it could play some other music formats (but not those championed by Microsoft or Real). Apple also started out with proprietary digital rights management (DRM) technology on the iPod and its iTunes store, creating problems with potential ecosystem partners as well as customers, although the service and the Apple devices are now more open.

The iPod, and not the Macintosh, seems to have taught Apple executives how to behave more like an *industry*-platform leader. In 2002, it introduced an iPod compatible with Windows and then opened a Windows version of the iTunes online store in 2003. By mid-2008, the iTunes store had become a near-monopoly in its own right, with about a 70% share of the worldwide market for digital music (Yoffie & Slind, p. 11).

Then, in 2007, Apple introduced the iPhone – probably the most exciting electronics product to hit the market since the Macintosh (Cusumano, 2008, p. 24). But quickly the debate ignited again over whether this was yet another "closed" product or a more "open" platform. The iPhone was distinctive first because of another remarkable user interface (there is a pattern here!) driven both by touch and virtual keyboard technology. But the original iPhone would not run applications not built by Apple, and it would not operate on cell phone networks not approved by Apple (initially only AT&T in the United States, but later Deutche Telekom/T-Mobile in Germany, Telefonica/O2 in the United Kingdom, and Orange in France). Fortunately for consumers, hackers around the world found ways to "unlock" the phone and add applications. A black market also developed for "hacked" devices. This market pressure again seemed to persuade Apple

I management that its latest great product was also becoming a great new platform, at least in the United States, and so the interfaces needed to be more open to outside application developers and other complement producers.

It is possible that Apple executives all along planned to open up the interfaces gradually, if the product won broad market acceptance. The facts are that the opening did happen, but slowly for many users and application developers. In March 2008, Steve Jobs announced that Apple would license Microsoft's email technology to enable the iPhone to connect to corporate email servers. By the end of 2009, there were a hundred thousand applications available for the iPhone through the official App Store. Some applications were free, and many vendors continued to sell unauthorized "illegal" applications over which Apple had no control – something to which Apple, unlike Microsoft, is unaccustomed (Kane, 2009; Wortham, 2009). Apple also had yet to allow consumers to use the iPhone on any service network they chose. Apple's repeated attempts to control applications that work on its iPhone platform led to several very public confrontations with Google, banning of some very useful technology (such as Google Voice), and the resignation of Google CEO Eric Schmidt from Apple's board of directors. Google's expansion into mobile operating system software and applications has transformed it from being Apple's partner in the competition with Microsoft over Internet search and desktop software applications ("the enemy of my enemy is my friend") into Apple's rival in the cell phone business (see Vascellaro & Kane, 2009; also Schroeder, 2009).

Despite positioning the original Macintosh computer more as a break-through product rather than as a new industry-wide platform, Apple finally figured out how to play both sides of the platform game and thereby create synergies and potential network affects across several of its product lines as well as complementary applications and services. For example, the iPod, iPhone, and iTunes service all work particularly well with the Macintosh computer, and all can take advantage of applications built for the iOS operating system as well as content delivered through iTunes. Apple devices and iTunes all have some interoperability with Windows as well and benefit from these users – a kind of "closed, but not closed" platform strategy. Apple is continually standardizing at least the user interface across the iPhone, iPod, iPad, and the Macintosh (Chen, 2012). In addition, providing or distributing the essential complements – like Microsoft has always done for DOS and Windows – has become critical to Apple's success. The iPod is not very valuable without external digital content such as music and video files. These complementary innovations also make the versatile iPhone and other smartphones much more valuable than ordinary cell phones. Here, Apple cleverly found a way to distribute the key complements – the iTunes Store and the iPhone App Store, which have themselves evolved into new types of distribution platforms. Moreover, these deliver *automated services*, with low costs and high potential profit margins. Apple is being smart and sharing most (70%) of these revenues with the content owners. For the past decade, Apple also has been creating more software applications for the Macintosh to reduce its dependence on Microsoft, Adobe, and other independent software vendors (Yoffie & Slind, p. 6).

We can see the results of these product and platform efforts in Apple's much-improved financial performance and market value (Table 2). In 1995, Apple was nearly *twice* the size of Microsoft in annual revenues (about $11 billion to $6 billion). However, Apple's market valuation was only about *40% of revenues*, whereas Microsoft's value was nearly *six times revenues*.

Table 2. Microsoft and Apple Financial Comparison.

	Microsoft			Apple		
	Revenues ($million)	Operating profits (%)	Year-end market value ($million)	Revenues ($million)	Operating profits (%)	Year-end market value ($million)
2011	69,943	39.0	218,380	108,249	31.0	376,410
2010	62,484	38.0	238,784	65,225	28.0	295,886
2009	58,437	34.8	246,630	36,537	21.0	180,150
2008	60,420	37.2	149,769	32,479	19.3	118,441
2007	51,122	36.2	287,617	24,006	18.4	74,499
2006	44,282	37.2	251,464	19,315	12.7	45,717
2005	39,788	36.6	233,927	13,931	11.8	29,435
2004	36,835	24.5	256,094	8,279	3.9	8,336
2003	32,187	29.7	252,132	6,207	(loss)	4,480
2002	28,365	29.2	215,553*	5,742	0.3	4,926
2001	25,296	46.3	258,033*	5,363	(loss)	7,924
2000	22,956	47.9	302,326*	7,983	6.5	5,384
1995	5,937	35.3	34,330*	11,062	6.2	4,481

Source: Calculated from data in Apple Inc., "Form 10-K," Washington, DC: United States Securities and Exchange Commission, September 24, 2011 and prior years; and Microsoft Corporation, "Form 10-K," Washington, DC: United States Securities and Exchange Commission, June 30, 2011 and prior years.
Note: Fiscal year data. Market value is for calendar year except when marked with asterisk, then fiscal year. 2010–2011 market values from Financial Times Global 500.
Units: $million, %.

Not surprisingly, Microsoft's operating profit margin was also about six times Apple's (35 to 6%). Apple's sales and market value shrunk in subsequent years whereas Microsoft's sales and value increased dramatically, as Windows became the basis for a new generation of Internet-enabled consumer and enterprise products, including Office. Not until iPod sales began to catch on in 2005 did Apple's revenues, profits, and valuation turn around. In the last few years, Apple's revenues have risen much faster than Microsoft's, which is focused primarily on the PC industry. They jumped from $6.2 billion in 2003, with an operating loss, to over $36 billion in 2009, with a 21% operating profit margin, and $108 billion in 2011, with a 31% operating profit margin. In addition, Macintosh computers in 2011 made up only 20% of Apple's revenues (see Box A1). By comparison, Macintosh sales were 79% of Apple's revenues in 2002 (Yoffie & Kim, p. 15, Exhibit 1B). The iPod (including the iPod Touch – in essence, an iPhone without the telephony function) accounted for 7% of 2011 revenues, music and software products and services a combined 9%, and the iPhone 43%.

It is particularly striking how Apple's market value remained less than its annual revenues for so many years while Microsoft's market value was 8 to 13 times revenues (Box A1). But here too, by 2005, the tide had turned. Apple's value has risen, reaching four times revenues by 2011 – at this point, ahead of Microsoft (three times revenues). Microsoft's valuation declined and then stagnated due at least in part to the apparent commoditization in PC hardware and software markets. In other words, competition among Windows PC manufacturers such as Hewlett Packard, Dell, Lenovo, and Acer has made it difficult to raise prices. For example, in their case study of Apple, David Yoffie and Renee Kim report that PC prices, despite a rise in average leels of memory and processing power, declined at a compound annual rate of 8% per year between 1999 and 2005 (Yoffie & Kim, p. 4). Microsoft remained more profitable than Apple through 2011 in terms of operating margins (39% compared to 31% – see Box A1). This was because Microsoft is primarily a software products company. Replicating software products has a marginal cost of close to zero, (Cusumano, 2004) unlike manufacturing (or paying others to manufacture) hardware systems like Apple's iPhone, iPad, iPod, or Macintosh. In contrast to Apple, which has a high cost of sales and therefore low gross margins (41% compared to 78% at Microsoft), Microsoft has much larger expenses than Apple in sales and marketing as well as R&D.

Most important for our purposes in this chapter is to suggest that Apple's resurgence reflects, at least in part, the value of a *platform company* compared to a product company. The remarkable financial turnaround since 2005 began with some new "hit" products, and this demonstrates the importance of having a strong product strategy to go along with a platform strategy. But Apple also now has a portfolio of products that have become or are becoming industry platforms, including essential complementary services platforms (iTunes and Apps Store). They all work together and reinforce each other, through strong direct and indirect network effects. Moreover, Apple now benefits from a vibrant ecosystem around the iPod and iPhone, which means it no longer has to do the lion's share of innovation itself! As of early 2012, for example, there were over 500,000 applications in the Apple App Store.[9] It is finally allowing ecosystems to form that can rival the Windows world, even though Apple at times has clashed with Google, Real, Palm, Microsoft, and other partners and users with regard to how open to make the iPhone and iTunes (see Kane, 2009; Schroeder, 2009; Vascellaro & Kane, 2009; Wortham, 2009).

In 2010, Apple also introduced the iPad. This is a more elegant tablet computer than Microsoft's earlier design, and uses the same remarkable touch-screen technology as the iPod Touch and the iPhone. The iPad has some technical limitations – such as the inability to run more than one application at a time, and no support for Adobe's rival Flash video technology (which the iPhone also does not support, even though Flash is used for the vast majority of videos and advertisements on the web) (Kenney & Pon, 2011; Shankland, 2010). But Apple was also reaching agreements with major book, textbook, and newspaper publishers as well as encouraging iPhone developers to build applications that have make the iPad a new platform for surfing the Internet and handling digital content (music, photos, books, videos, and documents) (Lohr, 2011; Yoffie & Kim, pp. 12–13).

Apple's recent successes illustrate the general point of this chapter: If Steve Jobs and Apple had tried to make "insanely great platforms" first and "insanely great products" second, then most personal computer as well as smartphone users today probably would probably be Apple customers. We would have lived much more in an Apple, rather than a Microsoft world. Apple has grown from being merely a fifth of Microsoft's size in terms of sales as late as 2003 to just over half by 2008, and then to a third larger in 2011 (see Box A1). Apple also passed Microsoft in market value in May 2010.

On these dimensions, Apple has improved markedly in just a few short years. But it still is less profitable than Microsoft in terms of operating margins and not likely to reverse this situation anytime soon. Apple may always struggle to maintain the distinctiveness of its products and to convince new customers beyond the first wave of early users to pay premium prices. Customers will spend more for a product when it is new and path breaking. The difficulty arises when the novelty wears off and cheaper copycat products appear that are "good enough." Bill Gates learned this lesson early on in his career and ruthlessly exploited this characteristic of the market. We can see this not only in the way Windows mimicked the look and feel of the Macintosh, but also in how Word and Excel in the 1980s and 1990s mimicked the functionality of WordPerfect and Lotus 1-2-3. Windows NT and Windows 2000 server also took billions of dollars in revenues from Novell and UNIX vendors.

Apple probably has the world's happiest and most loyal customers, but that may not enough to keep its growth rates high. To maintain these enormous growth rates, it needs to continually find new customers, especially outside the United States, and convince existing customers to upgrade to new models of its products. Apple probably cannot charge higher prices than it has done already in the past few years; in fact, it already dropped prices on the iPhone significantly after the initial introduction. For example, Apple dropped the price of the iPhone by $200 after it went on sale (Jobs, 2012). Both AT&T and Target, a major US retailer, also dropped the price of the iPhone 3GS to $49 in 2011, with a service contract (Reisenger, 2011, 2012). Prices on smartphones and other products such as the iPad may fall as well as competitors introduce similar tablet products and if price competition intensifies, as it did in the personal computer and smartphone industries.

The Microsoft–Intel ecosystem has at least one advantage: Its customers do not have to love their product to buy it and do not have to pay premium prices. Most users do not even choose Microsoft or Intel products directly. For example, as noted in Box A1, in fiscal 2011, only about 25% of Microsoft's Windows desktop (client) sales and 20% of Office sales were directly to consumers. This amounted to a little more than 5% of total revenues.[10] Overall, only 30% of Microsoft's sales were directly to consumers (20% of Windows desktop and 20% of the Office division, and all of Online Services and Entertainment and Devices sales). Most of the Windows desktop and server as well as Office sales are either to OEMs (the PC makers) or to enterprises and other large organizations. This remains true despite open-source and "free" software. In addition, Apple still has not created the enormous recurring revenues that Microsoft's ecosystem and enterprise customers generate, with those continuing sales of Windows and Office to PC manufacturers and corporations, as well as individuals – who will mostly upgrade their PCs if not their software products, eventually.

More importantly, Microsoft has very high operating profit rates generated from the software product business (Cusumano, 2004, pp. 43–46). As noted earlier, the cost of reproducing a software product is essentially zero. This is why, for the past decade, Microsoft typically has had gross margins of 65–80% and operating margins (profit before taxes and investment income) of around 35%. This compares to gross margins for Apple of 41% in 2011 and operating profit margins of 18–31% in 2007–2011, after years of much lower profit (and revenue) levels (see Table 2 and Box A1). In addition, though Apple won the battle for digital media players with the iPod, that product, like PDAs, was already declining in sales as of 2009 as the iPhone and other smartphones, which include digital media functional, increased in market penetration (Yoffie & Kim, p. 1). Apple may yet win the global smartphone battle, but Nokia, Samsung, and other firms using Google's Android software platform were introducing products that look and feel similar to the iPhone. Most smartphone makers today (Apple as well as Google, RIM/Blackberry, Nokia, and Microsoft) also now has online apps stores (Yoffie & Kim, p. 21, Exhibit 9). And Microsoft's Windows 7 operating system has been heralded as an important step forward in reducing the usability gap between PCs and the Macintosh, while the Windows 8 beta has been very well received and should make Microsoft much more competitive in the smartphone and tablet markets.

In the long run, if hardware and software products both continue to experience commoditization and declining prices, then the most valuable part of the Apple franchise might end up being iTunes, or the new iCloud service introduced in 2011, which lets Apple as well as Windows users access their content remotely. The hardware products may simply become platforms to sell high-margin automated digital services, including music and video content (Stone & Miller, 2009).[11]

PLATFORM, PRODUCT, OR BOTH?

Perhaps the most challenging question for managers gets into the heart of strategy and innovation: Is it possible for a firm with Apple's creativity, foresight, and independence to think "insanely great platform" first and still produce such great products? Based on Sony's experience with VCRs, or Microsoft's with DOS and Windows, it appears that platform companies do need to make technical and design compromises in order to work effectively with other industry players and encourage them to be partners and complementors rather than competitors. Nokia did this reasonably well by convincing some competitors to join its Symbian consortium to develop an alternative mobile operating system to Microsoft and then making this an independent nonprofit as well as open-source entity, though ultimately Nokia was the primary supporter, and the technology became outdated after the introduction of smartphones.

Recent biographical information and other company accounts suggest that Jobs and other executives were clearly aware of the product versus platform distinction and deliberately chose not to follow an "open" platform strategy until recently (Isaacson, 2011). They have historically preferred to control "the user experience" (and take most of the revenues and profits for Apple, though more recently with a "closed, but not closed" approach). It appears that a more open industry-platform strategy is only a secondary consideration. But the fact that Apple did open up its platforms eventually without losing their distinctiveness as products suggests the company could have pursued product and platform leadership simultaneously. The challenge here is to be open but not so open that the platform leader makes it too easy for competitors to imitate the essential characteristics that make the original product so appealing.

Of course, despite the many examples, not every market is or will become a platform industry (though most related to information or digital technology are) and not every product can become an industry platform. Annabelle Gawer and I considered this issue by reviewing several cases and concluded that, for a product or component technology to have platform potential, it should satisfy two conditions (Gawer & Cusumano, 2008). First, the product or technology should perform at least one essential function as part of a "system," like the scanning mechanism and playback format in a home video recorder, or the operating software and microprocessor hardware in a personal computer. The function is essential if it solves a critical system-related problem for the industry, such as how to encode video signals or control the operations of a personal computer or a smartphone. Second, the product or technology should be relatively easy for other companies to connect to with their own products, components, or services in order to improve or expand the functionality of the overall platform system, for both intended and unexpected uses.

Some complementors also become platform leaders within a platform. Adobe, founded in 1982 to make laser printer software for Apple computers, falls into this category. It has become one of the most profitable software companies in the world – with 2011 revenues of $4.2 billion, a gross margin of 90%, and an operating profit rate of 24%. It rivals Microsoft in sales productivity and profitability.[12] Adobe gives away or sells platform technologies and tools (Acrobat readers and servers, Photoshop, Illustrator, Flash and Dreamweaver, Air, etc.) for printing and editing digital files, including text, photos, and videos, as well as for creating web content. Other firms build complementary hardware and software products such as laser printers, special font sets and editing tools, or applications with Flash video clips that use Adobe technology. Still more firms use Adobe products to offer their own digital content and online services. But Adobe's main products (though not those using technologies which directly threaten alternatives from Microsoft and Apple) are also wonderful complements for the most common platforms in the software business – Windows personal computers and smartphones from Apple, RIM (Blackberry), Microsoft, and Google.[13]

It is important to realize as well that a company does not have to be first to market or have the best technology to become the platform leader and achieve the dominant market share in its industry. But platform leaders and wannabes do need to encourage innovation around their platforms at the broad industry level. The reason is that platform leaders usually do not themselves have the capabilities or resources to create all possible complementary innovations or even complete systems in-house. Yet the value of their platforms depends on the availability and innovativeness of these complementary products and services. In addition, based on the history of other platform technologies, where wars over incompatible standards often led to market confusion and wasted innovation, we can say that platform industries generally need architects. This is where the concept of a platform leader and measures to implement a platform strategy becomes important (see Gawer & Cusumano, 2002).

LESSONS FROM HISTORY

The cases of Apple versus Microsoft, and Sony versus JVS, in addition to other examples, suggest several lessons. First, it appears that implementing a platform strategy or a complements strategy requires a very different strategic mentality and set of actions and investments on the implementation side compared to a product strategy. There are different risks and higher short-term costs. But the long-term economic rewards from a successful platform or complements strategy – especially when one firm creates both, like Microsoft and now Apple have done – can be enormous. Second, it seems that managers still must invest in their own innovation and have a strong, multigeneration product strategy. But it is probably not necessary to have the "best" product all the time to win a platform contest. Platform leaders seem to win their battles by having the best platform, and that often requires building yourself or attracting the most compelling complements, which should then help attract the most users or other market participants, such as advertisers in the case of Google.

On this first point, we can say that platform companies and their competitors have clear tasks ahead of them. The four levers of platform leadership (Gawer & Cusumano, 2002) define the basic game plan: Design relatively open product architectures and correctly manage intellectual property rights. Decide what components and complements to build in-house versus to allow the ecosystem to provide. Work closely with external partners and share the financial pie with them. Figure out how to organize internally to minimize potential conflicts when stimulating and competing with partners. At the same time, companies that wish to become platform leaders or challenge incumbents need to solve system-level problems for users and competitors that draw them to the platform, and they must do whatever they can to help the market tip in their direction.

Complementors have a similar agenda, with equal or even greater risks: If there are competing platforms, they must decide which ones to support and how fully to give their support.[14] They have to select which complements to produce and which to let other ecosystem partners or the platform leader make. They need to work closely (but not too closely) with the platform leader or multiple leader wannabes, and always have something compelling and proprietary to offer. Otherwise, if the business opportunity is large enough, or if the complementor is too independent, the platform leader will likely try to absorb their product or service into its platform. This can be a delicate balancing act. But complementors also have their own power. It can be their product or service that causes a market to tip and stay tipped.

The benefits of success seem to be clear. Platform leaders can have significant leverage over an entire industry for decades – like Microsoft, Intel, Cisco, Google, Qualcomm, and Adobe, or even Wal-Mart with its chain of stores and Mattel with platform-like products such as the Barbie doll. They benefit from innovation across an entire network of firms, not just within their own boundaries. Moreover, even if one firm does not take a dominant share, platform initiatives can be invaluable for cultivating broad strategic partnerships to improve sales, profits, and innovation capabilities. If the market is growing and becomes very large, platform leaders will also grow and become large. Initial scale by itself, though, is not essential to establish a platform. It is obvious when you think about it, but all the leaders cited in this chapter began as small firms. In fact, Microsoft, Intel, Apple, Cisco, Google, Qualcomm, and Adobe *became large and enormously valuable* precisely because – and when – their platform or complement strategies became so successful.

But while we can distinguish a product from a platform strategy, my second point emphasizes the need to connect the two. It seems hard to succeed with an industry-platform strategy if you do not first have a very good (though not necessarily the "best") product. No amount of strategic maneuvering can make up for a product that customers do not want to buy or use. At the same time, platform-leader wannabes do not always have to produce the industry's best product generation after generation to get a market to tip and stay tipped. To strive for "insanely great" products like Steve Jobs has done at Apple is a wonderful way to compete for a firm with unique design capabilities. But, for most firms, it is probably smarter to adopt a strategy that does not depend on always having the most elegant or sophisticated product in the market.

A platform strategy, as well as the capabilities necessary to implement this effectively, also must be dynamic and evolve as technologies and competitive conditions change. In recent years, both Sony and JVC, as well as other Japanese consumer electronics firms, have been slow to develop or capitalize on new products as well as to create new platforms. They also must now compete with lower cost and dynamic competitors such as Samsung in Korea and other firms in China. Sony, for example, has been a major disappointment for its shareholders. After introducing the Betamax in 1975, the same chief engineer, Nobutoshi Kihara, invented the Walkman in 1979. This product is similar to Apple's iPod in many ways. Though a generation earlier, it is unfortunate for the company that Sony did not later on find a way to connect the Walkman to a library of digital media and then the Internet. At least some observers believe that Sony executives and engineers remained too tied to their hardware products and were late to understand the importance of the Internet and connecting their products to digital media (see, e.g., Tabuchi, 2012). The company did buy movie and music producers following the Betamax experience to get more control over content. It also went on to design new digital video recorders and many other successful audio and video products. But Sony's senior executives and engineers never seem to have fully understood the value of creating a new industry-wide platform or of investing more heavily in software program-ming skills and networking technology. This is a lapse in both strategy and capabilities. The Sony PlayStation has done relatively well, and Sony has made technically excellent PCs, high-definition TVs, and other audio and video equipment. But it would have done much better with a deeper appreciation for platform dynamics, software engineering, network dynamics such as the Internet, and the changes occurring in consumer technology.

JVC also struggled financially after VHS sales peaked and users replaced many VHS tapes with DVDs in the latter 1990s and 2000s (Chaney, 2005). It has always been an underdog of sorts, competing against much larger firms, including its parent, Panasonic/Matsushita. But it did not have another hit product or industry platform after VHS. Again, we can point to relatively weak capabilities in software, computers, and networks (there is a pattern here in Japan!). The VHS machine is a miracle of precision electronics and assembly. But it is a machine and not a computer or networked device. Like Sony, JVC went on to make excellent digital products for audio and video applications (displays, camcorders, home entertainment systems, car systems, projectors). Still, the firm struggled to make money from consumer electronics – tough to do without a platform strategy and without ownership of digital content or services such as iTunes. In 2008, Matsushita finally sold its holdings in JVC. This historic company then merged with another Japanese consumer electronics company and now operates under the name JVC KENWOOD.[15]

Again, the lesson seems to be that having great products does not necessarily help a firm remain competitive or win platform competitions; rather, the winners in the kinds of markets we see today in consumer electronics and digital technologies are more likely to be firms that have strong platform strategies – that means, their products have relatively open and accessible architectures, and they actively cultivate support from complementors. Complementary products and services create value for the platform and draw in users. In a platform market, garnering support from a broad ecosystem of innovative partners and users is far more important than winning a features contest or a product design award. And it generally requires a specific set of actions that come under the heading of a platform strategy.

NOTES

1. This chapter is a condensed and updated version of material drawn from Cusumano (2010b).

2. There is a large literature on product platforms, such as Meyer and Lehnerd (1997) and Sanderson and Uzumeri (1996). For more academic treatments, see Meyer and Utterback (1993), Ulrich (1995), Sanchez and Mahoney (1996), Baldwin and Clark (1999), Meyer and Dalal (2002), and Meyer and DeTore (2001).

3. I say "almost" because Kevin Boudreau suggests too many complementors can reduce the incentives of new complementors to invest (see Boudreau, 2011).

4. Annabelle Gawer (2009) recently published a book containing the latest platform-related research from multiple disciplines.

5. My thanks to Michael Bikard for this observation.

6. This section elaborates on an earlier discussion in Cusumano (2008).

7. For new details on the life of Steve Jobs and career in Apple, see Isaacson (2011).

8. See the discussion of Microsoft's strategy and product line during the 1980s and 1990s, as well as product strengths and weaknesses, in *Microsoft Secrets* (1995, pp. 127–185).

9. See http://www.apple.com/iphone/built-in-apps/app-store.html (accessed February 19, 2012).

10. According to its 2011 10-K report, Microsoft estimated that about 25 percent of Windows client (desktop) sales were directly to consumers. This is about 6.8 percent of total revenues of $70 billion.

11. Also for Apple information and demos of iCloud, see http://www.apple.com/icloud/ (accessed February 19, 2012).

12. These numbers are calculated from data available in Adobe Systems Incorporated, "Form 10-K," Washington, DC: United States Securities and Exchange Commission, December 2, 2011, p. 51. See also van Kooten (2012).

13. See all the various Adobe products, activities, and partnerships at www.adobe.com (accessed February 19, 2012). For a detailed description of Adobe's platform strategy, see Adobe Systems Inc. (2011), "Form 10-K."

14. In software, which platform to support was an issue with Netscape, and it decided to support Microsoft Windows as well as the Macintosh and UNIX. See *Competing on Internet Time*, pp. 157–180. Also, Cusumano and Yoffie (1999).

15. For more information on JVC KENWOOD Holdings in English, see http://www.jk-holdings.com/en/

ACKNOWLEDGMENT

Chapter adapted from *Staying Power: Six Enduring Principles for Managing Strategy and Innovation in an Uncertain World* (*Lessons from Microsoft, Apple, Intel, Google, Toyota and More*) (pp. 22–67, 151–152; including Table 1.2 on p. 38) by Cusumano, M. A. (2010) with permission of Oxford University Press.

REFERENCES

Adner, R. (2006). Match your innovation strategy to your innovation ecosystem. *Harvard Business Review*, *84*(4), 98–107.

Anvaari, M., & Jansen, S. (2010). *Evaluating architectural openness in mobile software platforms.* 2nd Workshop on Software Ecosystems, Copenhagen, Denmark.

Arthur, W. (1989). Competing technologies, increasing returns, and lock-in by historical events. *Economic Journal*, *99*(March), 116–131.

Bakos, Y., & Brynjolfsson, E. (1999). Bundling information goods: Pricing, profits and efficiency. *Management Science*, *45*(12), 1613–1630.

Baldwin, C., & Clark, K. (1999). *Design rules: The power of modularity* (Vol. 1). Cambridge, MA: MIT Press.

Boudreau, K. (2011). Let a thousand flowers bloom? An early look at large numbers of software 'apps' developers and patterns of innovation. *Organization Science*. (Published online September 2011, forthcoming 2012 in print).

Bresnahan, T., & Greenstein, S. (1999). Technological competition and the structure of the computer industry. *Journal of Industrial Economics, 47*(1), 1–40.

Chaney, J. (2005). Parting Words for VHS Tapes, Soon to be Gone with the Rewind. *The Washington Post*, August 25. Retrieved from http://www.washingtonpost.com/wp-dyn/content/article/2005/08/26/AR2005082600332.html. Accessed on May 3, 2012.

Chen, B. (2012). New apple operating system aims to knit together its products. *New York Times*, February 17, p. B6.

Cusumano, M. (2004). *The business of software* (pp. 1, 43–46). New York, NY: Free Press.

Cusumano, M. (2006). What road ahead for Microsoft and Windows? *Communications of the ACM, 49*(9), 21–23.

Cusumano, M. (2008). The puzzle of Apple. *Communications of the ACM, 51*(9), 22–24.

Cusumano, M. (2010a). Cloud computing and SaaS as new computing platforms. *Communications of the ACM, 53*(4), 27–29.

Cusumano, M. (2010b). *Staying power: Six enduring principles for managing strategy and innovation in an uncertain world* (pp. 22–67, 151–152). Oxford: Oxford University Press.

Cusumano, M., Mylonadis, Y., & Rosenbloom, R. (1992). Strategic maneuvering and mass-market dynamics: The triumph of VHS over beta. *Business History Review, 66*(1), 51–94.

Cusumano, M., & Nobeoka, K. (1998). *Thinking beyond lean* (pp. 9–17). New York, NY: Free Press.

Cusumano, M., & Selby, R. W. (1995). *Microsoft secrets* (pp. 384–397). New York, NY: Free Press.

Cusumano, M., & Yoffie, D. (1998). *Competing on internet time: Lessons from Netscape and its battle with Microsoft* (pp. 97–100, 133–138). New York, NY: Free Press.

Cusumano, M., & Yoffie, D. (1999). What Netscape learned from cross-platform software development. *Communications of the ACM, 42*(10), 72–78.

David, P. (1985). Clio and the economics of QWERTY. *American Economic Review, 75*(2), 332–337.

Eisenmann, T. (2006). Internet companies growth strategies: Determinants of investment intensity and long-term performance. *Strategic Management Journal, 27*(12), 1183–1204.

Eisenmann, T., Parker, G., & Van Alstyne, M. (2006). Strategies for two-sided markets. *Harvard Business Review, 84*(10), 92–101.

Eisenmann, T., Parker, G., & Van Alstyne, M. (2007, March). *Platform envelopment*. Unpublished working paper.

Farrell, J., & Saloner, G. (1986). Installed base and compatibility: Innovation, product preannouncements and predation. *American Economic Review, 76*(5), 940–955.

Farrell, J., & Shapiro, C. (1998). Dynamic competition with switching costs. *RAND Journal of Economics, 29*(1), 123–137.

Gawer, A. (Ed.). (2009). *Platforms, markets and innovation*. Cheltenham, UK: Edward Elgar.

Gawer, A., & Cusumano, M. (2002). *Platform leadership: How Intel, Microsoft, and Cisco drive industry innovation*. Boston, MA: Harvard Business School Press.

Gawer, A., & Cusumano, M. (2008). How companies become platform leaders. *MIT Sloan Management Review, 49*(2), 29–30.

Greenstein, S. (2012). Economic experiments and the development of Wi-Fi. In S. J. Kahl, B. S. Silverman & M. A. Cusumano (Eds.), *Advances in strategic management* (Vol. 29, pp. 3–33). Bingley, UK: Emerald Group.

Iansiti, M., & Levien, R. (2004). *The keystone advantage: What the new dynamics of business ecosystems mean for strategy, innovation, and sustainability.* Boston, MA: Harvard Business School Press.

Isaacson, W. (2011). *Steve Jobs* (pp. 138–139). New York, NY: Simon & Schuster.

Jobs, S. (2012). *Open iPhone letter.* Retrieved from http://www.apple.com/hotnews/open iphoneletter/. Accessed on May 3, 2012.

Kane, Y. (2009). Breaking Apple's grip on the iPhone: Firms launch sites selling unauthorized software for device, posing challenge to official online store. *Wall Street Journal*, March 6, p. B1.

Katz, M., & Shapiro, C. (1992). Product introduction with network externalities. *Journal of Industrial Economics, 40*(1), 55–83.

Kenney, M., & Pon, B. (2011). Structuring the smartphone industry: Is mobile platform OS the key? *Journal of Industrial Competition and Trade, 11*, 258.

Lampe, R., & Moser, P. (2012). Patent pools: Licensing strategies in the absence of regulation. In S. J. Kahl, B. S. Silverman & M. A. Cusumano (Eds.), *Advances in strategic management* (Vol. 29, pp. 69–86). Bingley, UK: Emerald Group.

Langlois, R. (1992). External economies and economic progress: The case of the microcomputer industry. *Business History Review, 66*(1), 1–50.

Leblebici, H. (2012). The evolution of alternative business models and the legitimization of universal credit card industry: Exploring the contested terrain where history and strategy meet. In S. J. Kahl, B. S. Silverman & M. A. Cusumano (Eds.), *Advances in strategic management* (Vol. 29, pp. 117–151). Bingley, UK: Emerald Group.

Levy, S. (1994). *Insanely great: The life and times of Macintosh, the computer that changed everything.* New York, NY: Viking.

Lohr, S. (2011). The power of the platform at Apple. *The New York Times*, January 30, p. BU3.

Meyer, M., & Dalal, D. (2002). Managing platform architectures and manufacturing processes for nonassembled products. *Journal of Production Innovation Management, 19*(4), 277–293.

Meyer, M., & DeTore, A. (2001). Perspective: Creating a platform-based approach for developing new services. *Journal of Production Innovation Management, 18*(3), 188–204.

Meyer, M., & Lehnerd, A. (1997). *The power of product platforms.* New York, NY: Free Press.

Meyer, M., & Utterback, J. (1993). The product family and the dynamics of core capability. *MIT Sloan Management Review, 34*(3), 29–47.

Mossberg, W. (2009). A windows to help you forget: Microsoft's new operating system is good enough to erase bad memory of Vista. *The Wall Street Journal*, October 8. Retrieved from http://online.wsj.com. Accessed on October 24, 2009.

Nalebuff, B. (2004). Bundling as an entry deterrent. *Quarterly Journal of Economics, 119*(1), 159–187.

Parker, G., & Van Alstyne, M. (2005). Two-sided network effects: A theory of information product design. *Management Science, 51*(10), 1494–1504.

Reisenger, D. (2011). *AT&T to Sell iPhone 3GS for $49.* CNET News, January 6. Retrieved from http://news.cnet.com/8301-13506_3-20027546-17.html?tag=mncol;txt. Accessed on May 3, 2011.

Reisenger, D. (2012). *Target Starts Selling iPhone 3GS for $49.* CNET News. Retrieved from http://news.cnet.com/8301-13506_3-20027984-17.html. Accessed May 3, 2012.

Rochet, J. C., & Tirole, J. (2003). Platform competition in two-sided markets. *Journal of the European Economic Association*, *1*(4), 990–1029.

Rochet, J. C., & Tirole, J. (2006). Two-sided markets: A progress report. *RAND Journal of Economics*, *37*(3), 645–667.

Rosenbloom, R., & Cusumano, M. (1987). Technological pioneering and competitive advantage: The birth of the VCR industry. *California Management Review*, *29*(4), 51–76.

Sanchez, R., & Mahoney, J. (1996). Modularity, flexibility, and knowledge management in product organization design. *Strategic Management Journal*, *17*(Special Winter Issue), 63–76.

Sanderson, S., & Uzumeri, M. (1996). *Managing product families*. New York, NY: Irwin.

Schmalensee, R., Evans, D., & Hagiu, A. (2006). *Invisible engines: How software platforms drive innovation and transform industries*. Cambridge, MA: MIT Press.

Schroeder, S. (2009, July 28). *Google voice thoroughly banned from the iphone; so much for an open platform*. Mashable: The Social Media Guide. Retrieved from http://mashable. com/2009/07/28/google-voice-banned/. Accessed on September 20, 2009.

Shankland, S. (2010) *HTML vs. Flash: Can a turf war be avoided?* CNET News, February 3. Retrieved from http://news.cnet.com/8301-30685_3-20000037-264.html. Accessed on May 3, 2012.

Shapiro, C., & Varian, H. (1998). *Information rules: A strategic guide to the network economy*. Boston, MA: Harvard Business School Press.

Stone, B., & Miller, C. (2009). Music forecast: The cloud. *The New York Times*, December 16, p. B1.

Tabuchi, H. (2012). How the tech parade passed Sony by. *The New York Times*, April 15, p. BU1.

Ulrich, K. (1995). The role of product architecture in the manufacturing firm. *Research Policy*, *24*(3), 419–440.

Utterback, J. (1996). *Mastering the dynamics of innovation*. Boston, MA: Harvard Business School Press.

van Kooten, M. (2012). *Global software Top 100 – Edition 2011*. Retrieved from http://www.softwaretop100.org/global-software-top-100-edition-2011. Accessed on May 3, 2012.

Vascellaro, J., & Kane, Y. (2009). Schmidt resigns his seat on Apple's board. *The Wall Street Journal*, August. Accessed on September 20, 2009.

Wortham, J. (2009). Unofficial software incurs Apple's wrath. *The New York Times*, May 13, p. B1.

Yoffie, D., & Kim, R. (2010). *Apple Inc. in 2010*. Harvard Business School Case No. 9-710-467, p. 17, Exhibit 3, Boston, MA.

Yoffie, D., & Kwak, M. (2006). With friends like these: The art of managing complementors. *Harvard Business Review*, *84*(9), 89–98.

Yoffie, D., & Slind, M. (2008). *Apple, Inc., 2008*. Harvard Business School Case No. 9-708-480, p. 6, Boston, MA, and other public sources.

APPENDIX

Table A1. VHS and Beta Group Alignments, 1983–1984.

Japan	United States	Europe
	VHS Group (40 firms)	
JVC	Magnavox (MA)	Blaupunkt (MA)
Matsushita	Sylvania (MA)	Zaba (J)
Hitachi	Curtis Mathes (MA)	Nordmene (J)
Mitsubishi	J.C.Penny (MA)	Telefunken (J)
Sharp	GE (Matsushita)	SEL (J)
Tokyo Sanyo	RCA (H)	Thorn-EMI (J)
Brother (MI)	Zenith (J) (from spring 1984)	Thomson-Brandt (J)
Ricoh (H)		Granada (H)
Tokyo Juki (H)		Hangard (H)
Canon (MA)		Sarolla (H)
Asahi Optical (H)		Fisher (T)
Olympus (MA)		Luxer (MI)
Nikon (MA)		
Akai Trio (J)		
Sansui (J)		
Clarion (J)		
Teac (J)		
Japan Columbia (H)		
Funai		
	Beta Group (12 firms)	
Sony	Zenith (S) (until spring 1984)	Kneckerman (SA)
Sanyo	Sears (SA)	Fisher (SA)
Toshiba		Rank (TO)
NEC		
General (TO)		
Aiwa		
Pioneer (S)		

Source: Cusumano et al. (1992, Table 5, p. 73). Reprinted with the permission of Cambridge University Press.
Note: Suppliers indicated by initiations (J = JVC, MA = Matsushita, H = Hitachi, MI = Mitsubishi, T = Tokyo Sanyo, S = Sony, TO = Toshiba, SA = Sanyo, P = Phillips, G = Grundig).

Table A2. VCR Production and Format Shares, 1975–1984.

	1975	1976	1977	1978	1979	1980
Beta group						
Sony	100	56	51	28	24	22
Others	–	5	5	12	15	11
Subtotal	*100*	*61*	*56*	*40*	*39*	*34*
VHS group						
Matsushita	–	29	27	36	28	29
JVC	–	9	15	19	22	18
Others	–	1	2	5	11	19
Subtotal	–	*39*	*44*	*60*	*61*	*66*

	1981	1982	1983	1984	–	1989
Beta group						
Sony	18	14	12	9		
Sanyo	9	10	8	6		
Toshiba	4	4	4	3		
Others	1	1	2	2		
Subtotal	*32*	*28*	*25*	*20*		*0*
VHS group						
Matsushita	28	27	29	25		
JVC	19	20	16	17		
Hitachi	10	10	11	15		
Sharp	7	7	9	9		
Mitsubishi	3	3	3	4		
Sanyo	–	3	4	5		
Others	2	2	2	5		
Subtotal	*68*	*72*	*75*	*80*		*100*

Source: "Strategic Maneuvering and Mass-Market Dynamics," Table 1, p. 55.
Unit: % of total industry production (both formats).

Box A1.   Detailed Apple and Microsoft Financial Comparison, 2011.

HOW APPLE MAKES MONEY

FY2011 Sales = $108 billion *(+ 66%)*, Operating Income = $34 billion (31%)
January 2012 Market Cap = $425 billion (4x revenues)
63,300 Employees. *Sales/Employee = $1.7 million*
Gross Margin = 41%, R&D = 2%, Sales/Mktg/G&A = 7%

Revenue Breakdown (61% International):

- *43% iPhone* and related products & services
- *20% Mac* (68% laptop)
- *7% iPod*
- *19% iPad* and related products & services
- *6% Music* and related products & services
- *3% Software and services* and other sales
- *2% Peripherals and other hardware*

HOW MICROSOFT MAKES MONEY

FY 2011 Sales = $70 billion (+ 12%), Operating Income = $27 billion *(39%)*
January 2012 Market Cap = $247 billion *(3x revenues)*
90,000 Employees. Sales/Employee = $778,000
Gross Margin = 78%, R&D = 13%, Sales/Mktg = 20%, G&A 6%

Revenue Breakdown (46% non-US):

- *90% Products* (Windows 27%, Office 31%, Servers/Tools 24%, Xbox 13%)
  Op. Profits: Windows 36%, Office 41%, Servers/Tools 19%, *Xbox 4%*
  Online Services lost $2.6 billion + Corporate expenses = $4.6 billion (e.g., marketing)
- *4% Online* (advertising)
- *5% Services* (estimated, from consulting & product support, mainly Servers/Tools)
- *1% Other* (income from investments, etc.)

- *Enterprise/OEM Revenues = 70% of sales*
  75% Windows, 80% Office, 100% Servers/Tools, 100% mobile/embedded
- *Consumer Revenues = 30% of total sales*
  20% Office, 25% Windows, 100% Online & Xbox

Source: Calculated from data in Apple Inc., "Form 10-K," Washington, DC: United States Securities and Exchange Commission, September 24, 2011; and Microsoft Corporation, "Form 10-K," Washington, DC: United States Securities and Exchange Commission, June 30, 2011.

PATENT POOLS: LICENSING STRATEGIES IN THE ABSENCE OF REGULATION

Ryan Lampe and Petra Moser

ABSTRACT

Purpose – *This chapter examines the licensing behavior of patent pools when they are unconstrained by antitrust rules.*

Design/methodology/approach – *Patent pools allow competing firms to combine their patents and license them as a package to outside firms. Regulators today favor pools that license their patents freely to outside firms, making it difficult to observe the unconstrained licensing strategies of patent pools. This chapter takes advantage of a unique period of regulatory tolerance during the New Deal to investigate the unconstrained licensing decisions of pools. Archival evidence suggests that – in the absence of regulation – pools may not choose to license their technologies.*

Findings/originality/value – *Eleven of twenty pools that formed between 1930 and 1938 did not issue any licenses to outside firms. Three pools granted one, two, and three licenses, respectively, to resolve litigation. Six pools issued between 9 and 185 licenses. Archival evidence suggests that*

History and Strategy
Advances in Strategic Management, Volume 29, 69–86
Copyright © 2012 by Emerald Group Publishing Limited
All rights of reproduction in any form reserved
ISSN: 0742-3322/doi:10.1108/S0742-3322(2012)0000029007

the pools studied in this chapter used licensing as a means to limit competition with substitute technologies.

Keywords: Patent pools; licensing

Patent pools allow competing firms to combine their patents and license them as a package to outside firms. Regulators today favor pools that license their patents freely to outside firms, making it difficult to observe the unconstrained licensing strategies of patent pools. This chapter takes advantage of a unique period of regulatory tolerance during the New Deal to investigate the unconstrained licensing decisions of pools. Archival evidence suggests that – in the absence of regulation – pools may not choose to license their technologies. Eleven of twenty pools that formed between 1930 and 1938 did not issue any licenses to outside firms. Three pools granted one, two, and three licenses, respectively, to resolve litigation. Six pools issued between 9 and 185 licenses. Archival evidence suggests that these pools used licensing as a means to limit competition with substitute technologies.

Patent pools allow competing firms, which own patents for individual components of a new technology, to combine their patents and license them as a package to outside firms. In recent years, pools have become a prominent mechanism to limit litigation risks and enable the adoption of new technologies, ranging from CDs and DVDs (Flamm, 2012) to genetic tests for breast cancer.[1] A key advantage of patent pools is that they facilitate licensing for technologies that are jointly owned by many firms. Thus, pools are expected to reduce transaction costs by creating "one-stop-shopping" opportunities for licensees and reduce license fees by eliminating royalty stacking, which occurs when firms charge inefficiently high prices for subsets of patents that cover complementary technologies (Merges, 2001; Shapiro, 2001, p. 134). Theoretical models of patent pools also predict a positive correlation between pools that improve welfare and pools that allow members to license their patents independently to outside firms (Lerner & Tirole, 2004).[2]

As a result, regulators typically treat liberal licensing strategies as a necessary condition for allowing pools to form. The U.S. Supreme Court argued as early as 1931 that

> If the available advantages (of a patent pool) are open on reasonable terms to all manufacturers desiring to participate, such interchange may promote rather than restrain competition. (U.S. Supreme Court in *Standard Oil v. United States*, 283 U.S. 163, 171 (1931))

Thus, pools with liberal licensing policies – such as the 1997 pool for the MPEG video and audio data compression standards, the 1998 DVD video and DVD-ROM standard pool, and the 2001 3G mobile platforms pool – are allowed to form.[3] Pools that restrict licensing, however, are typically prohibited. In 2007, for example, a report of the Department of Justice and Federal Trade Commission warned that pools that do not license technologies freely may "pose a barrier to entry if existing relationships make it harder for 'new firms to come in and overcome the patent thicket'" (2007). As a result of such policies, it is practically impossible to examine the unconstrained licensing strategies of pools.

This chapter takes advantage of a window of regulatory tolerance under the New Deal to investigate the licensing strategies of patent pools in the absence of effective regulation. After the Great Depression, New Deal policies, such as the National Industrial Recovery Act (NIRA, June 16, 1933) exempted most U.S. industries from antitrust. Even after the Supreme Court ruled on May 27, 1935 that the NIRA was unconstitutional, the U.S. government continued to tolerate collusion and price fixing in many industries (Haley, 2001, p. 8; Hawley, 1966).[4] Regulatory tolerance came to an end on March 11, 1938 when President Roosevelt appointed Thurman Arnold to reorganize the U.S. Department of Justice. From June 16, 1938 to April 3, 1941, Congressional hearings of the Temporary National Economic Committee investigated antitrust violations through cartels and pools.[5] In 1942, a district court decided to break up the *Hartford Empire* pool, which had suppressed competition by imposing production quotas and preventing licensees from adopting competing technologies.[6] After this, few pools formed until the Department of Justice revised its antitrust guidelines in 1995 and approved the MPEG-2 pool in 1997 (e.g., Gallini, 2011).

Anecdotal evidence suggests that pools may indeed facilitate the adoption of new technologies. Most prominently, the aircraft pool formed in 1917 after a congressional committee under Franklin D. Roosevelt encouraged the Wright brothers and Glenn Curtis to pool patents that the two firms had used to block each other from producing planes. Under the pool, production increased from 83 planes in 1916 to 11,950 in 1918 (Stubbs, 2002). There is, however, no systematic evidence to date on the unconstrained licensing strategies of patent pools.

This chapter uses archival documents for 20 pools that formed between 1930 and 1938 to investigate the unconstrained licensing decisions of pools. These sources indicate that, in the absence of effective regulation, most pools pursued relatively restrictive licensing strategies. Eleven of twenty pools issued no licenses, acting essentially like cross-licensing agreements that divided markets internationally and within the United States. Three of nine pools with licensees only licensed their technologies to a small number of firms in response to litigation.

Six pools issued licenses to a significant number of firms; court records suggest that these pools employed licensing as a means to limit competition with substitutes for pool technologies. Four of these pools formed after the Supreme Court ruled the NIRA to be unconstitutional in 1935.

Archival records may also help to shed light on related theoretical predictions about grant-back rules, pools as a mechanism to harbor weak patents, and the stability of patent pools. For example, theoretical models predict that pools, which include grant-back provisions that require members to offer new patents to the pool, are more likely to allow independent licensing (Lerner & Tirole, 2004). While court records do not allow us to separate pools that allow independent licensing from other pools, they reveal that the large majority of pools did require grant-backs; four pools without grant-backs were substantially more likely to license their inventions than the average pool. Court records also confirm that pools may serve as a mechanism to harbor weak patents (Choi, 2005; Gilbert, 2004).

ARCHIVAL SOURCES ON LICENSING

To document the licensing decisions of patent pools, we take advantage of a shift in regulatory tolerance after the *Hartford Empire* decision of 1942. This decision, which was taken against a particularly aggressive pool in the glassware industry, began a period of judicial activism against patent pools, which dissolved most of the pools that had formed during the New Deal. Eighteen pools were dissolved for violations of the Sherman Act after the *Hartford Empire* decision. Two pools – for furniture slip covers and machine tools – dissolved over internal disagreements while they were investigated. Court records between 1942 and 1955 – when the last patent pool (for stamped metal wheels) was forced to make its patents available at reasonable royalties – provide archival evidence on the licensing decisions of pools.

Pools in 20 Industries, 1930–1938

In the first step of the data collection, we searched regional depositories of the National Archives in Chicago, Kansas City, New York, and Riverside for records on all pools that are mentioned in Vaughan (1956), Gilbert (2004), and Lerner, Tirole, and Strojwas (2007). Records for all 20 pools describe licensing agreements in the final judgments. Additional information comes from written complaints for 16 pools and license agreements for 9 pools.

Pools cover a broad range of industries: high-tension cables to transmit electrical power at high voltages (1930–1948), water conditioning apparatus to purify drinking water (1930–1951), fuel injection equipment (1931–1942), pharmaceuticals (1932–1945), railroad springs, used in the production of railway cars (1932–1947), textile machinery (1932–1950), hydraulic pumps for oil wells (1933–1952), machine tools for grinding, boring, and drilling (1933–1955), Philips screws (1933–1949), color cinematography (1934–1950), dry ice (solid carbon dioxide used as a refrigerant, 1934–1952), electric generators (1934–1953), lecithin (1934–1947), variable condensers used for tuning devices in radios (1934–1953), aircraft instruments (1935–1946), stamped metal wheels for cars and trucks (1937–1955), wrinkle paint finishes (1937–1955), fuse cutouts (1938–1948), ophthalmic frames (1938–1948), and furniture slip covers (1938–1949) (Fig. 1).[7] All 20 pools include at least one U.S. firm, which makes them subject to the U.S. antitrust laws. Seven pools also included firms from Canada, Denmark, France, Germany, Italy, Japan, Switzerland, and the United Kingdom.

LICENSING STRATEGIES IN THE ABSENCE OF REGULATION

Of the 20 pools in our sample, 11 did not license their patents to outside firms. Three pools – for lecithin, variable condensers, and furniture slip covers – licensed sparingly to less than a handful of firms to resolve litigation. Six pools – for railroad springs, Phillips screws, stamped metal wheels, wrinkle finishes, fuse cutouts, and ophthalmic frames – licensed their patents to nine or more outside firms. Court records suggest that these pools chose to license to limit competition with substitutes for pool technologies. Four of these pools formed after the Supreme Court ruled the NIRA to be unconstitutional in 1935.

Most Pools Did not License to Outside Firms and Created Near Monopolies

Eleven pools did not issue licenses to outside firms and essentially operated as cross-licensing agreements (e.g., Shapiro, 2001) that created exclusive

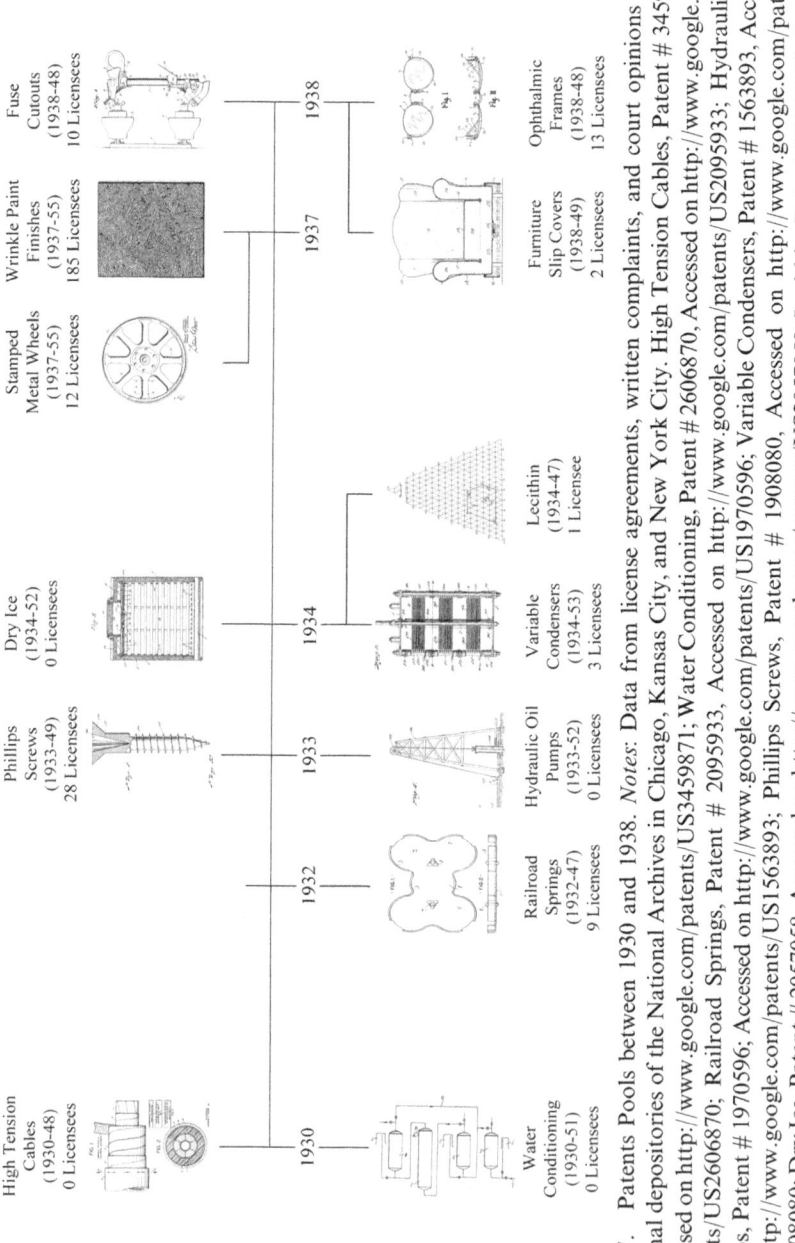

Fig. 1. Patents Pools between 1930 and 1938. *Notes:* Data from license agreements, written complaints, and court opinions from regional depositories of the National Archives in Chicago, Kansas City, and New York City. High Tension Cables, Patent # 3459871, Accessed on http://www.google.com/patents/US3459871; Water Conditioning, Patent # 2606870, Accessed on http://www.google.com/patents/US2606870; Railroad Springs, Patent # 2095933, Accessed on http://www.google.com/patents/US2095933; Hydraulic Oil Pumps, Patent # 1970596; Accessed on http://www.google.com/patents/US1970596; Variable Condensers, Patent # 1563893, Accessed on http://www.google.com/patents/US1563893; Phillips Screws, Patent # 1908080, Accessed on http://www.google.com/patents/US1908080; Dry Ice, Patent # 2057058, Accessed on http://www.google.com/patents/US2057058; Lecithin, Patent # 2726158, Accessed on http://www.google.com/patents/US2726158; Stamped Metal Wheels, Patent # 1682909, Accessed on http://www.google.com/patents/US1682909; Wrinkle Finishes, Patent # 1883408, Accessed on http://www.google.com/patents/US1883408; Fuse Cutouts, Patent # 2176227, Accessed on http://www.google.com/patents/US2176227; Ophthalmic Frames, Patent # 2346709, Accessed on http://www.google.com/patents/US2346709; Slip Covers, Patent # 2100868, Accessed on http://www.google.com/patents/US2100868.

sales territories and products for their members. Six of these pools involved foreign members. A pool for high-tension cables combined patents by firms from the United States, Italy, and Switzerland; pools for water conditioning apparatus and fuel injection devices combined patents by firms from the United States, France, Germany, and the United Kingdom; pools for pharmaceuticals and electric generators joined patents by the U.S. and German firms; and a pool for aircraft instruments combined patents by one U.S. firm with foreign firms from Denmark, France, Germany, Italy, Japan, Switzerland, and the United Kingdom.

Members of these pools granted each other exclusive sales territories and used their patents to prevent competing imports. For example, a pool for high-tension cables including General Electric refused to issue licenses to domestic competitors and prevented imports from the Italian pool member Pirelli. Their pool combined patents for electric conductors that were insulated from an outer sheath by oil or gas under mechanical pressure, and used to transmit electrical power at high voltage in industrial areas by railways and by public utilities. In 1930, General Electric and the U.S. General Cable Corporation agreed to pool their patents. Between 1931 and 1933, the pool added two domestic members, Okonite-Callendar Cable Company and Phelps Dodge Copper Products Corporation, and the Società Italiana Pirelli. When a Swiss firm, Protona, entered the U.S. market in 1938 with patents for fluid-filled cables and accessories that would be "more economical to the consumer than the type of fluid-filled cable and accessories manufactured by [the pool members]," the pool promptly acquired exclusive rights to the technology but then

> refrained from commercial exploitation of the cable and accessories which are the subject matter of the Protona patents

and, in fact,

> made unreasonable demands of other American electrical cable manufacturers who inquired as to the extension of such rights to them, so as to discourage and prevent such manufacturers from continuing to seek such rights, and to suppress the commercial exploitation of such cable in the United States.[8]

By 1947 pool members manufactured and sold all fluid-filled cable in the United States.

Five pools of domestic firms – for textile machines, hydraulic oil pumps, machine tools, color cinematography, and dry ice – issued no licenses and divided domestic markets according to fields of use. For example, the pool between Rodless and Old Kobe for hydraulic pumps to extract oil from wells (1933–1952) made Kobe the single U.S. manufacturer of hydraulic oil pumps. Although the initial agreement granted Rodless the right to use the pool patents, Rodlesss assigned exclusive manufacturing rights to Kobe within a year. In 1934, the pool acquired exclusive rights to a new type of pump, the "Gage" pump – an alternative hydraulic pump, which had threatened to become a successful competitor. When the Dempsey Pump Company entered with another pump in 1948, the pool sued for infringement. In 1952, the Court for the Northern District of Oklahoma held that the pool was guilty of monopolization by acquiring every important patent and denying licenses to outside firms.[9]

A pool in the dry ice industry (1934–1952) instigated price wars to drive competitors out of business, purchase their patents and plants, and add them to the pool. The expanded pool then allocated exclusive territories to pool members and, instead of licensing, threatened prospective manufacturers with litigation. By 1948, the pool combined "the only important patents in the dry ice field" and sold "over 75% of all the carbon dioxide and dry ice produced for sale and distribution in the United States."[10]

Licensing as a Means to Resolve Litigation

Three pools for lecithin, variable condensers, and furniture slip covers issued small numbers of licenses – 1, 2, and 3, respectively – to resolve litigation.

The lecithin pool (1934–1947) "impeded others ... from engaging in the production of lecithin in the United States, save upon conditions established by the defendants and enforced by means of litigation and threats of litigation based upon patents pool."[11] This pool had combined patents by American firms Glidden and Archer-Daniels Midland (ADM), the German Hansa-Muehle G.m.b.H., and the Danish Aarhus Oliefabrik.[12] Extracting lecithin from soybean oil, Glidden and ADM were the only large-scale manufacturers of lecithin in the United States until 1939. In 1939, the Refining Company entered with an alternative process to extract lecithin from corn, which it had patented. In 1940, Central Soya Company entered with another alternative process to extract lecithin from soybeans, which it had patented. Both companies refused to license the pool's technologies, and the pool sued Central Soya Company for patent infringement in 1940. This case was pending in 1946 when the Department of Justice filed its antitrust complaint. In 1943, the pool licensed its technology to Procter & Gamble after it learned that Procter & Gamble intended to produce lecithin with or without a license by the pool. In 1944, the two domestic members accounted for two-thirds of the U.S. production of lecithin. In 1947, the United States District Court for the Northern District of Ohio dissolved the pool.

The variable condensers' pool (1934–1953) combined patents by the Radio Condenser Company, General Instrument Corporation, and Dejur-Amsco Corporation, which jointly accounted for 75 percent of condensers in the U.S. radios when the pool formed. Immediately after the pool had formed, it filed infringement suits against two of three competing producers, Federal Instrument Company and Reliance Die and Stamping Company. In 1935, the pool settled its suit against Federal by licensing its technology, albeit at exceedingly high royalties; Federal became insolvent in 1938. In 1937, the pool settled litigation with Reliance with another license. In 1938, the pool granted a third license to a new entrant, the Variable Condenser Corporation, requiring that Variable would adhere to the pool's pricing scheme without challenging its patents. In the same year, the pool filed an infringement suit against the third original manufacturer, American Steel Package Company. This suit failed as the Second Circuit Court of Appeals held in 1940 that the patent in issue – U.S. patent 1,800,719 for electrical condensers – was invalid. The District Court of New Jersey dissolved the pool in 1953.[13]

The pool for furniture slip covers (1938–1949) instigated 10 lawsuits against retailers who had purchased slip covers from competing firms and forced them to stop purchasing competing products. It combined Surefit's patent 1,984,973 for the process of manufacturing ready-made slip covers from knitted fabrics with Comfy's patent 2,100,868 for "slip covers for furniture" (Fig. 2). Only nine days after the pool had formed, Comfy filed a lawsuit against Med-Vogue, a competing producer. In 1939 Med-Vogue agreed to cease the sales of knitted slip covers. In the same year, Comfy filed a lawsuit against Vatco; this suit settled when Vatco agreed to pay Comfy "a certain amount of money." The pool dissolved over an internal disagreement in 1949 after Surefit argued that its agreement with Comfy was "induced by false and fraudulent misrepresentations." At that time, the pool produced 62 percent of all U.S. slip covers in the United States.[14]

Licensing as a Means to Limit Competition with Substitutes

Six pools – for railroad springs, Phillips screws, stamped metal wheels, wrinkle finishes, fuse cutouts, and ophthalmic frames – issued nine licenses or more. Archival evidence suggests that these pools used licenses to limit competition with substitute technologies.

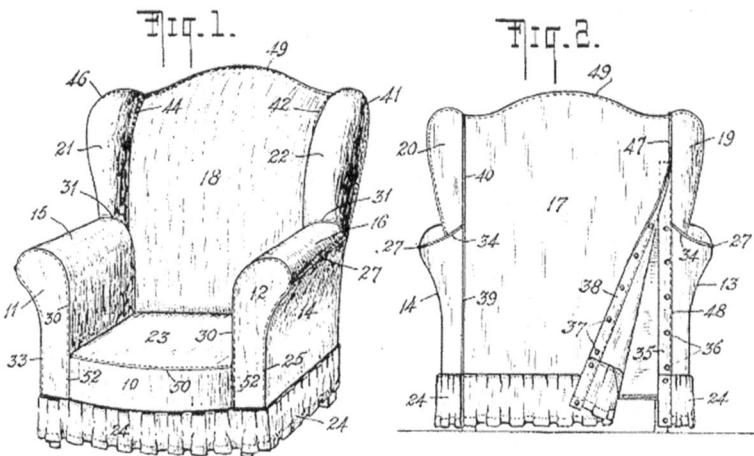

Fig. 2. Comfy's Patent 2,100,868 for Slip Covers for Furniture. *Notes*: Drawings from the original patent document for U.S. Patent 2,100,868 by Arthur Oppenheimer, filed on September 4, 1935, issued on November 30, 1937. Accessed on http://www.google.com/patents/US2100868.

The pool for "Universal" railroad spring plates and "Coil-Elliptic" railroad springs (1932–1947), for example, conspired with its licensees to fix prices through bid rigging. When railroads asked licensees to bid for contracts to produce springs and spring plates, the pool ensured that a licensee who was the existing supplier would submit the lowest bid; other licensees either refused to bid or submitted higher bids.[15] The pool also prevented licensees of the Coil-Elliptic springs – "a combination of coil and elliptic springs placed in what is called the 'window' of the trucks and freight cars"[16] – from manufacturing and selling "pressed steel plates competing and [interchangeable] with Universal plates." By 1942, the pool and its licensees produced and sold over "90 percent of railway coil or helical springs, and a substantial proportion of the spring plates that are manufactured in the United States." The United States Northern District Court of Indiana dissolved the pool in 1947.[17]

The pool for cross-recessed "Phillips" screws (1933–1949) between Henry Phillips and the American Screw Company also used licensing as a tool to limit competition with other cross-recessed screws, which were close substitutes for the pool's technology. The pool combined Henry Phillips' U.S. patent 1,908,080 on a "screw" with U.S. patent 1,908,081 on a matching screw-driver.[18] The closest substitute for the pool's technology was a screw based on U.S. Patent 308,246 by John Frearson, issued on November 18, 1884, and a written complaint of the Department of Justice complaint in 1947 observed that the "recess in the head of a Frearson screw differs only slightly in shape from the recess in the head of a Phillips screw."[19] In fact, sketches for the Frearson and the Phillips patents on the original patent grant documents reveal a striking similarity (Fig. 3).

Between 1937 and 1938, the pool had issued five licenses. After unlicensed screw and bolt manufacturers began to sell competing designs of cross-recessed screws, however, the pool issued another 23 licenses. The National Lock Company, for example, had begun to produce screws that were nearly indistinguishable from the Phillips screw, arguing that the Phillips pool's patent was invalid. The pool did not initiate legal proceedings but persuaded the National Lock Company in 1945 to license the pool's technology and abide by its price schedules. The Illinois Tool Works Company, for example, had prepared to manufacture a cross-recessed screw of its own design based on U.S. patent 2,129,440 (issued on September 6, 1938) when it agreed to license the pool's technology on August 4, 1939. In 1944, the pool and licensees sold 75 percent of the cross-recessed head screws in the United States; it was dissolved in 1949.

The largest producer of Frearson screws, however, Reed & Prince, never licensed the pool's technology. Without royalty payments to the pool, Reed & Prince was able to sell its screws at roughly half the price of comparable Phillips screws.[20]

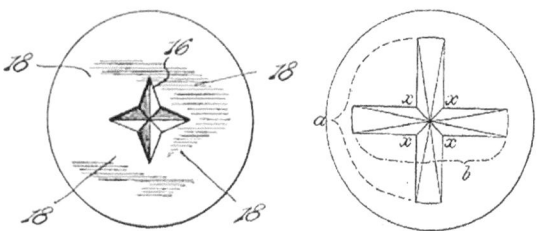

Fig. 3. Phillips Patent 1,908,080 (Left) and Frearson Patent 308,246 (Right) for Screws. *Notes:* Drawings from the original patent document for U.S. Patent 1,908,080 by John Thompson (assigned to Henry F. Phillips), filed on May 20, 1932 and issued on May 9, 1933, and US Patent 308,246 by John Frearson, filed on December 7, 1883 and issued on November 18, 1884. Accessed on http://www.google.com/patents/US1908080 and http://www.google.com/patents/US308246.

The pool for stamped metal wheels (1937–1955) also faced a large number of competing manufacturers who could have supplied the market had the pool not provided its technology. The pool technology consisted of patents from the Budd Wheel Company, the Kelsey-Hayes Wheel Company, and the Motor Wheel Corporation for stamped metal wheels, used in passenger automobiles and light-weight trailers. It was differentiated enough from producers of cast steel wheels, which were better suited to heavier vehicles such as heavy load trucks and trailers, but 20 alternative suppliers of stamped metal wheels, chose not to license the pool's technology, and may have competed on price.[21] In 1955, the pool was dissolved for restricting competition by allocating distributors of metal wheels to specific pool members.

The pool for wrinkle finishes – enamels, varnishes, and paints to produce a hard wrinkled surface coat on metal (1937–1955) – similarly used licenses to limit competition with a large number of manufacturers. To induce these firms to accept licenses, the pool initially set low royalty rates at 5 cents per gallon, relative to a sales price $2.85 per gallon.[22] Only after 12 of the largest manufacturers had accepted licenses, the pool began to enforce a minimum pricing scheme. Eventually, the pool managed to license its technology to 185 firms, which produced "substantially all wrinkle finishes produced in the United States" in 1948. In 1952, the Supreme Court dissolved the pool for fixing the price of wrinkle finishes.[23]

The "Line Material" pool for fuse cutouts (1938–1948) licensed its technology in the face of competition with alternative designs, such as "open dropouts," "open nondropouts," and "enclosed nondropouts." Line Material licensed its technology to 10 manufacturers, including General Electric and Westinghouse between 1940 and 1944. Together with these licensees, the pool was able to cover 41 percent of the average aggregate annual sales of all cutouts.[24]

The pool for eyeglasses and frames (1938–1948) covered three types of ophthalmic frames, "Ful-Vue," "Numont," and Loxit. Until the pool formed competitors sold alternative frames without patents at substantially lower prices. To eliminate lower priced alternatives, pool members issued licenses to 13 firms and required them to "establish, fix, and maintain a schedule of non-competitive prices for the sale of regular frames to wholesalers and retailers." Establishing minimum prices for the products of licensees enabled the pool to keep "the differential between prices of regular frames and license-controlled frames from being too great." By 1940, pool members and licensees accounted for 95 percent of all frames manufactured in the United States. In 1948, a consent judgment from the United States District Court for the Southern District of New York canceled the agreements.[25]

Related Evidence on Grant-Backs, Weak Patents, and Pool Stability

Archival evidence may also help to shed light on related predictions of the literature on patent pools, which could be explored in future work. Namely, theoretical models predict that pools with grant-back provisions, which require new patents to be "granted back" to the pool are more likely to allow independent licensing (Lerner & Tirole, 2004). Historical court documents do not separate pools with independent licensing from other pools, but they reveal that most pools – 16 of 20 pools in this sample – required grant-backs.

Three of the four pools without grant-backs licensed their technologies to outside firms – compared with 8 in 16 pools with grant-back rules. Only one pool without grant-backs – the 1932 pool for textile machinery – had no licensees. Three pools without grant-backs – for slip covers, fuse cutouts, and eyeglasses – issued 2, 10, and 13 licensees, respectively. These three pools formed after the Supreme Court declared the NIRA to be unconstitutional.

Theoretical models also predict that pools may act as an effective mechanism to harbor weak patents, because the private returns from overturning weak patents in a pool are relatively small (e.g., Choi, 2005; Gilbert, 2004). The experiences of pools for cross-recessed screws and variable condensers are consistent with these predictions. Even though the variable condenser pool's patent USPTO 1,800,719 was eventually ruled invalid, it remained unchallenged by outside firms until the pool itself initiated litigation. Similarly, outside firms did not initiate litigation to invalidate Henry Phillips' 1933 patent for the cross-recessed screw even though it was strikingly similar to Frearson's 1884 patent that formed the basis for most competing products.

Finally, Lévêque and Ménière (2011) predict that pools are more likely to dissolve if licensing terms are negotiated after licensees have incurred the fixed costs of entry. This prediction is confirmed by the case of the slip covers pool (1938–1949), in which two member firms *Surefit* and *Comfy* negotiated licensing terms after they had already entered with competing products, and their pool dissolved – before regulators could dissolve it – over an internal disagreement about these terms.

CONCLUSIONS

Antitrust guidelines, which favor pools that license their patents freely to outside firms, make it difficult to observe the unconstrained licensing strategies of patent pools. This chapter has taken advantage of a brief window of regulatory tolerance under the New Deal to examine archival evidence on the unconstrained licensing decisions of patent pools.

These sources document that – in the absence of effective regulation – the majority of patent pools did not license their technologies to outside firms. Eleven of twenty pools acted as cross-licensing agreements that did not issue licenses. Six of these pools included foreign firms; these pools assigned exclusive sales territories to individual members and used their patents to prevent imports of competing technologies. Five pools of domestic patentees divided U.S. markets into "fields of use" – specific technologies that could be produced only by one pool member under the pools' licensing terms. Two pools – for hydraulic oil pumps and color film – designated one member to be the sole producer of the pool's technology, effectively creating a monopoly. In addition to the eleven pools without licensees, three pools licensed to fewer than a handful of outside firms each to resolve litigation.

Only six pools licensed their technologies to a significant number of outside firms. Archival evidence suggests that their decisions to license were motivated by a desire to limit competition with substitute technologies. To avoid price competition, licensees were typically required to pay high royalties and adhere to the pool's pricing schemes. In some cases, pools acted as a coordination mechanism for bid-rigging and allocating distributors. Interestingly, four of the six pools that licensed formed after 1935, when the U.S. Supreme Court ruled the NIRA, which had relaxed antitrust enforcement, to be unconstitutional. This suggests that a shift toward stronger enforcement of antitrust laws, albeit imperfect, may have limited firms' ability to use patents as a means to soften competition, and forced pool members to use licensing as a mechanism to ensure that their technology would become the industry standard. The experience of the 20th-century software industry suggests that Apple's reluctance to license its Macintosh operating system may have helped Microsoft Windows to become the dominant operating system platform for personal computers (Cusumano, 2012).

If pools during the New Deal were aimed at limiting competition, how did they affect innovative activity? Analysis of changes in patent counts per year across pool technologies and a control group of related technologies in the same industry indicate a substantial decline in innovation after the formation of a pool (Lampe & Moser, 2012). This decline is strongest for technologies that pool members competed to improve before the creation of a pool, suggesting that a weakening of competition may, in fact, discourage innovation.[26]

NOTES

1. Patent pools are also instrumental in establishing technological standards, for example, for the MPEG-2 technology, for which a pool formed in 1997. In this volume, Greenstein (2012) examines the case of the 802.11b standard for wireless local area network communication, which encouraged the development of Wi-Fi technologies.

2. Licensing constrains prices only for welfare-reducing, but not welfare-enhancing pools (Lerner & Tirole, 2004). Using the existence of litigation by private parties and government as an indicator for anti-competitive pools, Lerner et al. (2007, p. 620) confirm this prediction. Specifically, they find that 36 percent of 28 pools that allowed independent licensing were litigated compared with 64 percent of 35 other pools that formed between 1895 and 2001. Brenner (2009) shows that the predictions of Lerner and Tirole (2004) only hold if incumbent pool members are allowed to prevent rivals from becoming members of the pool.

3. Licensees of these pools are free to use alternative technologies and the pooled patents can be licensed both individually and as a bundle (Gallini, 2011, pp. 14–15).

4. On May 27, 1935, the U.S. Supreme Court ruled in *Schechter Poultry Corp.* vs. *United States* that price and wage-fixing in the poultry industry, which were sanctioned under the NIRA, violated the U.S. Constitution by imposing restrictions on intrastate commerce (*A.L.A. Schechter Poultry Corp. v. United States*, 295 U.S. 495 (1935)).

5. The final report of the committee was released on March 31, 1941. See *Investigation of Concentration of Economic Power, Final Report and Recommendations of the Temporary National Economic Committee*. Washington, DC: U.S. G.P.O., 1941.

6. *United States v. Hartford Empire Co.*, 46 F. Supp. 541 (N.D. Ohio, 1942) and *Hartford Empire Co. v. U.S.* 323 U.S. 386 (Jan., 1945).

7. Lerner et al. (2007) identify 125 pools between 1856 and 2001 and obtain the pooling agreements for 63 of these pools from the National Archives, Congressional hearings, current-day pool administrators, the Department of Justice, and the Federal Trade Commission. Our sample includes 8 additional pools that formed between 1930 and 1938 and excludes 13 pools, which were subject to Congressional hearings, but were not litigated, so that detailed court records, which allow us to document licensing, are not available. Our sample also excludes a pool for television

and radio apparatus, because it consisted exclusively of Australian firms, a pool for male hormones (1937–1941), because it was short-lived, and a "pool" for grinding hobs (1931–1943) because it combined two patents by the same firm, the Barber-Colman Company. Our sample also omits a 1935 pool for acrylic acid and two 1938 pools for pour depressants and induction heat treatments, because we could not find records for these pools.

8. *United States v. General Cable Corp.*, CCH 1948–1949 Trade Cases ¶ 62,300 (S.D.N.Y. Civil No. 40-76; Complaint, 1947; Consent Judgment, 1948).

9. *Kobe v. Dempsey Pump Co.*, 198 F.2d 416 (10th Cir. 1952).

10. From a written complaint by the Department of Justice in 1948 (in *United States v. The Liquid Carbonic Corp.*, CCH Trade Cases ¶ 67,248 (E.D.N.Y. Civil No. 9179; Complaint, 1948; Final Judgment, 1952)).

11. *United States v. American Lecithin Co.*, CCH 1946-47 Trade Cases ¶ 57,542 (N.D. Ohio Civil No. 24115; Complaint, 1946; Consent Judgment, 1947).

12. Vaughan (1956) lists Ross and Rowe as a member, but court records show them to be sales agents only.

13. *United States v. General Instrument Corp.*, 115 F. Supp. 582 (D.N.J. 1953).

14. *United States v. Krasnov*, 143 F. Supp. 184 (E.D. Penn., 1956). *United States v. Krasnov*, Civ. A. No. 11024, United States District Court for the Eastern District of Pennsylvania, 109 F. Supp. 143; 1952 U.S. Dist. LEXIS 2118, December 22, 1952.

15. *United States v. American Locomotive Co.*, CCH 1945-47 Trade Cases ¶ 57,621 (N.D. Ind. Civil No. 545; Complaint, 1942; Consent Judgment, 1947).

16. *T. H. Symington & Son v. Symington Co.*, 9 F. Supp. 699 (1935).

17. *United States v. American Locomotive Co.*, CCH 1945-47 Trade Cases ¶ 57,621 (N.D. Ind. Civil No. 545; Complaint, 1942; Consent Judgment, 1947).

18. American Screw Company later contributed related patents for the manufacturing of screws and screw drivers.

19. *United States v. Phillips Screw Co.*, 1949 Trade Cases (C.C.H.) ¶ 62,394 (N.D. Ill. Civil No. 47-C-147; Complaint, 1947; Consent Judgment, 1949).

20. *United States v. Phillips Screw Co.*, 1949 Trade Cases (C.C.H.) ¶ 62,394 (N.D. Ill. Civil No. 47-C-147; Complaint, 1947; Consent Judgment, 1949).

21. During the interrogation, Kelsey-Hayes and Budd each produced a list of more than 20 alternative suppliers that did not license the pool's technology. *United States v. Kelsey-Hayes Wheel Co.*, CCH 1955 Trade Cases ¶ 68,093 (E.D.Mich. Civil No. 10-655; Complaint, 1951; Consent Judgment, 1955).

22. Equivalent to $25.80 in 2010 adjusted for the CPI (Officer and Williamson 2010).

23. *United States v. New Wrinkle, Inc.*, 342 U.S. 371 (1952). *United States v. New Wrinkle, Inc.*, 1955 Trade Cases (C.C.H.) ¶ 68,161 (S.D. Ohio).

24. *United States v. Line Material Co.*, 333 U.S. 287 (1948).

25. *United States v. American Optical Co.*, CCH 1948-49 Trade Cases ¶ 62,308 (S.D.N.Y. Civil No. 10-391; Complaint, 1940; Final Consent Judgment, 1948).

26. In fact, data on patents and alternative measures of innovation for a pool in the 19th-century sewing machine industry (1856–1877) indicate that even pools, which freely license may discourage innovation (Lampe & Moser, 2010, 2011). While the sewing machine pool was active, pool members, licensees, and other firms patented less and created fewer improvements in the technical performance, compared with the pre- and post-pool period (Lampe & Moser, 2010). Moreover,

licensees and other nonmember firms were less likely to enter with state-of-the-art pool technologies, while the pool was active, and more likely to produce and patent technologically inferior substitutes (Lampe & Moser, 2011). Even the aircraft pool, which is broadly believed to have facilitated the production of the airplane, was dissolved by the Department of Justice in 1976 because it was believed to have discouraged innovation (Bittlingmayer, 1988).

ACKNOWLEDGMENTS

We wish to thank Michael Cusumano, Steven Kahl, Brian Silverman, and seminar participants at AiSM Pre-Conference for helpful comments. Archivists at regional depositories of the National Archives in Boston, Chicago, Kansas City, New York City, Riverside, and San Francisco were instrumental in facilitating access to primary documents. Siyeona Chang, Josh Wagner, Aleksandra Goulioutina, and Marina Kutyavina provided valuable research assistance with collecting archival materials on patent pools. Moser thanks the Stanford Institute for Policy Research (SIEPR) and the Olin Center at Stanford for financial support.

REFERENCES

Bittlingmayer, G. (1988). Property rights, progress, and the aircraft patent agreement. *Journal of Law and Economics, 31*(1), 227–248.

Brenner, S. (2009). Optimal formation rules for patent pools. *Economic Theory, 40*(3), 373–388.

Choi, J. P. (2005). Live and let live: A tale of weak patents. *Journal of the European Economic Association, 3*(2–3), 724–733.

Cusumano, M. A. (2012). Platforms vs. products. Observations from the literature and history. In S. J. Kahl, B. S. Silverman & M. A. Cusumano (Eds.), *Advances in strategic management* (Vol. 29, pp. 35–67). Bingley, UK: Emerald Group.

Department of Justice and Federal Trade Commission. (2007). *Antitrust enforcement and intellectual property rights: Promoting innovation and competition.* Washington, DC: GPO.

Flamm, K. (2012, January). *A tale of two standards: Patent pools and innovation in the optical disk drive industry.* Working Paper, University of Texas at Austin, Austin, TX.

Gallini, N. (2011). Private agreements for coordinating patent rights. The case of patent pools. *Journal of Industrial and Business Economics, 38*(3), 5–29.

Gilbert, R. (2004). Antitrust for patent pools: A century of policy evaluation. *Stanford Technology Law Journal, 3* (April). Retrieved from http://stlr.stanford.edu/STLR/Articles/04_STLR_3

Greenstein, S. (2012). Economic experiments and the development of Wi-Fi. In S. J. Kahl, B. S. Silverman & M. A. Cusumano (Eds.), *Advances in strategic management* (Vol. 29, pp. 3–33). Bingley, UK: Emerald Group.

Haley, J. (2001). *Antitrust in Germany and Japan: The first fifty years, 1947–1998*. Seattle, WA: University of Washington Press.

Hawley, E. (1966). *The new deal and the problem of monopoly: A study in economic ambivalence*. Princeton, NJ: Princeton University Press.

Lampe, R., & Moser, P. (2010). Do patent pools encourage innovation? Evidence from the 19th-century sewing machine industry. *The Journal of Economic History, 70*(4), 871–897.

Lampe, R., & Moser, P. (2011, October). *Patent pools and the direction of R&D*. Retrieved from http://papers.ssrn.com/sol3/papers.cfm?abstract_id=1468062

Lampe, R., & Moser, P. (2012, April). *Do patent pools encourage innovation? Evidence from 20 U.S. Industries under the New Deal*. Stanford Law and Economics Olin Working Paper No. 417. Retrieved from http://ssrn.com/abstract=1967246

Lerner, J., Strojwas, M., & Tirole, J. (2007). The design of patent pools: The determinants of licensing rules. *RAND Journal of Economics, 38*(3), 610–625.

Lerner, J., & Tirole, J. (2004). Efficient patent pools. *American Economic Review, 94*(3), 691–711.

Lévêque, F., & Ménière, Y. (2011). Patent pool formation: Timing matters. *Information Economics and Policy, 23*(3–4), 243–251.

Merges, R. (2001). Institutions for intellectual property transactions: The case of patent pools. In R. C. Dreyfuss, D. L. Zimmerman & H. First (Eds.), *Expanding the boundaries of intellectual property: Innovation policy for the knowledge society* (pp. 123–166). Oxford University Press.

Officer, L. H., & Williamson, S. H. (2010). Measures of worth. *Measuring worth*. Retrieved from http://www.measuringworth.com/worthmeasures.php

Shapiro, C. (2001). Navigating the patent thicket: Cross licenses, patent pools, and standard setting. In A. Jaffe, J. Lerner & S. Stern (Eds.), *Innovation policy and the economy* (Vol. 1, pp. 119–150). Cambridge, MA: MIT Press.

Stubbs, K. (2002). *Race to the front: The material foundation of coalition strategy in the great war*. Westport, CT: Greenwood Publishing Group.

Vaughan, F. (1956). *The United States patent system: Legal and economic conflicts in American patent history*. Norman, OK: University of Oklahoma Press.

PART II
HISTORY AND INDUSTRY
EVOLUTION: CONVERGENCE,
DIVERGENCE, AND
INSTITUTIONAL BACKGROUND

MARRYING HISTORY AND SOCIAL SCIENCE IN STRATEGY RESEARCH

Johann Peter Murmann

ABSTRACT

Purpose – *This chapter is intended to encourage comparative-historical research in strategy by articulating a framework for the study of industry and firm evolution.*

Design/methodology/approach – *Strategy research at its core tries to explain sustained performance differences among firms. This chapter argues that one, out of the many ways to create a productive marriage between strategy research and historical scholarship, is to carry out historically informed comparative studies of how firms and industries gain and lose their competitive position. While much of current strategy research adopts a large N hypothesis testing mode with the implicit assumption that one discovers generalization just like a Newtonian law such as $F = m \times a$ that applies across all space and time, an historically grounded methodology starts from the opposite direction. It assumes that a process or event may be idiosyncratic and therefore seeks to establish with detailed evidence that a 2nd (and later 3rd, 4th, … nth) process or event is indeed similar before generalizing across observations.*

Findings/originality/value – *The chapter argues that the field of strategy would benefit from allocating more effort on building causal generalizations*

History and Strategy
Advances in Strategic Management, Volume 29, 89–115
Copyright © 2012 by Emerald Group Publishing Limited
ISSN: 0742-3322/doi:10.1108/S0742-3322(2012)0000029008

inductively from well-researched case studies, seeking to establish the boundary conditions of emerging generalizations. It articulates a comparative research program that outlines such an approach for the arena of industry and firm evolution studies.

Keywords: Industry evolution; firm evolution; comparative history

INTRODUCTION

Ever since sociology was institutionalized as a distinct academic discipline in the late 19th century, sociologists and historians have debated how these two fields and their methods differed. A prominent early example is the debate between Emile Durkheim, one of the founding fathers of sociology, and the historian Seignobos (Durkheim & Seignobos, 1982[1908]). The present volume attempts to make historical scholarship and its methods again more prominent in the field of strategy. Although Alfred Chandler's major writings, *Strategy and Structure* (1962), *The Visible Hand* (1977), and *Scale and Scope* (1990) are regarded widely as core books in the field of strategy, historical methods had become marginalized in the typical doctoral student education as the field was striving for scientific respectability in universities over the past four decades (see McKenna, 2012, in this volume on the parallel development of strategy as a consulting business).

In many ways the strategy field is now repeating a similar development that took place in sociology a few decades earlier. In the 1940s and 1950s, sociology tried to import a positivist philosophy of science with its focus on finding universalist laws among a few variables just as Newton had done so successfully in physics. In the context of this movement, historical research – with its emphasis on identifying how behavior differs across time and place – seemed to many academics antiquated at best and scientifically flawed at worst. However, when, after trying hard for a long time, sociology had not delivered powerful "universal laws," the positivist project itself became suspect. Leading sociologists such as Charles Tilly (1984) and Theda Skocpol (1984) sharply criticized the positivist agenda in sociology, arguing that macro sociology is fundamentally a historical science that tries to explain dissimilarity in outcomes across space and time as much as it looks for similarities. This paved the way for the emergence of the subfield of historical sociology in which Tilly, Skocpol, and Arthur Stinchcombe (1978, 1997) among others played an important role.

When I arrived in graduate school in 1991 to study for a Ph.D. in management, the new generation of researchers seemed to believe what historians do is both unsystematic and completely atheoretical: in short, the exact opposite of what a good social scientist would aspire to engage in. I spent my first couple of years as a "typical" doctoral student, running econometric analyses on large datasets about whose underlying empirical reality I knew little, learning all the reasons why what I was doing was so much more sophisticated than what those storytelling historians were engaged in. Trying to find stable relationships between variables, we were seeking the Newtonian laws of the social universe, while the intellectually feeble Ph.D. students in history, who did not even understand basic sample selection strategies, would at best learn how to become journalists of long-gone times and places. Their work would be totally useless for managing the affairs of today and tomorrow. While this description may appear to be a bit of an exaggeration, I think it captures well the spirit of how we were socialized to think about history.

My book *Knowledge and Competitive Advantage: The Coevolution of Firms, Technology and National Institutions* (Murmann, 2003) shows how dramatically I changed my view about the value of history for the social sciences in general and the study of how industries and firms develop in particular. One fundamental difference between an ahistorical natural science such as Newtonian physics and social science is that physical facts exist independent of the observer, whereas many social facts depend fundamentally on the agreement between human beings. Let me give an example: A $100 bill does not obtain its causal power from the paper it is printed on but from the fact that presently there is agreement in U.S. society that a $100 bill issued by the government serves as a storage unit of value and can be exchanged for any good in the economy. If no human being existed on this planet, the $100 bill would lose its power. Similarly, it is not difficult to imagine a future U.S. society that no longer knows any paper currency and instead relies solely on electronic currency. In this case the $100 bill would also have lost its causal power as a currency. There is a second key difference between a Newtonian ahistorical science and any science of society. While the financial crisis of 2008 may have some causes in common with the one that occurred in 1929, the world changed substantially in the intervening eight decades. This means that an explanation of the 2008 crisis will need to incorporate that the global financial systems had become more interconnected in part because of cheap computers and telecommunications technology that did not exist in 1929.

Historians take it as a premise that social conditions and the way society views the world change over time. For historians, to explain social action one needs to describe in some detail the larger conditions in which the action occurred. If one reads a bit of the historical literature describing how dramatically economic conditions changed in the course of human history – but especially since the industrial revolution in the 18th century – one realizes that the ahistorical Newtonian physics is the wrong model to imitate for any social science and the strategy field in particular. The historical natural sciences such as biology and geology are much better models but even they often don't capture the additional complexity that is created by self-aware human beings who have amazing capabilities to change their behavior in different conditions.

In the present context, it seems useful to briefly describe how my change of heart about the usefulness of history came about and why the field of strategy would benefit from a similar change in orientation that occurred in sociology earlier. Working with Michael Tushman on the question of how different types of technological innovations would affect the development of industries, I came across Hugh Aitken's books on the history of radio (1976, 1985); Thomas Hughes' (1983) history of the development of electric power networks in Chicago, Berlin, and London; and Walter Vincenti's (1990) work on the development of airplanes and the discipline of aeronautical engineering. It was simply not true that historians were merely telling one damn fact after another (see Gaddis, 2002, for a recent articulation of how historians work). The best historians don't shy away from abstractions and theory. Aitken, for example, in his history draws heavily on role theory from sociology, Hughes on general system theory, and Vincenti on evolutionary theory that my 2003 book builds on and tries to develop a little further. Joel Mokyr articulates in his book *The Gifts of Athena* (2002) an abstract theory of different kinds of knowledge and he then uses this theory to explain why and where the industrial revolution occurred. But historians always pay careful attention to formulating precisely the causal story that led to the outcome they are trying to explain. I also found that the thick descriptions— to use a term coined by the anthropologist Clifford Geertz (1973)—historians are using to lay out a causal sequence would, unlike summarizing one's key findings in a regression table, make it much easier to imagine and try alternative theoretical explanations for the phenomenon at hand. One's mind can more readily accept alternative explanations as compelling if one is presented with enough detail about what empirically happened.

I also discovered that the field of history includes an institutionalized practice that is important for any good empirical science: In their quest for professional recognition historians compete over who comes up with the more accurate description of what actually happened in the world. The conclusions regarding what the facts mean and how they should be interpreted from a causal point of view always come after trying to get the facts right. How much attention is the average reviewer in strategy journals presently paying on ensuring that an author got the facts right rather than ensuring that the statistical techniques used are valid? How many published articles in the field of strategy can you name whose main purpose is to overturn the empirical foundation that was used to confirm theoretical interpretations?[1] Would the field of strategy not benefit from imitating the field of history in this regard?

In this chapter, I will first describe the historically informed methodology that I used in my 2003 book and discuss how this methodology is conducive to making progress on many of the central questions in strategy research. It is useful to recall that if one tries to develop causal theories of performance differences among firms and claims that these differences are not random but are created through an intentional process on the parts of managers, then the burden of proof is quite steep. Given that most firms fail (Murmann, Aldrich, Levinthal, & Winter, 2003), the question arsises, how much managers can control the fate of their firms. When we want to argue that managers were responsible for the firm's superior performance, we ideally demonstrate the entire causal chain from the intentional action to the later performance differences. I will argue that causality about performance is easier to demonstrate in a comparative longitudinal research design that stays close to the historical phenomenon rather than a single case study.[2] There are many other ways to carry out research with historical sensibility and in no way do I want to give the impression that my proposal is the only approach to marrying strategy research and history. To get a sense of the many ways to use history, I refer the reader to other contributions in this volume, to the articles by O'Sullivan and Graham (2010) and Jones and Khanna (2006), and to the monographs by Charles Tilly (1997, 2008), Arthur Stinchcombe (1978, 2005), and Andrew Abbott (2001, 2004).

I will focus on formulating a call for collecting comparable data on firm and industry development that will provide a stronger foundation for constructing, refining, and testing theoretical ideas in strategy. (The contribution of Ingram, Rao, & Silverman, 2012, in this volume, outlines a complementary approach based on analytic narratives.) While my proposal is reminiscent of the call for a comparative database that John Freeman (1986) made when he was the editor of *Administrative Science*

Quarterly, it is closer in spirit to the *Human Area Relations File* (HARF) started in 1949 by a consortium of major universities under the leadership of Yale University. Until today, the HARF has the mission "to provide information that facilitates the cross-cultural study of human behavior, society and culture" (2012). The HARF project made it possible to systematically compare cultural practices, for example, marriage patterns across different areas of the world and determine how similar and different they are. If we had available similar data on many firms and industries, we could look for empirically grounded generalizations and articulate more precisely boundary conditions of such generalizations. To facilitate these comparisons, I will lay out a set of research questions and then articulate a list of variables[3] that would be very useful for scholars in strategy and history to collect. The novelty of this proposal is that it does not require one scholar to collect all variables and all time periods on a particular firm or industry. In fact, constructing a robust comparative framework makes it possible to divide the labor and pool efforts among strategy and organization scholars and their colleagues in business and economic history. The key in making such a project successful is to reduce the costs for people to contribute by publishing a common framework, so that at the same time as people engage in their particular research on a firm or industry they collect the information called for in the common framework. As will become apparent later in the chapter, the comparative framework is complementary to the FIVE Project organized by Connie Helfat[4] and to the efforts of the *Industry Studies Organization*[5].

STRATEGY AS HISTORICAL SOCIAL SCIENCE

One definition of the key task of strategy research that many scholars can agree on is: the field of strategy is concerned with providing explanations for sustained performance differences among firms (Nelson, 1991; Porter, 1996; Rothaermel, 2012; Rumelt, Schendel, & Teece, 1994). If we are trying to explain sustained rather than short-term or temporary advantages, the key question is: *How long does a competitive advantage have to exist before it would qualify as "sustained"?* Independent of the precise answer to this question,[6] the longer the time period one samples before pronouncing a sustained competitive advantage has existed, the more other scholars would agree with the finding.

After having taken course work as a doctoral student and read widely in strategy and related fields during the period from 1991 to 1994, I arrived at the working hypothesis that our real challenge was not that we lack theory of what causes competitive advantage on a very general abstract level. Comparing the most prominent perspectives at the time (main-line economics, organizational ecology, early-Porter (Porter, 1980, 1985), resource-based theory, etc.),[7] I found that across the main theories available in strategy virtually all external factors and internal factors that one could dream of were covered when conceived on an abstract level. Our challenge hence was and is not that we lack *theory* per se. Rather our challenge was and is (1) to identify the boundary conditions of existing theories, (2) to combine existing theoretical perspectives without ending up with 1,001 variables to analyze, and (3) to operationalize general categories of variables in a theory, so they capture concrete competitive dynamics in a particular industrial setting. Examining competitive advantage over long periods of time raises the fourth challenge that environments can shift quite dramatically, making it more likely that new factors play a role in determining how competitive a firm is. This means that a priori it is almost impossible to identify what are good ways to operationalize on a semi-abstract level the dimensions of a variable.

In the early 1990s and still today, most of strategy research is of the hypothesis testing nature. But this style of research is rather ill equipped to address the four aforementioned challenges. Michael Porter articulated this problem clearly in his 1991 SMJ article. He writes: "I concluded in my most recent research that detailed longitudinal case studies, covering long periods of time, were necessary to study [competitive success] ... This style of research nudges strategy research, and indeed industrial economics, into the world of the historian" (p. 116). Encouraged by Richard Nelson, who also believed that detailed empirical work on how industries and firms developed over time is going to bring about rich knowledge dividends (Mowery & Nelson, 1999), I set out to marry the sampling strategies developed by organizational ecologists (Hannan & Freeman, 1989) with methodologies developed by historians (Chandler, 1990; Hughes, 1983) and comparative sociologists (Skocpol, 1984; Tilly, 1984).

In the early 1990s virtually all full population studies that tracked the entry and exit of firms in the course of the development of an industry were carried out on the U.S. industries (Hannan & Carroll, 1992; Romanelli, 1989; Tushman & Anderson, 1986; Utterback & Suárez, 1993). Researchers had documented for a series of different U.S. industries that the number of producers initially started to rise and at some point the number declined, often quite substantially. This phenomenon was later dubbed *industry shakeouts* (Klepper & Simons, 1996). I had the suspicion that at least the timing and maybe even the patterns of industry evolution would be shaped by a country's institutional infrastructure. For this reason, one of the key issues that I wanted to examine in my dissertation was whether country-level institutions had an effect on patterns of industry evolution. Second, I wanted to get enough detail about the development of individual firms so that I could observe how industry-level forces have an impact on the life course of individual firms. Third, I wanted to trace performance not just in terms of birth and deaths but also in terms of level of profitability and market share.

To make developments comparable I canvassed a number of different industries: steel, chemicals, machine tools, car batteries, car brakes, water filters, and initially settled on the chemical industry for two main reasons. It had a history dating back to the 19th century and, unlike machine tools, the leading firms across different countries went public in the 1880s, leaving ample public records. I started to collaborate with Ashish Arora, Ralph Landau, and Nathan Rosenberg (1998), who at the time were organizing a comparative study of the development of the chemical industry in Britain, Germany, Japan, and the United States. Initially, I was asked to write the chapter on corporate strategies, but when Alfred Chandler joined the team, my task became to write a comparative history of the industry in Germany and Britain with Ralph Landau (Murmann & Landau, 1998). Because he had developed important petrochemical processes, Ralph Landau knew the technological history of the industry after World War II very well. But to be able to write a comparative history that would meet the quality standards of professional historians, I followed the standard process of historians to read as much as possible of the entire literature on the subject. As I was learning a great deal about the chemical industry, it became clear that the products in the industry were so diverse that I was effectively dealing with multiple industries.

For this reason, I decided to focus my dissertation research on one branch of the industry, synthetic dyes, which was special for a number of reasons. The industry displayed huge differences in performance both at the country level and at the firm level, which would make it much easier to detect the causes of those differences. Britain and France led the industry for the first 8 years until about 1865, but then Germany came to dominate the industry and had at least 75% world market share for three decades (Table 1, Row 5 provides detail on the development of country shares). Similarly, three German firms—Bayer, Hoechst, and BASF—overtook their British and French rivals by the early 1870s, and then steadily increased their output and market share. Each possessed 20% world

Table 1. Indicators for the Evolution of National Populations of Synthetic Dye Firms.

	Great Britain	Germany	France	Switzerland	U.S.
1. Total firm entries	53	118	68	32	28
Total firm exits	43	94	57	26	18
Firm failure rate	81%	80%	83%	81%	64%
2. Firm entries + exits	1861–1877: 50 1878–1893: 24 1894–1914: 15	1861–1877: 74 1878–1893: 72 1894–1914: 59	1861–1877: 44 1878–1893: 24 1894–1914: 15	1861–1877: 25 1878–1893: 8 1894–1914: 2	1865–1877: 5 1878–1893: 13 1894–1914: 28
3. Firm turnover[a]	1861–1877: 7.14 1878–1893: 1.71 1894–1914: 1.00	1861–1877: 12.33 1878–1893: 2.88 1894–1914: 1.74	1861–1877: 7.11 1878–1893: 2.18 1894–1914: 2.36	1861–1877: 8.33 1878–1893: 1.14 1894–1914: 2.62	1865–1877: 2.50 1878–1893: 4.33 1894–1914: 4.67
4. Share of all firms in the world	1860: 28% 1877: 22% 1893: 17% 1914: 14%	1860: 24% 1877: 38% 1893: 39% 1914: 31%	1860: 36% 1877: 15% 1893: 12% 1914: 15%	1860: 12% 1877: 11% 1893: 11% 1914: 8%	1860: 0% 1877: 5% 1893: 7% 1914: 13%
5. Share global market[b]	1862: 50.0% 1873: 18.0% 1893: 12.0% (est.) 1913: 6.5%	1862: 3.0% 1873: 50.0% 1893: 70.0% 1913: 74.1%	1862: 40.0% 1873: 17.0% 1893: 11.8% (est.) 1913: 5.4%	1862: 2.5% 1873: 13.0% 1893: 10% (est.) 1913: 7.0%	1862: 0.0% 1873: 0.2% 1893: 1.8% (est.) 1913: 3.3%

Source: Adapted from Murmann (in press).

[a]Turnover is calculated by adding up the firm entries and exits in the period and dividing it by the number of firms in the year before the period.

[b]The 1862 figures are from Leprieur and Papon (1979, p. 207). The authors report that Germany and Switzerland together held 5% of the market. I estimate that Germany's share amounted to 3% and the Swiss share to 2%. The 1873 figures were put together by Ernst Homburg from Hofmann (1873, p. 108), Wurtz (1876, p. 235), and Kopp, (1874, p. 153). The 1912 figures are from Thissen (1922). Except in the case of Germany, I did not have figures for the year 1893. I estimated the countries' market shares by assuming that market shares declined between 1877 and 1914 in a linear fashion.

market share in 1913. The biggest British firms at the time (Levinstein and Read Holliday) had 2.0% of the world market each and the biggest American firm (Schoellkopf) had 1.7% of the world market. Second, the synthetic dye industry started at roughly the same time in several countries—Britain (1857), France (1858), Germany (1858), Switzerland (1859), and the United States (1864). This would give the comparisons across the different national dye industries more face validity because in a contemporaneous comparison many factors are held constant that would probably be variable in those comparisons made across national industries that started at much different historical moments. Third, it was what historians dubbed the first science-based industry and constituted the high-tech branch of the chemical industry in the second half of the 19th century. Corporate R&D laboratories as a routine aspect of firms were pioneered in this industry. This meant the industry stayed in constant technological flux during its first six decades, requiring firms to do novel things and adapt to stay in the game.

It is convenient to describe the research design I selected using the typology Abbott (2004) laid out in his wonderful short book entitled *Methods of Discovery: Heuristics for the Social Sciences*. Abbott identifies three different ways of classifying research methods: by the type of data gathering (ethnography, surveys, record-based analysis, history—here he means old records and documents); by the type of data analysis (direct interpretation, quantitative analysis, formal modeling); and finally by how one poses the research question (case-study analysis, small-N analysis and large-N analysis). He then explains that one can mix and match these different strategies leading to 36 ($4 \times 3 \times 3$) possible subtypes. Abbott notes that while all 36 types have been tried, five types have been most widely used. They are: 1, ethnography; 2, historical narration; 3, small-N comparison; 4, standard causal analysis (by which he means large N, statistical models); and 5, formalization. In terms of this scheme, I married historical narration with small-N case comparison. The observed differences in performance outcomes in the synthetic dye industry from 1857 to 1914 both at the country and firm levels were so large that I did not need econometric tools to detect effects but could rely on small-N comparisons instead. Small-N comparisons try to overcome the disadvantages of single-case studies and large-N studies. With single-case studies, there is always a question of whether the findings generalize at all. Large-N studies, on the other hand, as Abbott explains (2004, p. 22) have the problem that they oversimplify and change the meaning of variables by removing them from their context. Furthermore, small-N comparisons do not assume that one already has been able to identify how to break a complex phenomenon into constituent parts, which is presumed in large-N studies with multiple independent variables. Ragin (1987) articulates in detail how it is possible to compare wholes (e.g. countries, national industries, firms) in small-N comparisons.

As mentioned before, to identify the causal processes that led to dramatic variations in performance across countries and firms in the period from 1857 to 1914, my study design was also going to marry the sampling strategies of organizational ecologists with the methods of small-N comparative sociologists and historians. Together with Ernst Homburg, a historian of technology, I put together a quantitative and qualitative database of all firms that left any trace somewhere in the historical records. (The database design is described in Appendix II of my 2003 book.) As a doctoral student more than a decade before, Homburg had participated in a project on the development of the dye industry (van den Belt, Gremmen, Homburg, & Hornix, 1984; van den Belt, Homburg, & Hornix, 1981) and had become the expert on the data sources for the industry and its relationship to science. Working together with a leading historian of the synthetic dye industry was invaluable for the quality of my work, preventing me from offering explanations that a person with knowledge of the details of the industry would not make. (I will give an example of this later.)

With simple descriptive data we could show that the patterns of firm entries, exits, and the number of producers over time showed substantial variation across the five major producer countries during the first 55 years of the industry's existence (see Fig. 1 taken from Murmann & Homburg, 2001). While France displayed a seemingly classic shakeout after 1862, the number of producers continued to rise in Germany until 1898 and then started to drop. If one has data only on the number of firms in the industry and no contextual knowledge, one could construct many equally plausible interpretations for the shakeout, for example, increasing returns to scale, pushing smaller players out of the industry. But in the case of the synthetic dye industry in France, the shakeout was caused in large part by a patent court ruling, which gave one firm, La Fuchsine, a monopoly. This firm used the police to shut down rival producers who sometimes set up shop across the border in Switzerland, where French law did not apply. The historical literature on the synthetic dye industry provided the details on the court case (van den Belt, 1992), which prevented me from misconstruing it as a shakeout primarily caused by increasing returns to scale. Here we already see how important the historians' emphasis is on getting facts right to safeguard against obviously false interpretations.

Fig. 1. Number of Synthetic Dye Firms by Country, 1857–1914. *Source*: Murmann and Homburg (2001). *Note*: To make the graphs easier to process for the eye, upon the request of the editor we reported 3-year moving averages in Murmann and Homburg (2001).

One other important advantage of using more than one case is that one can more confidently make causal inferences (Mahoney, 2000). If I had only studied the German synthetic dye industry and not compared it to Britain and the United States (Murmann, 2003) and later to Switzerland and France (Murmann, in press; Murmann & Homburg, 2001), it would have been more difficult to have confidence in my causal inferences.[8] For example, at the national level I cited the differences in university systems (which influenced the number of chemists available to start firms and later to staff R&D laboratories of existing firms) and patent laws as key causal factors behind Germany's success in the synthetic dye industry before 1914. Being able to show that Switzerland, the other country that became relatively more successful, also developed a stronger capability in training organic chemists, and that the other countries that became less successful, France, Great Britain, and the United States trailed Germany and Switzerland in that capability made the inferences about Germany more compelling. As far as the patent systems are concerned, being able to show with detailed data that Switzerland rejected granting patents for synthetic dyes until 1903–46 years after the start of the industry—so that Swiss firms could freely copy German dye inventions, lent strength to the interpretation that Germany benefited from not having an effective patent for the first 20 years of the industry until 1877, while Britain, France, and the United States offered patent protection.

One of the key predictions an evolutionary theory of industry evolution is that firm failures are absolutely necessary for developing some successful firms. Analyzing the underpinnings of creative thought, Campbell (1960, p. 395) pointed out: "The [...] variation-and-selection-retention model unequivocally implies that ceteris paribus, the greater the heterogeneity and volume of trials the greater the chance of a productive innovation. Doubling the number of efforts very nearly doubles the chance of a hit, particularly when trials are a small part of the total domain and the repetitiousness among trials is low. [...] unconventionality and no doubt numerosity [are] a necessary, if not sufficient condition of creativity." A similar prediction can be made regarding industrial development: More start-ups, ceteris paribus, increase the odds that some firms will be successful. While historians in different countries had written in detail about the synthetic dye industry, there had never been a systematic effort to collect data on all the firms that participated in the industry before 1914 to test such a prediction for the early history of the industry. One of the reasons why I collected with Ernst Homburg data on all the firms in the world before 1914 is precisely to be able to test whether this theoretical prediction held true in this industry and could explain why Germany overtook Britain and France and dominated the industry for decades. As you can see from Row 1 in Table 1, Germany's industry dominance was indeed built on having both a larger number of start-ups in all periods except for the first 4 years of the industry and a larger number of failures. Notice that I am turning the small-N case comparison into a much larger N comparison by focusing on all the firms within a country, although we know relatively little about all the firms except for what products they offered and when they entered and exited the industry.

To be able to verify the causal factors that I claimed operate at the country level and to account for country-level performance differences in this industry, it would have to be the case that causal processes impacted differentially on individual firms operating in different national contexts. For this reason, I conducted six detailed case studies of a winning firm and a losing firm in three countries: Germany, Great Britain, and the United States (see Murmann, 2003, Chapter 3). In the case of Germany, I was able to select two firms (Bayer and Jäger) that started in the same town (Elberfeld, now a part of Wuppertal). The firms also had the same background, namely the trading of natural dyes. This matched comparison held constant environmental factors, allowing me to isolate with greater confidence that managerial actions mattered for performance. (For a similar reason the contribution by Kipping & Westerhuis, 2012, in this volume, carefully selects two Dutch banks in the same country in order to be able to isolate the causal factors that led one firm to adopt the M-form earlier than the other firm.)

In analyzing what factors discriminated between the successful and unsuccessful firms in the three countries (even though the successful firm in Germany was a lot more successful for a lot longer than its British or American counterparts), three factors stood out: aside from making investments in Chandlerian organizational capabilities (in-house R&D, marketing, management, and manufacturing capabilities), those firms that went international earlier were more successful in the long run. But most importantly in the present context, the successful firms (Bayer, Levinstein [in Britain], and Schoellkopf [in U.S.], compared to the unsuccessful ones (Jäger, Brooke Simpson and Spiller [Britain], and American Aniline) secured better access to the centers of the organic-chemical knowledge network by recruiting students who had obtained their doctoral degrees in Germany. I thereby found support for the national-level argument that the German industry outperformed Britain and the United States because Germany became the leading country in organic chemistry. What differentiated the British and American successful firms from their less successful national counterparts was that they tried to overcome the problem of having an inferior national organic chemistry capability by hiring chemists from Germany, in the case of Levinstein in Britain, or by sending the son of the founder to Germany to study organic chemistry and acquire critical knowledge for running a synthetic dye business. Thirty percent of my 2003 book was devoted to tracing the entire life histories of the six firms until 1914, if they existed that long, because this provided the opportunity to detect national-level causal processes in the details of the firm histories. If I had not been able to confirm at the firm level that access to the German centers of organic chemistry mattered for performance, the country level explanations would have looked very suspect.

The strength of the historical method is precisely that it looks for evidence in all sizes and shapes to put together the most accurate account of what happened and why. I find it useful to draw an analogy between social science research and detective work. A good detective will not rely alone on DNA evidence that most advanced scientific methods from biology make available. She/he will always seek to see the crime scene, to interview not only the suspects, but also other people close to the crime scene or familiar with the suspects. In the case of historians, people are typically dead, so one needs to rely on written accounts. Some of the most useful empirical descriptions of what happened in the synthetic dye industry before 1914 were written by industry participants. Heinrich Caro, the first research director of BASF, wrote one of the best historical accounts of how Germany overtook France and Britain in the dye industry (Caro, 1892). Similarly, Carl Duisberg, one of Bayer's first research chemists, who later became the firm's CEO, left a sizable body of speeches and writings including an autobiography (1933) that provided me invaluable insights into how Bayer managed to outcompete every other firm except for BASF and Hoechst in this industry before 1914. Clearly, one needs to be cautious about the potential bias of any single participating observer. Just like a good detective, one is always skeptical of the accounts of single individuals and treats them as interesting hypotheses to be confirmed by other sources of information. While any one industry or academic participant may display a biased view of events, reading the accounts of many participants allows one to piece together an account where the individual biases largely cancel each other out.

What is true of historical research in my view is true of strategy research as well. In the end what makes an empirical argument compelling is a patchwork of different pieces of evidence that can include econometric analyses. But relying only on publicly available datasets and econometric analyses to determine causal relationships, as is often done in strategy research, is a fraught with danger. If one does not know anything about the context (as is the case if one only codes a trade directory), it is very easy to mistake correlations for causation because no alarm bells go off, as is the case with researchers who know something about the context.

In my view, strategy research would benefit if a larger number of studies would marry social science with historical methodologies as I articulated in the preceding pages. If we had more comparable research, we could start building up empirical generalizations from well-researched case studies of industry. In the next section I will put forward a proposal on how we could speed up the development of these industry case studies.

OUTLINING A COMPARATIVE INDUSTRY STUDY PROJECT

Evolutionary economists (Dosi, 2000; Nelson & Winter, 1982; Saviotti & Metcalfe, 1991) have articulated powerful theories about how industries change. During the last 20 years economists, sociologists, and business school scholars have begun to study empirically how particular industries develop over long periods of time. For example, Steven Klepper (2008) has studied the entry and exit patterns of firms in a number of different industries. He explicitly tried to make systematic comparisons across industries, asking why some industries experience a shakeout while other industries do not. Many other scholars have studied one particular national industry, focusing on particular aspects of the industry's evolution. Because scholars frequently do not analyze the same aspects (variables), it is often difficult to compare systematically across industries and figure out what causes lie behind the similarities and differences in patterns of industry evolution. The comparative effort by Mowery and Nelson (1999), which brought together authors of seven industry studies, showed that it would be fruitful to engage different industry studies with one another.

To make it easier in future studies to compare across industries and come up with causal explanations, it seems expedient to formulate an analytical framework, that is, a common list of characteristics that future studies could trace. The few existing cross-national comparisons (Chesbrough, 1999; Murmann, 2003; Murmann & Homburg, 2001) have highlighted that institutional differences can lead to very different patterns of industry evolution. Hence, a framework is called for that combines concepts from traditional industrial organization economics, evolutionary economics, innovation studies, and institutional theory broadly defined. Because industries within different national environments are also typically connected through flows of trade and investment, it is also vital to add a cross-national, integrative component that is able to detect cross-border interdependencies. Since the performance of an industry in one country often interacts with the performance of the same industry in another country, it is useful to find out, for example, whether these interactions create systematic differences in the timing of shakeouts.

There is yet another compelling reason for formulating such a framework. Business and economic historians are the custodians of a large empirical literature on how industries and organizations within industries have changed over time. When these scholars write up their own studies, they often do not provide all the evidence that an evolutionary economist or like-minded analyst would like to know for their analytical purposes. Articulating a common set of features to compare, contrast, and provide integrated explanations across industries would have the additional benefit of being able to recruit business and economic historians to share information they may have in their files but never published when they wrote about a particular firm or industry.

PRELIMINARY SKETCHES OF FRAMEWORK

The framework should be able to address two questions at the same time: Firstly, why do patterns of development in the organization of an industry differ? Secondly, why do patterns of development differ for the same industry in different countries? Klepper, for example, has shown that a shakeout in the number of producers started in the automobile industry already after 9 years (2007). But he also showed that there was no shakeout in the laser industry after 33 years (Klepper & Sleeper, 2005). Why? In the synthetic dye industry before 1914 Homburg and I (Murmann & Homburg, 2001) showed significant differences in national patterns of evolution. Do these differences exist in all industries or are they limited to a few industries? What explains these differences?

My initial work on the synthetic dye industry stopped in 1914 because World War I completely changed the industry dynamics. When the war broke out, the German government blocked German firms from supplying key foreign markets. As a result, some of the major consumer countries of dyes such as the United States no longer had enough dyes to color clothing, prompting the government to try to stimulate local production. Governments also discovered during the war that synthetic dye plants could be readily converted to making explosives, allowing Germany to ramp up its explosives production much faster than other countries that lacked large synthetic dye facilities. As a result, governments in Britain, France, the United States, and Japan took active steps to build significant national dye industries and afford these industries' protection after the war was over, so German firms would not wipe out local industries given their superior capabilities built up over 50 years.

The case of the United States after 1914 is instructive. Fig. 1 shows that the United States, unlike the other four major producer countries, experienced a rise in the number of industry participants just before World War I. The disappearance of German imports and the government's action to create a local industry had dramatic effects. In 1914, the

Murmann–Homburg database shows 14 firms producing dyes in the United States. According to Welsh (1944, p. 185) by 1918 the number had risen to 90. Then it started to fall to 49 by 1929 and to 29 firms by 1939, with five firms accounting for approximately 90–95% of total output (p. 186).[9] At the same time, the entire Germany dye industry was merged into one firm. This was possible in Germany because at the time the country allowed cartels that were illegal in the Unites States. What these numbers show is that World War I was an external event that reset the clock of industry evolution in the United States but not in Germany. This leads me to this general question: Under what circumstances show national industries the classical singular shakeout pattern versus when does the same industry[10] experience again a rise of producers after a shakeout?

After World War II, India and, after 1978, China became producers on the global synthetic dye market, initially fueled by the rise of their domestic textile industry. Industrial dye production started in India in 1956. Under strict state regulation, 20 firms started production during the first 10 years (Mandal, 2006). After 1974, the industry was deregulated, allowing many new firms to enter the industry on a small scale. India had 400 dye factories in 1985 (Mandal, 2006, p. 17) and 600 in 2005 (Mandal, 2006, p. 24). Similarly, in China an estimated 500 to 800 dye firms entered the market after liberalization of the economy (Jiang & Murmann, in press). Even in Germany the largest number of firms ever operating in the industry never reached more than 40. So what explains that the number of firms participating in the industry was so much higher in India and China than in any other producer country in the long history of the industry? At present I don't know enough to have well-founded answers. I simply present these numbers here to paint a vivid picture of what kinds of questions a comparative industry study framework will need to address.

Even more than previous work, the comparative industry study framework should focus on how producers are linked to users, how new users are brought into the market, and how the speed of market growth in their home environment affects the long-term global positions of firms that started in different countries.

Given the space limitation of the present chapter, I cannot go into articulating all the important questions that should be addressed. I will simply confine myself to presenting an outline. Here is the beginning of a list of candidate variables aside from the traditional industrial organization economics variables (size of market, rates of market growths, number of producers, export, import and international investment patterns, market shares in different countries, profit rates, cost structures, entry and exit rates of producers, capital intensity, etc.) that could form the core of the comparative framework: How big are the economies of scale or scope, and are they increasing or decreasing over time? What is the unit value and value per unit weight of the product? How numerous are the customers of the industry? What are the salient characteristics of users and how do they evolve over time? What is the frequency of product and process innovation in the course of the development of the industry? What is the frequency of innovations in organizations and in the institutional and regulatory frameworks shaping the evolution of different industries in different economies? How many of the skills needed by firms in the industry are created inside the firms and how many are created by external educational institutions? How are skills transferred from one producer to the next? What factors determine export versus international investment decisions? Does government have many policies tailored to the particular industry? How have policies in different countries shaped the evolution of the industry on a world scale? How did the regulatory pattern in the industry develop? What are the strategies and structures of firms that become the leading producers?

THOUGHTS ON THE PROCESS

In formulating a comparative framework it is necessary to balance the desire to develop a comprehensive framework (i.e., identifying all the causal mechanisms) with not having an endlessly long list of variables that would make these comparisons unwieldy. Thus, it should focus on some core evolutionary/managerial/policy questions. It also seems important to articulate what features of industry evolution are readily tracked quantitatively and what aspects call for more qualitative descriptions. I have created a beta version of the framework in Table 2. I invite other scholars to work me with on refining it. We should then subject it to a trial-run on a few industries, ideally where much of the material is accessible relatively quickly through secondary sources, and then refine it further.

Ideally, all industries should be traced from their beginning. For some industries this is easily feasible because the data is readily available after a bit of digging. For other industries only particular periods can be readily documented. Individual scholars may only possess part of the data on a particular industry. But collectively different scholars may be able to bring together all the data called for by the framework. For this reason, I have created a collaborative platform (called EEpedia on economic-evolution.net), which contains the beta version of the framework and where different

Table 2.   Comparative Industry Study (CIS) Framework.

	Country	World	Firm
Quantitative variables			
Demand	Size of market	Size of market	Sales
	Rates of market growth	Rates of market growth	Sales growth
	Imports	Imports	
	Number of consumers	Number of consumers	Number of customers
Supply	Number of producers	Number of producers	Variety of products offered
	Entry/Exit rates of producers	Entry/Exit rates of producers	Date of production start
	Concentration ratio	Concentration ratio	Market share
			Percentage of sales in particular industry
	Exports	Exports	Exports
	Cost structure	Cost structure	Cost structure
	Capital intensity	Capital intensity	Capital intensity
	Frequency of product and process innovations	Frequency of product and process innovations	Frequency of product and process innovations
	Capacity investment rates and distribution	FDI and portfolio control	Capacity investment rates
Finance	Profit rates	Profit rates	Profit rates
	Size of foreign direct investment	Size of foreign direct investment	Size of foreign direct investment
	Share of FDI of all investments	Share of FDI of all investments	Share of FDI of all investments
	Source of funds	Source of funds	Source of funds
			Investment in R&D
Qualitative variables			
Users	What are the salient characteristics of users and how do they evolve?	How diverse are the needs of users across countries?	What user segment is served? How does this change?
	How do producers find out about users' needs?		How does the firm find out users' needs?
Products	What is the type of product or service (final consumer good, intermediate good, primary good, standalone product, subassembly, component in system)?		How do products reach the users; does the firm market and sell directly, or are other organizations involved; are there changes?
Production	How are production skills formed (internal, other firms, or external organizations)?	Is global production concentrated in few countries?	What prior experience did the firm have?
			What factors determine export vs. international investment decisions?

Table 2. (*Continued*)

	Country	World	Firm
Policies/ regulations	Does government have many policies/ regulations tailored to the industry; do they have a demonstrable effect on country competitiveness in the industry?	What trade regimes exist and how do they change?	What is the strategy of the firm? What kinds of policies (routines) does the firm develop for its operation?
	How do policies/ regulations change over time?		What is the relationship among policies (routines)?
Supporting institutions	What is the role of trade associations and how do they change over time? Are there any other institutions that are crucial for the industry?	Are there any supranational nonfirm actors (e.g., UN, WTO)?	Does the firm have specific alliances with other actors?

scholars can deposit their findings. The hope is that with the help of the website and e-mail, the data collection on a particular industry can be done to some extent by virtual teams from all over the world.

DISCUSSION

When management scholars in the 1970s and 1980s endeavored to institutionalize strategy research as a separate field in business schools, they felt an imperative to imitate the then-reigning ideal of a social science in management to gain legitimacy for the subfield. Built on the positivist model of a natural science, this conception of science seeks to discover Newtonian-type universal laws (e.g., $F = m \times a$) independent of time and place by reducing social phenomena to abstract numbers and running econometric analysis of representative datasets to find the coefficients that relate a few explanatory variables to the outcome to be explained. This chapter argues that while econometric analyses are powerful tools in the mature final stages of a research problem, they typically have very limited power during the long period of research when one is trying to build an understanding of a social phenomenon. During this stage it is generally more productive to build deeper conceptual understanding by carrying out detailed empirical case studies about the causal processes driving a phenomenon (for an excellent example, see Danneels, 2011).

If one wants to look for a role model in natural sciences, it is the historical branches of natural science such as biology and geology that can serve as much better inspiration than Newtonian physics. Understanding how firms gain and lose competitive advantage in a larger industrial context that is changing quite dramatically within short periods of time requires contextual knowledge. The craft of historians has always been to place action in context, and this chapter argues that the field of strategy would be better off if more scholars would use historical methods because that would allow us to build generalizations from the ground up instead of trying to find Newtonian laws that either don't exist in strategy or are trivial (e.g., all profitable firms take in more money than they spend).

To give an illustration of how one can productively marry history with social science research in strategy, I described the methods I used in Murmann (2003). Since it is so easy to be misinterpreted, I would like to emphasize: I am not advocating that all strategy research should turn historical. My argument is more nuanced. I simply contend that the relative frequency in which different research methods are presently used in strategy research is leading to suboptimal outcomes. We need more careful empirical research based on case studies and small N-comparisons to articulate more clearly how firms gain and lose competitive advantage. When we have articulated with the help of these case studies more precisely the causal mechanisms and when we know more about boundary conditions where they apply, then it is fruitful to design large N studies that test more precisely stated theoretical statements.

The chapter advocated a comparative industry studies project that is in part inspired by the power of the Wikipedia model (Giles, 2005). Business historians reading these lines may fear that my proposal for a comparative industries studies project devalues the writing of traditional business histories of individual firms. That is not my aim and it would be unfortunate if I am understood that way. I simply wanted to point out that business history can have additional impact if we find a mechanism to more readily compare findings across different authors.

The comparative framework sketched in the preceding pages is only a start. We may find that important aspects of industry dynamics have been missed and we need to add them to the comparative framework. I am not a fan of preaching about research instead of doing it. In the next few years I will attempt to organize the study on an industry in open source way articulated in this chapter and validate that the concept can work in the realm of strategy research. Perhaps starting out with an industry that was recently born (e.g., solar industry) is the best way to involve many people, including industry participants who are eager to see the history of their industry documented. I have established a collaborative platform called EEpedia on Economic-Evolution.Net[11] to facilitate interaction among scholars. Would it not be fantastic if in 50 years we had something like the HARF in anthropology, allowing every university student in business to study industry dynamics by comparing the dynamics across particular industries of interest?

NOTES

1. A good example about fighting about facts occurred in the literature on transaction cost economics. See the debate about why General Motors merged vertically with Fisher Body in 1926 (Casadesus-Masanell & Spulber, 2000).

2. Precisely for this reason historians writing about a particular company often compare the firm under study with other firms in the industry and describe how typical or atypical the behavior of the firm was in the industry at a particular point in time.

3. I mean the term "variable" here to include qualitative features.

4. More information on the FIVE Project can be found here: http://five.dartmouth.edu/

5. More information on the Industry Studies Organization can be found here: http://www.industrystudies.org/

6. I invited the e-mail list members of the Business Policy and Strategy Division of the Academy of Management to complete a short survey to find out what scholars think about this issue. I am reporting here the responses of self-identified professors (112 out of the 154 respondents): 85% of professors believe that the time required to qualify for a sustained competitive advantage is 10 years or less; 54% think it is between 2 and 5 years; and 33% picked 5 years as the time required. The precise wording of the survey and its full results are available here: http://jpm.li/5

7. You can find the tables I prepared in comparing the major theories here: http://jpm.li/6

8. It is important to emphasize here that single cases can be quite easily turned into multiple cases by shifting the unit of analysis downwards. A single-country case can be – and often is – turned into multiple cases by studying the same phenomena in different regions within the country. A single firm study can also be decomposed into multiple cases by looking at different divisions or projects. Sophisticated practitioners of case studies frequently make the move of showing that explanations at the country level are empirically confirmed at smaller geographic units within countries. Hence one needs to be cautious to accuse case study practitioners that they only have an N of one because when you look into the details of the study a much larger N may become apparent.

9. At present I don't know how many of the five firms cannot be traced back to firms that existed in 1914. But I know for sure that DuPont was a new entrant in the industry, acquiring a significant position.

10. What counts as the same industry is theoretically not a straightforward question. Hannan, Pólos, and Carroll (2007) spent the past decade trying to bring some theoretical rigor to this question. Empirically, it is often quite easy to identify industries because participants typically will form a trade association and governments categorize firms into an industry for regulatory and policy purposes.

11. More information at http://economic-evolution.net

ACKNOWLEDGEMENTS

This chapter was largely written while I was the R. Graham Whaling Visiting Professor of Management at the Wharton School, University of Pennsylvania. I would like to thank the participants of the conference for the volume at the University of Chicago and the three editors for useful comments previous versions of the chapter.

REFERENCES

Abbott, A. D. (2001). *Time matters: On theory and method.* Chicago, IL: University of Chicago Press.

Abbott, A. D. (2004). *Methods of discovery: Heuristics for the social sciences.* New York, NY: W.W. Norton & Co.

Aitken, H. G. J. (1976). *Syntony and spark: The origins of radio.* New York, NY: Wiley.

Aitken, H. G. J. (1985). *The continuous wave: Technology and American radio, 1900–1932.* Princeton, NJ: Princeton University Press.

Arora, A., Landau, R., & Rosenberg, N. (Eds.). (1998). *Chemicals and long-term economic growth: Insights from the chemical industry.* New York, NY: Wiley.

Campbell, D. T. (1960). Blind variation and selective retention in creative thought as in other thought processes. *Psychological Review, 67,* 380–400.

Caro, H. (1892). Über die Entwicklung der Theerfarben-Industrie. [About the development of the coal-tar industry.] *Berichte der Deutschen Chemischen Gesellschaft, 25*(3), 955–1105.

Casadesus-Masanell, R., & Spulber, D. (2000). The fable of fisher body. *Journal of Law and Economics, 43*(1), 67–104.

Chandler, A. D. (1962). *Strategy and structure: Concepts in the history of American Industrial Enterprise.* Cambridge, MA: MIT.

Chandler, A. D. (1977). *The visible hand.* Cambridge: Belknap Press of Harvard University Press.

Chandler, A. D. (1990). *Scale and scope: The dynamics of industrial capitalism.* Cambridge: Harvard University Press.

Chesbrough, H. (1999). Arrested development: The experience of european hard disk drive firms in comparison with US and Japanese firms. *Journal of Evolutionary Economics*, *9*(3), 287–329.

Danneels, E. (2011). Trying to become a different type of company: Dynamic capability at Smith Corona. *Strategic Management Journal*, *32*(1), 1–31.

Dosi, G. (2000). *Innovation, organization and economic dynamics: Selected essays*. Northampton, MA: Edward Elgar Publishing.

Duisberg, C. (1933). *Meine Lebenserinnerungen*. [*My life*.]. Leipzig: P. Reclam jun.

Durkheim, E., & Seignobos, A. (1982[1908]). Debate on explanation in history and sociology. In E. Durkheim (Ed.), *The rules of the sociological method* (pp. 211–228). New York, NY: The Free Press.

Freeman, J. (1986). Data quality and the development of organizational social science: An ditorial essay. *Administrative Science Quarterly*, *31*(2), 298–303.

Gaddis, J. L. (2002). *The landscape of history: How historians map the past*. New York, NY: Oxford University Press.

Geertz, C. (1973). *The interpretation of cultures*. New York, NY: Basic Books.

Giles, J. (2005). Internet encyclopaedias go head to head. *Nature*, 900–901.

Hannan, M. T., & Carroll, G. R. (1992). *Dynamics of organizational populations*. New York, NY: Oxford University Press.

Hannan, M. T., & Freeman, J. H. (1989). *Organizational ecology*. Cambridge, MA: Harvard University Press.

Hannan, M. T., Pólos, L., & Carroll, G. R. (2007). *Logics of organization theory: Audiences, codes, and ecologies*. Princeton, NJ: Princeton University Press.

Hofmann, A. W. (1873). Einleitung. *Amtlicher Katalog der Ausstellung des Deutschen Reiches. Wiener Weltausstellung. Gruppe III: Chemische Industrie*. [*Official Catalog of Exhibit by the German Empire. Vienna World Exhibition. Group III. Chemical Industry*.]. Berlin, 95–139.

HRAF. (2012, December 21). About the Human Area Relations File: Cultural information for teaching and research. Retrieved from http://www.yale.edu/hraf/about.htm

Hughes, T. P. (1983). *Networks of power*. Baltimore, MD: The Johns Hopkins University Press.

Ingram, P., Rao, H., & Silverman, B. S. (2012). History in strategy research: What, why, and how? In S. J. Kahl, B. S. Silverman & M. A. Cusumano (Eds.), *Advances in strategic management* (Vol. 29, pp. 241–273). Bingley, UK: Emerald Group.

Jiang, H., & Murmann, J. P. (in press). Regional Institutions, Ownership Transformation, and Migration of Industrial Leadership in China. *Industrial and Corporate Change*.

Jones, G., & Khanna, T. (2006). Bringing history (back) into international business. *Journal of International Business Studies*, *37*(4), 453–468.

Kipping, M., & Westerhuis, G. (2012). Strategy, ideology, and structure: The political processes & introducing the M-form in the Dutch banks. In S. J. Kahl, B. S. Silverman & M. A. Cusumano (Eds.), *Advances in strategic management* (Vol. 29, pp. 187–237). Bingley, UK: Emerald Group.

Klepper, S. (2007). Disagreements, spinoffs, and the evolution of Detroit as the capital of the US automobile industry. *Management Science*, *53*(4), 616–631.

Klepper, S. (2008). Industry life cycles and market dominance. In W. D. Collins & J. Angland (Eds.), *Issues in competition law and policy* (pp. 695–722). Chicago, IL: ABA Press.

Klepper, S., & Simons, K. L. (1996). Innovation and industry shakeouts. *Business & Economic History*, *25*(1), 81–89.

Klepper, S., & Sleeper, S. (2005). Entry by spinoffs. *Management Science, 51*(8), 1291–1306.

Kopp, E. (1874). Wiener Weltaustellung 1873 [Vienna World Exhibition 1873]. *Bericht über Gruppe III, Chemische Industrie* [Report on Group III, Chemical Industrie]. Schaffhausen, 8.

Leprieur, F., & Papon, P. (1979). Synthetic dyestuffs: The relations between academic chemistry and the chemical inudstry in nineteenth-century France. *Minerva, 17*(2), 197–224.

Mahoney, J. (2000). Strategies of causal inference in small-n analysis. *Sociological Methods & Research, 28*(4), 387–424.

Mandal, P. (2006). *Synthetic dye industry in India: Strategies to increase sustainability.* MBA thesis, Indian Institute of Information Technology and Management.

McKenna, C. (2012). Strategy followed structure: Management consulting and the creation of a market for "strategy", 1950–2000. In S. J. Kahl, B. S. Silverman & M. A. Cusumano (Eds.), *Advances in strategic management* (Vol. 29, pp. 153–186). Bingley, UK: Emerald Group.

Mokyr, J. (2002). *The gifts of Athena: Historical origins of the knowledge economy.* Princeton, NJ: Princeton University Press.

Mowery, D. C., & Nelson, R. R. (Eds.). (1999). *Sources of industrial leadership: Studies of seven industries.* New York, NY: Cambridge University Press.

Murmann, J. P. (2003). *Knowledge and competitive advantage: The coevolution of firms, technology, and national institutions.* New York, NY: Cambridge University Press.

Murmann, J. P. (in press). The coevolution of industries and important features of their environments. *Organization Science.*

Murmann, J. P., Aldrich, H., Levinthal, D., & Winter, S. (2003). Evolutionary thought in management and organization theory at the beginning of the new millennium: A symposium on the state of the art and opportunities for future research. *Journal of Management Inquiry, 12*(1), 22–40.

Murmann, J. P., & Homburg, E. (2001). Comparing evolutionary dynamics across different national settings: The case of the synthetic dye industry, 1857–1914. *Journal of Evolutionary Economics, 11,* 177–205.

Murmann, J. P., & Landau, R. (1998). On the making of competitive advantage: The development of the chemical industries in Britain and Germany since 1850. In A. Arora, R. Landau & N. Rosenberg (Eds.), *Chemicals and long-term economic growth: Insights from the chemical industry* (pp. 27–70). New York, NY: Wiley.

Nelson, R. R. (1991). Why do firms differ, and how does it matter? *Strategic Management Journal, 12,* 61–74.

Nelson, R. R., & Winter, S. G. (1982). *An evolutionary theory of economic change.* Cambridge, MA: The Belknap Press of Harvard University Press.

O'Sullivan, M., & Graham, M. B. W. (2010). Guest editors' introduction to "moving forward by looking backward: business history and management studies." *Journal of Management Studies, 47*(5), 775–790.

Porter, M. E. (1980). *Competitive strategy.* New York, NY: Free Press.

Porter, M. E. (1985). *Competitive advantage: Creating and sustaining superior performance.* New York, NY: Free Press.

Porter, M. E. (1996). What is strategy? *Harvard Business Review, 74*(6), 61.

Ragin, C. C. (1987). *The comparative method: Moving beyond qualitative and quantitative strategies.* Berkeley, CA: University of California Press.

Romanelli, E. (1989). Environments and strategies of organization start-up: Effects on early survival. *Administrative Science Quarterly, 34*(3), 369–387.

Rothaermel, F. (2012). *Strategic management: Concepts and cases.* New York, NY: McGraw-Hill College.

Rumelt, R. P., Schendel, D. E., & Teece, D. J. (1994). *Fundamental issues in strategy: A research agenda.* Boston, MA: Harvard Business School Press.

Saviotti, P., & Metcalfe, J. S. (1991). *Evolutionary theories of economic and technical change.* Reading, MA: Academic Publishers.

Skocpol, T. (1984). *Vision and method in historical sociology.* New York, NY: Cambridge University Press.

Stinchcombe, A. L. (1978). *Theoretical methods in social history.* New York, NY: Academic Press.

Stinchcombe, A. L. (1997). Tilly on the past as a sequence of futures. In C. Tilly (Ed.), *Roads from past to future* (pp. 387–410). Lanham: Rowman & Littlefield.

Stinchcombe, A. L. (2005). *The logic of social research.* Chicago, IL: University of Chicago Press.

Thissen, F. (1922). *Die Stellung der deutschen Teerfarbenindustrie in der Weltwirtschaft (vor, in, und nach dem Kriege).* [*The position of the German tar color industry in the global economy before, during, and after the war.*] Doctoral dissertation, University of Giessen.

Tilly, C. (1984). *Big structures, large processes, huge comparisons.* New York, NY: Russell Sage Foundation.

Tilly, C. (1997). *Roads from past to future (With a review essay by Arthur Stinchcombe).* Lanham: Rowman & Littlefield.

Tilly, C. (2008). *Explaining social processes.* Boulder, CO: Paradigm Publishers.

Tushman, M. L., & Anderson, P. (1986). Technological discontinuities and organizational environments. *Administrative Science Quarterly, 31,* 439–465.

Utterback, J. M., & Suárez, F. F. (1993). Innovation, competition, and industry structure. *Research Policy, 22*(1), 1–21.

van den Belt, H. (1992). Why monopoly failed: The rise and fall of La Fuchsine. *British Journal for the History of Science, 25,* 45–64.

van den Belt, H., Gremmen, B., Homburg, E., & Hornix, W. (1984). *De Ontwikkeling van de Kleurstofindustrie.* [*The development of the synthetic dye industry.*]. Nijmegen: Faculteit der Wiskunde en Naturwetenschappen, University of Nijmegen. (Final Report of Research Project).

van den Belt, H., Homburg, E., & Hornix, W. J. (Eds.). (1981). *Development of the dye industry.* Nijmegen: University of NijmegenReport on Research Project.

Vincenti, W. (1990). *What engineers know and how they know it.* Baltimore, MD: Johns Hopkins Press.

Welsh, C. A. (1944). *The world dyestuffs industry: A study in the interrelationships of technology, industrial organization, and national economic policies.* Ph.D. dissertation, New York University.

Wurtz, A. (1876). *Progrès de L'industrie des Matières Colorantes Artificielles.* [The progress of the synthetic dye industry.]. Paris.

THE EVOLUTION OF ALTERNATIVE BUSINESS MODELS AND THE LEGITIMIZATION OF UNIVERSAL CREDIT CARD INDUSTRY: EXPLORING THE CONTESTED TERRAIN WHERE HISTORY AND STRATEGY MEET

Huseyin Leblebici

ABSTRACT

Purpose – *This paper focuses on a unique historical case study of industry evolution in order to develop a road map where historical and strategic research could develop a common ground for trans-disciplinary inquiry.*

Design/methodology/approach – *The industry I explore is the Universal Credit Card Industry since its inception with the Diners Club in 1949 until its maturity in late 1990s. My empirical objective here is to develop a historically detailed and theoretically rich case study in which evolutionary processes are discovered as a result of the historical narrative.*

History and Strategy
Advances in Strategic Management, Volume 29, 117–151
ISSN: 0742-3322/doi:10.1108/S0742-3322(2012)0000029009

Findings – *The historical account of the industry demonstrates how the evolution of alternative business models as organizing forms has led to the establishment of interorganizational platforms with unique ecosystems. These alternative business models, through various experimentations, have ultimately produced two critical interorganizational organizations, one based on an open-loop system represented by Visa and MasterCard, and the other based on a closed-loop system represented by Diners Club and the* American Express. *The historical account also shows that in a given industry competition is not only among specific firms in the industry but also among the business models and the platforms created by these models.*

Originality/value – *I conclude that historical analyses reveal the nature of competition not only among firms but also among alternative business models where traditional strategy research rarely covers.*

Keywords: Business models; credit card industry; historical case study

At the most fundamental level, the core concern of strategic research is to understand the nature of competition among firms and to explain why some firms perform better than others. It focuses on the underlying elements of firm success given a diverse *set of contingencies* including industry differences, firm characteristics, or managerial resources (Nag, Hambrick, & Chen, 2007). Its objective as a discipline is to develop generalizable theoretical arguments that can explain why certain firm behaviors produce desirable outcomes for various stakeholders, especially firms' shareholders.

In the last thirty years of strategic research, four major theoretical arguments have been developed to explain why firms fail or succeed. One set of arguments focuses on firms' managers. Firms could be run by incompetent managers who could not satisfy their constituencies and there are others who could do better. Firm-specific resources including managerial capabilities and their effective utilization could determine firm success. A second set of arguments focuses on the nature of firms' product or service offerings. The products or the services offered by individual firms or the industry may become obsolete. There could be mass extinction because the industry itself disappears. But, this does not mean that an individual organization cannot hire better managers, design better products, or move from one industry to another to avoid such a fate. The role of diversification especially unrelated diversification could become critical in explaining firm success. Thirdly, the nature of transactions within an industry or between industries could be used to understand the nature of division of labor among firms and why certain vertical integration/outsourcing strategies succeed or fail. Finally, the institutional rules may change because of the actions of the state or because of the changes in the conventional logic of an industry. Entrepreneurs could create new industries or reshape old industries by creating new industry recipes, which would make old strategies irrelevant. Such changes may lead to the extinction of certain organizational arrangements, forms, or industry structures. A diverse set of theories under various names ranging from transaction-cost perspective to resource-based view of the firm, strategic groups, and the industrial organization "structure-conduct-performance" (SCP) arguments has ultimately evolved to address the fundamental questions of competition and performance.

Historians are equally diverse in their approaches to historical inquiry. Historians including business historians provide alternative epistemological frameworks ranging from viewing history in terms of objective sequences of events to historians attempting to reconstruct and interpret events within a particular worldview. In other words, history can be simply viewed as a coherent chronological story of what actually happened within a particular period of "objective time." Or, history can be understood as a byproduct of particular theoretical perspective in which history includes not only factual conditions, events, and actions, but also an understanding of how they fit together as a dramatic story. Encapsulated within the framework of a "historical plot," narrative is intended to offer a coherent chronological story of "what actually happened." As Hall (1992) points out, the object of historical inquiry not only focuses on the events themselves but also provides forms of discourse on theoretical interpretations and explanations within a particular value set. For instance, in his book *Strategy and Structure*, Alfred Chandler (1962) has explicitly aimed at providing a narrative history of the development of large-scale enterprises in the United States together with a set of generalizable arguments on how strategy shapes structure of organizations.

HISTORY-FRIENDLY STRATEGY RESEARCH

Unfortunately, the epistemological perspectives mentioned above are problematic within the traditional discourse of explanation in strategy research. Rather than being concerned with a narrative content that may provide alternative historical plots, strategy researchers are interested in finding generalizable and statistically testable hypotheses driven from universal theories. Thus, even though there have been numerous calls to take history seriously, none of these attempts have been able to address the question of how we could navigate these contested terrains and find some common grounds (Kipping & Usdiken, 2009).

One partial solution offered has been to call for "history-friendly models" of strategy or industry evolution (Dosi, Malerba, & Teece, 2003; Malerba, Nelson, Orsenigo, & Winter, 1999). Malerba et al. have been arguing for some time that "history friendly models aim to capture in a stylized form, qualitative and 'appreciative' theories about the mechanisms and factors affecting industry evolution, technological advance and institutional change put forth by empirical scholars of industrial economics, technological change, business organization and strategy, and other social scientists." (1999, p. 3). Of course this is not new. A large number of scholars in sociology (Goldthorpe, 1991), in organization theory (Kieser, 1994; Leblebici & Shah, 2004), and in economics have been arguing that we all need to take history seriously.

But what does that mean specifically within strategy research? The field of sociology has had this debate without much success (Tilly, 1981). The obvious reason for such an argument is that our empirical data become more meaningful if we know something about the context in which strategic decisions are made or the gains in performance are accomplished. Without a clear understanding of the contextual conditions, our search for universal principles may be invalid. Theorizing in relation to specific historical periods increases our confidence in our analyses. A less obvious reason, which is at the core of this paper, is that historical strategic research with its narrative discourse enables us to look at critical phenomena from alternative levels of analyses. It helps us to rearrange known facts or data and to interpret them under alternative narratives. Generating new historical narratives encourages us to ask what and how questions could incorporate different levels of analyses as well as different conceptual tools at the same time (Stone, 1979).

My objective in this paper is to explore the second path by focusing on alternative conceptualizations of competition and extracting its multiple meanings within a historical narrative. The historical narrative I have selected is the evolution of the *charge card* (later on credit card) industry in the second half or the 20th century. In the next section, I will briefly discuss alternative theoretical conceptualizations of "competition" within strategic groups, industry recipes, and business models. What follows is a historical narrative where the questions of who, what, and how are answered and the basic analytic comparisons for different levels of analyses are presented. In the last section, I provide specific conjectures to reconceptualize competition within the historical narrative.

INDUSTRY RECIPES, STRATEGIC GROUPS, BUSINESS MODELS, AND THE NATURE OF COMPETITION

It is not an inaccurate generalization to state that most empirical research in strategy pays at least a lip service to the historical context in some form of another. Every paper in its presentation of the empirical setting discusses what is unique about the setting from a historical or contextual perspective. It usually goes like this:

> Because of its strategic diversity and economic significance, industry X is selected as a research context. This has been done in previous strategic research addressing questions such as .... (References). Furthermore, the industry X represents a turbulent environment with distinct boundaries with constantly changing environment because of government regulations, new entrants, and technological uncertainties. To study competitive positioning of firms and their strategic decisions, we developed a longitudinal study that makes use of archival data because governmental regulations make a host of secondary data readily available. Below we provide a short history of the industry and explain why certain operationalizations were selected ...

Different theoretical perspectives developed within strategy literature either constrain or necessitate much more expanded historical descriptions. This is especially true for research dealing with a specific industry evolution or various strategic groups in them. Fig. 1 is a simplified representation of various perspectives within strategic research depending on their emphasis on historical narrative.

Porter's theory of generic competitive strategy Porter (1980, 1985), which is fundamentally linked to IO economics, is unquestionably the most influential theoretical perspective within the study of strategic behavior in firms. Even though it is based on the traditional SCP paradigm, Porter argued that broader social, historical, and economic elements are required components of a theory that could describe firms' competitive strategies according to their market scope and their source of competitive advantage (e.g., cost or differentiation) (1981). As porter's descriptive theory was accepted and became the dominant paradigm of the field (Campbell-Hunt, 2000), however, the call for historically rich research is replaced with models looking for parsimonious, generalizable, and empirically oriented analyses.

Degree of Emphasis on Historical Narrative

	Weak	Strong
Industry Level Generic Strategies	Cell 1 IO Economics	Cell 3 Transaction cost & new Institutional Economics
Firm or group Level Differentiated Strategies	Cell 2 Strategic groups	Cell 4 Business Models

Conceptualization of Competitive Strategy

Fig. 1. Competitive Strategy and Historical Processes: Alternative Theoretical Perspectives and Their Degree of Engagement with Historical Research.

In this sense, generic competitive strategy research has progressively become void of historical analysis and narrative. As shown in Fig. 1, most of the historical analyses in Cell 1 are in the form of industry-level stylized facts that are developed within the paradigm of IO economics.

As the strategy research moved away from industry-level generic strategies to firm-level complex strategic decision making, it became more important to differentiate among firms within a given industry. The solution was the idea of strategic groups (Cell 2). Even though the concept of strategic groups was initially introduced within IO economics as an analytical device to explain performance differentials between firms within a single industry, it produced a substantial body of literature (McGee & Thomas, 1986). Because the original theory conceived strategic groups as cluster of firms within industries with similar strategies, it has been more important to understand how these groups are formed, how they stay stable, and how dynamic their boundaries are (Short, Ketchen, Palmer, & Hult, 2007). Such an approach required more detailed historical narrative. The critique of strategic group research in the 1980s has eventually led to more behavioral research arguing that strategic groups should be focusing on managerial decision making especially at top management teams to understand firms' strategic behaviors (Reger & Huff, 1993). By importing concepts from behavioral sciences such as psychology and sociology, strategic groups are now conceived as cognitive communities, reference groups, and led to conceiving strategic groups as cognitive communities that share a common identity (Dranove, Peteraf, & Shanley, 1998; Peteraf & Shanley, 1997).

The movement toward more behavioral perspective, however, reduced the need for extensive historical narrative.

Since the 1930s, institutional economics, under alternative names, has been promoting the idea that history matters. For instance, early intuitionalists (Commons, 1934) argued that the historical analysis of institutionalized economic practices whether they are informal in the form of conventions or formal in the form of laws and regulations that structure political, economic and, social interaction helps us understand the behavior of economic actors (Cell 3). As these institutions evolve and frame the incentive structures within an economy or the transactional practices within an industry, they shape the performance drivers for individual firms (North, 1978, 1991). Later, neo-institutional economics and the transaction-cost perspective (Williamson, 1981, 1991) have become mainstream frameworks within strategic research (David & Han, 2004) including the ideological controversies they created (Ghoshal & Moran, 1996).

Empirical research in neo-institutional economics and Transaction Costs Economics (TCE) utilize a variety of methodologies including historically rich case studies ranging from individual industry studies to contract analysis among exchange partners. In these research contexts, historically rich case studies have become an important supplement to the expected econometric analyses because the historical context highlights the heterogeneity of practices involving transactions or contracts as part of an evolutionary change in economic institutions (Masten, 2000). Even single-industry studies, which usually involve quantitative examination of transactional practices, require some degree of descriptive historical context (Silverman, Nickerson, & Freeman, 1997).

What I would like to argue in this paper is that the final cell – business models (Cell 4) – is where historical analysis would be most effective because it could include not only industry- level institutional practices but also the dynamic interaction patterns among individual firms. Since late 1990s, the term "business model" has become not only popular within the practitioners media but also a focus of attention within academic research. Even though there is a lack of agreement about its clear meaning, a recent survey indicates that there have been more than 1,700 research articles published on the subject (Zott, Amit, & Massa, 2011). Recent special journal issues and the application of the business model ideas in diverse literatures (e.g., innovation, e-business and IT technologies, entrepreneurship, strategic management, and organization theory) (Baden-Fuller & Morgan, 2010; Demil & Lecocq, 2010; Zott & Amit, 2007) indicate that it may serve as a way to integrate the perspectives mentioned above.

The beginning of the idea could be traced to industry recipes (Spender, 1989). A business model describes how a firm generates revenues within a reasonable cost and incorporates assumptions about how value is created in the industry in which the firm operates (Teece, 2010). At a very basic level, all firms must have a business model but some firms develop novel business models that shape the industry structure, create new platforms, and facilitate innovation (Gambardella & McGahan, 2010). In that sense, business models are not simple strategies but an amalgamation of how managers conceive their industries and their practices, strategic groups that operate within a specific platform, the ecology where interrelationship among firms spur collective survival, and the institutions within which taken-for-granted conventions are maintained and sometimes challenged. In a sense, it extends both the IO economics and the strategic group research by focusing on not only field-level forces but also the firm-level moves. In order to be an effective perspective, it must start with history.

Despite its long existence in popular business literature (Casadesus-Masanell & Ricart, 2011), the concept of business model has been criticized in academic circles because of its ambiguous conceptual foundations and its lack of theoretical grounding in economics or in management research (Perkmann & Spicer, 2010; Teece, 2010). As Teece argues, there is no real established place in economic theory for business models. But this is in a sense what makes the concept ideal for a historical/ strategic research. It stands against the general equilibrium models where change is always explained with exogenous forces. It incorporates the complexities of endogenous forces of economic life where historical narrative becomes relevant. Furthermore, it directly links to some of the recent concepts that are becoming part of the strategy literature – platforms and ecosystems.

Compared to more established macro constructs in economics, organization theory, or strategy such as industry, institutional fields, and organizational population, a business model defines the architecture of business within an industry, on one hand, and the value proposition offered by the firm' strategy to its customers, on the other. As firms develop their business models and build their growth strategies, they not only initiate new organizational practices, and acquire new partners by building transactional structures but also form narratives to construct meaning around the business idea to create a novel economic reality (MacKenzie & Millo, 2003; Perkmann & Spicer, 2010).

A business model, however, is insufficient in and of itself to understand how competitive advantage is achieved. Two additional constructs are necessary to convert a business model from being a story of how an enterprise works (Magretta, 2002) into a historically rich performativity through which new industries and enterprises are created (MacKenzie & Millo, 2003). The first is the idea of a platform (Cusumano, 2010; Gawer & Cusumano, 2002). As Cusumano (2010) argues, an industry platform is a mechanism by which multiple firms interact to produce the essential complements (p. 24) of a complex product or service. As the number of participants in an industry platform grows, it creates a network effect through positive feedback. As Cusumano describes (in this volume), through network effects and the positive feedback loops it creates, a platform could grow exponentially as more ecosystem partners add complementary innovations.

The second construct imbedded within the concept of business models is the idea of business ecosystem. As an industry platform gains momentum and brings together a very diverse set of players, it creates a complex ecosystem (Iansiti & Levien, 2004). An ecosystem extends beyond the traditional value chain within an industry and includes participants from other economic sectors similar to the notion of institutional fields developed in organization theory.

In short, business models that lead to the establishment of an industry platform within a highly complex ecosystem provide another level of analysis for understanding the nature of competition among firms. As firms introduce new business models, or refinements to existing ones, their success becomes dependent on the quality of the platform and the ecosystem they support. They collectively increase productivity, generate better value for the customers, and make replication more difficult for competitors.

Because of high technological or economic interdependencies among the players within the ecosystem, however, once established, business models are often inertial and are difficult to change. As will be shown later in this paper, American Express, Diners Club, and Discover Card have experienced a similar fate in trying to "morph to hybrid models where they issue cards themselves while simultaneously looking to persuade banks as partners to act as card issuers for them" (Teece, 2010, p. 181). On the other hand, Visa and MasterCard, which did not compete with banks, created an alternative ecosystem where highly diverse players could develop strong symbiotic relationships.

In the next section, I will provide a short historical analysis of universal credit card industry as it developed in the United States, and some of the major players in this industry. The history of this industry has been extensively covered by others with much more detailed analytical historical account of the industry by various historians (Evans & Schmalensee, 2005; Mandell, 1990; Nocera, 1994; Simmons, 1995). My objective is to demonstrate how historical account of the fifty years of an industry evolution could provide us not only explanations of why some firms perform better, or how competition among them manifest itself, but also how some of the new concepts in strategic research could be empirically explored.

THE EMERGENCE AND GROWTH OF THE UNIVERSAL CREDIT CARDS INDUSTRY[1]

In the last half of the 20th century, payment cards – credit, debit, and charge cards – have not only revolutionized how we pay for goods and services but also have created a completely new industry (Evans & Schmalensee, 2005). According to the U.S. Census Bureau, there are about 1.50 billion credit cards in the United States. The idea of a store or oil-company card has been around since 1910. Even today more than 200 million people have such cards (about three per individual).[2] Even though at the beginning of the 20th-century retailers and, specifically, department stores had issued their own-store-specific credit cards, they have been unable to create their own credit card industry. On the other hand, banks that lost large sums in the process of introducing the idea were the ones that ultimately created this global industry. The historical case study presented here focuses on a specific set of actors and the interplay among them in the development of the industry – the organizations that introduced alternative business models, that is, Diners Club and the American Express, and the two associations of banks, that is, Visa and MasterCard.[3] The evolution of the relationship among these actors along with institutional and technological changes can help us understand how selection and adaptation of these business models at the field level can simultaneously explain how individual firms compete, how division of labor within an industry evolves, and how the ecosystems created by different platforms structure the industry and the players in them.

The basic idea behind this new innovation was not that people could purchase goods on credit. This has been part of economic life for a long time. In the United States, a large proportion of retail sales, particularly of discretionary items, had always been made on credit (Mandell, 1990). The fundamental insight of these systems was the opportunity to use a card (now maybe a cell phone) to identify one's account to a centralized credit/debit system that was available at multiple locations and to multiple merchants within an industry-specific network.

In order to effectively establish such a system, three separate components had to be developed and integrated. The first, of course, was the recruitment of members who are either merchants or cardholders. It was not sufficient that the card holders were willing to use their cards but also that they were creditworthy and could pay their bills on time. For the merchants it was necessary to accept these cards and be willing to pay for the service. The second necessary component was the establishment of a centralized processing system that would track the ongoing transactions, pay the merchants minus the discount and possible fees, consolidate the card-holders' charges, bill them each month, and collect the payments. Finally, each system had to have a set of agreed rules on how the authorization and settlement of transactions would be carried out, who should decide the creditworthiness of future customers, and which merchants would be qualified to belong to the system.

In the beginning, alternative business models were introduced with various levels of success. The first model was the establishment of independent systems by large merchants or oil companies where all the components were integrated under one organization. A second alternative was to utilize an already existing industry-specific organization such as the National Hotel or Airlines Associations to act as the central processing system that also eliminated the need to recruit merchants in this industry. A third alternative model was a group of merchants in a region forming a cooperative and to assigning it the task of back-office operations. One final alternative design was the creation of third-party firms who were willing to be the central coordination unit. These systems differed from the single merchant, cooperatives, or the industry-specific payment card systems because the customers received their cards from the third party and all the risks as well as the profits of the system were captured by the third party.

The antecedents of universal credit cards

The forerunners of universal credit cards were the store-specific cards issued by a small number of hotels, oil companies, and department stores in the early 20th century. They were offered either by large merchants or by a network of merchants within a specific industry or geographic area. They were specifically designed to encourage consumers to purchase additional or higher-priced items than those who were paying with cash by providing them short-term credit and requiring full payment at the end of the billing cycle. Customers did not pay a fee to have or use these cards, nor did they pay interest on the short-term credit extended to them, so the systems themselves tended to lack profitability (Stearns, 2011). Moreover, it was believed that the customers would develop loyalty toward the store brand because such cards provided prestige and indicated to the customers that they were valued by the store.

The introduction of metal charge cards (later in plastic) was designed to prepare uniform-sales drafts with multiple copies for later processing. The early department store cards had been made of cardboard, and hand-copying the account information from the card to the sales draft caused constant errors. In late 1920s, the charga-plate systems together with imprinters were introduced. The account number, customer name, and address were stamped on one side of a metal plate and the other side included the name of the issuing store and a line for the customer's signature. These plates were used with an imprinter, which would press the plate against a uniform-sales draft. This draft contained an additional carbon paper layer, which automatically transferred the imprinted account details on the charga-plate to the top layer of the draft. The design of cards has not changed in any drastic fashion in the last ninety years (Stearns, 2011, pp. 6–9; also see Calder, 1999, Chapter 2).

For retailers, credit cards were merely a logical extension of their already existing installment plans. In 1914, several retailers began to issue cards to their wealthier customers to increase their store loyalty as well as to generate more sales. The main objective of these cards was to make these retailers more competitive against their rivals. Over the next thirty years, various innovations such as minimum monthly payments, finance charges, and the thirty-day grace period were developed and adopted by large retailers, such as Sears and J.C. Penney, to generate profits from their credit operations (Mandell, 1990, pp. 17–21).

Small merchants, facing the competitive pressures of store cards, developed the third alternative business model based on cooperative arrangements. In the late 1920s, the cooperative payment card systems would provide the opportunity for a cardholder to use the same card at multiple merchants. The cooperative usually would issue the cards and the individual merchants would bill their own customers separately. Such an arrangement, however, made the system to be inefficient to the merchants. Only in some rare instances, the central organization would extend the credit and collect from the customer with one bill. According to Mandell (1990, p. 18), for example, in 1936 the Retail Service Bureau of Seattle included over 1,000 retailers. The problem with these arrangements was that they neither helped the customer loyalty nor reduced the cost of back-office operations sufficiently. Merchants were still asked to send monthly bills and not expect any interest payments. These cooperatives were similar in concept to Visa (an association of banks), though they were owned by the retailers and not the banks, and were limited to a specific geographic area that limited their scope. Once the banks entered into the card game, there was no need for the existence of these cooperatives and they disappeared quickly.

Even though early experiments in the card business were proven mostly unprofitable, in 1920s, oil companies also introduced their "courtesy cards" for charging gas because they were also interested in customer loyalty. Later in 1936, the airline industry, led by the American Airlines, formed its own credit system called the Universal Air Travel Plan (UATP). The UATP credit plan later evolved into a credit card operation quite similar to and in direct competition with the universal third-party cards (Evans & Schmalensee, 2005, pp. 6–8; see also Mandell, 1990, pp. 19–21).

Table 1 provides a short chronology of some of the major events in this field. In my historical account below, I will specifically cover some of these critical events that are part of what is called "universal charge cards."

Creation of one card/one monthly bill idea – Diners Club

The era of the modern, third-party universal card began with the formation of Diners Club in 1950. Frank MacNamara, a businessman who came up with the idea of a universal charge card, designed the system mainly for the businessmen like himself. Instead of carrying a lot of cash, they would be able to pay for their travel and dining expenses with their cards and pay their total bill at the end of each month. By collecting 100 percent from the cardholders and reimbursing the merchants at 93 percent, Diners Club would keep 7 percent of the total receipts. At the beginning, the card was sent to prominent businessmen with a letter stating that there was no fee for membership (Simmons, 1995). Within one year, the membership increased to 100,000. Another 100,000 applied for membership but got rejected because of their poor credit ratings. Seeing the success of the Diners Club, other entrants across the country started to appear (Trip-Charge, Chicago; Dine&Sign, New York). Even though Diners Club decided to add a membership fee of about $6, the firm had 250,000 members at the end of 1952. And in 1955, it became international (Simmons, 1995, pp. 10–22).[4]

Table 1. A Short Chronology of the Charge Card Field.

1890	American Express introduces traveler's check
1914	Retailers issue credit cards
1924	General Petroleum (California gas station chain) issues cardboard credit card
1930	Airlines create Universal Air Travel Plan cooperative
1948	Major New York department stores form cooperative Charga-plate operation
1950	Diners Club becomes operational
1955	More than 100 banks enter the credit card business
1957	Oil companies refuse to honor universal credit cards
1958	BankAmericard launches its credit card and American Express introduces its charge card
1965	American Bankers Association introduces the first ATM machine that can be activated by a credit card
1966	Bank of America licenses its card across the United States, and Interbank Card Association is formed
1967	Approximately 600 banks in Illinois, Michigan, and Indiana form the Midwest Bank Card; New York City banks form the Eastern States Bankcard Association
1969	Interbank Card Association changed its card name to Master Charge
1970	Electronic Fund Transfer (EFT) systems are introduced in the United States
1972	City National Bank of Columbus, Ohio introduces its Debit Card to be used in the ATM machines
1974	Interbank Card Association and BankAmerica build first computerized networks (BASE-II and BankNet) to increase the speed of transactions and eliminate paper
1976	NBI changes BankAmericard to Visa and gives up its opposition to duality
1977	Midwest Payment Systems develops Jeanie, the first online shared ATM network; Visa and Master Charge introduce their debit cards (Entrée and Signet respectively)
1979	Visa and J.C. Penney reach an agreement for the use of its cards at JC Penney Stores
1980	Interbank changes its name from Master Charge to MasterCard
1982	CIRRUS, PLUS, and other national ATM networks (EFT) are established by banks
1985	First nonbank affinity cards (AT&T, GE, GM) are launched by Visa and MasterCard
1986	Sears introduces Discover card
1987	American Express introduces Optima Credit Card
1988	Citi Bank and American Airlines introduce AAdvantage frequent-flier reward bank card; Mastercard and Visa acquire CIRRUS and PLUS national ATM networks
1990	National EFT networks PLUS and CIRRUS enter duality agreement so that both networks could be used by cardholders
1991	Some restaurants in Boston start to refuse American Express Card
1999	Concord EFS, a nonbank, acquires the MAC EFT network

As mentioned earlier, the critical idea behind the Diners Club's business model was the introduction of a third party into the credit equation that existed between the retailers and the customers. Their company would become the middleman between them, extending credit to one, providing customers for the other, and charging one or both for their services. With no goods to sell or customer loyalty to promote, their interest was purely financial. They conceived of credit as a product to be sold, an end in itself rather than simply a means to an end, and the primary vehicle for extending credit was the credit card. The revenues needed to finance the company were generated by the merchant discount and by the yearly fees for cardholders.

Another important aspect of the business model was that compared to the earlier models of department stores, merchant cooperatives, or hotels, it required marketing to two parties, the merchants as well as the customers: consumers would not sign up for the card unless it was accepted by a large number of merchants, and merchants would not sign up until they saw a demand for the card from their customers. Just like any other two-sided platform business, Diners Club needed to convince two distinct groups that there is a benefit to both by linking with an intermediary who would coordinate their interactions without detrimental effect to Diners Club. In practical terms, the platform required the firm to sign up creditworthy customers who would pay their bills at the end of each month, to reimburse the merchants in a timely manner so that they stay in the system, and to process the paperwork as fast as possible to generate reasonable return. Moreover, as mentioned earlier, another obstacle facing the new universal charge card was the resistance of industries such as the airlines, oil companies, and the larger retailers who already issued their own credit cards. In addition to their reluctance to pay a discount to a third party, merchants feared that the acceptance of a third-party card would weaken their relationship with their customers (Stearns, 2011, pp. 10–16; see also Evans & Schmalensee, 2005, pp. 6–7).

The business model that was ultimately created by Diners Club is called the closed-loop model. As shown in Fig. 2, all the back-office activities were carried by Diners Club. This became the dominant model for the new entrants at least for a while. Most of the early participants in the "Travel & Entertainment" card business disappeared mostly because they issued cards to those with bad credit. In order to increase their market share and convince the merchants to be a member, they had to accept applications from customers who could or would not pay their charges on time. As the credit losses increased, they had no choice but to leave the field. Only Diners Club was successful to retain wealthy patrons who not only paid their bills on time but also spent more because of their cards (Stearns, 2011, pp. 14–15).[5]

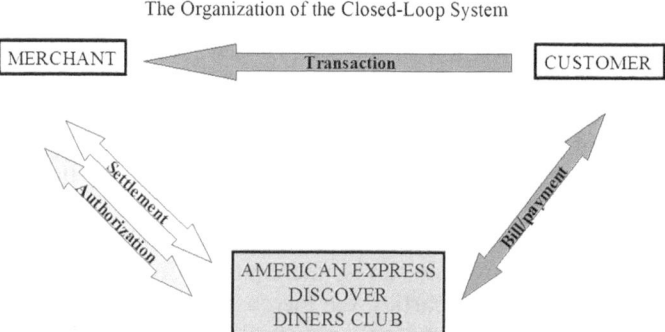

Fig. 2. The Closed-Loop Business Model as the Organizing Form Established by
         Diners Club and Later Institutionalized by American Express.

Entrance of powerful competitors: American Express and Carte Blanche

In 1958, American Express, the traveler's check giant, and Carte Blanche, the private credit card operation of the Hilton Hotel Corporation, both entered the universal credit card field. American Express had been in business for more than 100 years before it entered the payment card industry. It was formed in 1850 with the merger of two express mail companies but it was known for its invention of American Express Travelers Check as an alternative to money order. The product had quickly become one of the company's signature products after its introduction in 1891. As Americans started traveling abroad in increasing numbers, they took American Express Travelers Checks, which they could cash at a growing network of American Express offices in Europe and the rest of the world (Stearns, 2011, pp. 16–17).[6]

At the time when Diners Club was founded and introduced a charge card with closed-loop payment system, American Express was the world's largest travel agency and operated the world's largest private mail service. The boom in international travel after the end of the Second World War helped the firm to increase its travel agencies from 50 at the end of the war to nearly 400 ten years later. The company sold approximately $12.5 billion of traveler's checks in 1955 and claimed to control 75 percent of the worldwide market. Because Diners Club started to expand into other travel and entertainment segments such as hotels, restaurants, and florists, American Express contemplated of its acquisition but decided instead to enter the charge card industry itself as an extension of its other travel-related activities. It had already more than 17,000 merchant locations and 250,000 cardholders when it started on October 1, 1958, compared to close to million cardholders for Diners Club. It initially set its annual fee 20 percent higher than Diners Club, thereby suggesting that it was the more "exclusive" card. But it set the initial merchant discount slightly lower in order to motivate additional merchants to accept its cards: 5–7 percent for restaurants and 3–5 percent for hotels and motels (Simmons, 1995, pp. 61–70).

Development of another business model and new players

The year that American Express entered the credit card business using the closed-loop model, the country's largest and second-largest banks, Bank of America and Chase Manhattan Bank, launched their credit card operations but using an alternative business model. They targeted people "who wanted to buy but who couldn't, or didn't want to pay in thirty days." (Simmons, 1995, p. 93). They were soon joined by a number of smaller banks all looking to test their own business models in this new industry. And the bank card was born.

As shown in Fig. 3, the new model comprised customers and their banks (card issuers), as well as merchants and their banks (known as acquirers), along with a network operator and other participants that facilitated these transactions and that evolved with the industry. The transactions involved a set of interrelated bilateral transactions. In order for a credit card transaction to be started, a consumer has to establish a relationship with an issuer (usually a bank) and receive a credit card. Similarly a merchant is capable of accepting payment card transactions.

In order to complete a given credit card transaction, three separate but related activities involving multiple parties must take place. The first activity, which is usually called "authorization," takes place when customer A uses a credit card to pay a merchant B. Then, merchant B sends the encrypted transaction data to its card merchant processor for authorization. Many merchant banks hire a third party (sometimes called "acquiring processor") for bank card processing. The processor provides credit card processing, billing, and reporting services that are necessary to complete the transaction. The card merchant processor sends the transaction data to the consumer A's (issuing) bank over the Visa or MasterCard network. The issuing bank is a licensed member of Visa or MasterCard and holds agreements with, and issues cards to, consumers. Once the issuing bank

The Organization of the Open-Loop System

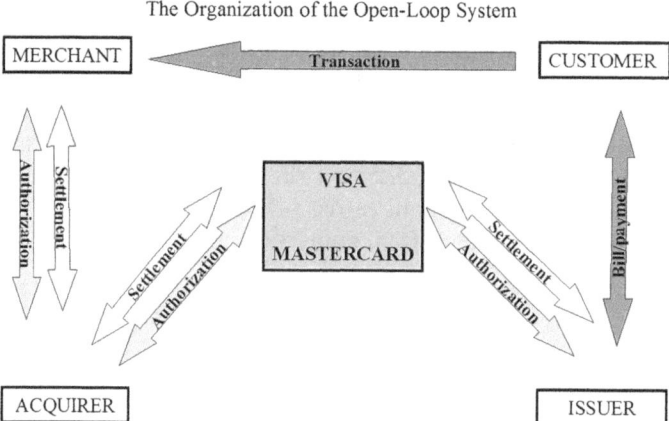

Fig. 3.   The Open-Loop Business Model as the Organizing Form Instituted by Bank
Associations such as Visa and MasterCard.

authorizes the amount and issues an authorization, the card merchant
processor notifies the merchant that the transaction has been authorized and
the Merchant B asks the customer A's signature.[7]

The second set of activities, that is, processing, starts once the purchase is
authorized and is called "capture." The capture process uses the
authorization to charge the authorized amount of money to the consumer's
credit card. The merchant will then submit these credit transactions in
batches at the end of a specific period (e.g., day) to its card merchant
processor to finalize the transactions. The final set of activities is usually
called "settlement." Once the card merchant processor receives the information and settles the batch, then it sends the necessary information to the
issuing and merchant banks using an authorized clearinghouse (ACH)
operator. The third-party ACH operator, which links the issuing and
merchant banks, settles transactions between them, and the merchant's
bank credits the merchant B's account.

After its initial introduction, the next few years saw a gradual shakeout of
the industry as banks struggled to learn and overcome the idiosyncrasies of
the credit card business. Some, such as Chase Manhattan, which sold its
operation in 1962, were unable to make their credit card companies a viable
concern. Many of the operational problems they faced, such as processing
difficulties and various forms of credit card fraud, would continue to plague
the industry for the next twenty years (Stearns, 2011, p. 18).

In 1960s, most banks could only do business in their own states. This was also true for Bank of America cardholders. Even though Bank of America could open branch banks in California, it could not operate in other states. In other states, the banking laws were even more restrictive. For instance, in Illinois, banks could not even operate a branch on the next street.[8] In different states alternative models were tried to overcome these limitations. For instance, in Chicago, five major banks developed a common credit card operation called Midwest Bank Card Operation in 1966. Just before Christmas, they collectively mailed five million unsolicited credit cards to unexpecting bank customers. Without any careful credit checks, cards were sent to children, family dogs, and even customers who were dead. The final fiasco was major credit card losses because of fraud and mismanagement. Banks eventually realized that this is not an easy business. It became very clear early on that the he primary obstacle to growth was the lack of a national network, which particularly affected the many smaller banks that maintained local credit card operations (Evans & Schmalensee, 2005, pp. 61–67; see also Mandell, 1990, pp. 29–32 and Nocera, 1994, pp. 19–20).

In 1966, Bank of America took a major step toward solving this problem by franchising its new BankAmericard that was started in California to be available across the United States. It established BankAmerica Service Corporation (BSC) as a national licensing arm. BSC enabled local banks in different states to issue a card that could be used nationally and provided an arrangement for coordination between the merchant banks and the issuing bank. By the late 1960s, however, the BankAmericard franchise system became unworkable. The infrastructure of the franchise system became increasingly inadequate for handling growing numbers of franchisees and transactions. Moreover, franchisees wanted to have more voice in the system's future direction. As a result, Bank of America spun off its credit card licensing organization by forming National BankAmerica, Inc. (NBI) as a nonstock membership corporation in 1969. NBI changed its name to Visa USA in 1976 (Stearns, 2011, pp. 19–21)[9] (see Table 1).

The decision by Bank of America, the nation's largest bank, to expand its operations across the country encouraged several other large banks to join together to form a second national card system, known as the Interbank Card Association (Master Charge) as a joint venture (or consortium). By 1978, more than 11,000 banks had joined one or both of these networks. Annual sales reached to $44 billion, and fifty-two million Americans had at least two bank credit cards. Interbank later changed its name to MasterCard in 1980. The result of these various experiments in franchising and joint ventures was the creation of the open-loop business model (Mandell, 1990, pp. 38–40).[10]

The open-loop business model was more inclusive and also more complicated. As Fig. 3 shows, member banks could operate as issuers or/and acquirers using their association's brand name. They could even be a member in both associations (duality rule) creating much more intricate network of relationships between banks, their customers, the merchants, and the network organizations. Later on, it was possible for nonbank entities to operate as issuers or acquirers. The boundaries that clearly separated cooperation and competition between banks and the networks became fuzzier, and a new ecosystem with complex forms of division of labor among the participating firms was firmly established.

Although some banks continued with their own private-label cards, the vast majority issued either Master Charge or Visa. In 1970, Master Charge had enjoyed a solid lead over BankAmericard in both the domestic and the international markets. But at the end of the decade, Visa was able to overtake and eventually pass its rival. From 1969 to 1981, the number of participating MasterCard banks increased from 4,461 to 12,504, while the number of participating Visa banks increased from 3,751 to 12,518. By the late 1980s, Visa had increased its lead over its rival to more than a third (Mandell, 1990, p. xiv).

The competition between the two came to a head in the mid-1970s over the issue of duality. Duality referred to the issuance of both major credit cards by the same bank. Initially, both Visa and MasterCard had prohibited this practice. However, under pressure from the courts, which maintained that such a prohibition violated antitrust laws, they were forced to give the banks free rein to issue both cards. The introduction of duality initiated a tremendous marketing war among issuing banks to increase the number of their cardholders. Banks stepped up their marketing efforts to consumers in an attempt to place a second card in the hands of all their customers. The results of this marketing war for the banks were lower profits because of increased costs. As banks attempted to increase card membership, they used mass mailings without careful credit checks. Unsolicited credit cards not only increased the banks back-office operations but also let to losses because of fraud and unpaid credit card bills (Evans & Schmalensee, 2005, pp. 70–71; see also Nocera, 1994, pp. 144–148).

Competition and growth also led to increased concentration in the Travel and Entertainment card (T&E) industry. With its far superior resources, American Express quickly overtook both Diners Club and Carte Blanche. By 1970, it had twice the number of cardholders as Diners Club, and four times the number of Carte Blanche cardholders. By 1976, its cardholder base numbered nearly seven and a half times that of Diners Club, and ten times that of Carte Blanche (Evans & Schmalensee, 2005, pp. 78–80). By the middle of the 1970s, the American Express card was well established throughout the country. It had become the dominant card in the travel and entertainment sector, with more than five times as many cards issued as Diners Club in the T&E category. Many upscale restaurants, hotels, rental car companies, stores that relied on tourists, and other travel and entertainment-related businesses accepted the American Express card even though it was more expensive for the consumers in terms of its annual fees. At the start of the 1980s, American Express had a merchant discount that was almost 50 percent higher than that charged by Visa and MasterCard: 3.6 percent versus 2.5 percent. And it charged cardholders an annual fee of $60 for its standard Green Card and $85 for its Gold Card. By 1984, the Gold Card fee had been raised to $96, and American Express' net profits from its charge card business alone were estimated to total $370 million (*ibid.*, pp. 151–153).

These developments, however, did not change the attitudes of the large national retailers and their refusal to accept universal credit cards. The large retail stores in the United States, which had operated credit card plans on their own for much of the 20th century, issued far more cards than all of the third-party companies combined and continued to do so in the 1980s. In 1981, Sears alone issued more cards than either Visa or MasterCard (*ibid.*, pp. 77–80).

Unlike third-party issuers, who run their credit operations to make a profit, retailers used their credit card operations as a means to facilitate sales and ensure customer loyalty. Generally, retail credit card operations broke even or operated at a loss. The larger retailers, such as Sears, Montgomery Ward, and J. C. Penney, had resisted third-party credit companies from the outset. As the universal cards grew in size, however, smaller retailers found them appealing. As the earlier experiments had shown, small retailers even collectively were unable to run their own credit operations because of the high back-office operation costs; and thus it made sense for them to accept third-party cards. Furthermore, many small retailers, particularly the specialty stores, had very little interest in increasing the loyalty of their customers who visited their shops only occasionally (Mandell, 1990, Chapter 1).

Despite the inroads the third-party cards made into the ranks of the smaller retailers in the early 1970s, they still could not gain access to the larger stores. National chains such as J.C. Penney and Sears continued to operate their own credit card plans. Large regional retailers, meanwhile, joined together to pool their credit operations by using an outside credit management company to handle all of the transactions. Although more expensive than allowing the use of third-party cards, private-label card operations had the singular advantage of maintaining the retailer's identity and its relationship with its customers.

The breakthrough for the bank cards finally came in 1979 when J.C. Penney surprised the industry by signing an agreement with Visa. Although J.C. Penney had been an early and vocal opponent of third-party credit cards, the new arrangement with Visa not only gave the retailer a strong competitive edge but also reduced its total cost of card operations by getting a very favorable discount rate from Visa (*ibid.*, pp. 46–51).[11]

In addition to convincing the large retailers to accept universal credit cards, Visa and MasterCard started to enter competition for the lucrative high end of the marketplace. The attraction of this segment had been clear since the start of this industry – high-end customers generally have higher monthly bills because they spend more and have significantly lower credit risks. Throughout the 1970s, the prestige card field was dominated by the T&E industry. American Express, with its gold card, Diners Club, and Carte Blanche were the primary issuers. In the early 1980s, however, both Visa and MasterCard introduced their own prestige cards and very quickly established themselves as serious competitors, surpassing both Diners Club and Carte Blanche and challenging the supremacy of American Express. American Express responded to this incursion into its territory with the introduction of the Optima card in 1987. This was American Express's first credit card (regular American Express cards are charge cards; the balance must be paid in full each month). Within a year, Optima was able to acquire more than 2.5 million members. Unfortunately, in the 1990s American Express lost its dominance as the premier charge card company as it lost its customers' loyalty. Intense competition from no-fee bank cards and debit cards and the loss of merchants accepting its card because of high fees were sufficient to increase losses for the firm. It was also revealed in 1992 that Optima card had lost close to $300 million even though it was presented as a successful initiative (Grossman, 1987).

In addition to the increased competition among existing credit card companies, the 1980s has also seen the introduction of a new major competitor – the Discover card. Launched in 1986 by Sears, the Discover card was intended for Sears to enter into the financial services industry. Following its acquisition of the Caldwell Banker real estate company and the Dean Witter brokerage company in the 1980s, Sears was looking for another opportunity to expand its financial services. Already the largest issuer of credit cards in the world through its retail operations, it decided to launch a universal credit card using its already existing large customer base. By 1991, the Discover Card was accepted by more merchants than the American Express Card (Mandell, 1990, pp. 83–85).

As Fig. 4 clearly shows, by the late 1980s, several developments weakened the business model that had served American Express extremely well since the inception of its charge card thirty years earlier. First, many consumers had bank credit cards that were widely accepted and could do roughly as much as American Express charge cards. Consumers could easily do without their American Express cards because they could charge purchases at almost all the U.S. locations that took American Express cards and at many other merchant locations that did not. As with American Express cards, they could pay for the charges on the next billing cycle to avoid

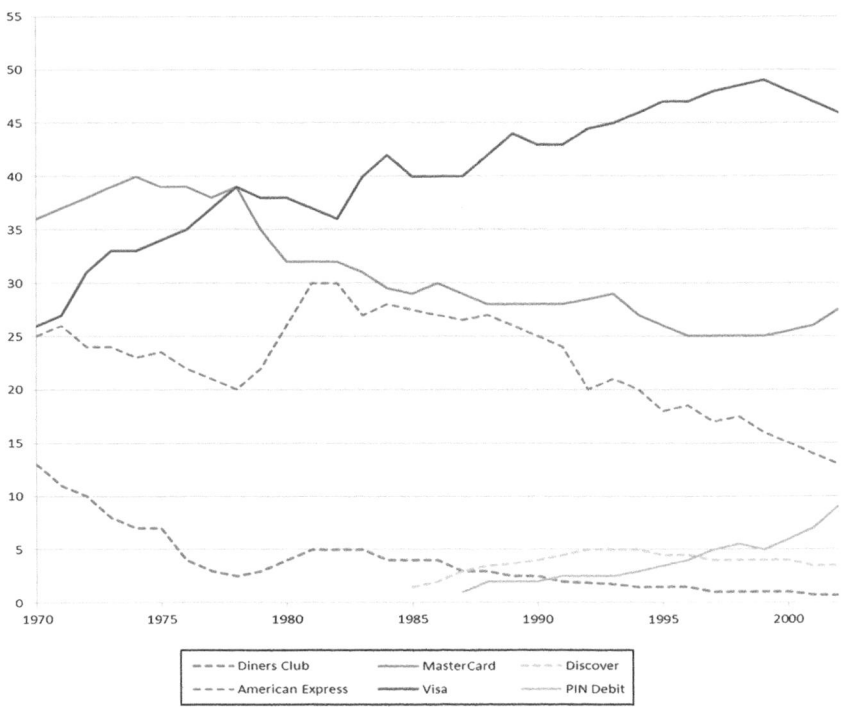

Fig. 4. Competition among Business Models and Dominant Players (% Share of Dollar Values of Transactions).

interest charges. In addition, however, the credit cards let their bank customers take out an instant loan at any time to finance their purchases. Second, because most American Express cardholders also had MasterCard or Visa cards, the business case for merchants to take American Express cards was weakened. In 1991, for example, almost 90 percent of American Express cardholders also had either a MasterCard or a Visa card (Evans & Schmalensee, 2005, pp. 13–14). Finally, the pricing strategies adopted by the open-loop credit card systems like Visa severely constrained the pricing strategies available to closed-loop charge card systems like American Express. In the closed-loop system, card issuers have only two levers to make their systems succeed. They could either subsidize their cardholders (e.g., Diners Club) by charging less for the cards to their customers or they could subsidize their merchants by lowering merchant discounts (e.g., American Express). In an open-loop system, however, each individual bank could make these decisions separately depending on their own unique economic conditions. Moreover, they could also negotiate alternative interchange fees depending on their transaction volume (e.g., Visa). Such arrangements provide more flexibility for the system as a whole.

American Express' decision to join the others by introducing its Optima credit card in the early 1990s as an open-loop system necessitated a complete reconfiguration of the exiting closed-loop system by bringing in banks and other financial institutions into the game. However, this new hybrid model had one major drawback – it put American Express competing against its own partner banks when it not only issued its own cards but also attempted to convince the partner banks to issue American Express cards. As mentioned earlier, its flawed introduction of the Optima credit card in 1987 had resulted in large losses from unexpectedly high charge-offs, adding to other severe losses at its travel-related services division (Pederson, 2001).[12]

*Introduction of Electronic Funds Transfer and the Automated
Teller Machines (ATM): The Birth of Debit Cards*

As the credit card industry developed in the late 1970s and early 1980s, another supporting element of the ecosystem started to grow. The electronic fund transfer (EFT) systems were an expected addition to the credit card system. They were designed to eliminate the third parties who were responsible to move the funds from a customer's bank account to a merchant's bank account. Even though their beginnings were difficult and slow, in the late 1980s there were more than 80,000 ATM machines in the United States (Hayashi, Sullivan, & Weiner, 2003).[13]

The formation of ATM networks by regional banks accelerated the process with the establishment of more than six national networks. In 1982 PLUS, RIA (Regional Interchange Association), and CIRRUS Networking helped to place ATM machines in locations other than banks such as airports, train stations, grocery stores, hotels, and other retail establishments. CIRRUS and PLUS were later acquired by MasterCard and Visa, respectively (*ibid.*, pp. 5–7).

As in the case of a credit card, a debit card transaction involves the purchase of a good or service. In this case, the consumer presents a debit card (which again was issued by the bank holding the checking account) to a merchant, and the consumer either enters a PIN (online debit) or signs a receipt (offline debit) to verify the consumer's identity. The merchant, in turn, sends information about the transaction across one or more debit card networks, and if the transaction is approved, the consumer receives the good or service. At the same time the consumer's checking account is debited and the merchant is reimbursed by a credit to its bank account. Online debit requires the use of a PIN and funds are debited immediately, while offline debit does not require a PIN but a signature and funds are not debited immediately. Online debit transactions are processed over an EFT network. By contrast, offline debit transactions are processed over credit card networks. Online debit allows the consumer to obtain cash (e.g., an ATM), while offline debit does not.

What is critical about these new payment processing schemes is the introduction of a chain of activities that led a new division of labor and new players. Specialized activities such as transaction initiation, transmission of payment information, sorting and aggregating payment information, and transfer of funds to appropriate parties required a new set of third-party processors. They were able to provide a variety of services, all related to this chain of activities, including ATM services, merchant services, account maintenance and authorization services, transaction routing and gateway services, offline debit processing services, and clearing and settlement services. As shown in Fig. 4, since the early 1990s, the fastest growing segment of the charge card industry has been the PIN-based debit cards (Mandell, 1990, pp. 123–135).[14]

With a complex division of labor that centered around various card payment networks, banks were becoming less dependent on the brand names of Visa or MasterCard even though most of these payment networks were ultimately acquired by these core players. The future is not clear about whether or not banks will feel the need to rely on the brand images of these two major players. This is especially true as the concentration ratios among credit card issuing banks have reached to about 80 percent in recent years (in 2007 four-firm concentration ratio was 79.2 and eight-firm concentration ratio was 87.4) even though concentration ratios in commercial banking were about 40 percent.[15]

Open- versus closed-loop systems: business models and
the nature of competition

As shown in Figs. 2 and 3, open- and closed-loop systems perform the same functions but with different structural organization. The open-loop system is based on complex joint ventures involving thousands of independent firms, each with its own shareholders, strategic objectives, and internal management problems. In addition, both of the two associations (Visa and MasterCard) have their own staff of employees who work for them directly and thus work indirectly for the thousands of member banks.

American Express, Diners Club, and Discover, the major single-firm systems, are often referred to as "closed-loop" systems because all transaction data is captured within the system. Because a single owner has contracts with all cardholders and merchants that belong to its system, it sees and captures all of the data that flow between the cardholder and the merchant. It authorizes and settles all transactions.

By contrast, the Visa and MasterCard joint ventures, known as "open-loop" systems, must transmit data among thousands of members. When the participant who signed up the cardholder differs from the participant who signed up the merchant, the transaction between the two is processed through a centralized authorization and settlement system. The system receives the details of the transaction and transmits them to the issuer, and it executes the transfer of charges between the issuer and acquirer. Each issuer independently sets the prices (fees and finance charges) for the cards it issues, and each acquirer independently sets the prices (fees and merchant discount) for the merchants it services. Under these local conditions parties could set prices depending on the local competition among banks and other third-party organizations as well as set subsidies for one side or the other in these two-sided markets (Eisenmann, Parker, & Alstyne, 2006). Both the closed-system and the early system of franchise contracts governing the BankAmericard enterprise proved to be less flexible and workable in a world of complex, uncertain, and rapidly changing credit card business. Open-loop system, on the other hand, has shown some advantages when it comes to system expansion. Expansion could take place whenever any of the individual members of the open-loop system perceive profit opportunities, without any approval from centralized management. Any member of the system can implement issuer-level innovations without the need to obtain a consensus at the network level.

At the beginning of the 1990s, the major universal credit card systems were firmly established and developed their brand images and the closed-loop system was in decline. The two open-loop systems developed distinct set of electronic transfers and rules for processing transactions, seeking verifications, getting approvals, transferring funds, and capturing billing information. As Table 2 clearly shows, at the turn of the 21st century, the competition between the closed and open systems that had evolved as a result of constant experimentations since the beginning of 1960s, has come to a close.

It is clear that these systems evolved slowly after much experimentation. It, probably, is surprising that the Visa and MasterCard joint ventures perform as well as they did. These uniquely large joint ventures have evolved considerably over the last quarter century. They have had to improvise and learn from their mistakes as they have grappled with a set of unique managerial and operational problems they faced. The competition between

Table 2. A Comparison of the Five Major Universal Credit Card Systems at the Turn of the New Century.

Card System	Type	Entry Date	Cards Issued (millions)		
			1990	2000	2010
Closed loop					
Diners Club	Charge	1950	1.4		
American Express	Charge	1958	20.3	33	48.9
Discover	Credit	1985	47.8	50	54.4
Optima (Am. Express)	Credit	1987	9.3		
Open loop					
Visa	Credit	1966	240.7	255	302
MasterCard	Credit	1966	164.5	200	203

Notes: In 2004, Diners Club agreed to use MasterCard logo and 16-digit account number on the front. In a transaction completed on July 1, 2008, Discover Financial Services purchased Diners Club International from Citi for $165 million.
Since July 2009, American Express no longer accepts applications for the Optima cards.

MasterCard and Visa is especially interesting because both systems have essentially the same members. Intense competition also takes place among the thousands of issuers of MasterCard and Visa cards even though these issuers collaborate through the bank card associations. Fig. 4 shows the evolution of this competition in terms of its outcomes as reflected in the volume of transactions processed within each model and the competing systems within each.

Theoretically, part of the explanation for the success of the open-loop business model comes from "spill-over" effect or network externality. There is a network externality when the value existing users get from the network increases when another user joins the network. A card system can survive only if it has a critical mass of both cardholders and merchants. The problem is even more complicated for the bank card associations: if Bank A issues more Visa cards, the merchant customers of Bank B will be made better off, and Bank B will benefit.

To some extent, this is true in many industries. Network externalities result in "increasing returns." The more customers a network gets, the more valuable the network becomes on average to each customer because of direct or indirect externalities. The organizations that are the coordinators of these networks end up being the transactional monopolist and ultimately determine industry structure as well as individual firm's behavior. When network externalities are important, multiple networks that do not inter-connect can survive only if they are offering consumers substantially different services. In the case of credit cards, multiple networks exist in part because these networks offer consumers and merchants somewhat different products.

What we learn from this history is ultimately what makes any organizing form (firm, industry, or global markets) successful is to effectively structure its two basic elements – division of labor among its parts and integration of these parts. What Visa and MasterCard (and later on debit cards) were able to accomplish is expanded decentralization with simultaneous integration (Sassen, 2006). With the growth of EFT networks, highly specialized third parties, banks, other commercial organizations, and coordinating parties could enter the ecosystem by participating in the industry platform. Local banks and commercial players could easily become part of a global network of financial transactions. Once established, these new platforms provide the means of participating in the industry-level business model with very little investment on their parts. In our case study, through expanded decen-tralization with simultaneous integration, one business model was more effective in terms of two critical performance measures of its ecosystem. It was able to persist in the face of constant environmental change, for example, robustness, and it was capable of niche creation by producing variety and supporting diversity (Iansiti & Levien, 2004).

Discussion and Conclusion: Conjectures and Relations to Extant Literature

In this paper, I have attempted to explore different strands of theories in strategy research with their propensity for historical analysis. Despite the strategy researchers' traditional focus on analytical models and their dislike of nontheoretical qualitative methodologies, most of the perspectives presented in Fig. 1 encourage not only longitudinal but specifically historical research. I have sketched a short historical analysis of the U.S. credit card industry to show how competition could be conceived not only as rivalries among firms but also as the business models in which industry conventions are established, formal rules of interactions are developed, and specific strategies are formulated. Business models as organizing forms establish the basic transactional mechanisms and the institutionalized conventions in an interorganizational network. At the level of interorganizational fields, competition cannot be conceived in terms of the density of a set of homogeneous organizations as the ecologists suggest, or in terms of strategic moves developed by competing firms, or even in terms of a set of institutionalized practices as the institutionalists argue.

At the field level, where competing platforms are developed with their own ecosystems, the competition for resources and legitimacy occurs among business models that form the alternative interorganizational networks. Each network, and the business model it is based on, may need different resource mix, collective learning strategies, and a core logic for the division of labor among member organizations. What determines the longevity and dissolution of organizations is ultimately the competition among business models that are the organizing forms of interfirm organizations. Similar ideas have also been discussed in organization theory (Durand, Rao, & Monin, 2007), economic sociology (Lounsbury, 2007; Uzzi, 1999), and the neo-institutional economics (Williamson, 1998) with a strong emphasis to historical analysis.

These preliminary ideas presented in this paper are designed to show that history and strategy research could be mutually beneficial for each other. By focusing on three critical elements of historical research, it is possible to build fruitful strategies for developing historically informed strategic research (Hall, 1992). The first element of such an approach is what some historians call the situational history (Roth, 1976). Even though it does not offer a meta-theoretical scheme for interpretation (as might be expected in strategy research), it makes us focus on the historical plot that reveals the actors and "traces the unique course of events, processes, and institutional developments that have given rise to the current situation" (Hall, 1992, p. 184). The payment card history is such a situational history. The second element is the constant focus on the explanation of a particular historical phenomenon. Hall (1992) defines this as sociohistorical object where a relatively self-contained set of events and sequences are used to develop the historical narrative that reveals the phenomenon and its development, such as the idea of alternative business models in the evolution of the payment card industry. The third element is the convergence of the historical narrative with a particular theoretical configuration. At this stage the narrative is decomposed into a series of historically emergent components via a particular theory in strategic research. Such an analytic framework makes the causal argument emerge out of the historical narrative. The most successful examples of this strategy are contained in Max Weber's writings in his research on bureaucracy and the emergence of capitalism. Here the objective is to identify a series of historically emergent components that are necessary but not sufficient to understand how and why events evolved in a particular fashion. In the case outlined in this paper, the ideas borrowed from diverse domains of strategy research, such as platforms and ecosystems, help us not only conceptualize the individual historical events covered in the narrative of the business models in the credit card industry but also rethink the concept of competition.

By using the lenses offered by historical analysis, we are able to uncover how historical narrative unfolds by creating the opportunities for the social actors to imagine the future and take actions that lead to that future. The business models as organizing forms are the products of collective actors and they are the fundamental building blocks of interorganizational networks. This is definitely different from the traditional models of competition that have dominated the strategy and organizational studies thus far.

NOTES

1. For the historical account of the payment card history, I relied heavily on several sources on this topic: Mandell (1990), Evans and Schmalensee (2005), and Nocera (1994).

In terms of the cultural and regulatory aspects of credit card use and its impact on American consumers, several books could be considered to be classic works: Nocera (1994), Calder (1999), and Mann (2006).

For specific company histories, I relied on the following books: for Diners Club, Simmons (1995); for American Express, Friedman and Meehan (1992) and Grossman (1987); for Visa, Chutkow (2001); and for retail and department store histories including Sears, Emmet, Rosenwald, and Goodkind (1950).

For statistical information, various research divisions of the Federal Reserve System and FDIC were critical sources for the historical account. In addition, various private sources including the Nelson Report were used. A listing of these sources could be found in the Appendix at the end of this chapter.

2. Various sources for this statistical information are available. I used the data provided by Credit Card News (http://www.creditcards.com/credit-card-news/credit-card-industry-facts-personal-debt-statistics-1276.php). Other sources are listed in the Appendix.

3. For the early history of Diners Club, please see Simmons (1995). A more general coverage of the early period could be found in Mandell (1990, pp. 1–11).

4. Simmons provides a colorful description of the early years of Diners Club and the nature of the competition with American Express.

5. Evans and Schmalensee (2005, pp. 175) call the closed-loop model the Go-It-Alone system and the open-loop model the co-opetitives system.

6. A more expanded history of American express and its entrance into the charge card business could be found in Grossman (1987).

7. The description provided here is a very simplified version of the whole process. A more detailed description could be found in Hayashi, Sullivan, and Weiner (2003). Federal Reserve Banks of Chicago and Philadelphia also provide more detailed transactional flowcharts.

8. According to Stearns (2011), 19 states and the District of Columbia allowed statewide branching at the time, 16 allowed limited branching, and 15 enforced unit banking as in Illinois.

9. See also Chutkow (2001), especially the chapter on the formation of the franchise.

10. A short chronology of this transformation could be found at "Master Card Milestones". *Milestones/Mastercard*. MasterCard. http://www.mastercard.com/us/company/en/ourcompany/company_milestones.html. See also Evans and Schmalen see (2005, pp. 65–66).

11. American Banker covered this story extensively in 1979 and 1980. See Kutler (1979).

12. Additional information about the Optima card could be found in American Express, Annual Reports 1990, 1991, 1992, and 1993.

13. Federal Reserve Bank of Kansas City has additional research publications that are more technical in nature (see Bradford, Davies, & Weiner, 2003).

14. This part of the credit card history is usually associated with the ever changing nature of technology. It is, however, important to realize that these technological changes also produce new business models as well as new platforms.

15. Statistics are based on the official figures of the U.S. Census Bureau, http://www.census.gov/econ/concentration.html.

REFERENCES

Baden-Fuller, C., & Morgan, M. S. (2010). Business models as models. *Long Range Planning*, *43*(2–3), 156–171.

Bradford, T., Davies, M., & Weiner, S. E. (2003). *Nonbanks in the payment System: Federal Reserve Bank of Kansas City*. Kansas City, Kansas: Federal Reserve Bank of Kansas City.

Calder, L. (1999). *Financing the American dream: A cultural history of consumer credit*. Princeton, NJ: Princeton University Press.

Campbell-Hunt, C. (2000). What have we learned from generic competitive strategy? A meta-analysis. *Strategic Management Journal*, *21*(2), 127.

Casadesus-Masanell, R., & Ricart, J. E. (2011). How to design a winning business model. *Harvard Business Review*, *89*(1/2), 100–107.

Chandler, A. D. (1962). *Strategy and structure: Chapters in the hisory of the industrial enterprise*. Cambridge, MA: MIT Press.

Chutkow, P. (2001). *Visa: The power of an idea*. New York, NY: Harcourt.

Commons, J. R. (1934). *Institutional economics*. Madison, WI: University of Wisconsin Press.

Cusumano, M. A. (2010). *Staying power: Six enduring principles for managing strategy and innovation in an uncertain world*. Oxford: Oxford University Press.

David, R. J., & Han, S.-K. (2004). A systematic assessment of the empirical support for transaction cost economics. *Strategic Management Journal*, *25*(1), 39–58.

Demil, B., & Lecocq, X. (2010). Business model evolution: In search of dynamic consistency. *Long Range Planning*, *43*(2–3), 227–246.

Dosi, G., Malerba, F., & Teece, D. (2003). Twenty years after nelson and winter's an evolutionary theory of economic change: A preface on knowledge, the nature of organizations and the patterns of organizational changes. *Industrial and Corporate Change*, *12*(2), 147–148.

Dranove, D., Peteraf, M., & Shanley, M. (1998). Do strategic groups exist? An economic framework for analysis. *Strategic Management Journal*, *19*(11), 1029.

Durand, R., Rao, H., & Monin, P. (2007). Code and conduct in French cuisine: Impact of code changes on external evaluations. *Strategic Management Journal*, *28*(5), 455–472.

Eisenmann, T., Parker, G., & Alstyne, M. W. V. (2006). Strategies of two-sided markets. *Harvard Business Review*, *84*(10), 92–101.

Emmet, B., Rosenwald, J. E., & Goodkind, E. (1950). *Catalogues and counters: A history of sears, roebuck and company*. Chicago, IL: University of Chicago Press.

Evans, D. S., & Schmalensee, R. (2005). *Paying with plastic: The digital revolution in buying and borrowing*. Cambridge, MA: MIT Press.

Friedman, J., & Meehan, J. (1992). *House of cards: Inside the troubled empire of American Express*. New York, NY: Putnam.

Gambardella, A., & McGahan, A. M. (2010). Business-model innovation: General purpose technologies and their implications for industry structure. *Long Range Planning*, *43*(2–3), 262–271.

Gawer, A., & Cusumano, M. A. (2002). *Platform leadership: How intel, microsoft, and cisco drive industry innovation*. Boston, MA: Harvard University Press.

Ghoshal, S., & Moran, P. (1996). Bad for practice: A critique of the transaction cost theory. *Academy of Management Review*, *21*, 13–47.

Goldthorpe, J. H. (1991). The uses of history in sociology: Reflections on some recent tendencies. *British Journal of Sociology, 42*(2), 211–230.

Grossman, P. Z. (1987). *American express: The unofficial history of the people who built the great financial empire.* New York, NY: Crown Publishers.

Hall, J. (1992). Where history and sociology meet: Forms of discourse and sociohistorical inquiry. *Sociological Theory, 10,* 164–193.

Hayashi, F., Sullivan, R., & Weiner, S. E. (2003). *A guide to the ATM and debit card industry.* Kansas City, MO: Federal Reserve Bank of Kansas City.

Iansiti, M., & Levien, R. (2004). Strategy as ecology. *Harvard Business Review, 82*(3), 68–78.

Kieser, A. (1994). Why organization theory needs historical analyses – and how this should be performed. *Organization Science, 5*(4), 608–620.

Kipping, M., & Usdiken, B. (2009). Business history and management studies. In G. Jones & J. Zeitlin (Eds.), *The Oxford Handbook of Business History* (pp. 96–119). Oxford: Oxford University Press.

Kutler, J. (1979). Penny to honor Visa: First big retailer to accept bank cards. *American Banker.* April 5, p. 2.

Leblebici, H., & Shah, N. (2004). The birth, transformation, and regeneration of business incubators as new organizational forms: Understanding the interplay between organizational history and organizational theory. *Business History, 46*(3), 353–380.

Lounsbury, M. (2007). A tale of two cities: Competing logics and practice variation in the professionalizing of mutual funds. *Academy of Management Journal, 50*(2), 289–307.

MacKenzie, D., & Millo, Y. (2003). Constructing a market, performing theory: The historical sociology of a financial derivatives exchange. *American Journal of Sociology, 109*(1), 107–145.

Magretta, J. (2002). Why business models matter. *Harvard Business Review, 80*(5), 86–92.

Malerba, F., Nelson, R., Orsenigo, L., & Winter, S. (1999). History friendly models of industry evolution. *Industrial and Corporate Change, 8,* 3–40.

Mandell, L. (1990). *The credit card industry: A history.* Boston, MA: Twayne Publishers.

Mann, R. J. (2006). *Charging ahead: The growth and regulation of payment card markets.* Cambridge: Cambridge University Press.

Masten, S. E. (2000). Transaction-cost economics and the organization of agricultural transactions. In M. R. Baye (Ed.), *Advances in applied microeconomics-industrial organization* (Vol. 9, pp. 173–195). New York, NY: Emerald Group Publishing.

McGee, J., & Thomas, H. (1986). Strategic groups: Theory, research and taxonomy. *Strategic Management Journal, 7*(2), 141–160.

Nag, R., Hambrick, D. C., & Chen, M.-J. (2007). What is strategic management, really? Inductive derivation of a consensus definition of the field. *Strategic Management Journal, 28*(9), 935–955.

Nocera, J. (1994). *A piece of the action: How the middle class joined the money class.* New York, NY: Simon & Schuster.

North, D. C. (1978). Structure and performance: The task of economic history. *Journal of Economic Literature, 16*(3), 963–978.

North, D. C. (1991). Institutions. *Journal of Economic Perspectives, 5*(1), 97–112.

Pederson, J. P. (2001). *International directory of company histories* (Vol. 38). New York, NY: St. James Press.

Perkmann, M., & Spicer, A. (2010). What are business models? Developing a theory of performantive representation. In M. Lounsbury (Ed.), *Technology and organization: Essays in Honour of Joan Woodward* (Vol. 29, pp. 265–275). Research in the Sociology of Organizations. Bingley, UK: Emerald Group.

Peteraf, M., & Shanley, M. (1997). Getting to know you: A theory of strategic group identity. *Strategic Management Journal, 18*, 165–186.

Porter, M. (1981). The contributions of industrial organization to strategic management. *Academy of Management Review, 6*, 609–620.

Porter, M. E. (1980). *Competitive strategy*. New York, NY: Free Press.

Porter, M. E. (1985). *Competitive advantage*. New York, NY: Free Press.

Reger, R. K., & Huff, A. S. (1993). Strategic groups: A cognitive perspective. *Strategic Management Journal, 14*(2), 103–123.

Roth, G. (1976). History and sociology in the work of Max Weber. *British Journal of Sociology, 27*, 306–318.

Sassen, S. (2006). *Territory, authority, rights: From medieval to global assemblages*. Princeton, NJ: Princeton University Press.

Short, J. C., Ketchen, D. J., Jr., Palmer, T. B., & Hult, G. T. M. (2007). Firm, strategic group, and industry influences on performance. *Strategic Management Journal, 28*(2), 147–167.

Silverman, B. S., Nickerson, J. A., & Freeman, J. (1997). Profitability, transactional alignment, and organizational mortality in the U.S. trucking industry. *Strategic Management Journal. Special Issue: Organizational and Competitive Interactions, 18*(Summer), 31–52.

Simmons, M. (1995). *The credit card catastrophe: The 20th century phenomenon that changed the world*. New York, NY: Barricade Books.

Spender, J. C. (1989). *Industry recipes: The nature and sources of managerial judgement*. Oxford: Blackwell.

Stearns, D. L. (2011). *Electronic value exchange: Origins of the VISA electronic payment system*. London: Springer.

Stone, L. (1979). The revival of narrative: Reflections on a new old history. *Past and Present, 85*, 3–24.

Teece, D. J. (2010). Business models, business strategy and innovation. *Long Range Planning, 43*(2–3), 172–194.

Tilly, C. (1981). *As sociology meets history*. New York, NY: Academic Press.

Uzzi, B. (1999). Embeddedness in the making of financial capital: How social relations and networks benefit firms seeking financing. *American Sociological Review, 64*(4), 481–505.

Williamson, O. E. (1981). The economics of organization: The transaction cost approach. *American Journal of Sociology, 87*(3), 548–577.

Williamson, O. E. (1991). Strategizing, economizing, and economic organization. *Strategic Management Journal. Special Issue: Fundamental Research Issues in Strategy and Economics, 12*, 75–94.

Williamson, O. E. (1998). The institutions of governance. *American Economic Review, 88*(2), 75–79. Papers and proceedings of the Hundred and Tenth Annual Meeting of the American Economic Association.

Zott, C., & Amit, R. (2007). Business model design and the performance of entrepreneurial firms. *Organization Science, 18*(2), 181–199.

Zott, C., Amit, R., & Massa, L. (2011). The business model: Recent developments and future research. *Journal of Management, 37*(4), 1019–1042.

APPENDIX

A listing of the government and private data sources used for the historical narrative

Credit Card News (http://www.creditcards.com/credit-card-news/credit-card-industry-facts-personal-debt-statistics-1276.php)

Payments Source (http://www.paymentssource.com/statistics/)

American Banker

ABA Banking Journal

Bankers Monthly Magazine

Cards and Payments (Formerly Credit Card Management)

Board of Governors of the Federal Reserve System Statistics: Releases and Historical data

Federal Reserve Bank of Boston Consumer Payments Research Center (http://www.bos.frb.org/economic/cprc/index.htm)

Federal Reserve Bank of Chicago (http://www.chicagofed.org/webpages/markets/index.cfm)

Federal Reserve Bank of Kansas City, Banking and Payments Research (http://www.kansascityfed.org/research/bankingandpayments/)

Federal Reserve Bank of Philadelphia Payment Card Center (http://www.philadelphiafed.org/consumer-credit-and-payments/payment-cards-center/)

Other useful web pages

For the history of credit cards

http://www.creditcards.com/credit-card-news/credit-cards-history-1264.php

For the history of credit card processing

http://www.gotmerchant.com/history_of_credit_card_processing.php

STRATEGY FOLLOWED STRUCTURE: MANAGEMENT CONSULTING AND THE CREATION OF A MARKET FOR "STRATEGY," 1950–2000

Christopher McKenna

ABSTRACT

Purpose – *This chapter traces the creation of a market for strategy by management consulting firms during the second half of the twentieth century in order to demonstrate their impact in shaping debates in the subject and demand for their services by corporate executives.*

Design/methodology/approach – *Using historical analysis, the chapter draws on institutional theory, including institutional isomorphism. It uses both primary and secondary data from the leading consulting firms to describe how consultants shifted from offering advice on organizational structure to corporate strategy and eventually to corporate legitimacy as a result of the changing economic and regulatory environment of the time.*

Findings/originality/value – *This study provides a historical context for the emergence of corporate and competitive strategy as an institutional*

History and Strategy
Advances in Strategic Management, Volume 29, 153–186
Copyright © 2012 by Emerald Group Publishing Limited
All rights of reproduction in any form reserved
ISSN: 0742-3322/doi:10.1108/S0742-3322(2012)0000029010

practice in both the United States and around the world, and provides insights into how important this history can be in understanding the debates among consultants and academics during strategy's emergence as an academic subject and practical application.

Keywords: History of strategy; management consulting; legitimacy; Boston Consulting Group; McKinsey & Company; institutional isomorphism

Popular writers and management theorists have long acknowledged that the academic subject of strategy has been profoundly influenced by those management consultants who theorized, packaged, and sold the new discipline to their corporate clients starting in the early 1960s (Business Week, 1973a; Hayes, 1979; Lieberman, 1987; Peters, 1994; Seeger, 1984).[1] From the infamous "BCG Box" to the "McKinsey Matrix," the names of the leading management consulting firms remain imprinted on the academic discipline of strategy as it is taught to students in business schools around the world (Mintzberg, 2004). Far from a purely theoretical subject, pragmatic MBAs have come to accept that developing a new strategy is as much about weighing the competing claims advanced by rival consulting firms as it is about evaluating the particular value of the relevant theories in academic texts (Bower, 1982).

Strategy theorists, however, have done far less research in understanding how the ideas emanating from these professional firms have reflected the particular "core competence" and regulatory environment in which the consultancies were themselves situated.[2] It is noteworthy, for example, that the Boston Consulting Group (BCG) revolutionized management consulting by offering novel theories about strategy during the 1960s and 1970s that their consultants claimed were universally applicable across all industries in part because the BCG consultants had to overcome the potential liability that they were not trained as industry specialists. During the 1960s, when antitrust laws encouraged corporate executives to look beyond industrial boundaries and create conglomerates, BCG's universalistic approach would be particularly well received (Berg, 1965; Lubatkin, 1983; Reed & Luffman, 1986). Yet, conversely, McKinsey & Company re-emerged as a leading strategy consultancy during the mid-1980s just as the crisis in corporate liability gave their industry expertise particular weight as professional gatekeepers (Coffee, 2006). Thus, the strategic theories proffered by the leading management consulting firms were a product not only of economic cycles and marketing acumen, but also of the interaction between legislative and regulatory changes set against the firms' idiosyncratic historical competencies. While BCG's promotion of the conglomerate form of organization declined during the 1980s, their initial support for conglomeration was itself a natural consequence of the consultancy's expertise in guiding the construction of corporate portfolios (Kipping, 1999).[3] In the historical development of consulting, management consultants crafted strategies to reflect and accentuate their particular skills and the broader economic environment in which they were operating.

Management consultants, of course, were particularly influential in reshaping large organizations to resemble one another. Following Paul DiMaggio and Woody Powell's work on "institutional isomorphism," management theorists have recognized that consultants have been one of the most powerful forces in the dissemination of corporate structures, strategies, and management tools to their clients across economic sectors and throughout the world; like "Johnny Appleseeds" in Powell and Dimaggio's evocative description (DiMaggio & Powell, 1983). Yet, once those norms are set – new structures installed, corporate strategies agreed, and management tools institutionalized – just how do the established institutional models change? The missing links are the management consultants who have an economic incentive to promote and sell new organizational models, thus restarting the process of institutional isomorphism. The leading management consulting firms have operated as both the enforcers of institutional isomorphism and the institutional entrepreneurs who actively devised new ways to rethink their clients' operations. Thus, the commercial logic of these agents of institutional isomorphism is not simply convergence upon a single standard but also the constant search for new models to be commodified and resold to the large organizations that are already clients of the consultants.

This chapter explores the relationship between the academic discipline of strategy as generally presumed by theorists to be the interaction of theoretical concepts and evolving economic circumstances, and the more messy reality that novel strategic frameworks have tended to emerge from the sale of new models derived from the particular operational strengths of the leading management consulting firms within the context of changing regulatory environment. Drawing on the internal archival records of the leading consulting firms and their corporate clients, this historical analysis will contextualize the changing and contingent nature of strategy over the fifty-year history of the American consulting firms that dominated the production and distribution of strategy during its emergence as an academic field. In particular, this chapter will review the three epochs of strategy as demanded by corporate clients, sanctioned by government officials, and provided by entrepreneurial consultants: the 1950s to mid-1960s when strategy was equated with organizational structure, the mid-1960s to mid-1980s, when strategy was considered a form of economic theory, and the mid-1980s to the end of the 1990s when strategy became a system of corporate legitimacy. To understand the origins and impact of any market, and particularly the market for strategy, one must first understand the influence of the consultants who have guided its development over the past fifty years.

THE EARLY HISTORY OF MANAGEMENT CONSULTING

From the 1920s on, a new type of professional service emerged that focused on controlling the white-collar bureaucracy of large companies, not their line workers. They provided "business surveys" for companies interested in learning new methods of cost accounting and departmental organization. Unlike the self-taught engineers who led the scientific management movement, the university-trained accountants, engineers, and lawyers who founded the leading management engineering firms – Stevenson, Jordan & Harrison and Ford, Bacon & Davis in New York, and Booz Allen & Hamilton and James O. McKinsey & Company in Chicago – offered executive-level advice on administration and organization. Management engineers assisted not only large corporate clients but also the bankers for these companies by restructuring troubled companies, merging rival firms, or analyzing possible acquisition targets.[4]

In the 1930s and 1940s, management engineering firms, now better known as management consulting firms, proved themselves increasingly useful to American corporations both as sources of new ideas and, equally important, as a means to avoid corporate liability for malfeasance.[5] In the depths of the Great Depression, and with the creation of the Securities and Exchange Commission (SEC), corporations believed that they could avoid shareholder lawsuits if they hired consultants to certify their actions. As a result, between 1930 and 1940, the number of management consulting firms grew, on average, 15 percent a year from an estimated 100 firms in 1930 to 400 firms by 1940, and, during the 1940s, the number of new firms continued to grow at nearly 10 percent a year so that by 1950 there were an estimated 1,000 management consulting firms in existence (Association of Consulting Management Engineers, Inc. (ACME), 1964, Table 2). In the late 1930s and the early 1940s, contemporary observers, from both the academic and the business world, perceived that this rapid growth of management engineering was distinct from the scientific management movement – eschewing the ideology of Taylorism, management engineers studied the top of the organizational pyramid, not its base.[6]

It is important to be clear what role these companies played – as specialists in organizational design and structure – and what advice they did not give – namely, advice on shop floor productivity. From the 1930s on, the pioneering management consulting firms like McKinsey & Company and Booz Allen & Hamilton largely replaced Taylorist consulting firms in America, even though Taylorist consulting firms continued to dominate the market for organizational advice in Europe through the 1950s. Although a few early American Taylorist consulting firms, like the one founded by Harrington Emerson, managed to stay in business during the postwar era, in the United States, the leading management consulting firms neither were founded by Taylorists nor promoted scientific management techniques.[7] After World War II, these new "management consultants" (as they renamed themselves in the 1940s) worked to establish themselves as close advisors to top management, likening themselves to corporate lawyers by arguing that they were the true professional advisors to the board of directors.

From the outset, management consultants used their principal management tool, the general survey, to identify and solve organizational problems. The general survey was a detailed overview of a company's organizational structure and, as a leading consulting firm described the general survey in 1934, "such a survey appraises the effectiveness of the management, checks the organization procedures, the nature of records, the standards, budgets, quotas, and the like" (Stevenson, Jordan, & Harrison, 1934). At James O. McKinsey & Company, as at Stevenson, Jordan & Harrison, the general survey was the preferred means of studying a company, and staff consultants first performed a general survey before tackling any specific organizational problems (Wolf, 1978).[8] By the end of the 1940s, administrators, whether in the corporate, state, or nonprofit sectors had generally accepted the utility of management consultants as the acknowledged outside experts on organizational structure.

THE PROPHETS (AND PROFITS) OF THE MULTIDIVISIONAL STRATEGY

The work that McKinsey & Company and Booz Allen performed in the 1940s and 1950s included helping corporate boards calculate executive compensation and installing budgetary control systems, but the most prestigious and visible assignments for consulting firms involved the restructuring of corporations, most often using the "decentralized" or "multidivisional" model. In the 1930s, executives from DuPont, General Motors, and Sears Roebuck published widely on the decentralized model that they had developed in the 1920s to manage their national, multiproduct corporations (Chandler, 1962). Indeed, Peter Drucker's best-selling management book from 1946, *The Concept of the Corporation*, was simply an extended description of how General Motors divided its product lines (Chevrolet, Buick, Cadillac, etc.) into autonomous divisions that competed against one another yet were ultimately responsible to the chief executive officer (Drucker, 1964). But, even if executives recognized the form of the multidivisional corporate model, the majority of large American firms did not decentralize until the immediate postwar era; and when they did decide to divisionalize, their executives invariably hired the leading management consulting firms to help them make the transition. Consultants from Booz Allen & Hamilton decentralized IBM in 1956, Cresap, McCormick and Paget divisionalized Westinghouse in 1951, and McKinsey & Company installed the multidivisional structure at Chrysler in the 1950s.[9] In 1962, the business historian, Alfred Chandler, could comfortably write the history of decentralization in the United States, arguing that the multidivisional structure had become the dominant organizational form among American industrial companies in large part through the work of management consulting firms (Chandler, 1962, pp. 381–382).[10] By 1967, 86 percent of the 500 largest companies in America had adopted the decentralized organizational model (Wrigley, 1970).

In the 1950s and 1960s, management consultants repeatedly recommended that large organizations adopt the decentralized model, an organizational "formula" that came to dominate American industrial companies. As many academics have already argued, by the 1940s and 1950s, management consulting firms like Booz Allen & Hamilton, Robert Heller & Associates, and Cresap, McCormick & Paget were the primary disseminators of the multidivisional form to public and private organizations across the United States (Fortune, 1952; Hewes, 1975, pp. 72–74).[11] Nevertheless, as historian Alfred Chandler has written, even if corporate executives generally understood the form of the multidivisional model, they specifically hired the leading management consulting firms to help them install it in their companies. Management consultants, thus, believed in the virtues of decentralized organization and, as the "visible hand" of institutional isomorphism, they spread it among the institutions with which they worked, including prominent assignments in the state and nonprofit sectors.

Although internal memos from the corporate archives of McKinsey & Company in the late 1950s and early 1960s make it clear that the consultants did not set out to "sell" decentralization to their European clients, the final result would not have been very different if that had been McKinsey's strategy.[12] In Britain, McKinsey & Company decentralized 22 of the largest 100 companies, and in Germany McKinsey "alone was involved in, and largely shaped, over a dozen divisionalizations of major German firms" (Channon, 1973, p. 239).[13] In contrast, as Mauro Guillen has demonstrated, because McKinsey and the other leading American management consulting firms did not set up offices in Spain during the 1960s, not a single large Spanish company adopted the decentralized organizational form before the 1980s (Guillén, 1994).[14] As one German academic summarized the trend toward corporate decentralization: "the main driving force in Germany, as elsewhere, has been provided by the American management consultants McKinsey (Fiedler-Winter, 1974). In the Netherlands, as Matthias Kipping and Gerarda Westerhuis show in this volume, both McKinsey and Arthur D. Little installed the multidivisional structure in the leading banks (Kipping & Westerhuis, 2012). In a very direct and central way, American management consulting firms, and especially consultants from McKinsey & Company, were responsible for spreading the multidivisional organizational model in Europe during the 1960s.

In Britain, where McKinsey had the greatest impact in persuading companies to decentralize, 72 of the 100 largest businesses adopted the multidivisional structure by 1970. Of course, many firms like Unilever and Royal Dutch/Shell had already decentralized their production into regional divisions in the 1950s, so when growth strained their organizations, their executive boards felt comfortable hiring McKinsey & Company to further divisionalize their companies (Jones, 2005). Thus at Royal Dutch/Shell, prior to McKinsey's reorganization, the joint Anglo-Dutch directors managed the company through regional divisions supported by functional departments located in London (marketing, finance, and distribution) and The Hague (exploration, manufacturing, and research) (Engle, 1959). In the late 1950s, however, this structure became increasingly unwieldy as Shell began diversifying into petrochemical production, yet executives still tried to manage the worldwide production and sale of specialty chemicals from their London offices (Channon, p. 115). Unable to install the multidivisional form on their own, and unwilling to hire either Dutch or British consultants for fear that the other group would rebel, John Loudon, the Dutch managing director at Shell, turned to an American consultancy to divisionalize Shell. When the U.S. petroleum industry went through the same diversification into chemicals in the postwar era, it provided American executives, in Alfred Chandler's words, with a "powerful pressure for decentralization" (Chandler, 1962, p. 353). Thus during the 1960s, despite the many cultural and structural differences among the European multi-nationals, management consultants installed the decentralized organizational structure in dozens of British, Swiss, French, German, and Dutch companies.

The rapid growth of management consulting firms in the 1950s and 1960s, however, eventually posed a problem for the leading management consulting firms. Even if corporate executives understood the value of management consultants, by the early 1950s, consultants had already divisionalized many of the large companies in America and, likewise, by the end of the 1960s they had also carried their models throughout Europe. Like the earlier Taylorist efficiency engineers who had installed incentive systems, management consultants were rapidly working themselves out of a job even as their numbers swelled. The Association of Consulting Management Engineers, the professional association of management consulting firms, estimated that by 1950 there was one management consultant for every 150 salaried managers in the United States, but by 1965 the ratio had risen to one consultant for every 100 managers.[15] Consulting firms soon decided that the solution to their problem was a simple one – instead of selling general surveys, management consulting firms offered increasingly promoted specialized studies to their clients. General management consulting firms like McKinsey & Company offered to make detailed studies of specific departments, products, and markets for companies whose organizations had already been "surveyed" by management consultants.[16] In turn, this frequent use of consultants for smaller surveys made their presence less ad hoc and more a part of the corporate routine, institutionalizing the role of management consultants in the ongoing administration of companies.

Yet, even as they tried to diversify their own product offerings, by the end of the 1960s, American consultants had become synonymous with the installation of the decentralized organizational model. As Marvin Bower, the former Managing Director of McKinsey & Company, noted, the publicity surrounding their assignments in the United States, and particularly in Europe, meant that McKinsey "became known, exclusively to many, as reorganizers" (Bower, 1979, p. 97). That reputation served the consulting firm well when the decentralized model was new and uncommon, but by the early 1970s, McKinsey & Company had, quite literally, decentralized most of the largest companies in the world. As Allen Stewart, a partner in McKinsey's Paris office, subsequently admitted:

> What happened in France is that in 5 or 6 years [1965–1971] we had gone through what London went through in about 12 years [1959–1971]. And that initial phase of restructuring came to an end. Also that favorable climate of the early days of the Paris office – respect for all things American – also diminished. There was probably a feeling in the marketplace that these McKinsey people have been just about everywhere and what have they achieved?[17]

This decline in business was not limited to McKinsey & Company, but McKinsey felt it more acutely because the general downturn in the market for consulting services during the 1970s recession came at the same time that McKinsey had exhausted the market for their organizational studies (Business Week, 1973c). Although McKinsey denied in the *Financial Times* that it was "feeling the economic squeeze more than the major U.K. consulting firms," the head of the London office later remembered, "Somewhere about 1970 the phone stopped ringing" (Financial Times, 1971; McCreary, 1964).[18] The answer, of course, was not for management consultants to exit the profession but instead to consider offering a different form of consulting advice.

THE STRATEGIC ALTERNATIVE FOR CONSULTING

In contrast to the broad decline of consulting in organizational design, in the late 1960s and 1970s, no management consulting specialty grew faster than the emerging practice of "strategy" consulting. Between 1963, when Bruce Henderson founded The BCG, and 1973 when his partner Bill Bain broke away from BCG to found Bain & Company, The BCG grew rapidly from only 2 consultants to 142 consultants. Although the relative growth of BCG would slow to 10 percent a year in the firm's second decade, the swift rise of Bain & Company from 1974 onwards – an annual compound growth rate of 40 percent in Bain's first decade – would only reinforce the widespread perception that organizational consulting was past and strategy consulting was the new frontier (Hemp, 1991). The founder of LEK, a prominent strategy consulting firm in the 1990s, summarized the shifting fortunes of the leading consultancies in the following way, "McKinsey & Co. was No. 1 in the 1960s, BCG was on top in the 1970s, [and] Bain and Co. had the momentum in the 1980s ..." (McKibben, 1990). By the middle of the 1970s, the older management consulting firms like McKinsey and Booz Allen realized that their future laid in strategy consulting, not in resuscitating the general survey nor in trying to popularize a new organizational structure (The Wall Street Journal, 1976b). In contrast, for example, to the orphaned products that Damon Phillips describes in this volume, consultants shifted their products to suit the needs of the time (Phillips, 2012). After all, organizational structures only needed to be changed every few years, but corporate and competitive strategy was any ever-changing question. But an important question still remained: what was strategy consulting and how did one successfully compete in this newly created field?

The irony, of course, was that consultants had always implicitly dealt with corporate strategy when they were installing the multidivisional organizational structure. From 1962 on, after business historian Alfred Chandler had explicitly linked corporate strategy and organizational structure through his famous dictum that "structure follows strategy," management theorists understood the causal relationship between the "determination of the basic long-term goals and objectives of an enterprise" and the decision to adopt a new organizational structure (Chandler, 1962, p. 13). But from 1959 through 1965, the year when Bruce Henderson would first describe his firm's specialty as "business strategy," McKinsey & Company's total revenues from "strategic examinations" averaged only 3 percent of the firm's total revenues while the "organizational" studies for McKinsey's clients provided 25 percent of the firm's revenues on average.[19] The problem, of course, was in first identifying *this* particular practice area as the potential source of long-run growth and, equally difficult for the consulting firms, in defining what form this new "strategy" advice would take. Indeed, as the corporate lore from The BCG makes clear, the consultants in BCG were no more certain than their competitors precisely what "strategy" consulting really meant. An early member of BCG's consulting staff, Robert Mainer, remembered Bruce Henderson's decision to describe his firm's specialty as "business strategy" was intentionally vague, even if clearly distinctive:

> Bruce [Henderson] called a staff meeting for a Saturday morning in the fall of 1965. He explained that to survive, much less grow, in a competitive landscape occupied by hundreds of larger and better-known consulting firms, we needed a distinctive identity. He had concluded that we shouldn't fight the competitive battle as generalists, but

should instead stake out a special area of expertise. [Henderson] asked what we thought that specialty should be. Many suggestions were offered, but in each case we were able to identify several other firms that already had strong credentials in that particular area. The discussion began to stall. Then Bruce asked a momentous question: "What about business strategy?" I objected: "That's too vague. Most executives won't know what we're talking about." Bruce replied, "That's the beauty of it. We'll define it." (The Boston Consulting Group, 2005)

The new form of strategy consulting that the consultants in The BCG offered their clients was novel not because it offered a common theoretical model but because BCG's strategy practice fused the universalism of economic theory with the hard-nosed fiscal and operational concerns of business (Warsh, 1994).

While Bruce Henderson was not the only theoretically oriented consultant in the BCG – both Alan Zakon, a former finance professor at Boston University, and James Abegglen, a leading academic expert on the Japanese economy, were also prominent BCG partners – Henderson's theories would become the most widely known primarily because of his constant promotion of the consulting firm. Starting in 1964, Henderson began writing a series of opinion pieces that he sent to executives roughly once a month, entitled "Perspectives" that BCG subsequently bundled into a series of books with the same name (The Boston Consulting Group, 1968). From 1966, with Henderson's promotion of the "Experience Curve," which described how the production cost of manufactured products declined at a predictable rate because of the increase in manufacturers' "accumulated experience," Henderson's ideas would spread far beyond his clients' walls (Arthur Young & Company, 1982). As Henderson's obituary described his intellectual legacy, Henderson's "seemingly simple concepts, once scorned by academics, are now fixtures in business school curriculums" (Hayes, 1992). Although Henderson would eventually complain about the widespread misapplication of BCG's models, there was little doubt that his popularization of these simplified concepts contributed to the rapid rise of The BCG's professional reputation.

The concept of BCG's "experience curve" was similar to the already established principle in economics of a "learning curve," in which repetitive tasks performed by manual workers resulted in a predictable decline in labor costs (Andress, 1954; Hirschmann, 1964). The consultants at BCG first developed the idea of the "experience curve" based on their consulting work within Texas Instruments, which allowed them to predict the rate at which the cost of semiconductors fell as the volume of production increased (Henderson, 1998). The Texas Instruments assignment, however, was not the end of the idea but its beginning; as Henderson would later say, "a real understanding [of the experience curve] required many, many, client assignments" (Henderson, 1998). Not only were executives encouraged by BCG's "experience curve" to underbid their rivals in order to gain production capacity and thereby lower their costs, but the logic of the "experience curve" also suggested that it was better to enter markets earlier and at higher volumes in order to preempt potential competitors (Rothschild, 1992). As Bruce Henderson put it in simple terms, "either invest in greater market share or get out" (Thackray, 1979). Although semiconductors were clearly a particularly vivid example of continually falling production costs, the consultants from BCG argued that their model could be applied across all manufacturing industries and, by the late 1960s, Henderson's theories were already hotly debated among academics – not only in policy but also in marketing – and had begun to strongly influence the strategies of leading corporate executives (Catry & Chevalier, 1974). Consider, for example, this jargon-laden comment on Nabisco's introduction of the new "Chips Ahoy" chocolate chip cookie in 1969 by John T. Gerlach, who was then a vice president in General Mills:

> If you are involved with new-product programs you must understand such things as how the implication of market share as hypothesized by experience curve theory relates to the product life cycle and how the combination of the two influences new-product pricing. (Dougherty, 1969)

Although the *New York Times* reporter would follow this apparently baffling analysis with the remark, "which is one way to put it," clearly the consultants from BCG had already made themselves understood in the boardroom of General Mills, which by the late 1960s was a conglomerate producing not only cookies and frozen vegetables, but also the board game "Monopoly," Lionel toy trains, and domestic kitchen appliances (Wojahn, 2003).

That BCG's concept of the "experience curve" should have had such a forceful impact on the corporate executives in General Mills, which was rapidly diversifying in the in the late 1960s, was not coincidental. As late as 1980, when support for the conglomerate form was quickly fading in the United States, Bruce Henderson remained a cheerleader for unrelated diversification by large companies. As Henderson defended the conglomerates, "[they] are the normal and natural business form for efficiency and channeling investment into the most productive use. If nature takes its course, then conglomerates will become the dominant form of business organization, particularly in the United States" (Warsh, 1980). Or to put it more bluntly, the conglomerate was the natural home for the products developed by the "strategy" consultants from The BCG (Seeger, 1984). Bruce Henderson, who had first worked for the large, diversified company, Westinghouse, and then Arthur D. Little, the consulting firm where Royal Little devised the tools he used to manage Textron (the first American conglomerate), was well positioned to become a supporter of the modern conglomerate form (Little, 1979). Not only did Henderson's notion of the "experience curve" encourage executives to invest in market share, but it also encouraged their diversification into industries that exhibited similar returns to scale. And aiding these executives' analysis of potential acquisitions and divestitures was Henderson's other famous model, the "growth/share matrix" that integrated the experience curve with an analysis of growth markets in order to promote the use of internal cash flow to invest in potential industry "stars" (Seeger, 1984, p. 95).

The growth share matrix, which segmented the product divisions of large companies into four quadrants based on the two dimensions of market share and market growth, gave the executives within multidivisional companies a simple tool to model their corporate portfolio based on a simplified analysis of cash flow (Wind & Mahajan, 1981). The immediate benefits of The BCG's model, moreover, grew in proportion to the scale and diversity of the corporation itself. As Michael Allen, a vice president and "planner" at General Electric noted in 1979, "previously all companies had the know-how of allocating capital in a single product business, which was quite inadequate for resource allocations between different industries" (Thackray, 1979, p. F4; see also Allen, 1979). It is not surprising, therefore, that General Electric, one of the earliest proponents of the growth/share matrix, was also one of the largest conglomerates in the United States – and thereby became the most reliant on formalized models to guide its corporate strategy for diversification (Wind & Mahajan, 1981).

By focusing not on reorganizing the structure of a company but on rethinking its corporate strategy, the BCG showed its clients which businesses were "dogs," which were "cash cows," and which were "stars" in the growth/share matrix (Catry & Chevalier, 1974; Lieberman, 1987). And, like the other strategy tools that BCG pioneers, the growth/share matrix did not require expertise in the industry – either for the clients or for the executives who followed this strategy. With this new focus on corporate strategy, and not simply corporate structure, the work of management consultants began to parallel that of investment bankers since consultants recommended that clients divest themselves of divisions that were "dogs" and buy existing companies that were "stars," a choice made possible by their common multidivisional structure.[20] Of course, even as BCG was expanding, rival management consulting firms were also creating their own models to guide the leading conglomerates. In 1981, when Robin Wensley wrote about the "boxes" employed by consultants to analyze the impact of market share versus growth, his analysis would cover not only BCG's model but also Arthur D. Little's and McKinsey's competing growth share matrices (Wensley, 1981). These models, moreover, were not simply academic exercises but the very real basis for corporate strategy formulation. For example, during the late 1960s, the consultants in McKinsey & Company provided detailed advice for Sun Oil on what companies to acquire and how to integrate the acquired company into their existing decentralized organizational structure while the consultants at Cresap McCormick & Paget were advising Lukens Steel on the purchase of fastener companies in order to diversify the company's product lines.[21] Thus, the management consulting firms helped to feed the merger and acquisition boom in the late 1960s, during the famous "Go-Go Years," by advising their clients on how to diversify their business lines to resemble the rapidly growing conglomerate corporations (Brooks, 1973; Lubatkin, 1983).

By the mid-1970s, the energy crisis and the extended recession of the early 1970s made the U.S. business system appear less worthy of emulation. In response, the consultants from the BCG and McKinsey & Company began promoting organizational models imported from Japan to their American and European clients who were struggling against the apparently superior management methods of Asian manufacturers. In particular, the consultants from the BCG had the advantage over McKinsey & Company because BCG had established its first overseas office in Tokyo in 1966, five years before McKinsey & Company first opened its office in Japan. It was in Europe, however, that consultants found their most lucrative market by advising governments on industrial policy in response to foreign competition.

THE STRATEGY OF THE STATE: THE EUROPEAN MARKET FOR CONSULTANTS

In contrast to growth in conglomerate assignments in the United States, as corporate demand for American consultants dried up in Western Europe during the early 1970s, the competition for public sector consulting assignments intensified (Randall, 1970). As their reputation grew during the 1960s,

American consultants shifted from working for the subsidiaries of giant multinationals (IBM, Shell, and Hoover) to decentralizing European corporations (ICI, Rhône-Poulenc, and Geigy) in the mid-1960s, and then to reorganizing large government departments (British Rail, BBC, and the Bank of England) in the late 1960s. By the early 1970s, paralleling developments in the United States during 1950s and 1960s, European governments had become a significant customer of the American consultancies (The Times, 1972a). The importance of state assignments increased still further as corporate customers cut back on their use of consultants during the extended recession following the energy crisis in the 1970s.

In the early 1970s, British officials began to employ American consulting firms not simply to reorganize the administration of government departments, but to evaluate "objectively" the economic performance of industrial sectors (Corina, 1971; The Times, 1972a, p. 18). Between 1970 and 1975, for example, McKinsey & Company surveyed the economic viability of the British automobile industry, Booz Allen & Hamilton studied the commercial prospects of the British shipbuilding industry, and, infamously, the BCG evaluated the international market for the British motorcycle industry (The Times, 1972b, 1975a, 1975b). Not surprisingly, the ministers in the Department of Trade and Industry decided to employ consultants to analyze state-owned enterprises just when bipartisan support in parliament for nationalization vanished as deficits surged (Wickham-Jones, 1996; Wilson, 1979). Each successive consulting study of a national industry, therefore, served as an implicit referendum on whether particular British industries should be supported by the state (The Times, 1974). British cabinet ministers, faced with limited means to fund their growing portfolio of troubled companies, learned how to shift the blame for closing troubled factories from themselves to the consultants (Wickham-Jones, 1996, p. 99). Although a potentially lucrative market for management consulting as legitimacy, American consultants soon began to wonder whether these public assignments, despite the depressed market for consulting, were really worth the inevitable notoriety.

The American consulting firms naturally differed on their estimates of the value of these high-profile assignments. For example, while McKinsey may have gained more than it lost from its reorganization of the Bank of England (in 1972, McKinsey would bid to reorganize the World Bank in part based on the firm's international experience at the Bank of England and Royal Dutch Shell), the firm became increasingly wary of public sector assignments (Galambos & Milobsky, 1995). In comparison, for a rising consultancy like the BCG, the immediate benefit in accepting a high-profile assignment in Britain, where the firm was still relatively unknown, was too appealing to forego even if it opened the firm to potential criticism. In particular, the consultants from BCG expected that they could avoid much of the potential controversy in their study of the British motorcycle industry since the British government did not ask them to provide a conclusive opinion but instead to offer a range of potential strategic options (House of Commons, 1975). As it turned out, the BCG consultants underestimated the potential risks since their study of the British motorcycle industry eventually became the most famous and controversial case in the history of management consulting when prominent management theorists later criticized its emphasis on what they argued was a linear view of business strategy (Mintzberg, 1996). Yet, even if one accepts the academic criticism of BCG's report, the BCG study also foreshadowed the crucial trends that would come to dominate management consulting over the next decade (Mair, 1999).

The BCG's report on the British motorcycle industry combined three distinct elements that would become increasingly influential among consultants during the 1970s and early 1980s: a focus on competitive strategy and not just administrative structure; the use of explicit theoretical models (including the "experience curve," which showed that the Japanese motorcycle manufacturers had beaten their British rivals through the volume of their production); and, lastly, a detailed analysis of the apparently superior Japanese system that had overtaken the American model (Ghemawat, 2002b). As historian Robert Locke has argued, European preoccupation with the American corporate model only disappeared when the Japanese "economic miracle" was touted during the early 1980s: "for Europeans *le défi américain* had turned into the *le défi japonais*" (Locke, 1996).

STRATEGY AS LEGITIMACY: RETURNING TO THE ROOTS OF MANAGEMENT CONSULTING

In the late 1970s, the partners at McKinsey responded to almost a decade of turmoil by reexamining the consultancy's past successes – the firm's professional growth and culture – through a series of firm histories, in order to plan for the future (Bower, 1979, pp. x–xi; Business Week, 1973b; Neukom, 1975; The New York Times, 1973; The Wall Street Journal, 1976a). Equally important were initiatives undertaken by the younger partners to analyze what rival consulting firms were doing and to propose new "products" that the consultants from McKinsey could offer (McKinsey & Company, 1981). Although the McKinsey consultants had scrambled to catch up the BCG's innovative strategy practice, McKinsey's own internal studies agreed with industry analysts like James Kennedy of *Consultants News* that the BCG had "taken the initiative away from McKinsey" (Thackray, 1979, Sect. 3, 4). As Michael Porter described McKinsey & Company's dilemma in 1979:

> ... partly as a result of BCG's [The Boston Consulting Group's] success, managers are very interested in concepts. BCG has had something specific to say to people, rather than having a client betting on its competence. McKinsey has reacted to that, by setting up a bunch of task forces within the firm to try and pull together their practice and codify what they've learned.[22] (Hayes, 1979)

So, instead of repeatedly protesting that the early versions of BCG's "matrix strategy analysis and the product portfolio ... were developed by McKinsey," or that BCG's oversimplified frameworks were "a poor mirror of the real world," the consultants from McKinsey & Company began to create and promoted its own simplified, copyrighted models (Thackray, 1979, p. 4). In particular, the McKinsey 7-S[©] framework was the most influential product from this initiative (Pascale & Athos, 1986, p. 9). Popularized by Tom Peters and Bob Waterman's *In Search of Excellence*, the 7-S[©] model for analyzing corporate strategy, would bring McKinsey tremendous prominence during the early 1980s as the experts on "corporate culture" based in large part on the internal culture of the consulting firm itself (Wilson, 1994). As a reporter from the *New York Times* explained, "in the 1960s, decentralization was the vogue in management. In the 1970s, corporate strategy became the buzzword. Now, corporate culture is the magic phrase that management consultants are breathing the ears of American executives" (Salmans, 1983). Yet, corporate culture was not the crucial concept that saved McKinsey & Company as the consulting firm had hoped. Instead, the most important development for management consultants during the 1980s did not arise from within their firms but from the external regulatory environment – the rapid return of the "management audit," a consulting product that had gone out of fashion more than forty years earlier.

When the consultants from McKinsey began investigating their own history in order to find new products for their corporate clients, they never returned to the roots of consulting in the 1930s but instead looked at the origins of their own corporate culture in the 1950s. The irony is that had they looked another twenty years earlier in their history, they would have rediscovered the "management audit," a product that later dominated management consulting through the end of the twentieth century. The "management audit," a variation of the "management survey," was not, however, a new way to introduce knowledge into a company but a much older means, first employed during the 1930s, for corporate executives to avoid legal liability for their actions.

In the aftermath of the stock market crash in 1929, American legislators, concerned that corporate executives had been negligent in their duties, created a host of new financial regulations and the SEC in order to stiffen the legal liability of corporate boards (Douglas & Bates, 1933; Manne, 1962). In response, the directors and officers of American corporations addressed the new regulatory requirements of the New Deal legislation by hiring accountants, investment bankers, and consultants to certify that their actions were both legal and prudent (Allen, 1940; Freedman, 1983; Rohrlich, 1935). In particular, the early management consulting firms produced "general surveys" or, by another name, "management audits," that paralleled the "financial audits" produced by the accountants and the "valuation reports" produced by investment bankers. The "management audit," like a financial audit, did not bring new methods into the firm or seek to change the way that a firm was run, but rather served as independent, external confirmation of management's judgment (Markham, 2003). Corporate boards quickly concluded, with a not-so-gentle push from the SEC, that their first line of defense against increased legal liability would be to pay, "experts such as accountants, engineers, and appraisers whose professions give authority to their statements" to certify their actions according to William Douglas (who succeeded James Landis as Chairman of the S.E.C.) (Brooks, 1969; Douglas & Bates, 1933; Murphy, 2003). During the 1930s, boards of directors shrewdly marshaled the legitimacy of professional opinion, in part through the use of management consultants, to reduce their potential liability in the face of increased regulation.

In the early 1940s, however, corporate boards began to employ an even more straightforward device to protect themselves from shareholder lawsuits: liability insurance. The immediate result was a rapid increase in the number of corporations purchasing indemnity insurance for their officers. As an article in the *Harvard Business Review* explained:

> In 1938, stockholders had not heard of agreements for general indemnification of directors and officers for expenses incurred by them in connection with litigation to which they might become subject by virtue of their corporate positions. The few proposals made in 1939 and 1940 were shown in 1941 to have been merely the precursors

of a fad that a host of corporations would scramble to adopt. (Bates & Zuckert, 1942, p. 244; Frampton, 1958)

What have initially seemed a "fad" for the provision of directors' indemnity insurance, or "directors and officers (D&O) liability insurance" as it would come to be known, soon became a *de facto* corporate policy for the protection of executives in large corporations (Baxter, 1995; Romano, 1989). With the introduction of insurance policies to bear the potential risks of litigation, the use of professionals, like management consultants, as a hedge against legal liability faded away except where federal and state laws explicitly required their use. As the percentage of American public corporations holding directors' and officers' liability insurance rose, an increasing number of insurance companies began offering D&O coverage (Bishop, 1968). With few corporate lawsuits and even fewer guilty verdicts against directors and officers, there seemed to be little reason to worry about corporate liability. Management consultants returned to selling advice, not due diligence, as their primary product, until the next crisis in American corporate governance more than forty years later.

Corporate executives were initially right not to be concerned about their exposure to corporate liability, because they were generally well protected from litigation by the "business judgment rule." As Marvin Bower, the consultant who would go on to re-found McKinsey & Company in the late 1930s, explained to the readers of the *Harvard Business Review* in 1931, "fortunately, the law has so developed that the honest and careful director can usually avoid personal liability without keeping counsel constantly by his side" (Bower, 1931). In essence, the business judgment rule that evolved in American common law presumed, as the courts interpreted the concept, that "in making a business decision the directors of a corporation acted on an informed basis, in good faith, and in the honest belief that the action taken was in the best interest of the company" (*Aronson v. Lewis*, 1984). Thus, dissident stockholders challenging executives' actions could not base their claim on the economic outcome but instead had to challenge the legal presumption that the board of directors had acted in good faith and to the best of their abilities in reaching a decision (Gilson, 1986; Manne, 1967; Williamson, 1991). For most of the twentieth century, the business judgment rule turned on the process of corporate decision making, therefore board members could be held liable for mistakes only if shareholders could prove that the board had demonstrated gross negligence. In 1985, however, just as demand for corporate culture and all Japanese things was starting to fade, the issue of directors' and officers' liability insurance would become a national crisis when a board of directors was found negligent in a prominent legal decision that led to a full-blown crisis in corporate governance (Herzel & Katz, 1986; Hilder, 1985).

STRATEGY AS AN AUDIT OF CORPORATE GOVERNANCE

In 1985, the Delaware Supreme Court ruled that the board of directors of the Trans Union Corporation had failed to exercise "informed business judgment" in approving the acquisition of the company in 1980 by Jay Pritzker, the billionaire whose family built the Hyatt Hotel chain (*Smith v. Van Gorkom*, 1985; The Wall Street Journal, 1980).[23] In particular, in the precedent-setting *Smith v. Van Gorkom* case, the Delaware Supreme Court overruled the lower Chancery Court that despite an emergency two-hour meeting by the board of directors and despite the fact that Pritzker's offer price was significantly above the stock market price, the board members were "grossly negligent" in approving the sale of the company (*Smith v. Van Gorkom*, 1985, p. 874). As Bayliss Manning, former Dean of the Stanford Law School, described the resulting turmoil, the court's decision in the Van Gorkom case had "exploded a bomb" (Manning, 1985). Stunned corporate lawyers, searching for a way to insulate their clients against potential liability, seized upon the court's criticism of the Trans Union board for not seeking outside advice (Manning jokingly referred to this decision as the "Investment Bankers' Relief Act of 1985") even though the justices claimed that external studies were *not* essential "to support an informed business judgment" (Manning, 1985, p. 3; *Smith v. Van Gorkom*, 1985, p. 876). Jonathan Macy and Geoffrey Miller explained in the *Yale Law Journal* that as a practical matter the Van Gorkom decision virtually guaranteed the increased "use of investment bankers and lawyers in corporate decision making" (Macey & Miller, 1988).[24]

It was not only investment bankers and lawyers, however, who benefited, since one of the key pieces of evidence used by the dissenting justice to show that the Trans Union board had exercised "informed business judgment" was the fact that less than two months earlier, "the board had reviewed and discussed an outside study of the company done by The Boston Consulting Group" (*Smith v. Van Gorkom*, 1985, p. 897). As lawyers from Wachtell Lipton, echoing comments from other leading law firms, would announce to a staff reporter from *The Wall Street Journal*, "this decision underscores once again the critical need for the retention of independent experts" (Bleakely, 1985; Koenig, 1985). In short, by toughening the standard interpretation of the business judgment rule in 1985, the Delaware court had resuscitated the dormant logic of the "management audit" that had once been the central product of the leading management consulting firms during the 1930s.

The Van Gorkom decision quickly led to a national crisis in the United States over corporate liability insurance. Emboldened by the judgment, American corporate lawyers launched a barrage of class action lawsuits against public companies with the result that between 1984 and 1987, the number of lawsuits against directors and officers rose by a factor of five and the associated monetary judgments rose by 750 percent (Trieschmann & Leverett, 1990). The editors of *The Wall Street Journal* explained the subsequent chain of events in an editorial criticizing the new legal standard:

> The problem began with the Delaware Supreme Court rule last year in *Smith vs. Van Gorkom* ... The 10 directors were held liable for $23.5 million, only $10 million of which was covered by insurance. The rest would have come out of their pockets if the Pritzkers hadn't picked up the tab. Premiums skyrocketed when insurers realized that directors could be held personally liable even when their corporation is sold at a huge profit. (The Wall Street Journal, 1986b)

The problem, however, was not simply that insurance companies increased their premiums but that for some corporations, in industries where shareholder lawsuits had been decided against corporate executives, there was no available supply at any price (Huber, 1988). As the *New York Times* reported, despite significantly reduced coverage and premiums rates that rose as much as tenfold, "... in certain industries – such as steel, petroleum, and electronics – there may be a problem simply finding an insurer" (Lewin, 1986). Even though corporations had no choice but to pay the higher rates for directors' and officers' liability insurance, many of the large insurance companies withdrew from the market for D&O insurance, canceled long-standing policies, and forced large corporations to self-insure (Harrington, 1988; The Wall Street Journal, 1985b, 1985c; Winter, 1991).

With corporations unable to offer boards of directors adequate liability coverage to cover the increase in shareholder lawsuits, outside directors began to defect (Perkins, 1986). In September 1985, for example, the chairman of the board and six external directors resigned from the eleven-member board of Continental Steel when the corporation ceased to carry D&O liability insurance because, in the words of the corporate spokesman, "the cost of providing the coverage wasn't 'economically viable' " (The Wall

Street Journal, 1985a). To the rich and powerful executives who remained on the boards of the largest American companies, their financial exposure to unlimited personal liability was simply unacceptable and the directors and officers of the giant corporations were willing to pay a great deal for some – even any – form of personal protection (Cooter, 1991). So, corporate boards once again embraced the "management audit" of the 1930s to protect themselves from possible liability.

Corporations dealt with the D&O liability crisis by pursuing three parallel lines of defense: purchasing what little insurance they could, pushing their legislatures for tort reform, and employing external professional counsel (Slaughter, 1987).[25] Executives bought as much insurance as they could at the newly inflated rates. Contemporary accounts make clear, however, that what D&O insurance was available was simply not enough to cover the potential liability that boards faced. As a leading insurance broker from Alexander & Alexander explained in 1986, "where it used to be possible to get $200 million of coverage for a client, it would now be an outstanding feat to put together $35 million" (Lewin, 1986). Meanwhile, companies began to agitate for new legislation and revised corporate statutes to limit their exposure. In Delaware, for example, the state legislature quickly passed a new law that allowed shareholders to vote to "exempt outside directors from liability [in order to] reduce director liability and thus the cost of premiums" (The Wall Street Journal, 1985b). Eventually, the clamor for tort reform that began in the aftermath of the Van Gorkom decision would result in the American Congress passing the Private Securities Reform Act of 1995 and the Securities Litigation Uniform Standards Act of 1998 in order to reduce the number of class action lawsuits by corporate shareholders.[26] Nevertheless, directors and officers solicited external opinions on their important corporate decisions since, as the Van Gorkom decision had made clear, the courts did not consider a two-month-old study from The BCG to be relevant. With increased liability came the natural instinct to offset potential losses by increasing corporate legitimacy through outside affirmation of specific internal decisions (The Wall Street Journal, 1986a). The "Strategic Audit," what Gordon Donaldson, in the *Harvard Business Review,* called a "new tool," for corporate boards to lessen their liability, was in fact a very old idea rediscovered by executives and academics when the need arose once again (Donaldson, 1995).

Where management consultants had previously proposed a suggested course of action to be ratified by independent board members – whether an organizational design, an acquisition strategy, or a new perspective on corporate culture – the tables were turned during the late 1980s and early

1990s, when consultants, in practice, became the independent outsiders who endorsed the "internal" board's previous decisions. Management consulting advice, of course, had always been used as a political tool to legitimate executive decisions, but, beginning in the late 1980s, consultants' role in conferring legitimacy began to be more openly employed as a legal hedge against corporate liability (Mallen & Evans, 1987). In particular, two influential cases in American corporate law involving Fortune 500 corporations illustrate how corporate boards came to depend on management consultants to prove that the directors had exercised good judgment in their decisions. In the first case, the Delaware Chancery Court (subsequently upheld on appeal) ruled in *QVC v. Paramount* (1993) that the board of directors of QVC had been negligent in approving a merger with Paramount. The court based its decision, in part, on evidence that the QVC Board of Directors had relied upon a Booz Allen & Hamilton report that was only a preliminary "first cut" and not an exhaustive analysis of the benefits that would come from the proposed merger (Fabrikant, 1993; *QVC Network v. Paramount Communications*, 1993). In the second case, the Superior Court of North Carolina ruled in *First Union v. Suntrust Banks* (2001) that the board of directors of Wachovia Bank had conclusively demonstrated good judgment in pursuing a merger with First Union. The court based its decision on evidence that the Wachovia Bank Board of Directors had followed the corporate strategy outlined in a McKinsey & Company report that included the consultants' analysis of a possible merger with First Union (*First Union v. Suntrust Banks*, 2001). Thus, both cases made it clear that a board of directors needed to commission a management consulting study – preferably exhaustive – of any significant strategic decision. When the board of directors relied only on their own judgment or an outdated or incomplete report – as in Trans Union's reliance on an old BCG report in 1985 or QVC's use of a preliminary study by Booz Allen in 1993 – the directors could well be found negligent (Cowan, 1993; Mollenkamp, 2001; Norris, 1993). It is no wonder that during the 1990s, American corporations like AT&T hired management consultants with abandon, since consulting reports came with the added bonus that they also represented a form of insurance against shareholder lawsuits (Byrne, 1994).

In general, professional expertise functioned as promised and most lawyers counseled disgruntled shareholders who brought suits against corporate boards to settle the case quickly if a leading consulting firm had backed up the board's decision. Those cases that did go to court were generally dismissed (Quinn & Levin, 2001). As a result, insurance under-writers offered the leading strategy consulting firms far better terms for

professional liability insurance than other professional service firms since
strategy consultants were the least likely to be found guilty in a shareholder
lawsuit (Skapinker, 2002). Conversely, with consulting studies from
McKinsey, Bain, BCG, or Booz Allen serving to bolster the business
judgment rule, executives understood that the exorbitant fees they paid were
as much a premium for corporate liability insurance as a direct payment for
consulting advice. Thus, management consultants had come full circle to
provide the same service nearly fifty years after they first emerged as
professional gatekeepers during the corporate governance crisis of the
1930s. Where in the 1950s, consultants offered strategy in the tangible form
of organizational structure, and during the 1960s and 1970s they sold
strategy as a form of intellectual justification, in the 1980s and 1990s they
returned to selling strategy as a form of corporate insurance. Strategy, as
reconfigured by management consultants, would take many forms depending on the needs of executives.

EMBEDDING STRATEGY IN MARKETS

The title of this chapter, "strategy followed structure," is meant to invoke
three separate references, only two of which may be immediately obvious to
readers. The first, of course, is Alfred Chandler's famous dictum, that
"structure follows strategy," upon which the academic field of strategy was
founded and we now understand as the underlying logic for the emergence
of the multidivisional form in the 1920s and its dissemination during the
1950s and 1960s. The second is the historical reality that the demand among
the large American corporations in the 1950s, and later their European
cousins in the 1960s, for the multidivisional form meant that consulting
firms like McKinsey & Company were first concerned with organizational
"structure" and only later did the new corporate "strategy" consulting firms
like BCG emerge during the 1960s. But there is a third reference that only a
few readers may immediately recognize – an article by Tom Peters, when he
still published under the name "Thomas J. Peters," in the *California
Management Review* entitled: "Strategy Follows Structure." In that long
forgotten article, Peters argued that existing corporate structures were as
much at the heart of strategy as theoretical predictions of future markets
(Peters, 1984). But in a particularly telling section of the article, Peters
chronicled his own professional and intellectual trajectory as a consultant –
a career path that intersected with the most volatile years in the evolution of

strategy as a new academic discipline and the emergence of strategy consulting as a mainstream institution.

In 1976, when Thomas Peters returned to McKinsey & Company after completing a Ph.D. in business at Stanford, he was asked by McKinsey's new managing director, Ronald Daniel, to study "the next generation of organizational structure." (Peters, 1984, p. 114) This was the era when McKinsey & Company, in Peters' words, was:

> ... going will-nilly down the path of becoming a "strategy boutique," in response to competitive threats (the first ones in the company's history) from the Boston Consulting Group and Bain & Company. Indeed, McKinsey in the mid seventies was populated by young men almost entirely enamored with the nuances of the ideological debate going on amongst strategists – the Porter view, the PIMs view, and the McKinsey (or GE) portfolio/nine box, versus the BCG/four box versus the ADL/24 box.[27] (Peters, 1984, p. 114)

McKinsey's new managing director hoped that Tom Peters could explain why the new organizational structure (the matrix) that McKinsey had recommended to its clients was not working and how the consulting firm could continue to be a leader in "radical decentralization" as the means to achieve lasting competitive advantage. Peters would then go on to chronicle how, in responding to this assignment, he and his partner, Bob Waterman, sought to move beyond the "simple structure-strategy-systems" formulation to understand basis of "excellent" corporations in their corporate culture. In short, Tom Peter's summary of the project that he began, at roughly the halfway mark of the fifty-year span of this chapter, captured two of the three epochs in the changing use of strategy consulting by corporate executives. What Peters could not see in 1984, was that in trying to move past the systems approach to strategy to embrace corporate culture, he and his partners had missed the potential return of the "strategic system" of corporate legitimacy. Indeed, during the second half of the twentieth century, the arc of strategy had moved from strategy expressed as structure, to strategy expressed as models, to strategy expressed as legitimacy and in each era management consultants, responding to regulatory changes, quickly addressed the needs of corporate executives for these new forms of strategy.

In the second half of the twentieth century, like any human practice, strategy constantly evolved to suit the needs of its time. Management consultants, eager to seek out new markets, refashioned strategy to suit the contemporary needs of corporate executives from the "organization man" of the 1950s concerned with corporate structure to the "boardroom executives" of the 1990s concerned with legal liability. Yet, over this fifty-year cycle, corporate executives and the leading strategy consultants were intellectually flexible enough to successfully recreate strategy to suit the tenor of the times. Instead, it was the academic strategists who became locked into a particular construction of "strategy" from mid-1960s when it first emerged in Bruce Henderson's pronouncements in his "Perspectives." Like a satellite launched into stratospheric orbit, the academic discipline of strategy became locked into a theoretical trajectory even as new practical uses of strategy evolved in the world below. High above the world, strategists may still believe that their theoretical models hold true, but for those consultants who inhabit the earth below, strategy has always been, and always will be, first and foremost a pragmatic business with strategy its core product.

NOTES

1. For the broader influence of the consulting firms on the development of strategy, see Kiechel (2010).
2. For a broad history of competitive strategy, see Ghemawat (2002a). For specific strategy models, see Hambrick, MacMillan, and Day (1982) and Bracker, (1980).
3. For a similar evolutionary process in the development of the credit card industry, see Huseyin Leblebici's analysis in this volume.
4. The strong historical links between the needs of merchant banks and the services of management consulting firms are more fully described in McKenna (2006). This article draws heavily on that previous book.
5. Although the contemporary term was "management engineering," in the late 1940s, under pressure from engineers in New York who complained that management "engineers" frequently lacked professional training in engineering and lacked an engineer's license, leading firms like McKinsey & Company increasingly adopted the term "management consultant" to describe themselves. Thus, the description "management engineering" or "management consulting" can be used interchangeably without historical imprecision.
6. Columbia University economist Joel Dean (1938) noted the rapid growth of management engineering in *The Harvard Business Review*. For an industry perspective available to executives at Lukens, see Bankers Monthly (1941).
7. For the distinction between Taylorists and these management experts, see Aitken (1960).
8. Edwin Booz, the founder of Booz Allen & Hamilton, also specialized in general surveys. In 1924, Booz changed the description on his office door from "Business Engineering Service" to "Business Surveys" (Bowman, 1984).
9. For IBM's decentralization, see Watson and Petre (1990). For Cresap's work for Westinghouse, see Fortune (1952). On the reorganizations of Chrysler, see Reich and Donahue (1985).
10. By 1967, 86 percent of the 500 largest U.S. companies had adopted the multidivisional model (Wrigley, 1970).
11. Microfilm, Cresap Archives, Chandler (1962, p. 325).

12. As Marvin Bower, the Managing Director of McKinsey & Company and the architect of McKinsey's expansion into Europe, wrote in February 1960, "Our *secondary* objective [after 'serving American business overseas'] is to serve European business enterprises – to the degree that they are interested in our unique services. We are *not* trying to 'sell them service' and therefore looking for what they will 'buy.'" Marvin Bower to Gil Clee, "Developing our European Practice," 5 February 1960, *Supplement to Perspective on McKinsey* (Mimeographed, McKinsey & Company, 1979), 20 [italics in original].

13. Quotation from Dyas and Thanheiser (1976, p. 112). Unfortunately, no comparable estimates exist on the number companies divisionalized by McKinsey & Company in France, Switzerland, or the Netherlands.

14. McKinsey's directors decided not to open an office in Spain during the mid-1960s because Marvin Bower, with Gil Clee, argued that Spain's position outside the European Common Market and the risk of operating under a dictatorship mitigated the potential gains from establishing yet another European office. It was, for a time, the source of some disagreement within the firm (Bower, 1969, pp. 111–112).

15. This is based on an estimated 10,000 practicing management consultants in 1950 (Association of Consulting Management Engineers, Inc. (ACME), 1964, Table 4). See also Management Review (1954) and Business Week (1965).

16. In the late 1950s, the general survey began to fall out of everyday use although an outline of it appeared in McKinsey & Co.'s training manual as late as 1962 (Wolf, 1978, p. 52).

17. Allen Stewart notes for "A McKinsey Scrapbook." Corporate Archives, McKinsey & Company.

18. Hugh Parker notes for "A McKinsey Scrapbook," Corporate Archives, McKinsey & Company.

19. McKinsey & Company, "All Offices: Analysis of Practice by Type of Study, F/Y 1959-1965 Incl." See also, McKinsey & Company, "Dollar Distribution of Total Billings among Industrial Categories: Fiscal Year 1966 Through 1970 Inclusive," 1971, both in Corporate Archives, McKinsey & Company, New York.

20. So similar was McKinsey & Co.'s work and culture to investment banking that the Directors of McKinsey and Co. seriously considered a merger with the elite Wall Street firm of Donaldson, Lufkin & Jenrette. They were stopped only by an impassioned plea by the retired Managing Director, Marvin Bower, who had worked for thirty years to keep McKinsey & Co. independent (Bower, pp. 288–289). See also Bower (1982) and Reed and Luffman (1986).

21. The reports for Sun Oil prepared by McKinsey & Co. between 1965 and 1969 are deposited in Archives and Manuscripts at the Hagley Museum and Library, Acquisition 1317, Series 1e, box 339. Although the records of Cresap, McCormick & Paget's first study of the "Markets for Heads and Job Stampings" survive (see note 93), the records of their subsequent study have not survived in Lukens' corporate archives deposited at the Hagley Museum and Library. The reports that Cresap, McCormick & Paget prepared, however, do survive in the archives of Towers Perrin, the corporate successor to Cresap, McCormick & Paget, in Valhalla, New York. See Cresap, McCormick, and Paget (1968).

22. Michael Porter would find his own strategy consulting firm, Monitor, just three years later.

23. Trans Union is one the three leading companies (alongside Equifax and Experian/TRW) that sell consumer credit reports in the United States.

24. In retrospect, however, at least one subsequent study could not firmly establish whether the number of "Fairness Opinions" really increased or not, see Bowers (2002).

25. For nonlawyers, a "tort," under the law, is when someone has been held liable for damages that are the result of an injury to a person or property that is not a criminal act nor based on a contract.

26. Pub. L. No. 104-67, 109 Stat. 737 (1995); Joseph A. Grundfest and Michael A. Perino, "Ten Things We Know and Ten Things We Don't Know About the Private Security Reform Act of 1995," Joint written testimony before the Subcommittee on Securities of the Committee on Banking, Housing and Urban Affairs, United States Senate, 24 July 1997; Lerach (1998).

27. Tom Peter's, of course, is wrong that these competitive threats were the first significant ones in McKInsey's history, but the important point here is his perspective (and those of his colleagues) in the 1970s that this was the first time that their consulting firm had been threatened by significant competitors.

REFERENCES

Aitken, H. G. J. (1960). *Scientific management in action: Taylorism at watertown arsenal, 1908–1915* (pp. 17–18). Princeton, NJ: Princeton University Press.

Allen, J. (Ed.). (1940). *Democracy and finance: The addresses and public statements of William O. Douglas as member and chairman of the securities and exchange commission* (pp. 175–180). New Haven, CT: Yale University Press.

Allen, M. G. (1979). Diagramming G.E.'s planning for what's WATT. In R. J. Allio & M. W. Pennington (Eds.), *Corporate planning: Techniques and applications* (pp. 211–220). New York: AMACOM.

Andress, F. J. (1954). The learning curve as a production tool. *Harvard Business Review, 32*(January–February), 87–97.

Aronson v. Lewis, 473 A2.d 805, 812 (Del. Sup. 1984).

Arthur Young & Company. (1982). Management consulting – its history and potential: A study of the marketplace. *Mimeograph* (pp. 4–5). New York: Arthur Young & Company.

Association of Consulting Management Engineers, Inc. (ACME). (1964). *Numerical data on the present dimensions, growth, and other trends in management consulting in the United States* (Table 2). New York, NY: ACME.

Bankers Monthly. (1941). Management engineers help renew borrower's earnings. *Bankers Monthly*, March (Reprinted by George S. May Company in file 14, box 2019, Lukens Steel).

Bates, G. E., & Zuckert, E. M. (1942). Directors' indemnity: Corporate policy or public policy? *Harvard Business Review, 20*, 244.

Baxter, C. (1995). Demystifying D&O insurance. *Oxford Journal of Legal Studies, 15*(4), 557–558.

Berg, N. (1965). Strategic planning in conglomerate companies. *Harvard Business Review, 43*(3), 79–92.

Bishop, J. W., Jr. (1968). Sitting ducks and decoy ducks: New trends in the indemnification of corporate directors and officers. *The Yale Law Journal, 77*(6), 1078.

Bleakely, F. R. (1985). Business judgement case finds directors liable. *The New York Times*, January 31, pp. D1–D4.

Bower, J. L. (1982). Business policy in the 1980s. *Academy of Management Review, 7*(4), 630–638.

Bower, M. (1931). Becoming a director – A business honor or a financial boomerang? *Harvard Business Review, 9*(April), 372.

Bower, M. (1979). *Perspective on McKinsey* (pp. 111–112). New York: McKinsey & Co. Inc.

Bowers, H. M. (2002). Fairness opinions and the business judgement rule: An empirical investigation of target firms' use of fairness opinions. *Northwestern University Law Review, 96*(2), 567–578.

Bowman, J. (1984). *Booz Allen & Hamilton: Seventy years of client service, 1914–1984* (p. 7). Chicago, IL: Booz Allen & Hamilton.

Bracker, J. (1980). The historical development of the strategic management concept. *Academy of Management Review, 5*(2), 219–224.

Brooks, J. (1969). *Once in Golconda: A true drama of wall street, 1920–1938* (pp. 241–242). New York, NY: Harper & Row.

Brooks, J. (1973). *The go-go years: The drama and crashing finale of Wall Street's bullish 60s* (pp. 233–234). New York: Wiley.

Business Week. (1965). What management consultants can do. *Business Week*, January 23, p. 88.

Business Week. (1973a). Selling business a theory of economics. *Business Week*, September 8, pp. 85–90.

Business Week. (1973b). Surprise at McKinsey: Walton steps down. *Business Week*, April 28, pp. 44–45.

Business Week. (1973c). The consultants face a competition crisis. *Business Week*, November 17, p. 72.

Byrne, J. A. (1994). The craze for consultants. *Business Week*, July 25, p. 60.

Catry, B., & Chevalier, M. (1974). Market share strategy and the product life cycle. *Journal of Marketing, 38*(4), 29–34.

Chandler, A. D., Jr. (1962). *Strategy and structure: Chapters in the history of the American industrial enterprise*. Cambridge, MA: MIT Press.

Channon, D. F. (1973). *Strategy and structure of British enterprise* (p. 239). London: Macmillan.

Coffee, J. C. (2006). *Gatekeepers: The professions and corporate governance*. New York: Oxford University Press.

Cooter, R. D. (1991). Economic theories of legal liability. *Journal of Economic Perspectives, 5*(3), 18.

Corina, M. (1971). Consultants stalking Whitehall's corridors. *The Times*, January 26, p. 17.

Cowan, A. L. (1993). Caution signal for corporate boards. *The New York Times*, November 25, p. D6.

Cresap, McCormick, & Paget. (November 1968). *Lukens steel company: A plan for growth by corporate acquisition, Phase I*, 3–4, microfilm, Towers Perrin Corporate Archives.

Dean, J. (1938). The place of management counsel in business. *The Harvard Business Review, 16*(4), 451–465.

DiMaggio, P. J., & Powell, W. W. (1983). 'The iron cage revisited:' Institutional isomorphism and collective rationality in organizational fields. *American Sociological Review, 48*(April), 147–160(Quotation from page 153).

Donaldson, G. (1995). A new tool for boards: The strategic audit. *Harvard Business Review*, *73*(July/August), 99–107.

Dougherty, P. (1969). Advertising: A cookie that didn't crumble. *The New York Times*, May 23, p. 62.

Douglas, W. O., & Bates, G. E. (1933). The Federal Securities Act of 1933. *The Yale Law Journal*, *43*(2), 195.

Drucker, P. F. (1964). *The concept of the corporation*. New York, NY: Mentor Executive Library.

Dyas, G., & Thanheiser, H. (1976). *The emerging European enterprise* (p. 112). London: Macmillan.

Engle, A. (1959). Organisation and management planning in the royal Dutch/Shell group. In R. S. Edwards & H. Townsend (Eds.), *Business enterprise: Its growth and organisation* (pp. 348–353). London: Macmillan.

Fabrikant, G. (1993). Delaware court ruling aids QVC in struggle to acquire paramount. *The New York Times*, December 10, p. A1.

Fiedler-Winter, R. (1974). Divisionalisierung als Hilfsmittel: Beratung als Assistenz – Unruhe Unvermeidlich. *Management International Review*, *14*(6), 96.

Financial Times. (1971). Gloom sets in as squeeze hits consultants. *Financial Times*, March 5, p. 17.

First Union v. Suntrust Banks, WL 1885686 (N.C.Super.), 25, 35 (2001).

Fortune. (1952). *Fortune*, December, p. 184.

Frampton, G. T. (1958). Indemnification of insider's litigation expenses. *Law and Contemporary Problems*, *23*(2), 330.

Freedman, M. V. (1983). The Securities and Exchange Commission. In K. Louchheim (Ed.), *The making of the new deal: The insiders speak* (p. 142). Cambridge: Harvard University Press.

Galambos, L., & Milobsky, D. (1995). Organizing and reorganizing the World Bank, 1946–1972: A comparative perspective. *Business History Review*, *69*(Summer), 180.

Ghemawat, P. (2002a). Competition and business strategy in historical perspective. *Business History Review*, *76*(1), 37–74.

Ghemawat, P. (2002b). Competition and business strategy in historical perspective. *Business History Review*, *76*(Spring), 45–46.

Gilson, R. (1986). *The law and finance of corporate acquisitions* (p. 741). Minneola, NY: Foundation Press.

Guillén, M. F. (1994). *Models of management: Work, authority and organization in a comparative perspective* (pp. 200–201). Chicago, IL: The University of Chicago Press.

Hambrick, D. C., MacMillan, I. C., & Day, D. L. (1982). Strategic analysis and performance in the BCG matrix – a PIMS-based analysis of industrial product business. *Academy of Management Journal*, *25*(3), 510–531.

Harrington, S. E. (1988). Prices and profits in the liability insurance market. In R. E. Litan & C. Winston (Eds.), *Liability: Perspectives and policy* (pp. 42–43). Washington, DC: The Brookings Institution.

Hayes, T. C. (1979). McKinsey & Co., problem solvers. *The New York Times*, August 19, p. D8.

Hayes, T. C. (1992). Bruce Henderson, 77, consultant and writer on business strategy. *The New York Times*, July 24, p. D16.

Hemp, P. (1991). Did greed destroy Bain? *The Boston Globe*, February 26, p. 35.

Henderson, B. D. (1998). The experience curve reviewed: History. In C. W. Stern & G. Stalk, Jr. (Eds.), *Perspectives on strategy from the Boston Consulting Group* (pp. 12–14). Wiley.

Herzel, L., & Katz, L. (1986). Smith v. Van Gorkom: The business of judging business judgment. *Business Lawyer, 41*(August), 1188–1189.

Hewes, J. E. (1975). *From root to McNamara: Army organization and administration, 1900–1963.* Washington, DC: Center of Military History, U.S. Army.

Hilder, D. B. (1985). Risky business: Liability insurance is difficult to find now for directors. *The Wall Street Journal*, 10. July, p. 1.

Hirschmann, W. B. (1964). Profit from the learning curve. *Harvard Business Review, 42*(January–February), 125–139.

House of Commons. (1975). Dramatic fall in British motor cycle exports: Further state funds for industry ruled out. *The Times*, August 1, p. 8 (The original Parliamentary debate is also available in *Hansard*).

Huber, P. W. (1988). *Liability: The legal revolution and its consequences* (p. 135). New York, NY: Basic Books.

Jones, G. (2005). *Renewing Unilever: Transformation and tradition* (pp. 46–48). New York: Oxford University Press.

Kiechel, W., III. (2010). *The lords of strategy: The secret intellectual history of the new corporate world.* Boston: Harvard Business School Press.

Kipping, M. (1999). American management consulting companies in Western Europe, 1920 to 1990: Products, reputation, and relationships. *The Business History Review, 73*(2), 190–220.

Kipping, M., & Westerhuis, G. (2012). Strategy, ideology and structure: The political processes of introducing the M-form in two Dutch banks. In S. J. Kahl, B. S. Silverman & M. A. Cusumano (Eds.), *Advances in strategic management* (Vol. 29, pp. 187–237). Bingley, UK: Emerald Group.

Koenig, R. (1985). Court rules Trans Union's directors used poor judgement in sale of firm. *The Wall Street Journal*, February 1, p. 7.

Lerach, W. S. (1998). "The Private Securities Litigation Reform Act of 1995 – 27 months later": Securities class action litigation under the Private Securities Litigation Act's Brave New World. *Washington University Law Quarterly, 76*, 597–644.

Lewin, T. (1986). Director insurance drying up. *The New York Times*, March 7, p. D1.

Lieberman, M. B. (1987). The learning curve, diffusion, and competitive strategy. *Strategic Management Journal, 8*(5), 441–452.

Little, R. (1979). *How to lose $100,000,000 and other valuable advice.* Little, Brown and Company.

Locke, R. (1996). *The collapse of the American management mystique* (p. 164). Oxford: Oxford University Press.

Lubatkin, M. (1983). Mergers and the performance of the acquiring firm. *Academy of Management Review, 8*(2), 218–225.

Macey, J. R., & Miller, G. P. (1988). Trans Union reconsidered. *The Yale Law Journal, 98*(1), 129–139.

Mair, A. (1999). Learning from Honda. *Journal of Management Studies, 36*(1), 25.

Mallen, R. D., & Evans, D. W. (1987). Surviving the directors' and officers' liability crisis: Insurance and the alternatives. *Delaware Journal of Corporate Law, 12*, 439–464.

Management Review. (1954). Consultants numbers grow. *Management Review*, March, p. 9.

Manne, H. (1967). Our two corporate systems: Law and economics. *University of Virginia Law Review, 53*, 259–285.

Manne, H. G. (1962). The 'higher criticism' of the modern corporation. *Columbia Law Review, 62*(3), 400.

Manning, B. (1985). Reflections and practical tips on life in the boardroom after Van Gorkom. *Business Lawyer, 41*(1), 1.

Markham, J. W. (2003). Accountants make miserable policemen: Rethinking the federal securities laws. *North Carolina Journal of International Law & Commercial Regulation*, 765.

McCreary, E. A. (1964). *The Americanization of Europe: The impact of Americans and American business on the uncommon market* (p. 165). New York, NY: Doubleday & Company.

McKenna, C. D. (2006). *The world's newest profession: Management consulting in the twentieth century*. New York: Cambridge University Press.

McKibben, G. (1990). 'Strategy' consulting firm bucks tradition. *The Boston Globe*, October 21, p. A1.

McKinsey & Company. (1981, March 18–20). *Competitor Analysis Project*. Montsoult: McKinsey & Company (Corporate Archives, pp. 3–4).

Mintzberg, H. (1996). The 'Honda effect' revisited. *California Management Review, 38*(4), 78.

Mintzberg, H. (2004). *Managers not MBAs* (pp. 85–86). Harlow: FT Prentice Hall.

Mollenkamp, C. (2001). SunTrust assails wachovia at hearing. *The Wall Street Journal*, July 18, p. A4.

Murphy, B. A. (2003). *Wild bill: The legend and life of William O. Douglas*. New York, NY: Random House.

Neukom, J. G. (1975). *McKinsey memoirs: A personal perspective* (pp. 1–2). New York, NY: Privately Printed.

Norris, F. (1993). Delaware law: From a muddle, owners win. *The New York Times*, November 28, p. F1.

Pascale, J., & Athos, R. T. (1986). *The art of Japanese management* (p. 9). London: Penguin Books Ltd.

Perkins, R. B. (1986). Avoiding director liability. *The Harvard Business Review, 64*(3), 8.

Peters, T. (1994). Pioneering executives and management 'thinkers' do exist. *The Academy of Management Review, 19*(3), 387.

Peters, T. J. (1984). Strategy follows structure: Developing distinctive skills. *California Management Review, 26*(3), 111–125.

Phillips, D. J. (2012). Orphaned jazz: Short-lived start-ups and the long-run success of depression-era cultural products. In S. J. Kahl, B. S. Silverman & M. A. Cusumano (Eds.), *Advances in strategic management* (Vol. 29, pp. 315–350). Bingley, UK: Emerald Group.

Quinn, M. S., & Levin, A. D. (2001). Directors and officers liability insurance: Probable directions in Texas law. *The Review of Litigation, 20*(Spring), 381–480.

QVC Network v. Paramount Communications, 635 A.2d, 1245, 1255, 1270 (1993).

Randall, J. C. (1970). U.S. abroad: New competition. *The Washington Post*, January 11, p. 101.

Reed, R., & Luffman, G. A. (1986). Diversification: The growing confusion. *Strategic Management Journal, 7*(1), 29–35.

Reich, R. B., & Donahue, J. D. (1985). *New deals: The Chrysler revival and the American dream* (p. 17), New York, NY: Penguin Books.

Rohrlich, C. (1935). The new deal in corporation law. *Columbia Law Review, 35*(8), 1170–1171.

Romano, R. (1989). What went wrong with directors' and officers' liability insurance? *Delaware Journal of Corporate Law, 14,* 1–10.

Rothschild, M. (1992). The Henderson revolution. *Upside Magazine,* December.

Salmans, S. (1983). New vogue: Company culture. *The New York Times,* January 7, p. D1.

Seeger, J. A. (1984). Reversing the images of BCG's growth/share matrix. *Strategic Management Journal, 5*(1), 93–97.

Skapinker, M. (2002). Slippery counsel. *The Financial Times,* July 23, p. 16.

Slaughter, S. R. (1987). Statutory and non-statutory responses to the director and officer liability insurance crisis. *Indiana Law Journal, 63*(Winter), 181–189.

Smith v. Van Gorkom, Del.Supr., 488 A.2d 858 (1985).

Stevenson, Jordan, & Harrison. (c. 1934). *Management engineers, "principles and practices"* (p. 16). Business Pamphlet Collection, New York Public Library.

Thackray, J. (1979). Winning the game with a hot theory: Companies seek advice of Boston Consulting Group. *The New York Times,* April 15, p. F1.

The Boston Consulting Group. (1968). *Perspectives on experience.* Boston: The Boston Consulting Group.

The Boston Consulting Group. (2005). *BCG history* (p. 4). Boston: The Boston Consulting Group.

The New York Times. (1973). McKinsey manager to step down. *The New York Times,* April 27, p. 49.

The Times. (1972a). Consultancy boom in public sector. *The Times,* June 12.

The Times. (1972b). Whitehall names management firm for shipbuilding advisory role. *The Times,* June 6, p. 17.

The Times. (1974). Planning another bankrupt state industry. *The Times,* August 1, p. 15.

The Times. (1975a). Future of the motor cycle industry. *The Times,* August 7, p. 13.

The Times. (1975b). Government faces new clash over 'McKinsey Study of Car Industry'. *The Times,* May 30, p. 17.

The Wall Street Journal. (1976a). How's business? Among consultants it depends on whom you ask. *The Wall Street Journal,* February 26, p. 1.

The Wall Street Journal. (1976b). McKinsey & company names a new managing director. *The Wall Street Journal,* July 15, p. 22.

The Wall Street Journal. (1980). Trans Union holder sues to halt merger with Pritzker Firm. *The Wall Street Journal,* December 22, p. 7.

The Wall Street Journal. (1985a). Continental Steel Corp says its chairman, 6 directors resigned. *The Wall Street Journal,* September 24, p. 22.

The Wall Street Journal. (1985b). Corporate liability crisis. *The Wall Street Journal,* August 21, p. 22.

The Wall Street Journal. (1985c). Liability insurance is difficult to find now for directors, officers. *The Wall Street Journal,* July 10, p. 1.

The Wall Street Journal. (1986a). Businesses struggling to adapt as insurance crisis spreads. *The Wall Street Journal,* January 21, p. 31.

The Wall Street Journal. (1986b). Corporate liability crisis. *The Wall Street Journal,* August 21, p. 22.

Trieschmann, J. S., & Leverett, E. J., Jr.. (1990). Protecting directors and officers: A growing concern. *Business Horizons, 33*(6), 52.

Warsh, D. (1980). Views from the Top. *The Boston Globe,* June 3, p. 26.

Warsh, D. (1994). Michael porter abandons models for frameworks. *The Boston Globe*, June 26, p. 29.

Watson Jr., T. J., & Petre, P. (1990). *Father, Son & Co.: My life at IBM and beyond* (pp. 284–295). New York, NY: Bantam Books.

Wensley, R. (1981). Strategic marketing: Betas, boxes, or basics. *Journal of Marketing, 45*(3), 173–182.

Wickham-Jones, M. (1996). *Economic strategy and the labour party: Politics and policy-making, 1970-83* (p. 147). London: MacMillan.

Williamson, O. (1991). Comparative economic organization: The analysis of discrete structural alternatives. *Administrative Science Quarterly, 36*(June), 106.

Wilson, H. (1979). *Final term: The labour government, 1974-1976* (pp. 34–35). London: Weidenfeld & Nicolson.

Wilson, I. (1994). Strategic planning is dead – it changed. *Long Range Planning, 27*(4), 12–24.

Wind, Y., & Mahajan, V. (1981). Designing product and business portfolios. *Harvard Business Review, 59*(1), 155–165.

Winter, R. A. (1991). The liability insurance market. *The Journal of Economic Perspectives, 5*(3), 115.

Wojahn, E. (2003). *The general mills/parker brothers merger: Playing by different rules.* Washington, DC: Beard Books.

Wolf, W. B. (1978). Management and consulting: An introduction to James O. McKinsey (p. 48). Ithaca, NY: New York State School of Industrial and Labor Relations.

Wrigley, L. (1970). *Divisional autonomy and diversification.* Ph.D. dissertation, Harvard Business School, Boston, p. 50.

STRATEGY, IDEOLOGY, AND STRUCTURE: THE POLITICAL PROCESSES OF INTRODUCING THE M-FORM IN TWO DUTCH BANKS

Matthias Kipping and Gerarda Westerhuis

ABSTRACT

Purpose – *The broader aim of the research is to better understand the origins of firm heterogeneity in terms of strategy and structure, looking beyond convergence pressures resulting from economic and institutional forces.*

Design/methodology/approach – *To identify firm-specific differences, the paper uses an in-depth analysis of two matched cases, comparing the introduction of diversification strategies and decentralized organizational structures in two Dutch banks. Based on detailed archival research it tries to understand how different outcomes were shaped by political processes involving a variety of internal and external actors.*

Findings – *The research shows the importance of these processes and, in particular, the role of management succession as a trigger for organizational changes as well as the potential power of management consultants based on a combination of their own "political" skills and*

History and Strategy
Advances in Strategic Management, Volume 29, 187–237
ISSN: 0742-3322/doi:10.1108/S0742-3322(2012)0000029011

the opportunity provided by internal divisions. Moreover, the study confirms the view that organizational change requires a change in dominant ideology.

Research limitations/implications – *The research was able to go beyond the limitations of extant studies based on cross-sectional data or single cases. It demonstrates the usefulness of historical analysis when examining changes in strategy and structure. Its results need to be confirmed by conducting similar studies in different contexts.*

Originality/value – *The paper provides new insights into the complex and dynamic processes of organizational change and shows how external consultants – within a specific set of circumstances – were able to manage these processes. The results are valuable to scholars studying organizational change and those looking at consultants and their role. They might also provide insights for practicing managers working or planning to work with consultants.*

Keywords: Consulting; strategy and structure; M-form; multidivisionalization; banking

INTRODUCTION

The multidivisional structure or M-form has been characterized as the most important organizational innovation of the 20th century (e.g., Whittington and Mayer, 2000; Williamson, 1971). It is marked by a separation between relatively autonomous operational divisions with profit responsibility and a corporate center, which makes firm-level strategic decisions and supervises the divisions through financial control mechanisms (e.g., Strikwerda and Stoelhorst, 2009, pp. 13–15; Williamson, 1985, p. 284). In much of the literature the term M-form, divisionalization, or decentralization is used interchangeably (e.g., Freeland, 2001, p. 1). Most studies consider the creation of product or geographic divisions as evidence for M-form adoption, while some also describe a more broadly defined decentralized organization with the delegation of decision making and accountability driven deep into the hierarchy – a principle that has, at times, even been seen to provide a model for managing society as a whole (e.g., Drucker, 1993 [1946]; Ouchi, 1984).

Historically, the multidivisional structure is widely believed to have originated during the 1920s in a number of increasingly diversified US companies, notably General Motors and DuPont (Chandler, 1962; Drucker, 1993 [1946]; Sloan, 1964; cf. however Fear, 2005), and to have spread more widely and quite rapidly after World War II, both in terms of its geographic expansion – first in the United States and then in Western Europe (e.g., Binda, 2013; Channon, 1973; de Jong, Sluyterman, & Westerhuis, 2011; Dyas & Thanheiser, 1976; Rumelt, 1986 [1974]; Whittington and Mayer, 2000) – and in terms of the sectors covered – with banking and other financial services among the last to adopt it from the late 1960s onwards (Channon, 1977, 1978). At the beginning, companies diversified into related businesses, but they soon also expanded into unrelated activities, often through acquisitions, leading to a growing number of conglomerates. While the latter became largely de-institutionalized during the 1980s (Davis, Diekmann, & Tinsley, 1994) and have tended to disappear (albeit not completely), predictions about the demise of divisionalized organizations more broadly speaking (Bartlett & Ghoshal, 1993) seem to have been premature, with a recent article in the *McKinsey Quarterly* extolling the virtues of an independent corporate center (Hall, Huyett, & Koller, 2012; see also Colli, Iversen, de Jong, 2011; Gooderham & Ulset, 2002; Whittington, Mayer, & Curto, 1999).

In addition to tracing its dissemination, the literature on the M-form has largely focused on identifying the factors driving its widespread adoption, coalescing into two dominant schools of thought (see also Palmer, Jennings, & Zhou, 1993): one focusing on economic efficiency and the other on institutional conformity pressures – reflecting a broader dichotomy within the literature on the dissemination of management innovations (Abrahamson, 1991, 1996). The efficiency argument was developed theoretically by Williamson (esp. 1971), building on the path-breaking empirical research by Chandler (1962). While the latter identified geographic and/or product diversification as a major driver, as compared to more broadly defined growth for the former, both coincided in arguing that the adoption of a divisional structure and its associated controls allowed for better monitoring and led to a more efficient allocation of resources among the different divisions. However, subsequent empirical tests yielded only mixed results regarding the predicted superior profitability of decentralized organizations (for an overview Hoskisson, Hill, & Kim, 1993). The institutional explanation for M-form adoption, by contrast, focused less on competitive markets and efficiency improvements and more on pressures toward conformity exercised, among others, by management consultants and business schools, ultimately leading to "isomorphism." It was theorized by DiMaggio and Powell (1983) in terms of coercive, normative, and mimetic mechanisms and, more recently, by Abrahamson (1991, 1996) with respect to the role of "fashion-setting communities." This approach could rely on growing evidence for the role of consulting firms in promoting decentralization (Chandler, 1962; Channon, 1973; Kipping, 1999) and clear indications that the background of CEOs, namely in terms of a graduate degree from an elite business school (Palmer et al., 1993, p. 120) and of a previous focus on sales and finance within the company (Fligstein, 1985), made the adoption of the M-form much more likely.

While authors in each school stressed their differences, even incompatibilities (e.g., Fligstein, 1985; Whittington & Mayer, 2000), others found some statistical validity for both (e.g., Palmer et al., 1993) and yet others tried to integrate them (Roberts & Greenwood, 1997). What needs to be stressed here is that – for all their differences – both the efficiency and institutional approaches are highly deterministic in terms of identifying a series of drivers that are seen to increase the likelihood of M-form adoption. This leaves little, if any room for firm-specific factors, in the sense that despite sharing similar characteristics, organizations might differ considerably in the timing or depth of decentralization. Such a deterministic view stands in clear contrast with recent findings from the strategy literature, which have highlighted firm heterogeneity as the major source for sustainable competitive advantage (e.g., Barney, 2001; Hoopes, Madsen, & Walker, 2003; Teece, Pisano, & Shuen, 1997; for an empirical example Noda & Collis, 2001).

Within the extant M-form literature, there are some starting points for building an alternative approach based on firm-specific differences. Thus, in deriving broader conclusions from his study of M-form adoption in US corporations, Fligstein (1985, pp. 388–389) highlights the need for powerful internal actors to identify or construct problems based on their interpretation of the internal and/or external environments and to implement what they perceive as the most appropriate solution given their own position within the organization (see also Pettigrew, 1985). Similarly, Freeland (2001) in his in-depth, archive-based study of the M-form in General Motors has exposed the ongoing power struggles between owners, senior executives, and middle managers regarding their respective responsibilities, leading over time to differences in the separation between strategic and operational decision making – with, in his view, a more consensual approach resulting in superior economic outcomes. However, neither study looked at management consultants, whose rather contentious role in the process of M-form implementation has been described in a number of historical case studies (e.g., Cailluet, 2000; Hilger, 2000; for a summary Kipping & Armbrüster, 2002).

To advance this type of analysis, what is needed is a systematic comparison of two organizations, which share similar characteristics, but show significant differences in terms of the timing and depth of M-form adoption. This paper will present the results of such a study, comparing two Dutch banks. It suggests that only by examining the underlying dynamic processes involving a variety of internal and external actors can these different outcomes be understood. More in general, the paper argues that studying these kinds of "political" processes can supplement the economic efficiency and institutional perspectives toward the introduction of management innovation and that comparative historical case studies are well suited to examine these processes and their outcomes in the necessary detail, thus ultimately contributing to better understand how firm-specific differences drive sustainable competitive advantage (see also the contribution by Ingram, Rao, & Silverman, 2012).

What follows consists of four major parts. The next section examines in more detail the drivers for M-form adoption identified in the extant literature, focusing on the dominant efficiency and institutional approaches and their shortcomings in terms of explaining firm heterogeneity. Building on some previous studies and more general ideas in the relevant literature, the section then outlines an alternative, less deterministic and more dynamic view, which looks at the "political" processes of management innovation. The subsequent section explains the selection of cases for our empirical study as well as the data and methodology used. Next is the presentation of the results from our analysis, organized chronologically: a brief overview of the context, summarizing the changes in the Dutch banking sector after WWII, followed by the in-depth examination of the two cases with respect to (i) the motivation for introducing a more decentralized organization; (ii) the process of top-level organizational change and the role of internal and external actors involved; and (iii) the outcome in terms of the depth of decentralization, understood as the degree of autonomy (and the corresponding accountability) of lower-level managers. The final section discusses the broader insights from this study regarding the extant literature on the M-form, namely in terms of how political processes shape the relationship between strategy and structure; the introduction of management innovations more in general; and, last not least, the possible contribution of a historical approach to the strategy literature.

REVIEWING AND ADVANCING THE LITERATURE

The first part of this section summarizes the extant research on the M-form. In an earlier review of the literature, Hoskisson et al. (1993) had distinguished three perspectives: transaction cost economics (mainly Williamson's M-form hypothesis), strategic management (which suggested that efficiency outcomes depend on a variety of contingencies), and sociological approaches (which looked at the role of power struggles among competing groups within the organization on the one hand and at the attempt to gain legitimacy on the other). Combined with the more recent research, one can actually identify two dominant schools of thought, which highlight, on the one hand, economic efficiency as a major driver for the development and dissemination of the multidivisional structure and, on the other, the pressures toward organizational isomorphism exercised by coercive, normative, and mimetic forces. We will argue that, despite their different focus, both approaches are rather deterministic, predicting M-form adoption based on a series of organizational characteristics. Building on part of the limited literature subsumed by Hoskisson et al. (1993) under the "sociological" label, the section will then develop an alternative, political approach (see also Palmer et al., 1993), which looks at the dynamic interplay between different actors to better understand firm-specific outcomes.

The Dominant Economic and Institutional Views

The first to describe what subsequently became known as the M-form was Peter Drucker in his book *Concept of the Corporation* (1993 [1946]), which examined the case of General Motors (GM) "as an example of the social structure and of the institutional problems of the big-business corporation" (p. 41). He observed that GM had not only created a separation between central and divisional management, but had also driven the decentralization principle further down the hierarchy, with the larger divisions of the company themselves being further decentralized. Academic study and a more widespread interest in the multidivisional structure originated with the work of Alfred Chandler (1962), who studied the four pioneering US companies, DuPont, General Motors, Standard Oil (of New Jersey) and Sears Roebuck, in depth and also examined the diffusion of the new decentralized, "product-division structure" among the largest industrial firms in the United States, identifying different patterns in different industries (Chandler, 1962, Chapter 7) – an examination later complemented and completed by Rumelt (1986 [1974]).

Chandler's work became the starting point for both of the approaches that came to dominate subsequent research. On the one hand, he put efficiency at the center of his argument, summarized in the oft-quoted dictum: "Unless structure follows strategy, inefficiency results" (Chandler, 1962, p. 314). He found that after the four companies adopted a diversification strategy, expanding either geographically or into related products, their senior executives became "too enmeshed in operational activities" to the detriment of strategic, entrepreneurial decision making (p. 315). The resulting "administrative overload" eventually prompted them "to establish a structure consisting of divisional offices to administer each of the major product lines and a general or corporate office to administer the enterprise as a whole" (here from Chandler, 1990, p. 43). While representatives of the institutional approach have, consequently, tended to characterize him as part of what some call "efficiency theory" (Abrahamson, 1991; see also Fligstein, 1985), Chandler (1962) also stressed a number of other elements driving the companies he studied to review and revise their organizational structures. Thus, concerning the dissemination of the new organizational form, he points to "the very significant role that management consultants [...] have had in bringing about the adoption of the new structure as well as introducing many other administrative innovations and practices" – but did not provide further details (pp. 381–382). Moreover, he notes a mimetic effect – without using that term – since organizations wanting to introduce a divisional structure "could look to the model" of the pioneering companies – with their example also providing a possible incentive for those wanting to embark on diversification, but having previously been held back by the absence of an adequate structure (p. 394).

Drawing on Chandler's empirical findings, Oliver Williamson (esp. 1971, also 1985) developed a theoretical reasoning for the adoption of the M-form based on economic efficiency. Looking at transaction and information costs, it sees size rather than diversification as the primary driver. As the functionally based unitary or U-form organizations became larger, so the main argument, "[t]he ability of management to handle the volume and complexity of demands placed upon it became strained and even collapsed," leading lower-level managers to behave opportunistically. This behavior was corrected by the introduction of a multidivisional structure, which empowered top managers to allocate cash flows "among divisions to favor high-yield uses." For Williamson (1985, pp. 280–281), such a structure can therefore be usefully understood as "a miniature capital market," which allowed for a more efficient allocation of resources among the different divisions – the superiority over external capital markets explained by the lower information costs of the internal hierarchy. "Altogether, so Williamson (1971, p. 368), the M-form enterprise tends, through *internal* organization, to provide institutional underpinning for the prima facie standing ordinarily accorded to the profits-maximization assumption" (emphasis in original). Taking this logic further, Williamson (1985, p. 288) endorsed unrelated diversification, characterizing the conglomerate "as a logical outgrowth of the M-form mode for organizing complex economic affairs," which also lead him to see takeovers of unrelated businesses as a way for these companies to grow (*ibid.*). Finally, Williamson and Bhargava (1972) developed a taxonomy, distinguishing in particular the "pure" M-form, with a clear separation between the strategic center and the divisions, and the "corrupt" M-form, where the former retained some operational control over the latter.

While there are a number of studies examining the role of size as predictor for M-form adoption (Grinyer, 1982; Grinyer & Yasai-Ardekani, 1981; cf. Donaldson, 1982), much of the empirical testing has focused on the superior performance supposedly resulting from divisionalization. This research has yielded mixed results. Thus, in their review of the extant literature, Hoskisson et al. (1993) identified thirteen studies of which nine found some, usually qualified, support for what had become widely referred to as the "M-form hypothesis," while four did not (see also Ezzamel, 1985). Among the former was a study of 28 US oil companies, which not only found a statistically significant positive relationship between M-form adoption and profitability, but also showed that any such superior performance was temporary and vanished as the new structure became more widely diffused within the industry (Armour & Teece, 1978; see also Teece, 1981), which is not surprising, given that widespread adoption of an innovation tends to erode any competitive advantage of the first movers. Efficiency, or as most would say "performance," was also an explicit or at least implicit assumption in many of the studies tracing the diffusion of the M-form (e.g., Rumelt, 1986 [1974]). For instance, a fairly recent study of the largest 100 industrial firms in the UK, Germany, and France concluded that in terms of both survival over time and financial results "the multidivisional is a solid and consistent performer" (Whittington & Mayer, 2000, p. 187).

Within this broader school of thought, there was some debate about the relative merits of the different types of M-forms posited by Williamson (see above). Thus, based on a questionnaire survey of the top 500 commercial and industrial firms in the UK, Hill (1985a) found broad support for a link between the "pure" multidivisional organizational structure and superior profitability, but also noted that pure M-forms constituted only a small subset of his sample, 26 of 144 respondents (p. 215). In another analysis of the same data, he confirmed the superior profitability of the "pure" M-form but only for cases of unrelated diversification, while for related diversification what he calls the "centralized" and what Williamson calls the "corrupt" M-form performed better (Hill, 1988, pp. 79–80). As possible explanations Hill suggested the failure of the pure M-form to exploit interrelationships between the divisions and, possibly, the role of financial controls, which prompted divisional managers to sacrifice long-term investments, for example, in R&D, to improve short-term profit maximization (pp. 80–81; see also Hill & Hoskisson, 1987; Hoskisson, 1987).

A more recent longitudinal, in-depth, archive-based case study of GM (Freeland, 1996, 2001) came to conclusions broadly similar to those derived from the questionnaire-based cross-sectional data by Hill. It showed that the company operated as a "textbook" M-form only during very limited time periods, usually preferring "governance by consent" among owners, senior executives, and middle managers. This, in Freeland's (1996, p. 512) view, "did not necessarily lead to suboptimal performance." On the contrary, he argued, it was only when the owners imposed a stricter separation between the strategic center and the operational divisions that GM's performance suffered. While both Hill (see esp. 1985b) and Freeland used their findings to launch a more theoretical critique of Williamson (rebuffed in the latter case by Shanley, 1996), their findings can be reconciled with a view focusing on economic efficiency as a major driver for and result of the M-form. Thus, building on these and similar findings Hoskisson et al. (1993, pp. 281–285) suggested distinguishing between what they called "cooperative" and "competitive" M-form organizations, with the former exploiting economies of scope through related diversification and the latter functioning as an internal capital market for unrelated divisions (see also Hoskisson & Hitt, 1990; Hoskisson & Turk, 1990).

More or less explicitly, all of the studies focusing on efficiency as the main driver for M-form adoption have highlighted the importance of market competition as a necessary condition, putting pressure on companies to close the performance gap arising from an inefficient structure. This had already been pointed out by Drucker (1993 [1946]), who argued that the major advantage of a decentralized organization like GM stemmed from its superiority "in developing and training leaders capable of decisions and assuming responsibility," with markets supplying "objective performance tests for managerial ability" (pp. 128–129). Equally, in discussing the differences in M-from adoption among different industries, Chandler (1962) pointed not only at the different levels of diversification but also at their respective exposure to "market demand." Or, in banking, where only the UK case has been studied in some detail, what was seen to have precipitated the introduction of decentralized structures were (i) the move toward a more oligopolistic industry structure through a series of mergers, (ii) the "awakening of competition" through deregulation, and (iii) the competitive threat from foreign, in particular US banks (Channon, 1977, 1978). There were also suggestions that some of the country-based differences in M-form diffusion, notably its later adoption in Europe, could be attributed to less competitive and more collaborative, even collusive interfirm relations there (e.g., Franko, 1974; more in general Chandler, 1990).

However, both empirical findings and theoretical developments prompted a growing number of scholars to question the role of economic efficiency and the underlying assumptions about market pressures and led to the development of alternative explanations for the widespread diffusion of the M-form – and management innovations more in general. Empirically, there was the observation of the "significant role" played by management consultants in the dissemination of the M-form, first made by Chandler (1962), and then confirmed, among others, in subsequent studies of the adoption of the new structure in Great Britain, Germany, and France (Channon, 1973; Dyas & Thanheiser, 1976), and also highlighted by those examining the historical development and global expansion of management consulting firms (Kipping, 1999; McKenna, 2006). Theoretically, the foundation for the new approach was (neo-)institutional theory, which posits the need for companies to achieve social legitimacy (Meyer & Rowan, 1977) and highlights the impact of coercive, normative, and mimetic pressures on managers leading to widespread "isomorphism" (DiMaggio & Powell, 1983, 1991). Both were brought together namely in the work of Abrahamson (1991, 1996), who questioned the assumption that organizations necessarily adopted the most efficient management innovations, and instead stressed the importance of fashion-like processes and the role of "fashion-setting communities" for the widespread adoption of structures such as the M-form.

Additional empirical support for this approach came, for instance, from Thompson (1983), who examined a sample of 138 large, publicly quoted nonfinancial UK firms between 1958 and 1976. Among the 102 firms that had adopted a broadly defined M-form, he found that its diffusion resembled the symmetric patterns typical for complex process innovations (p. 302). More important was the work of Fligstein (1985, 1991), who empirically tested five different theories of organizational change to see which of them seemed best placed to explain the spread of the multidivisional form (MDF). These included Chandler's historical approach, where changes in strategy toward diversification were – presumably – followed by changes in structure; Williamson's transaction cost economics, which suggests that increasing size leads to control loss and inefficiency – supposedly remedied by M-form adoption; population ecology, which according to Fligstein (1985, p. 379), would predict "that younger and smaller firms would be more likely to adopt the MDF than older and larger ones." Based on a detailed examination of the 100 largest industrial firms in the US between 1919 and 1979, he finds no support for the latter two. By contrast, M-form adoption seemed positively affected by (i) a diversification strategy – consistent with Chandler's predictions, (ii) top managers having a sales or finance background – explained by what he calls a "power perspective," which suggests that M-form "adoption would be favoured by those who stood to gain most" from growth and diversification strategies (p. 380); and (iii) in industries where other firms have altered their structures – lending support to what he, based on DiMaggio and Powell (1983) calls "organizational homogeneity theory."

A study by Palmer et al. (1993) comes to similar conclusions. It explicitly tests for economic drivers, defined as poor firm performance preceding the M-form adoption, and "institutional factors," divided into tradition and, building on DiMaggio and Powell (1983), mimetic, coercive, and normative pressures. Using discrete-time event history analysis, they examined a sample of 105 companies from the largest 500 industrial corporations in the US in 1962 that previous studies had found to be using the U-form for six one-year intervals from January 1, 1963 to December 31, 1968. They did find support for economic factors, with an increase in industrial or geographic scope, also through acquisition, significantly increasing the likelihood of M-form adoption, while size per se and low profitability did not (p. 117). And, like Fligstein, they found that having a CEO with sales experience did exert a significant influence (pp. 118–119). In terms of institutional conformity, they confirmed a mimetic effect with the number of firms in an industry with an M-form significantly increasing the likelihood of others adopting it; they also found an influence of coercive pressure in terms of financial dependence, measured as a higher debt-to-equity ratio, and, most importantly, support for normative pressures, namely in terms of Board interlocks and of the CEO holding a graduate degree from an elite business school, which increased the probability of adopting the M-form by .369, "about the largest increase observed in the study" (p. 120). Their analysis also revealed an increase in the adoption rate over the period and, as institutional theory would predict, the different pressures being associated with each other (p. 121). Interestingly enough, in an earlier study based on a structural equation model they had found no support for what they then called an "ecological" explanation, referring to the lasting legitimacy of dominant organizational forms in a given industry and the structural inertia of more established firms (Palmer, Friedland, Jennings, & Powers, 1987).

These studies, while confirming the influence of diversification strategies first identified by Chandler, highlight the importance of isomorphic pressures, in particular the adoption rate within a given sector and the business school and/or sales background of CEOs. Given the apparent role of both economic and institutional factors, Roberts and Greenwood (1997, p. 358) proposed integrating these approaches, arguing that "the extent to which an organization is driven to evaluate the efficiency of its current design is influenced by its institutional environment" and using the M-form as an illustration for what they call the "constrained-efficiency framework." Nevertheless, what needs to be stressed here is that the institutional perspective remains equally, if not more, deterministic in orientation than the efficiency-based approach, leaving little room for firms in the same country and industry to differ in terms of the speed and extent to which they adopt a multidivisional structure. Or, as Schneiberg and Clemens (2006, p. 195) put it for institutional theory more generally:

> The behavior of actors – whether individuals or other social entities – is attributed not to the characteristics or motives of that entity, but to its context or to higher-order factors. Thus, individual action derives from scripts or schemas drawn from shared cultural systems. Firm behavior and attributes are shaped by the organization of industries, fields, or national polities.

This clearly contrasts with recent insights from the strategy literature that point at firm-specific "resources," "capabilities," or "competencies" as the major sources of sustainable competitive advantage (e.g., Barney, 2001; Hoopes et al., 2003; Teece et al., 1997). Differences in the adoption of the M-form between companies from the same sector and country, therefore, need to be explained by other, more firm-specific factors. Institutional theory does leave the option open that, while organizations adopt changes following external conformity pressures, they might do so only superficially, leaving their operating core untouched – a process generally referred to as "decoupling" (Meyer & Rowan, 1977). But while such a "symbolic" adoption seems feasible for equal opportunity practices (Edelman, 1992) or shareholder value (Fiss & Zajac, 2006), it is more difficult to imagine for the changes in the organizational structure and in the attribution of responsibilities and accountability required when introducing the M-form. And even if one admits this possibility, the question remains what would drive one organization toward a symbolic adoption, while another profoundly changes its operating core. However one puts it, the drivers for such profound differences need to be found within those firms. The following section outlines these firm-specific drivers building on some of the factors identified in the M-form literature under the label "political."

Toward a Complementary, "Political" Approach

Faced with the deterministic nature of both the efficiency and institutional approaches, one can go back once again to Chandler, who in the Introduction to the 1990 reprint of *Strategy and Structure* has stressed that the relationship between the two was not as unidirectional as the book title – and subsequent interpretations – might have suggested: "My goal from the start was to study the complex interconnections in a modern industrial enterprise between structure and strategy, and an ever-changing external environment." At a more conceptual level, he also distanced himself quite clearly from Williamson, highlighting that his primary unit of analysis was the firm (and its context) rather than the transaction (Chandler, 1992).

Among the different theories tested by Fligstein (1985), what he calls the "power perspective" probably comes closest to what we refer to as a political approach in terms of the relationships and interplay between various actors. As noted, in his analysis of longitudinal cross-sectional data Fligstein found support for this perspective, operationalized as the background of top managers. In interpreting these findings, he characterized "shocks" or "turbulence" in an organizational field as "a necessary, although not sufficient, impetus to change," highlighting instead the crucial role of "key actors" within an organization in using these external conditions to articulate a different view of a firm's strategy and "the power to implement that view" (here Fligstein, 1991, pp. 334–335). He also stressed that the implementation of these solutions did not necessarily improve the performance of the organization, as the economic efficiency approach would argue (Fligstein, 1985, pp. 388–389):

> This model of organizational change does not imply that the most important organizational problems are being solved. Instead, it suggests that actors have to construct such problems, have the claim to solve those problems, and be able to

implement their solutions. It is also the case that the organizational change may or may not aid the organization in surviving.

Such a model, while consistent with his results, is difficult to prove or even illustrate based on the kind of statistical analysis conducted in his article. It has, however, found support in a number of case studies. Thus, based on his in-depth history of British company Imperial Chemical Industries (ICI), Pettigrew (1985) also rejected a simplistic causal relationship between changes in the environment and internal changes, arguing instead that "a change in business strategies has to involve a process of ideological and political change, which eventually releases a new concept of strategy that is ideologically acceptable" (here Pettigrew, 1987, p. 666). Moreover, like Fligstein, he stressed that such a change is not always successful, because it pitches corporate leaders, who are often new to their position, against "dominating ideas and power groups of the organization" (*ibid.*). More specifically with respect to the M-form, there is the already mentioned in-depth, archive-based analysis of General Motors by Freeland (1996, 2001). He argued that in order to understand the shifting balances between centralization and decentralization in terms of the involvement of the corporate center in operational issues, "governance must be recast as a social process" (Freeland, 1996, p. 485), pointing namely to the ongoing struggles between owners and the different levels of managers.

However, none of these studies, whether specific or general, has looked at the role of management consultants as additional actors. Their – often contentious – interaction with various internal actors, and in particular middle managers, has been examined in a number of largely descriptive, historical case studies of the introduction of the M-form in resource-based and industrial firms (e.g., Cailluet, 2000; Hilger, 2000; in general Kipping & Armbrüster, 2002). Moreover, all these detailed studies have looked at single cases, which, while providing a richness of detail, make it difficult to derive broader generalizations (Eisenhardt, 1989). Chandler (1962), in his original study, did compare four companies, but his key interest was in identifying the commonalities, driving these organizations to pioneer a multidivisional structure. More importantly, these companies came from very different sectors, which does not allow identifying firm-specific differences in terms of M-form implementation within an otherwise largely similar context. We, therefore, now turn to such a comparative study of two organizations in the same context and with broadly similar characteristics in order to examine the impact of such firm-specific political processes on the adoption of the M-form in terms of the timing and depth of decentralization.

METHOD, CASES, DATA

In order to identify these political processes and their possible influences on the patterns of decentralization, our analysis will have to study three crucial aspects:

(i) *The developments over the long term*, which include (a) the earlier history of the selected organizations to identify the "dominating ideas and power groups" (Pettigrew, 1987), which were eventually challenged following external turbulences; (b) the actual "process of ideological and political change" (*ibid*.), where a new view of the organizations' strategy and structure was being constructed by "key actors" (Fligstein, 1985); and, finally, (c) the outcomes, first regarding the extent to which these actors were able to implement these changes – even if only symbolically – and then regarding the consequences these changes had in terms of solving the organizational problems and contributing – or not – to the survival of the organization over the long run – neither of which, as Fligstein (1991) has stressed, should be taken for granted.

(ii) *The relationship between the organization and its context*, focusing in particular on (a) "shocks" or "turbulences" in the organizational field (Fligstein, 1991) preceding the M-form adoption; (b) the interpretation of these environmental changes by powerful groups within the organization, but possibly also by external actors such as management consultants; and (c) the extent to which the various actors and their interpretations succeeded in "challenging and changing the core beliefs, structure, and strategy of the firm" (Pettigrew, 1987, p. 650).

(iii) *The interplay between the key actors*, examining namely (a) the "social process" of governance (Freeland, 1996), that is, the shifting balance of interests and power between owners, represented by the company's Board, and the different levels of managers; (b) the possible influences of changes in leadership (Pettigrew, 1987); and (c) the – still little understood – role of external consultants in legitimizing certain actors and courses of action within such internal power struggles (Jackall, 2009 [1988]; Kipping, 2000; Kipping & Armbrüster, 2002).

Only a historical study can satisfy these requirements in terms of the time horizon, contextualization, and in-depth analysis (Berg & Lune, 2012, Chapter 9; Goodman & Kruger, 1988; Pettigrew, Woodman, & Cameron, 2001, pp. 699–701). The key issues identified above provided the "explicit *sampling frame*" (Miles & Huberman, 1994, p. 29; emphasis in original) for the selection of two cases for in-depth study – a selection which had to be theory-driven, purposive, and ex-ante: Thus, in order to isolate the influence of the political processes, the selected organizations needed to be from the *same* country, the *same* sector, and as *similar* as possible in terms of their main characteristics. In addition, there had to be, on the one hand, sufficient information on the context and its evolution and, on the other hand, unrestricted access to internal, confidential documentation of the organizations, making it possible to examine the various actors and political processes in detail. The organizations meeting all these criteria are the two Dutch banks AMRO and ABN, which had both been established in 1964, each based on the merger of two other banks (see below) – and eventually merged in 1990 to form ABN AMRO. As Table 1 shows, at the time they were very similar in terms of their major characteristics.

Based on these characteristics, one would have expected ABN to adopt an M-form organization earlier, because it was more geographically diversified and displayed a notable performance gap vis-à-vis AMRO. However, the latter actually became the first mover, hiring McKinsey to study its

Table 1. Key Characteristics of AMRO and ABN in 1964.

	AMRO	ABN
Type	Listed	Listed
Ownership	Dispersed	Dispersed
Creation	Merger	Merger
No. of executives	9	11
No. of nonexecutives	14	36
Assets (in mill Euros)	2,707.27	2,573.85
Return on equity	0.160	0.078
Return on assets	0.009	0.004
Liquidity[a]	0.073	0.096
Leverage[b]	0.055	0.054
Share noninterest income (in total net operating income)	0.42	0.33
No. of domestic branches	544	358
No. of foreign branches	0	36
No. of domestic employees	10,634	7,950
No. of foreign employees	0	1,760
No. of total employees	10,634	9,710

[a]Cash plus securities divided by total assets.
[b]Total equity divided by total assets.

organization in 1968, while the former only considered revising its structure in 1972, asking Arthur D. Little (ADL) for assistance. This somewhat unexpected outcome further highlights the need for an in-depth study of the underlying political processes in each organization and should make our findings more robust (Miles & Huberman, 1994, p. 29).

The extant literature on the M-form, reviewed in the previous section, has almost exclusively focused on resource-based or industrial organizations and sectors. Channon (1977) has conducted the only in-depth study of strategy and structure in the banking sector, looking at both clearing and merchant banks in the UK (summarized in Channon, 1978). His conclusions are in line with the economic efficiency approach, stressing the role of "increased competition in the late 1960s, the diversification of domestic services and the spread of overseas activities" as major drivers, while nevertheless highlighting "the widespread use of consultants" (Channon, 1978, p. 78). In terms of outcomes, he found that all banks had adopted a similar three-division structure: UK banking, international banking, and related banking/financial services, but that decentralization within each of these divisions was uneven, with the UK banking divisions still being largely centralized, while the other two were operated more on a "holding company basis." In terms of the accompanying measures supporting decentralization, he found that "modern budgetary control procedures" had been introduced at these banks, while "long range planning systems and clearly allocated profit responsibility were still rare." With respect to performance effects, he stated that it was only possible to derive an "impressionistic" picture, due to that fact that banks were legally entitled to mask their "true profitability" (*ibid.*). He nevertheless suggested that the first movers in terms of divisionalization and internationalization showed higher growth in net assets, which, he admitted, might be the result of favorable exchange rates, "but, so he continued, *speed of reaction* and *degree of aggression* certainly appeared to be greater among the divisional companies" (Channon, 1978, p. 86; emphasis added).

While pioneering, his study remains marred by the fact that he did not have access to internal company documents (which would have allowed him to study the divisionalization and implementation process in greater detail) and that it was conducted too close to the actual organizational changes to evaluate the depth of decentralization and its longer-term impact. By contrast, both were possible in our cases, since the necessary confidential files were fully available in the ABN AMRO historical archives (hereafter AAHA). Moreover, there was sufficient historical distance to better evaluate the changes and their results in the context of the Dutch banking sector.

We were thus able to cover all the prerequisites for the empirical analysis, outlined above, relying namely on three different types of data:

(i)   the extant secondary literature on the evolution of the banking sector in the Netherlands, which has been studied fairly comprehensively. In addition, there has also been some work on the role of consultants in the sector, examining in particular the special relationship between AMRO and McKinsey (Arnoldus, 2000; Arnoldus & Dankers, 2005), which provides important context information for our analysis.

(ii) extensive and comprehensive internal archival documents from both banks. These include the various reports written by the consultancies involved, McKinsey and Arthur D. Little; the very detailed – often secret – minutes of – at times seemingly endless – discussions during the Board meetings at ABN; and the rich internal correspondence at AMRO, where Board minutes tended to only record the decisions reached. Incidentally, these differences in terms of the archival sources are already indicative of the rather different processes and corporate cultures at both banks.

(iii) a database covering the main characteristics (e.g., revenues, assets, income) and performance indicators (e.g., return on equity/assets, liquidity) of the 20 largest listed and nonlisted Dutch banks for each year from 1957 through 2007. This data was collected from the annual reports of the banks and the industry publication *het Bankenboekje*. It provides important information about the evolution of the sector and the relative position of both banks.

The secondary literature was mainly used to provide the context for the analysis of our case studies. The primary source documents were examined using what Ventresca and Mohr (2002, pp. 814–815) call the "historio-graphic" mode of archival analysis, which is most appropriate for a small number of cases, involves "the careful and detailed scrutiny of the archival materials" and requires that "the researcher reads through large amounts of archival information (often from unstandardized sources) in a disciplined fashion as a way to gain insights, make discoveries and generate informed judgments about the character of historical events and processes." Since there was little doubt about the genuineness of the archival material, our analysis focused on the internal rather than the external source criticism, trying to uncover the "deeper level of meaning" of the various documents, identifying for instance the author's motives and intended messages (Berg & Lune, 2012, pp. 312–316). While the eclectic nature of the archival sources was a limitation – which is, incidentally, a challenge shared with all process studies (Langley, 1999, pp. 693–694) – we increased the validity and robustness of our findings through the matched case study design (Eisenhardt, 1989) and the comparison with the extant literature, both conceptual and empirical (Berg & Lune, 2012, p. 317). The next section summarizes the main results of our analysis.

EMPIRICAL ANALYSIS AND MAJOR FINDINGS

This section traces, in some detail, the decentralization processes in AMRO and ABN. The first sub-section puts the firm-specific developments into their broader context by examining the transformation of the Dutch banking sector after the 1950s and the consequent strategic changes at the major banks. The remainder of the section examines the underlying political processes in each of the banks, analyzing internal as well as external actors and their interplay. Table 2 provides an overview of the main events in each bank between 1964 and 1978. These are analyzed in some more detail in the following narrative, which is subdivided chronologically: (i) the period leading up to the decision to change the organizational structure, made in 1967 at AMRO and 1972 at ABN, comparing in particular their respective motivations; (ii) the process of top-level change toward an M-form, namely concerning the separation between corporate center and operational divisions; and finally (iii) the extent to which decentralization was driven further into the organization, providing more autonomy and accountability at lower levels of the hierarchy.

Context: Increasing Consolidation, Competition, and Isomorphism

The introduction of the M-form in both AMRO and ABN has to be seen within the context of profound changes in the Dutch banking sector. Both banks played an active role in those changes, but they were also affected by them, namely because they became pitched more closely against each other following the mergers leading to their formation in 1964. Before the 1950s, the banking sector in the Netherlands had been segregated along functional lines. The field consisted of four large commercial banks: Nederlandsche Handel-Maatschappij (NHM), De Twentsche Bank (DTB), Amsterdamsche Bank (AB), and Rotterdamsche Bank (RB). All were mainly active in the West of the country, and their business focused on attracting deposits from large companies and, to a lesser extent, from wealthy customers.

Table 2.   Chronology of Organizational Changes at AMRO and ABN,
1964–1978.

	1964	1967	1968
Amro	Merger between Amsterdamsche Bank and Rotterdamsche Bank; first chairman Klaasse from AB; complex structure with two headoffices, one in Amsterdam, the other in Rotterdam; duplication of many functions; limited integration	Upon Klaasse's illness/ retirement dual chairmanship: Karsten (RB) and Van den Brink (AB); both ambitious and fairly "Americanized"; adds personal dimension to rivalry between predecessor banks	Hire McKinsey, initially to restructure top-level organization; first prelimenary report in June 1968, followed by three progress reports (October 30, 1968, November 27, 1968, January 9, 1969); when Board rejects initial suggestions, McKinsey proposes "compromise," creating Executive Committee of two Chairmen and three divisions (Domestic, International, Securities)
ABN	Takeover of De Twentsche Bank (DTB) by Nederlandsche Handel-Maatschappij (NHM), officially disguised as merger; first chairman van der Wall Bake from NHM; inherits NHM's strong corporate culture; considering itself an "eminent" bank due to venerable age (founded in 1824); perpetuates decentralized structure, with a separate division for extensive international activities (also from NHM); but centrally controlled by Managing Board	Weight of foreign activities increased further with takeover of Hollandsche Bank Unie (HBU), which has a large international branch network	

Table 2. *(Continued)*

	1969	1970	1972	1973
Amro	Final progress report on January 9, followed by meeting in May to inform second echelon and letter to all employees; McKinsey stresses new "integrative" management philosophy of delegation and individual responsibility; further, related projects look at domestic branch network and planning and control systems	Bank starts implementing new divisional structure with General Managers reporting to Executive Committee; remainder of Board members assigned to five "Steering Groups" with increasingly limited influence; further delegation of decision making (including for loans) in domestic branch network with area, district and branch managers		Additional McKinsey projects regarding the organization of domestic banking activities and their relationship with the center; efforts to increase commercial orientation of retail banking
ABN		van der Wall Bake succeeded by Wurfbain from DTB	Wurfbain succeeded by dual chairmanship: Dijkgraaf (DTB) and Batenburg (NHM); concerns about possible adverse effects of well know animosity between them lead Supervisory Board to demand recourse to an external advisor	Hire Arthur D. Little as "second best", when AMOR opposes use of McKinsey; asked to review top level management structure; voices similar concerns and makes similar proposals as McKinsey at AMOR; however, Managing Board refuses to make any radical changes; adds one functional division and establishes new level of *Directeuren Generaal* to head divisions

Table 2. (*Continued*)

	1974	1976	1977	1978
Amro	McKinsey proposes Overhead Value Analysis (OVA) to reduce cost; Co-Chairman hesistant because of possible redundancies involved; increased costs partially due to additional hierarchical levels added following earlier recommendations by the consultants	OVA starts, but encounters resistence from Board Members and Personnel Manager due to its sensitive nature; decision to rename it "cost management" and direct it internally without project members from McKinsey; consultants to provide ad hoc advice upon request	McKinsey proposes to develop international strategy for the bank; foreign activities had so far been limited to few joint subsidiaries with European partner banks, despite having an International division; several projects over the following decade, focusing eventually on establishing a presence in the United States	End of dual chairmanship with Vogelenzang becoming single Chairman; had been involved in restructuring efforts and attended McKinsey training programs
ABN	Implementation of revised structure; but central authority of *Raad van Bestuur* reasserted: ABN as a whole "the only profit centre"; limited delegation of authority to lower hierarchical level, in particular with respect to credit granting, which is carried out by three newly created loan committees; return to single chairmanship following premature death of Dijkgraaf removes potential for major political conflicts and need for further reorganization			

The deposits were placed as short-term loans to the corporate sector. There were also two major cooperative banks with a countrywide presence, deep roots in the local farming communities and close links with companies in the food sector, a number of building societies and many local savings banks, with usually just one branch. The two cooperative banks, the National Postal Savings Bank (*Rijkspostspaarbank*), and the individual savings banks dominated the market for household savings.

This well-defined system came under pressure as a result of postwar economic growth and the development of retail banking. This led the originally focused banks to develop more diversified – but now increasingly similar – product portfolios and prompted a process of consolidation (van der Lugt, 1999). Moreover, while Dutch business had initially financed its postwar growth mainly via retained earnings, since the late 1950 profits became lower due to rising wages and benefits as well as increasing taxes (de Jong, Röell, & Westerhuis, 2010). To fill the gap, the commercial banks started financing Dutch companies. The lower profitability also led to a relative decline in deposits maintained by corporate clients, which had been the traditional source of funds for the four commercial banks. Thus, to provide the corporate sector with medium- and long-term loans, the banks had to attract other sources of funds. They, therefore, started looking for household savings, which were rising fast due to increases in private incomes. The four commercial banks approached the savings market aggressively, offering more attractive interest rates on savings accounts and providing transfer payments free of charge. Consequently, their share of savings grew from less than 1 percent in the early 1950s, to 8.4 percent in 1960, 15.3 percent in 1970, and 27.4 percent in 1980s, after which it stabilized (van Zanden & Uittenbogaard, 1999).

The automation of administrative processes, which started in 1963, has been an important contributing factor (Bosman, 1989). This made it possible to use computers for the administration of wages, salaries, and pensions, and for the payment of salaries into bank and giro accounts rather than as cash (Bosman, 1989; van der Lugt, 1999; van Zanden & Uittenbogaard, 1999). To offer the new products and services to private households, the banks built up a countrywide network of branches, which had to be managed, with decisions needed about how much autonomy to grant each of them. Thus, the number of branches increased rapidly at AMRO from 544 in 1965, to 673 in 1970, and 873 in 1980. The branch network of ABN was somewhat less widespread in 1965 with 359 branches, but expanded quickly to 528 in 1970, and 718 in 1980 (van Zanden & Uittenbogaard, 1999).

Due to these changes, the formerly specialized banks gradually trans-formed themselves into nationally active general banks during the following decades (de Leeuw, 1996). As general banks, they began to offer a comprehensive array of banking services. The increase in competition led to a wave of mergers and acquisitions, which in turn accelerated the process further. As a result, the total number of banks declined from 145 in 1958 to 40 in 1973 (own database). The concentration process culminated in the two mergers in 1964 – one between NHM and DTB into ABN and the other between AB and RB into AMRO. These mergers created by far the two largest banks in the Netherlands. Another important merger, leading to an increasingly oligopolistic competition, was the one between the two cooperative banks into Rabobank in 1972, which was as large as ABN or AMRO (Sluyterman, Dankers, van der Linden, & van Zanden, 1998). The consolidation process ended in 1975 when ABN and AMRO bought two private banking firms, Mees & Hope and Pierson, Heldring & Pierson, respectively.

The formation of ABN and AMRO in 1964 created an intense rivalry between them. For example, when large companies wanted to issue shares on the capital market, the two banks battled as to which one would lead the syndicate. However, the uneasiness of major clients about this rivalry quickly prompted ABN and AMRO to start holding confidential "evening talks" every six months, aiming to smooth ruffled feathers caused by any perceived wrongdoing (van Zanden & Uittenbogaard, 1999). Both also met in more broadly based interbank meetings, such as the ones of the *Nederlandse Bankiersvereniging* (Dutch Association of Bankers). Moreover, since ABN and AMRO both had the most central position in the Dutch corporate network during the 1960s (Westerhuis & de Jong, 2010), their top managers held many positions as nonexecutive directors (*commissarissen*) in Dutch companies and, consequently, met each other in the network of industrial decision makers.

These close contacts also led to mimetic behavior reflected for example in the way they developed their retail activities, opened domestic branches, and acquired other banks. The decision to reorganize their top-level structure has to be partially seen in this context. The exact timing of the reorganization differed, however, with AMRO starting the process in 1967 and ABN in 1972 – a difference that, as the following sub-section will show, was mainly related to the structures and the succession planning they had adopted following their respective mergers, combined with marked differences in corporate culture.

Motivation: Leadership Politics

As the following sub-sections will show, in both banks top management succession and the associated political conflicts were the main trigger for reconsidering the top-level organizational structure and hiring consultants as advisers – with the timing of the succession explaining the difference in the timing of these efforts. In addition, at AMRO mimetic factors played a role, while at ABN, there were some concerns about the administrative problems resulting from its fast growth. All of these issues can ultimately be traced back to the mergers that established both banks in 1964.

AMRO: Internal Rivalries and Americanization

The formation of AMRO in 1964 was the result of a merger not only between two rival banks, but also between two banks located in the two major Dutch cities, Amsterdam and Rotterdam, which had a long-standing and intense rivalry. The merged entity tried to soften potential conflicts by adopting a structure with *two* head offices, one in each city with the members of the Managing Board (*Raad van Bestuur*, in Dutch) divided accordingly: three members located in Rotterdam and four in Amsterdam, with Board meetings often taking place by teleconference (see "Structure Amsterdam-Rotterdam Bank," February 1965 and an internal note from the Managing Board to all employees, February 15, 1965, both at AAHA, AMRO 3591; and an internal note on the structure of AMRO from H. N. Wakkie to the other members of the Managing Board, September 7, 1967, AAHA, AMRO 4814). Many positions at lower levels were also held by two people, one from each predecessor bank, in order to advance, so the stated reason, the integration between the two (internal note from the Managing Board to directors, vice-directors, and department directors, February 15, 1967, AAHA, AMRO 2139). But because responsibility was held jointly at many levels of management, accountability for the departments was often shared and diffused. Adding to the complexity was the fact that over 40 departments reported directly to the Managing Board, regardless of their importance or size.

The bank did appoint a single person as Chairman of the *Raad van Bestuur*, the former president of Amsterdamsche Bank (AB), C.A. Klaasse, who was the most senior member of the Managing Boards of the predecessor banks. His integrative role should, however, not be overstated, since Dutch organizations had statutory collegial management, where all Board members together were responsible for decision making. They discussed things in meetings trying to come to a consensus, with the

Chairman leading the discussions and summarizing final decisions, rather than imposing their own ideas, like a CEO in an Anglo-American context might be able to do (van Zanden, 2002). More importantly, already at the time of the merger AMRO created a ticking political time bomb by stipulating that upon Klaasse's retirement in 1968 he would be succeeded by two Chairmen, one each from the two predecessor banks, J.R.M. van den Brink from the former AB and C.F. Karsten from the former Rotterdamsche Bank (RB). This decision was apparently made to provide incentives for both to stay in the merged entity (Arnoldus & Dankers, 2005). De facto, they took the reins of the Managing Board already in 1967, when Klaasse went on extended sick leave, before officially retiring in 1968 (internal note of the Managing Board on mutations, January 29, 1968, AAHA, AMRO 3591).

Both van den Brink and Karsten were ambitious, which seems to have added a personal dimension to the already tense relations between the two former entities and their host cities. Before joining AB, the former had been the Dutch Minister of Economic Affairs between 1948 and 1952 and as such played an important role in the first steps toward Western European integration (Cuppen, 1986). Karsten had already been Chairman of RB between 1959 and 1964, when the merger forced him to take a – temporary – step back. His actions at the time suggest that he was not content with the traditional, consensus-building task of the Chairman, but tried to emulate the role of an Anglo-American CEO. Thus, finding the RB Managing Board too preoccupied with daily operations and not enough with overall strategy, he changed the way Board meetings were held by introducing an agenda with the most important items and by no longer giving priority to the interventions of members with more seniority. His interest in and familiarity with the American way of doing business probably stemmed from his dissertation on the US banking sector (Karsten, 1952). And his penchant for "Americanization" could also be seen in the introduction of a budget for marketing and advertising during his reign at RB (van der Werf, 1999b). Van den Brink was also familiar with US business, having overseen the distribution of Marshall Plan aid and trying to foment investment by American companies in the Netherlands as a Minister.

These preferences explain to a large extent why AMRO decided to ask a US consulting firm to advise them on simplifying the organizational structure and improving decision making, after officially declaring the integration of both banks as successfully completed (Internal note, February 15, 1967, AAHA, AMRO 2139). Another driver might have been the examples of ongoing or planned reorganizations of its European partners, Deutsche

Bank, Midland Bank in the UK, and Société Générale in Belgium, with which AMRO had cooperated since the early 1960s and formed the European Banks' International Company (EBIC) in 1970. To compete with the US banks both in Europe and in the United States, EBIC started opening joint international offices/branches and subsidiaries (AAHA, AMRO: EBIC's international problems with special reference to the competition of American banks. Second report from the Foreign Managers' Group, October 1968, mentioned in van Zanden, and Uittenbogaard (1999)). Economic efficiency, by contrast, seems to have played less of a role. Even McKinsey recognized in his first progress report that AMRO had managed to "become the most profitable of Dutch Commercial banks" – a finding confirmed by our database – while at the same time stressing the potential threats to this position requiring, so the underlying logic, immediate action ("Organizing to Maintain Leadership in the Banking Community," Progress Report I, October 30, 1968, AAHA, AMRO 2131).

According to the available evidence, Van den Brink and Karsten considered Booz-Allen Hamilton, at the time the largest US consulting firm, as well as McKinsey, since both had an office in Amsterdam, but only contacted and then met the latter (internal note, undated, AAHA, AMRO 337/2). On June 18, 1968, the consulting firm submitted a proposal entitled "Organizing to Maintain Leadership in the Banking Community" and "developed on the basis of preliminary discussions held with Messrs. J.R.M. van den Brink and C.F. Karsten and after a review of the Bank's Annual Reports" (AAHA, AMRO 2139). It was approved by the *Raad van Bestuur* in its meeting on June 20 and formally accepted by the bank in a letter dated June 25, 1968 from Karsten to McKinsey Director Everett Smith in New York (AAHA, AMRO 2435). Smith had been the one developing the consulting firm's blueprint for the reorganization of banks (see below).

This sequence of events highlights the central role of both Van den Brink and Karsten in promoting reorganization and hiring McKinsey. This still somewhat tentative coalition of interests between the two Co-Chairmen and the consulting firm would prove crucial for the subsequent process, as will be discussed below.

ABN: Growing Pains and Board-Level Disagreements
In terms of "politics," the case of ABN was different, since there was no rivalry similar to the one between Amsterdam and Rotterdam and, consequently, much less of a need to keep a balance within the Managing Board. Despite being billed as a merger, the creation of ABN was actually a takeover of De Twentsche Bank (DTB) by Nederlandsche Handel-Maatschappij

(NHM) (van der Werf, 1999a, 1999b). This was also reflected in the fact that former NHM President H.W.A. van den Wall Bake became ABN's first Chairman (1964–1970). Moreover, ABN already had a somewhat decentralized structure consisting of two main directorates: Domestic and International, and some additional functional directorates. This was in continuation of its predecessor bank NHM, which had managed its international activities separately. And the weight of ABN's international activities was further reinforced in 1967 with the acquisition of Hollandsche Bank Unie (HBU). Thus, being already somewhat decentralized at the operational level, while more integrated at the top, ABN originally felt less of an immediate need for reorganization, despite some concerns being expressed in the Managing Board about the complexities resulting from the fast growth of the bank (Secret minutes of the Managing Board meeting, February 9, 1970, AAHA, ABN D2326).

It was once again the introduction of a dual chairmanship, which caused divisions at the top management level and prompted a reflection about the future composition and role of the Managing Board at its meeting on March 25, 1972 (Secret minutes, AAHA, ABN S298). Following the retirement of Wall Bake's successor Wurfbain, the bank appointed two Chairmen, Andre Batenburg from the former NHM and Tom Dijkgraaf from the former DTB. It is not clear what prompted this decision; it was certainly not agreed at the time of the merger, and the bank returned to a single Chairman after Dijkgraaf's premature death in 1974 (see the reports to the ABN Managing Board, by A. Batenburg and H. Langman, respectively September 16 and 19, 1974, AAHA, ABN D4505). Nevertheless, it was clear and well known that the relationship between the two Chairmen was rather problematic. It seems therefore not surprising that at a meeting on February 28, 1972 certain members of the Managing Board expressed their concerns about the planned dual chairmanship due to "the fear that Dijkgraaf and Batenburg could not get along, which would frustrate the bank's policy-making and would ultimately harm the bank" (Minutes AAHA, ABN D2326; see also the Secret minutes, Managing Board meeting, March 25, 1972, AAHA, ABN S298).

The main resistance against the dual chairmanship, however, came from the bank's Supervisory Board (*Raad van Commissarissen*), which would have preferred Dijkgraaf as a single chairman. Moreover, the Supervisory Board was rather unhappy about not having been properly consulted in the appointment process. In the meeting of the Managing with the Supervisory Board on March 3, 1972, the Chairman of the latter, J. Th. van der Lecq, stressed that "it is of utmost importance that the bank's Supervisory Board has a say in the suggestions that are put to the meeting. This is a requirement of democratic treatment. It is certainly not desirable that certain solutions are more or less forced upon the Supervisory Board."

While ultimately agreeing to the dual chairmanship, the Supervisory Board insisted, in the words of van der Lecq, that the Managing Board solicited "the opinion of an external advisor about the question whether the future composition of the Managing Board, as currently decided, meets the requirements of efficiency and representativeness, internally as well as externally" (Secret minutes, AAHA, ABN D2326). It was thus ABN's Supervisory Board that more or less forced the Managing Board to hire a consultant. It should not come as a surprise, given the mimetic behavior described above, that the bank's preference would have been for McKinsey (Secret minutes, Managing Board meeting, May 9, 1972, AAHA, ABN S298). However, after having been informed by ABN about their intention, AMRO intervened and convinced McKinsey not to accept the assignment, apparently threatening to end what had turned into a very lucrative relationship for the consulting firm (Arnoldus & Dankers, 2005; see also below). ABN continued to covet a US consultancy, but had to go for "second best," hiring Arthur D. Little, which had no office in the Netherlands but conducted the project from a base in Brussels.

Despite a difference in timing, AMRO and ABN seem to have made similar decisions for a similar reason: the introduction of a dual chairmanship in 1968 and 1972 respectively, which prompted the reorganization of top-level management with the help of an external advisor. However, these similarities are superficial. The AMRO organization was clearly more divided based on the previous rivalry among the constituent banks, their home cities, and, now, two ambitious co-chairmen. ABN, by contrast, was a more unified organization, since it had been created through a (dissimulated) takeover, and at the same time had a more decentralized operational structure due to its significant international activities – making the personal dislike among the two Chairmen appointed in 1972 a notable, but ultimately passing phenomenon. Moreover, McKinsey, who was hired by AMRO on an – as it would turn out – exclusive basis, could rely on strong internal support from the two chairmen, whereas ADL was handicapped from the outset, since the hiring of an external adviser was imposed by the Supervisory Board and the firm itself had only been the second choice of the Managing Board.

The following sub-section will discuss how these and other differences in the role and relative weight of the different actors also drove the processes of M-form adoption in both organizations.

Restructuring the Top-Level Organizations

As we will show in this sub-section, the choice of consultant, ultimately somewhat involuntary for ABN, proved highly consequential for the subsequent divisionalization process. We first discuss the reorganization at AMRO, and then compare it with the one at ABN, showing in particular the different roles McKinsey and ADL played at both banks. The degree of influence that the consultants could impose upon outcomes depended, as repeatedly noted, not only on the structures adopted directly after the mergers in 1964, but also on the banks' corporate cultures, and, last not least, on the consultants' working procedures.

AMRO: McKinsey as the Master of Ceremonies

Two fundamental drivers shaped the reorganization of top-level management at AMRO. First of all, in its meeting on June 4, 1968, that is, even before the arrangement with McKinsey was formalized (see above), the Managing Board discussed whether reaching "a certain coordination and harmony of opinion among top management was desirable" before being interviewed by the consultants, but ultimately decided to let each Board member "express their opinions as freely as possible" with respect to what were anticipated to be the key issues: a single or two headquarters, the structure and responsibilities of the *Raad van Bestuur*, its relationship with middle managers (*directeuren*) as well as the equality among Board members, both current and future (Meeting minutes, AAHA, AMRO 337). This decision was crucial, since it exposed to the consultants – and to us as researchers – the deep rifts within the Managing Board about all of these questions. It also enabled McKinsey to exploit, at least to a certain extent, these divisions when managing the reorganization process.

This became even more important in light of the second fundamental driver, the fact that McKinsey came with a fairly clear blueprint what a "modern" bank organization should look like contained for instance in an address by McKinsey Director Everett Smith to the American Bankers Association, entitled "Bank management: the unmet challenge," published in the *McKinsey Quarterly* and *The Bankers*, July 1967 or a detailed 39-page study on "Developing Future Bank Management" prepared by McKinsey for the US-based Association of Reserve City Bankers. Copies of all these documents can be found in the files of Karsten pertaining to the top-level restructuring (AAHA, AMRO 337/2), incidentally together with a document by the British–Dutch oil company Shell, which had also been advised by McKinsey in its own restructuring at the beginning of the 1960s

(Howarth & Jonker, 2007; Kipping, 1999). While this suggests both mimetic and normative pressures, it needs to be stressed again that much of the outcome was shaped by the political processes, which AMRO set in motion at the time of the 1964 merger. When the Board decided to let its members express their opinions freely, it exposed the internal divisions to the consultants, enabling them to dominate the political process – usually with hidden rather than open support from the two co-chairman. McKinsey first conducted an analysis of the existing structure of the bank, concluding that

> the present AMRO organization did not meet the changing needs of the banking community nor satisfy the interests of senior employees and clients. Therefore the organization in its present form could not systematically manage the very important branch network; it restrained the development of individual accountability for results; it did not adequately motivate second level managers; and it did not facilitate the development of new and essential skills. (Progress Report I, October 30, 1968, AAHA, AMRO 2131)

Then, based on interviews with all *Raad van Bestuur* members, who were also asked to note down their activities in minute detail, with many *directeuren* and with select lower-level managers, the consultants proposed two possible structures, one including an "Operations Committee" and the other a "Presidium." Both structures caused quite some discussions within the Board especially regarding the related issue of the Board's collective responsibility. The first option, presented as an interim structure, "provided a link between *Raad van Bestuur* and operating management by formation of an Operations Committee, assisted by a General Manager responsible for directing and controlling the line and staff departments of the bank" (Progress Report II, November 27, 1968, *ibid.*). To this structure the Board raised the following objections. First, it would give little job satisfaction to most Board members, because of the exclusive emphasis on policy-making. Second, the task of the General Manager would be beyond the capacity of any one man. And lastly, they had doubts whether second-level managers were sufficiently well qualified to perform key operating jobs (Progress Report III, January 9, 1969, AAHA, AMRO 2132). The second option, to move collective responsibility from the Managing Board to a "Presidium," providing leadership and authority, was not accepted by AMRO either, because it violated joint responsibility of the Managing Board. Moreover, Board members were afraid of a demotion of the status of those not elected to the Presidium, and of the need for too high a degree of specialization of those members not elected (Progress Report II, *op. cit.*).

After discussing both alternatives with the Board members individually, it became clear that no overall consensus of opinion emerged, which would satisfy even the majority of the Board. This "political" impasse allowed McKinsey to become the final arbiter in the restructuring of the bank. Thus, the irreconcilable differences about the respective merits of both alternatives eventually led to a "compromise," creating an Executive Committee responsible for policy-making and three operational divisions: Domestic Banking, International Banking, and Securities, each run by a General Manager, as well as two functional divisions: Controller and Personnel. The "Executive Committee that in the name of the Managing Board stimulates, coordinates and controls the banks activities," was supported by five Steering Groups: Branches and Retail Banking; Wholesale Banking; International Banking; Credit Policy; and Personnel. The fact that the Executive Committee was made up of the two Co-Chairmen, while the other *Raad van Bestuur* members would join some steering group, shows who the political winners of this solution were. The other Board members nevertheless accepted the proposal, partially because they were allowed to (i) compete for the General Manager positions – unsuccessfully as it eventually turned out, not surprisingly; (ii) stay in their original home city, while Karsten had to move to Amsterdam, which was determined as the location of the Executive Committee and the General Managers; and, relatedly, (iii) retain their positions on other Supervisory Boards as well as high-level client contacts – even if the latter were being hollowed out through the creation of account managers, also proposed by McKinsey (Memorandum on "Account Management," December 11, 1968, AAHA, AMRO 873).

But McKinsey not only dominated the process politically, guiding the bank to a solution close to its original blueprint, but also dominated it philosophically and linguistically, which was equally, if not more, important. Thus, in the first round of interviews, the consultants noted "a minor communications gap surrounding such complex words as policy formulation, accountability, strategic planning, management and so forth" and therefore sent Karsten, and possibly other Board members, a copy of Marvin Bower's book *The Will to Manage*, which "is an easy, conversationally styled book to read and defines all the terms we generally employ" (Covering letter to Karsten, September 16, 1968, AAHA, AMRO 337/2). More importantly, the consultants stressed the need for a change in philosophy from bankers to managers and the need for individual autonomy and accountability: "the responsibilities for activities that influence the performance of the bank should be assigned to individuals. This could only be made possible by delegation and the implementation of information and control systems" (Final report to General Managers, March 3, 1969, AAHA, AMRO 873).

Nevertheless, despite the significant political and linguistic prowess, McKinsey in the end did not fully control the process and the result was somewhat hybrid, with elements of the old structure and ideology surviving alongside a multidivisional organization. Despite attempts by the consultants to clearly define the various roles, significant potential for political conflict therefore remained and, as we will show, flared up during the subsequent period, when McKinsey worked relentlessly to drive decentralization and its management philosophy further down AMRO's hierarchy.

ABN: Remaining True to Its Roots
By contrast, ABN did not let the consultants dominate the political process. When hired by the bank in 1972, Arthur D. Little (ADL) was asked to address three issues: (i) the top management structure, (ii) the relationship between the Managing Board and the Directorates; and (iii) the role of the Supervisory Board. In March 1973, ADL presented its first report on "Top-Level Management Organization" stating that ABN "suffered a lack of commonly understood goals, excessive centralization of power, over-emphasis on collegial management, often wasteful utilization of management talent, and an insufficient commercial orientation" (AAHA, ABN 23). These observations were quite similar to the ones McKinsey had made at AMRO. However, the ultimate outcomes at both banks were quite different, which was due to ADL being politically less powerful and, possibly, less astute than McKinsey. Most importantly, ADL had not been ABN's first choice – its suggestions therefore having less legitimacy from the outset. Second, due to the limits on time and expenses set by ABN (Arnoldus & Dankers, 2005), the consultants interviewed fewer internal managers than McKinsey did at AMRO and none of ABN's clients. Third, in contrast to AMRO, ABN already had a somewhat more decentralized structure, which suited its (international) growth ambitions quite well. Fourth, ABN was more confident in what it was doing and less open to be manipulated by external advisors, considering itself a very distinguished bank given that its predecessor NHM could trace its origins back to 1824. AMRO, by contrast, had a more businesslike image, which was a reflection of its predecessor Rotterdamsche Bank known for its aggressive growth (van Zanden & Uittenbogaard, 1999). The different corporate cultures were also reflected in the background of their respective Chairmen with AMRO's Van den Brink and Karsten both holding a degree in economics, while ABN's first Chairman Van den Wall Bake came from an eminent family.

A specific example for the fact that ABN did not take everything that ADL suggested for granted was the decision by the Managing Board in its meeting on October 19, 1973 to cancel the planned assignment on the Supervisory Board (Secret minutes, AAHA, ABN S299). Many of ABN's important clients actually sat on its Supervisory Board, which explains the unusually high number of members: 27 as compared to an average of just under 7 for the 100 largest listed nonfinancial Dutch companies in 1968 (Westerhuis & de Jong, 2010). ABN was apparently concerned that ADL might suggest a reduction in the number of Supervisory Board members thus jeopardizing high-level personal ties with major industrial companies.

ADL was therefore limited to making – largely marginal – improvements to the bank's existing structure. As noted, its recommendations had to be less radical, since ABN already had a structure consisting of several Directorates, in particular Domestic Banking and International Banking, supported by several functional ones providing support to these. As a result, the consultants only suggested adding two more directorates, Credit and Customer Services, bringing together activities, which were until then spread throughout the bank. Once again demonstrating its independence from the consulting advice, ABN's Managing Board decided to only create the latter. In its opinion, with respect to the credit function the creation of three permanent loan committees, the Netherlands Loan Approval Committee, the International Loan Approval Committee, and the Executive Loan Committee, was sufficient to increase the speed and efficiency of the lending process. Their creation had been discussed for the first time at a Managing Board meeting on October 31, 1968 (Secret minutes, AAHA, ABN D2326), but was only decided in 1973. The Executive Loan Committee functioned as the ultimate loan approval committee of the bank (Report on credit granting procedures, May 24, 1973, AAHA ABN D2538).

ADL did nevertheless manage to introduce some significant changes in the top-level organization, moving it somewhat closer to an M-form with a corporate center and more autonomous operational divisions. Before the reorganization, the *Raad van Bestuur* had collectively made decisions regarding operational matters, which were then executed by the managers (*Directeuren*) in the various Directorates. As the bank grew, this structure had created an increasing workload for the Managing Board and its members – in particular given the traditional tendency to discuss all decisions at length. ADL, therefore, proposed to create a more streamlined decision making at the top, by turning its purely coordinating "Presidium" into an executive body – similar to the Executive Committee introduced at AMRO by McKinsey. This proposal caused significant commotion, when it was discussed at the Board meeting in January 1973, and was ultimately rejected (Secret minutes, AAHA, ABN S299). The Presidium itself was abolished in

1974. ABN did, however, accept the subsequent proposal to create the position of several *Directeuren Generaal*, each in charge of one Directorate and reporting to the Managing Board – comparable to the General Managers at AMRO, but with somewhat reduced authority since the Board members continued to interfere in certain operational decisions (Secret minutes, Managing Board meetings on January 2 and 8, 1973, AAHA, ABN S299).

Overall therefore, the top-level reorganization went into the same direction at both banks: toward a separation between a corporate center and (relatively) autonomous divisions. However, both the process and the outcome were less radical at ABN, since it already had operational divisions – albeit with limited autonomy, which was now increased with the establishment of *Directeuren Generaal* to head them. An attempt to centralize the top level with the creation of a more autonomous Presidium was rejected by the Managing Board, which retained its collective responsibility and sufficient control over operations, namely through several loan committees that made major lending decisions. AMRO created not only operational divisions but also more centralization at the top though an Executive Committee, consisting of the two Co-Chairmen and located, together with the top of the line organization and most support functions, in Amsterdam, while diffusing the influence of the Managing Board by maintaining its members in two locations and dispersing them into various, largely impotent steering groups.

These differences resulted not only from the previous structures but also from the differential ability of the consultants to influence the political process, very limited for ADL at ABN, while significant for McKinsey at AMRO. And while the former was not retained after the end of the top-level restructuring, the latter established a quasi-permanent presence, driving decentralization deep down into AMRO's hierarchy and also creating activities for its new international division, given the almost exclusive domestic focus of the bank so far.

The Depth of Decentralization

This section examines the extent to which AMRO and ABN subsequently decentralized their respective organizations beyond the top level and identifies the drivers behind these decisions. At AMRO, over the next decade McKinsey – with the now more open support from the two Co-Chairmen – drove decentralization deep into the organization, and in particular into the domestic branch network. By contrast, ABN went hardly beyond the very moderate level of decentralization it had already introduced following the merger, with no clear separation of strategic from operational control and little, if any, autonomy given to lower levels of the hierarchy, in particular the branch managers.

AMRO: Going Deep

In May 1969, once the decision was made to create an Executive Committee and five divisions, three of them operational, AMRO's Managing Board organized a meeting to inform the second-level managers. It also sent a letter to all other managers informing them about the changes, which – not surprisingly – was drafted by McKinsey. The letter stressed that despite the success of the merger in terms of access to funds, a nation-wide branch network, and the availability of qualified personnel, "further integration was needed," which "applies in particular to the development of a common management philosophy, serving as a guiding principle (in Dutch: *rode draad*) for the whole business and aligning the daily activities of bank employees at all levels towards a common goal" (Discussion draft, sent by McKinsey to the *Raad van Bestuur*, AAHA, AMRO 873). This common philosophy, so the letter, consisted of four key elements: (1) the need for higher-level employees to act like managers rather than bankers in the narrow sense; (2) the assignment of responsibilities for activities that influence the profitability of the bank to individuals; (3) the delegation of responsibilities toward lower levels of the hierarchy; and (4) the introduction of a planning and control system.

Over the next two decades McKinsey set out to realize what could be understood as the new dominant ideology of the bank – as well as promoting its internationalization. This process can be traced through more than two dozen consulting reports and the internal discussions they prompted. The consulting firm, in agreement with AMRO's top management, first focused on the Domestic Banking division, including the branch network, because "here is where profits will be made." McKinsey, therefore, stressed the need to put more emphasis on the "commercial side of activities" and, consequently, to strengthen retail banking and sales & marketing by putting them under a unified leadership. Its report about the reorganization of the branch network from September 1969 (AAHA, AMRO 2132) recommended a more elaborate hierarchical structure below the General Manager of the Domestic Banking division. The recommendation, subsequently implemented by the bank (see "Adjusting the Organization to Support Domestic Branch Banking," Progress Report #1, September 19, 1973, AAHA, AMRO 2134), was to create half a dozen areas, then a series of districts, which each had their own line manager as well as some functional managers and in turn oversaw a number of branches. Next was the creation of a Management Control and Planning system, intended, so the McKinsey project proposal of March 25, 1969 (AAHA, AMRO 280), to "assist the restructured top organization of AMRO in establishing its initial operating techniques and controls, to recommend ways of improving the organization and control methods for the branch network, and to design a management information system."

Many of these recommendations had increased the bank's cost by creating a significant number of new line management and functional positions, which prompted McKinsey to propose a project about overhead value analysis (OVA) in a confidential letter to Van den Brink and Karsten on December 30, 1974 (AAHA, AMRO 74.3). Being aware of the potential political repercussions of such a project, given that it basically focused on "redundant employees," van den Brink and Karsten for the first time hesitated to head McKinsey's advice and delayed the start of the project until 1976. Even then, the "new McKinsey drive" did indeed generate controversy within the organization. In a preliminary internal meeting on February 10, 1976, the General Manager of the Personnel division suggested "not to involve McKinsey," because, in his opinion, "the OVA methodology of McKinsey was too much focused on the employees, whereas it should be dealing with cost management in general" (AAHA, AMRO 422). Similarly, in the meeting of February 19, 1976 some Board members asked "why can't we do this internally without external assistance" (AAHA, AMRO 76.1). It is clear that in this instance McKinsey had touched upon a very sensitive issue that threatened the core of Dutch labor relations (Nijhof & van den Berg, 2012). The consultants, therefore, had to back peddle and let the bank control the process rather than directing it themselves: AMRO created a – temporary – Cost Management Committee with only bank mangers as members, who could, however, if they so wished, draw on the expertise of McKinsey. Moreover, as a largely linguistic concession to these concerns, the controversial OVA methodology was renamed "cost management" (Meeting of March 25, 1976, AAHA, AMRO 76.1).

The next series of projects, which kept the consultants busy well into the 1980s, concerned AMRO's international activities. While the bank had followed McKinsey's advice and created an International Banking division with the top-level reorganization in 1969, it had few operations outside the Netherlands, except a few joint branches through EBIC (see above). And since McKinsey had been busy reorganizing AMRO's admittedly much more important domestic operations, it was only in 1977 that it wrote a proposal "aimed at developing an international strategy for the bank" (AAHA, AMRO 2136), which was followed by a series of reports, which eventually, in 1983, focused on developing a strategy for AMRO in the United States (AAHA, AMRO 2137).

What should be stressed here is an important difference between the divisions, resulting from all the changes recommended by McKinsey, with respect to their autonomy in making – inherently risky – decisions. Thus, in the International Banking and the Securities divisions, most operating decisions required Board approval because of the amount of risk involved and because of the bank's financial reputation at stake. In the Domestic Banking division, by contrast, responsibility was much more decentralized. Following McKinsey's idea that profits were best made when individuals were held responsible and accountable, AMRO focused its efforts to increase profitability on the domestic branch network. In this respect, an important "concession" to the McKinsey philosophy was the decision made in the Board meeting of October 9, 1969, "to give more responsibility to district managers concerning the granting of credits" (Minutes, AAHA, AMRO 2439) – which, as we will see, would ultimately promote more risk-taking at lower hierarchical levels.

At ABN, by contrast, decentralization did not go as far and the center remained more firmly in control.

ABN: Retaining Central Control
Unlike at AMRO, where McKinsey continued to drive decisions regarding structure and strategy based on their management philosophy until the late 1980s, Arthur D. Little was asked to leave ABN very quickly. Already at its meeting on March 13, 1973 the bank's Managing Board decided that after the first phase of implementation, the Board would take over the management of the process, with ADL intervening in an advisory and supporting role on an ad hoc basis only (Secret minutes, AAHA, ABN S299). And when the Managing Board, at its meeting on September 25, 1973, decided to ask the consulting firm to formulate task descriptions for the directorates, it also made clear that this should be ADL's last assignment with one of the Board members urging "to phase out ADL's activities as per 31 December 1973" and Co-Chairman Dijkgraaf suggesting that "it could at the very most overrun to the end January 1974" (Minutes, AAHA, ABN D2538).

The speedy removal of the consulting firm, which never had much legitimacy or leeway to begin with, combined with end of the dual chairmanship due to the premature death of Dijkgraaf in 1974, removed much of the political conflict potential that continued to drive changes at

AMRO. Rather than decentralizing further as its rival did, ABN retained centralized control over most operating decisions. Thus, with respect to the newly created *Directeuren Generaal*, who were in charge of the operational and daily management of the divisions, the Managing Board in its meeting on September 25, 1973 clearly stated that they had budget, *not* profit responsibility, stressing that "there is only one profit center: ABN as a whole" (Minutes, AAHA, ABN D2538; see also the report on the relations between the directorates, September 21, 1973, *ibid.*). And while the introduction of this additional hierarchical level freed up more time in the *Raad van Bestuur* for long-term planning and policy-making (Secret minutes, Managing Board meeting, January 11, 1973; AAHA, ABN D4400; see also Westerhuis, 2008), in practice there was no clear separation between strategy and operations. Thus, the Board members, the *Directeuren Generaal*, and the chairmen of the loan committees met on a regular basis, forming what was called the Executive Management Committee of the bank, which coordinated the bank's daily activities (ABN Annual Report 1973). This was different from AMRO, where the Executive Committee also met regularly with the General Managers of the different divisions, but consisted only of the two Co-Chairmen and had exclusive power over policy-making, ultimately creating a more profound separation between strategy and operations.

Concerning the Domestic Banking operations, ADL, similar to McKinsey, considered that ABN had an insufficient commercial orientation. However, in sharp contrast to McKinsey, it did not suggest a far-reaching decentralization of responsibilities into the branch network. In general, ABN's Managing Board was more hesitant than that of AMRO to delegate responsibilities, wanting to control the important aspects of banking operations, in particular the approval of loans and issues. Thus, applications for large – domestic as well as foreign – loans had to be sent to head office for approval by the three newly created Loan Committees. Loans and issues above a certain amount had to be approved by the Managing Board itself. ABN was of the opinion that these decisions could have such an impact on the bank's solvency, that they should not be delegated but managed carefully at a central level (Report on credit granting procedures, May 24, 1973, AAHA, ABN D2538). Consequently, the most important recommendation of ADL with respect to a more commercial organization structure was not so much a delegation of (credit) responsibilities, but an emphasis on customer rather than product orientation. To this end, ABN followed the suggestion by ADL (see above) and created a Customer Services directorate, responsible for the development and marketing of new financial products.

There are some indications that these differences in the depth of decentralization might have impacted how both banks fared during the economic crisis of the early 1980s. This crisis was the result of an expansionary credit policy during the 1970s, fueled by low interest rates, which came to an abrupt halt in 1979 as a result of the global recession following the second oil shock. Between 1980 and 1983 a wave of bankruptcies hit Dutch business, creating serious problems for the commercial banks for the first time since 1945 – further aggravated by the international debt crisis of 1982 (van Zanden & Uittenbogaard, 1999). AMRO was particularly hard hit by these developments, reporting huge losses, which eventually led to a temporary lowering of its credit rating by Standard & Poor in late 1984. The crisis revealed two organizational problems at the bank. First, the decision-making process for loans was too decentralized, apparently leading lower-level managers to extend too many dubious credits – which now became exposed. Second, many EBIC subsidiaries had also been too independent, allowing them to over-extend their activities, leaving AMRO and its European partners on the hook for the mounting losses (Metze, 1993; van Zanden & Uittenbogaard, 1999).

By contrast ABN was less affected. It had pursued a more conservative policy, both at home and abroad, with management having a firmer grip on the organization, notably with decisions about loans taking place at the top level (van Zanden & Uittenbogaard, 1999; Westerhuis, 2008). While it might be difficult to establish a causal link between the organizational changes of the early 1970s and the way both banks fared in the crisis of the early 1980s, it seems clear that the "degree of aggression," lauded by Channon (1978) as a positive feature of the divisionalized banks in the UK (see above), might not have served AMRO all that well in this context.

SUMMARY AND DISCUSSION

As the preceding in-depth analysis has shown, political processes played an important part in the adoption of the M-form at both Dutch banks with the roles of various actors and their interplay explaining much of the variation of outcomes in terms of the timing and depth of decentralization.

Thus, in the first instance a change in top management – rather than a change in strategy – prompted both AMRO and ABN to reconsider their organizational structure and bring in outside consultants. Since this change occurred at different moments in time, 1967/1968 and 1972, respectively, decentralization was proposed and considered earlier at one and later at the other. It was not the change in leadership per se, but the creation of a dual chairmanship that led to the subsequent courses of action. In the AMRO case both leaders seem to have pushed for change to enhance their own powers, making them more akin to US CEOs rather than consensus-building Dutch Chairman, and tried to further their agenda with the help of US consultants. At ABN, the dual chairmanship introduced a level of personal conflict that worried other members of the Managing Board and, in particular, the Supervisory Board, which, therefore, insisted on hiring external advisers. But while the dual chairmanships triggered the reconsideration of organizational structures at both banks, the root cause for these developments has to be sought in the mergers leading to their formation in 1964 and the decisions made at the time: At AMRO, these decisions installed permanent rivalries, culminating in the dual chairman-ship, while at ABN they created a more stable structure, which, so the concern among Managing and Supervisory Board members, might be disturbed by having two Chairmen – concerns that ultimately proved unfounded though.

These deeply rooted differences also explain, in part, the role consultants were able to play in the subsequent divisionalization processes. Thus, at AMRO McKinsey was able to exploit the deep divisions within the organization and its Managing Board, taking charge of the process: It initially proposed two rather complex solutions, neither of which found a majority among the Board members, then suggested a "compromise" very much in line with the M-form structures they introduced at banks in the United States and the UK (see Channon, 1977) with a corporate center comprising the two Co-Chairmen, called Executive Committee, and three operating divisions (domestic, international, securities). The rest of the Managing Board members retained certain operational activities in terms of client relationships – gradually being hollowed out by the introduction of account managers – and participated in "steering groups," which had some oversight but little actual power. While in terms of outcome this appears like a kind of normative isomorphism, in particular since it goes hand in hand with a change in management philosophy and terminology, it was made possible only by the political processes and the way these were managed by McKinsey with tacit support from Van den Brink and Karsten.

At ABN, the consultants were never given the same leeway to guide the process. This was due partially to their reduced legitimacy from the outset – given that Arthur D. Little had only been chosen as the second best following AMRO's refusal to let ABN hire McKinsey – partially to the absence of a rift similar to the one at AMRO, which the consultants there were able to exploit both in terms of the political process and as an argument in favor of reorganization. Thus, after discussing the suggestions made by ADL at length, the Managing Board decided to make only very moderate changes to the top-level organization by adding one (functional) division.

The differences in terms of the underlying political tensions and the role of external advisers continued throughout the implementation process following the top-level restructuring. At AMRO, through a series of additional projects over the subsequent decade McKinsey managed to drive decentralization – in terms of decision-making autonomy and account-ability – deep into the hierarchy, namely by creating several intermediate decision-making levels (areas and districts) and also by attributing significantly increased responsibilities to district and branch managers. In a way, this was a process of implementing the new management philosophy, or ideology, of individual responsibility the consultants had been advocating and disseminating in the bank from the outset, portraying it as a way to promote the integration of the two predecessor banks. These initiatives had the backing of the two Co-chairmen, who warded off the – very rare – critiques from other *Raad van Bestuur* members by making largely symbolic concessions. Last but not least, McKinsey started pushing AMRO to internationalize, namely in the United States, thus kind of filling in one of the divisions created during the top-level restructuring – showing that at least in this instance structure clearly preceded strategy.

At ABN, unsurprisingly, the consultants were not retained beyond the initial reports on the top-level structure, which themselves had been implemented only partially. In any case, the premature death of one of the Co-Chairmen in 1974 removed most of the conflict potential, which had prompted their hiring in the first place. ABN maintained its already somewhat decentralized structure, which had not only granted some limited autonomy to its operational divisions, but also reaffirmed central control over important decisions, in particular regarding credit granting. This was in marked contrast to AMRO, where lower-level managers were given more autonomy in this respect, which increased risk-taking behavior and might have contributed to the bank's problems during the economic crisis of the early 1980s – problems largely avoided by ABN.

More in general, our analysis has confirmed the importance of a political approach for understanding M-form adoption – an approach that had already been suggested in parts of the extant literature. We have shown in particular how these factors help explain firm-specific differences in two cases that were largely identical in their competitive and institutional contexts and very similar in terms of economic performance and diversification strategy – with the bank that, theoretically, could be expected to be more driven to decentralize actually doing so not only later, but also less deeply. In this context, the personalities of top managers, their backgrounds, and ambitions as well as their (potential) conflicts assumed an important role (see also Greenstein (2012) for the idiosyncratic but lasting influence of such personalities on technological change). And so did the consulting firms chosen to assist in the restructuring process and their ability to persuade internal audiences (for the importance of persuading – in that case – an external audience, see also Kahl, Liegel, & Yates, 2012). Nevertheless, what turned out to be of crucial importance were the structures and "cultures" put in place at the time both organizations had been established though mergers: a dualistic and largely conflictual culture at one of the banks, nourishing itself from a variety of sources; compared with a more balanced culture at the other, which combined elements of centralization and decentralization, and was restored quickly following the short-lived disturbance of the dual chairmanship in the early 1970s (for the lasting impact of earlier choices see also the contribution by Leblebici (2012)).

It should be stressed that "politics" is not a substitute for the economic and institutional drivers identified by previous research. Both of these are present in the two cases studied here. But these factors were translated and brought alive because of political conditions at each of the organizations and through the interplay of various actors mobilizing them in their interest. Thus, the consultants, and more specifically McKinsey, highlighted the threat for competitive performance resulting from inaction and also created mimetic pressure by drawing the attention of top managers to the reorganization at other banks. Probably even more important was their insistence on the need to change the mindset from "bankers" to "managers" and to adopt a new management philosophy of individual responsibility. This confirms the views expressed earlier by Fligstein and Pettigrew that an organizational change first and foremost requires a change in ideology. But, with respect to their research, it adds consultants as an important actor into the equation. These factors came into play the way they did, because – for a variety of reasons – one of the two banks studied was more open for consulting advice and, in addition, McKinsey was very skilled at understanding and exploiting its organizational politics.

The first more general contribution from our research, therefore, concerns the relationship between strategy and structure, which is so fundamental not only to research on the M-form but also to organizational change more generally (e.g., Whittington, 2002). What we show is that this is not a one-directional process in terms of changes in structure being driven by changes in strategy, which in turn are prompted by external disturbances or shocks. Rather, our case study analysis suggests, it is an ongoing, interactive process, where external turbulences, such as increasing competition in a specific sector, and also internal shocks, like a merger, lead to the adoption of structures, which make the organization more or less open for certain types of strategies – without necessarily leading to an entirely path-dependent process. Moreover, our research confirms the crucial mediating role of ideology in this process, both in terms of confirming or solidifying extant strategies and structures and of opening the organization for new strategic directions or structural arrangements.

Secondly, our research suggests that this process needs to be conceptualized as a kind of negotiation involving a wide variety of actors: owners (Freeland, 1996, 2001), corporate leaders (Pettigrew, 1987), powerful groups of managers (Fligstein, 1985), and also, this is the major contribution from our study, management consultants. However, while one of our cases clearly shows the persuasive power of – at least certain – consulting firms, their influence should not be overestimated or overgeneralized, as some of the extant literature has done (e.g., Kieser, 2002; cf. Sturdy, 1997). Their skills of managing ideological change need to meet with the opportunity to deploy them – determined largely by the political constellation within the client organization (see also Kipping, 2000) and the legitimacy to propose and enact a new ideology. Thus, while the consultants were very influential in one of the two cases, where these conditions were present, their influence was marginal in the other, where they were absent. (It is an interesting counterfactual question whether McKinsey might have been able to affect more fundamental change at ABN, had AMRO let them accept the project. We doubt it.). Moreover, whatever the consultants proposed had to be in tune with the *Zeitgeist*, which was the case at the time since the idea of "decentralization" was both popular and legitimate. When that changed and managerial concerns and attention shifted to other issues, even the seemingly all-powerful McKinsey could do little to halt the swing of the pendulum and actually struggled to maintain its discursive – and market – position (as McKenna, 2012 shows).

The third, and much more tentative, insight from our research concerns the relationship between the M-form and competitive performance – one if not *the* issue most widely discussed in the extant literature (see, most recently, Higgins & Toms, 2011), albeit with few definite findings. There is some suggestion, emanating from the M-form literature, that its adoption – and the diffusion of management innovations more generally – provides some advantage to the first movers, but that this advantage is quickly being eroded as the innovation becomes more widely adopted (see above). What our research shows is that a simple dichotomy, M-form, or no M-form, which has driven many of the quantitative studies, might be misplaced to answer this question. Confirming some earlier research, namely by Hill and Freeland, based respectively on questionnaires and archival data, our results suggest that a "hybrid" or "coordinated" M-form, where the corporate center retains some or even considerable control over operational matters, might lead to superior performance in the medium to long term. This seems at least true for the banking industry, where giving too much autonomy to lower hierarchical levels might lead to high levels of risk-taking – with their cumulative impact potentially being disastrous, as the recent credit crisis has once again demonstrated. Be that as it may, future research on the performance aspects of the M-form or other organizational innovations should make sure to adopt a more fine-grained analysis when trying and to different structural features to superior performance.

Relatedly, our research also demonstrates the benefits of a historical analysis when examining changes in strategy and structure. Despite well-known limitations, namely due to the eclectic nature of the data, a historical approach can yield excellent results when it comes to studying long-term processes involving a broad variety of internal as well as external actors (see also Goodman & Kruger, 1988; Lawrence, 1984; Pettigrew et al., 2001). This becomes very apparent, when comparing our approach to studying the M-form with those by Channon (1977, 1978) and Fligstein (1985, 1991). The former relies only on publicly available information and has little distance to the still unfolding events, which makes the resulting insights highly preliminary and somewhat superficial given the absence of an understanding of the underlying change processes and their medium- to long-term outcomes. The latter conducts a sophisticated quantitative analysis to test various models explaining M-form adoption, derived from the literature. While his research design inspires sufficient confidence regarding the statistical results, it does little to support his ultimate suggestions regarding the ideological–political nature of organizational change processes, which can only be observed using historical data and analysis, such as the ones performed by Pettigrew (1985, 1987), Freeland (1996, 2001), or in our paper – the latter with additional robustness being derived from a matched case study design (Eisenhardt, 1989). One can only hope that these benefits of historical studies become more widely recognized among scholarly communities in strategy and other areas of management (see also Ingram et al., 2012).

ACKNOWLEDGMENTS

We would like to thank Doreen Arnoldus for sharing her previous research on consultants in AMRO and ABN with us and also express our gratitude to the participants of the Strategy and History Workshop in Chicago on February 3–5, 2012 and the Economic History Seminar at the University of Utrecht on April 19, 2012 for their stimulating and helpful comments and suggestions on earlier drafts and to the volume editors for their diligence and patience. As customary, the ultimate responsibility for this paper remains ours.

REFERENCES

Abrahamson, E. (1991). Managerial fads and fashions: The diffusion and rejection of innovations. *Academy of Management Review*, *16*(3), 586–612.

Abrahamson, E. (1996). Management fashions. *Academy of Management Review*, *21*(1), 254–285.

Armour, H. O., & Teece, D. J. (1978). Organizational structure and economic performance: A test of the multidivisional hypothesis. *The Bell Journal of Economics*, *9*(1), 106–122.

Arnoldus, D. (2000). The role of consultancies in the transformation of the Dutch banking sector, 1950s to 1990s. *Entreprises et Histoire*, *25*, 65–81.

Arnoldus, D., & Dankers, J. (2005). Management consultancies in the Dutch banking sector, 1960s and 1970s. *Business History*, *47*(4), 553–568.

Barney, J. B. (2001). Is the resource-based theory a useful perspective for strategic management research? Yes. *Academy of Management Review*, *26*(1), 41–56.

Bartlett, C. A., & Ghoshal, S. (1993). Beyond the M-form: Toward a managerial theory of the firm. *Strategic Management Journal*, *14*, 23–46.

Berg, B. L., & Lune, H. (2012). *Qualitative research methods for the social sciences* (8th ed.). Boston, MA: Pearson.

Binda, V. (2013). *The dynamics of big business: Structure, strategy, and impact in Italy and Spain*. New York, NY: Routledge.

Bosman, H. W. J. (1989). *Het Nederlandse bankwezen* (Vol. 1). Serie Bank- en Effectenbedrijf. Amsterdam: NIBE.

Cailluet, L. (2000). McKinsey, Total-CFP et la M-Form. Un exemple français d'adaptation d'adaptation d'un modèle d'organisation importee. *Entreprises et Histoire*, *25*, 26–45.

Chandler, A. D., Jr. (1962). *Strategy and structure. Chapters in the history of the industrial enterprise*. Cambridge, MA: MIT Press.

Chandler, A. D., Jr. (1990). *Scale and scope. The dynamics of industrial capitalism.* Cambridge, MA: Harvard University Press.

Chandler, A. D., Jr. (1992). Organizational capabilities and the economic history of the industrial enterprise. *Journal of Economic Perspectives, 6*(3), 79–100.

Channon, D. F. (1973). *The strategy and structure of British enterprise.* London: MacMillan.

Channon, D. F. (1977). *British banking strategy and the international challenge.* London: MacMillan.

Channon, D. F. (1978). *The service industry: Strategy, structure and financial performance.* London: MacMillan.

Colli, A., Iversen, M. J., & de Jong, A. (2011). Mapping strategy, structure, ownership and performance in European corporations: Introduction. *Business History, 53*(1), 1–13.

Cuppen, J. H. Th. M. (1986). J. R. M. van den Brink: wetenschapper, minister en bankier. *Politieke Opstellen, 6,* 73–83.

Davis, G. F., Diekmann, K. A., & Tinsley, C. H. (1994). The decline and fall of the conglomerate firm in the 1980s: The deinstitutionalization of an organizational form. *American Sociological Review, 59*(4), 547–570.

de Jong, A., Röell, A., & Westerhuis, G. (2010). Do national business systems change? Evidence from the organization of corporate governance and financing in the Netherlands, 1945–2005. *Business History Review, 84*(4), 773–798.

de Jong, A., Sluyterman, K., & Westerhuis, G. (2011). Strategic and structural responses to international dynamics in the open Dutch Economy, 1963–2003. *Business History, 53*(1), 63–84.

de Leeuw, J. (1996). *Financiële conglomeraten in Nederland* (Vol. 38). Serie Bank- en Effectenbedrijf. Amsterdam: NIBE.

DiMaggio, P. J., & Powell, W. W. (1983). The iron cage revisited: Institutional isomorphism and collective rationality in organizational fields. *American Sociological Review, 48,* 147–160.

DiMaggio, P. J., & Powell, W. W. (1991). Introduction. In W. W. Powell & P. J. DiMaggio (Eds.), *The new institutionalism in organizational analysis* (pp. 1–38). Chicago, IL: The University of Chicago Press.

Donaldson, L. (1982). Divisionalization and size: A theoretical and empirical critique. *Organization Studies, 3*(4), 321–337.

Drucker, P. F. (1993 [1946]). *Concept of the corporation.* London: John Day.

Dyas, G. P., & Thanheiser, H. T. (1976). *The emerging European enterprise: Strategy and structure in French and German industry.* London: MacMillan.

Edelman, L. B. (1992). Legal ambiguity and symbolic structures: Organizational mediation of civil rights law. *American Journal of Sociology, 97*(6), 1531–1576.

Eisenhardt, K. M. (1989). Building theories from case study research. *Academy of Management Review, 14*(4), 532–550.

Ezzamel, M. (1985). On the assessment of the performance effects of multidivisional structures: A synthesis. *Accounting and Business Research, 16*(Winter), 23–34.

Fear, J. R. (2005). *Organizing control: August Thyssen and the construction of German corporate management.* Cambridge, MA: Harvard University Press.

Fiss, P. C., & Zajac, E. J. (2006). The symbolic management of strategic change: Sensegiving via framing and decoupling. *Academy of Management Journal, 49*(6), 1173–1193.

Fligstein, N. (1985). The spread of the multidivisional form among large firms, 1919–1979. *American Sociological Review, 50*(3), 377–391.

Fligstein, N. (1991). The structural transformation of American industry: An institutional account of the causes of diversification in the largest firms, 1919–1979. In W. W. Powell & P. J. DiMaggio (Eds.), *The new institutionalism in organizational analysis* (pp. 311–336). Chicago, IL: The University of Chicago Press.

Franko, L. G. (1974). The move towards a multidivisional structure in European organizations. *Administrative Science Quarterly, 19*, 493–506.

Freeland, R. F. (1996). The myth of the M-form? Governance, consent and organizational change. *American Journal of Sociology, 102*, 483–526.

Freeland, R. F. (2001). *The struggle for control of the modern corporation: Organizational change at general motors, 1924–1970.* Cambridge: Cambridge University Press.

Goodman, R. S., & Kruger, E. J. (1988). Data dredging or legitimate research method? Historiography and its potential for management research. *Academy of Management Review, 13*(2), 315–325.

Gooderham, P. N., & Ulset, S. (2002). 'Beyond the M-form': Towards a critical test of the new form. *International Journal of the Economics of Business, 9*(1), 117–138.

Greenstein, S. (2012). Economic experiments and the development of Wi-Fi. In S. J. Kahl, B. S. Silverman & M. A. Cusumano (Eds.), *Advances in strategic management* (Vol. 29, pp. 3–33). Bingley, UK: Emerald Group.

Grinyer, P. H. (1982). Discussion note: Divizionalization and size: A rejoinder. *Organization Studies, 3*(4), 339–350.

Grinyer, P. H., & Yasai-Ardekani, M. (1981). Strategy, structure, size and bureaucracy. *Academy of Management Journal, 24*, 471–486.

Hall, S., Huyett, B., & Koller, T. (2012). The power of an independent corporate center. *McKinsey Quarterly, March*(2), 39–42.

Higgins, D. M., & Toms, S. (2011). Explaining corporate success: The structure and performance of British firms, 1950–84. *Business History, 53*(1), 85–118.

Hilger, S. (2000). American consultants in the German consumer chemical industry: The Stanford Research Institute at Henkel in the 1960s and 1970s. *Entreprises et Histoire, 25*, 46–64.

Hill, C. W. L. (1985a). Internal organization and enterprise performance: Some UK evidence. *Managerial and Decision Economics, 6*(4), 210–216.

Hill, C. W. L. (1985b). Oliver Williamson and the M-Form firm: A critical review. *Journal of Economic Issues, 19*(3), 731–751.

Hill, C. W. L. (1988). Internal capital market controls and financial performance in multidivisional firms. *Journal of Industrial Economics, 37*(1), 67–83.

Hill, C. W. L., & Hoskisson, R. E. (1987). Strategy and structure in the multiproduct firm. *Academy of Management Review, 12*, 331–341.

Hoopes, D. G., Madsen, T. L., & Walker, G. (Eds.). (2003). Guest Editors' introduction to the special issue: Why is there a resource-based view? Toward a theory of competitive heterogeneity. *Strategic Management Journal, 24*(10), 889–902.

Hoskisson, R. E. (1987). Multidivisional structure and performance: The diversification strategy contingency. *Academy of Management Journal, 30*, 625–644.

Hoskisson, R. E., Hill, C. W. L., & Kim, H. (1993). The multidivisional structure: Organizational fossil or source of value? *Journal of Management, 19*, 269–298.

Hoskisson, R. E., & Hitt, M. A. (1990). The antecedents and performance outcomes of diversification: Review and critique of theoretical perspectives. *Journal of Management, 16*, 461–509.

Hoskisson, R. E., & Turk, T. (1990). Corporate restructuring: Governance and control limits of the internal market. *Academy of Management Review, 15*, 459–477.

Howarth, S., & Jonker, J. (2007). *Geschiedenis van Koninklijke Shell, deel III: Stuwmotor van de koolwaterstofrevolutie, 1939–1973.* Amsterdam: Boom.

Ingram, P., Rao, H., & Silverman, B. S. (2012). History in strategy research: What, why, and how. In S. J. Kahl, B. S. Silverman & M. A. Cusumano (Eds.), *Advances in strategic management* (Vol. 29, pp. 241–273). Bingley, UK: Emerald Group.

Jackall, R. (2009 [1988]). *Moral mazes: The world of corporate managers.* Oxford: Oxford University Press.

Kahl, S. J., Liegel, G. J., & Yates, J. (2012). Audience structure and the failure of institutional entrepreneurship. In S. J. Kahl, B. S. Silverman & M. A. Cusumano (Eds.), *Advances in strategic management* (Vol. 29, pp. 275–313). Bingley, UK: Emerald Group.

Karsten, C. F. (1952). *Het Amerikaanse Bankwezen.* Rotterdam: Drukkerij M. Wyt.

Kieser, A. (2002). Managers as marionettes? Using fashion theories to explain the success of consultancies. In M. Kipping & L. Engwall (Eds.), *Management consulting: Emergence and dynamics of a knowledge industry* (pp. 167–183). Oxford: Oxford University Press.

Kipping, M. (1999). American management consulting companies in Western Europe, 1920 to 1990: Products, reputation and relationships. *Business History Review, 73*(2), 190–220.

Kipping, M. (2000). Consultancy and conflicts: Bedaux at lukens steel and the Anglo-Iranian Oil Company. *Entreprises et Histoire, 25*, 9–25.

Kipping, M., & Armbrüster, T. (2002). The burden of otherness: Limits of consultancy interventions in historical case studies. In M. Kipping & L. Engwall (Eds.), *Management consulting: Emergence and dynamics of a knowledge industry* (pp. 203–221). Oxford: Oxford University Press.

Langley, A. (1999). Strategies for theorizing from process data. *Academy of Management Journal, 24*(4), 691–710.

Lawrence, B. S. (1984). Historical perspective: Using the past to study the present. *Academy of Management Review, 9*(2), 307–312.

Leblebici, H. (2012). The evolution of alternative business models and the legitimization of universal credit card industry: Exploring the contested terrain where history and strategy meet. In S. J. Kahl, B. S. Silverman & M. A. Cusumano (Eds.), *Advances in strategic management* (Vol. 29, pp. 117–151). Bingley, UK: Emerald Group.

McKenna, C. D. (2006). *The world's newest profession. Management consulting in the twentieth century.* New York, NY: Cambridge University Press.

McKenna, C. D. (2012). Strategy followed structure: Management consulting and the creation of a market for "strategy," 1950–2000. In S. J. Kahl, B. S. Silverman & M. A. Cusumano (Eds.), *Advances in strategic management* (Vol. 29, pp. 153–186). Bingley, UK: Emerald Group.

Metze, M. (1993). *De geur van geld. Een opmerkelijk bankafschrift.* Nijmegen: SUN.

Meyer, J. W., & Rowan, B. (1977). Institutionalized organizations: Formal structure as Myth and ceremony. *American Journal of Sociology, 83*, 340–363.

Miles, M. B., & Huberman, M. A. (1994). *Qualitative data analysis* (2nd ed.). Thousand Oaks, CA: Sage.

Nijhof, E., & van den Berg, A. (2012). *Het menselijk kapitaal. Sociaal ondernemersbeleid in Nederland.* Amsterdam: Boom.

Noda, T., & Collis, D. J. (2001). The evolution of intraindustry firm heterogeneity: Insights from a process study. *Academy of Management Journal, 44*(4), 897–925.

Ouchi, W. G. (1984). *The M-form society.* Reading, MA: Addison-Wesley.

Pettigrew, A. M. (1985). *The awakening giant: Continuity and change in imperial chemical industries*. Oxford: Blackwell.

Pettigrew, A. M. (1987). Context and action in the transformation of the firm. *Journal of Management Studies, 24*(6), 649–670.

Pettigrew, A. M., Woodman, R. W., & Cameron, K. S. (2001). Studying organizational change and development: Challenges for future research. *Academy of Management Journal, 44*(4), 697–713.

Palmer, D., Friedland, R., Jennings, D. P., & Powers, M. (1987). The economics and politics of structure: The multidivisional form and the large U.S. corporation. *Administrative Science Quarterly, 32*, 25–48.

Palmer, D., Jennings, D. P., & Zhou, X. (1993). Late adoption of the multidivisional form by large U.S. corporations: Institutional, political and economic accounts. *Administrative Science Quarterly, 38*, 100–131.

Roberts, P. W., & Greenwood, R. (1997). Integrating transaction cost and institutional theories: Toward a constrained-efficiency framework for understanding organizational design adoption. *Academy of Management Review, 22*(2), 346–373.

Rumelt, R. P. (1986 [1974]). *Strategy, structure and economic performance*. Cambridge, MA: Harvard University Press.

Schneiberg, M., & Clemens, E. S. (2006). The typical tools for the job: Research strategies in institutional analysis. *Sociological Theory, 24*(3), 195–227.

Shanley, M. (1996). Straw men and M-Form myths: Comment on Freeland. *American Journal of Sociology, 102*(2), 527–536.

Sloan, A. P., Jr. (1964). *My years with general motors*. New York, NY: Doubleday.

Sluyterman, K. E., Dankers, J., van der Linden, J., & van Zanden, J. L. (1998). *Het coöperatieve alternatief. Honderd jaar Rabobank 1898–1998*. The Hague: Sdu Uitgevers.

Strikwerda, J., & Stoelhorst, J. W. (2009). The emergence and evolution of the multi-dimensional organization. *California Management Review, 51*(4), 11–31.

Sturdy, A. (1997). The consultancy process – an insecure business? *Journal of Management Studies, 34*(3), 389–413.

Teece, D. J. (1981). Internal organization and economic performance: An empirical analysis of the profitability of principal firms. *The Journal of Industrial Economics, 30*(2), 173–199.

Teece, D., Pisano, G., & Shuen, A. (1997). Dynamic capabilities and strategic management. *Strategic Management Journal, 18*(7), 509–533.

Thompson, R. S. (1983). The spread of an institutional innovation: The multidivisional corporation in the UK. *Journal of Economic Issues, 17*(2), 529–538.

van der Lugt, J. (1999). Het commerciële bankwezen in Nederland in de twintigste eeuw. Een historiografisch overzicht. *NEHA-Jaarboek, 62*, 388–420.

van der Werf, D. C. J. (1999a). The two Dutch bank mergers of 1964: The creations of Algemene Bank Nederland and Amsterdam-Rotterdam Bank. *Financial History Review, 6*(1), 67–84.

van der Werf, D. C. J. (1999b). *Banken, bankiers en hun fusies. Het ontstaan van de Algemene Bank Nederland en de Amsterdam-Rotterdam Bank. Een studie in fusiegedrag over de periode 1950–1964*. Amsterdam: Nederlandse Instituut voor het Bank- en Effectenbedrijf.

van Zanden, J. L. (2002). Driewerf hoera voor het poldermodel. *Economisch Statistische Berichten, 87*(4358).

van Zanden, J. L., & Uittenbogaard, R. (1999). Expansion, internationalisation and concentration, 1950–1990. In J. de Vries, W. Vroom & T. de Graaf (Eds.), *Worldwide banking. ABN AMRO 1824–1999* (pp. 335–392). Amsterdam: ABN AMRO Bank.

Ventresca, M. J., & Mohr, J. W. (2002). Archival research methods. In J. A. C. Baum (Ed.), *The Blackwell companion to organizations* (pp. 805–828). Oxford: Blackwell.

Westerhuis, G. (2008). *Conquering the American market. ABN AMRO, Rabobank and Nationale-Nederlanden working in a different business environment, 1965–2005*. Amsterdam: Boom.

Westerhuis, G., & de Jong A. (2010). The Dutch Corporate Network: Structural changes in the period 1903–2003. Paper presented at the workshop "Corporate Networks in Europe in the 20th Century," November 12–13, Utrecht.

Whittington, R. (2002). Corporate structure: From policy to practice. In A. M. Pettigrew, H. Thomas & R. Whittington (Eds.), *Handbook of strategy and management* (pp. 113–138). London: Sage.

Whittington, R., & Mayer, M. (2000). *The European corporation: Strategy, structure, and social science*. Oxford: Oxford University Press.

Whittington, R., Mayer, M., & Curto, F. (1999). Chandlerism in post-war Europe: Strategic and structural change in France, Germany and the UK, 1950–1993. *Industrial and Corporate Change, 8*(3), 519–551.

Williamson, O. E. (1971). The multidivisional hypothesis. In R. Marris & A. Wood (Eds.), *The corporate economy: Growth, competition, and innovative potential* (pp. 343–386). London: Macmillan.

Williamson, O. E. (1985). *The economic institutions of capitalism: Firms, markets, relational contracting*. New York, NY: Free Press.

Williamson, O. E., & Bhargava, N. (1972). Assessing and classifying the internal structure and control apparatus in the modern corporation. In K. Cowling (Ed.), *Market structure and corporate behaviour* (pp. 125–148). London: Gray-Mills.

PART III
ANALYTIC NARRATIVES: HISTORICAL NARRATIVE MEETS ECONOMIC AND SOCIOLOGICAL THEORY

HISTORY IN STRATEGY RESEARCH: WHAT, WHY, AND HOW?

Paul Ingram, Hayagreeva Rao and
Brian S. Silverman

ABSTRACT

Purpose – *This chapter is intended to help strategy scholars evaluate when, why, and how to employ historical research methods in strategy research.*

Design/methodology/approach – *Drawing on theory and practice of historical research as well as on key examples from the history and strategy literatures, we develop a typology of research approaches to highlight the areas of potential complementarity between historical methods and "traditional" empirical methods in strategy. We then provide annotated examples of historical strategy research to highlight the benefits of this approach and to demonstrate how to make research-related decisions when employing such methods.*

Findings – *The chapter provides a step-by-step conceptual roadmap for conducting historical strategy research, primarily using an analytic narratives approach.*

History and Strategy
Advances in Strategic Management, Volume 29, 241–273
ISSN: 0742-3322/doi:10.1108/S0742-3322(2012)0000029012

Originality/value – The chapter fulfills an explicit need for strategy scholars on the boundary of history. We anticipate that it will be a useful reference for those who are considering the use of history in their strategy research.

Keywords: Analytic narratives; history and strategy

Most fields of social science have active debates about the relative utility of historical approaches. In fields such as political science and sociology, the historical method is well represented, and perhaps more so among the most senior faculty at the most prestigious institutions. In economics, many classic ideas have their roots in history, and economic history is a legitimate and stable subfield. In management there is little explicit attention as to whether, when and how to use history. This is surprising on the face of it. Management derives from a practical interest in phenomena, and history has some notable advantages when it comes to taking phenomena seriously. Moreover, the prevalence of case teaching in management indicates that most management scholars accept that induction from rich descriptions of past episodes has potential for improving understanding in this area.

Ironically, the significance of cases for teaching in management may actually hint at why history is underappreciated as a research method in the field. While there are commonalities between learning from cases and learning from history – specifically an appreciation for context and in the inductive method – cases do not typically meet (or aspire to meet) generally accepted criteria for good history. There is no particular reason that they should, given their function to facilitate students' learning rather than to push forward the vanguard of knowledge of a field. Still, we speculate that familiarity of management faculty with cases, and therefore with their limits as research tools, may have in their minds damned by association the practice of history. This is all the more reason to take up in the context of management the questions we do in this chapter: What is history; why do history; and how to do history?

WHAT IS HISTORY?

Historians are notoriously and maddeningly opaque about their methods. We offer two clear attributes that, when combined, can differentiate between history and other research methods. These two attributes of history are both discussed explicitly by Gaddis (2002), although he labels them a little differently than we do. The juxtaposition of the two attributes to define history relative to other forms of scholarly inquiry is, we think, our own.

Remote Sensing, not Direct Observation

The first is that historians use structures to infer processes. Gaddis (2002, p. 41) compares history to fields such as astronomy, paleontology, or evolutionary biology where "phenomena rarely fit within laboratories, and the time required to see results can exceed the life spans of those who seek them." Practitioners in such fields conduct thought experiments where they use logic to infer the processes that could have produced observed structures, as when geologists propose geological uplift resulting from plate tectonics to explain the fact that strata that could have only been laid down horizontally are now observed to be tilted or vertical. "Historians too start with surviving structures, whether they be archives, artifacts, or even memories" (p. 41) and conduct thought experiments as to what could have happened in the past to produce this residue. The notable distinction here is between fields such as history and geology that interpret residual structures and others, most obviously those that depend on experiments that can "rerun history" or otherwise observe it unfolding.

Gaddis offers the label "remote sensing" to describe the method of inferring processes from residual structures. He offers an example of the onset of the Cuban Missile Crisis, which began when a U-2 spy plane took high-altitude pictures of installations. In his memoir *Thirteen Days*, Robert F. Kennedy says that the pictures looked to him to be "no more than the clearing of a field for a farm or the basement of a house" and that President Kennedy observed that they looked to him like a football field (1969, pp. 23–24). But to those responsible for the photoreconnaissance, who had not been expecting to find missiles in Cuba, the pictures looked like those taken of missile sites in the Soviet Union. Using that comparison, the experts convinced Kennedy and others that their conclusion made sense. The episode then has three stages: a reality on the ground that is not directly observable; an interpretation of the reality that experts made from afar; and the consensus of that interpretation that the experts were able to persuade others to accept. This is a good description of what historians (or geologists) seek to do: To understand a reality, observed from afar, where the quality of the understanding is judged by whether it convinces others.

This last point, about convincing others, is an important one for those who consider using history as a method for strategy research. As we have developed this chapter and discussed it with colleagues, one not uncommon reaction we've heard is that history is not science. Some historians would echo this position with pride. Fischer (1970, pp. xxi–xxii) makes this observation of the field:

> The work of too many professional historians is diminished by an antirational obsession – by an intense prejudice against method, logic and science. In their common speech, "scientism" has become a smear word, and "scientific history" is a phrase which is used merely to condemn the infatuation of an earlier generation. In the process of this reaction, historians have not merely severed their ties with the natural sciences, but have also turned away from science in the larger sense of a structured, ordered, controlled, empirical, rational discipline of thought ... . History, it is said, is an inexact science. But in fact historians are inexact scientists, who go blundering about their business without a sufficient sense of purpose or procedure. They are failed scientists, who have projected their failures to science itself.

Of course, Fischer is criticizing the antiscience bent of some historians, not advocating antiscience as a fundament of history. And he goes on to identify a number of historians' fallacies, with an eye to overcoming the failings identified in the paragraph above. Gaddis (2002) takes a similar position that history should aspire to the same goal of consensus regarding interpretations among the widest set of observers. Experimental science achieves this through replication. In history, as in geology, astronomy, paleontology, and most of evolutionary biology, all that can be replicated are the thought experiments used to deduce processes from structures, to estimate what happened before from what was left behind. The connection between structure and process rests on logic, and there is a test for its quality, and it is exactly the same test used in experimental science: whether there is a consensus among others that it exists.

Contextualism not Reductionism

At the early stages of thinking about this chapter, one of us had lunch with Chris Brown, the noted historian of abolition and the slave trade. One of the things he told us is that historians love to point out that "it is more complicated than that." This sets off alarms in our social-scientific brains. Most social scientists learn Occam's Razor in the socialization phase of their professional education, and the drive to parsimony is one of our mobilizing forces. In the world of social science, "it's more complicated than that" is often taken as a marker that the speaker doesn't understand the point of the enterprise. Good social scientists simplify, they don't aspire to represent all of the complexities of a thing.

Historians, of course, must also simplify. If James Joyce could fill the 700 pages of *Ulysses* describing an average day in the life of one man, imagine the length of an exhaustive written account of all of the complexities of the Battle of Gettysburg, with its tens of thousands of protagonists! That said, historians draw the line of what to exclude at a different place than social scientists. A telling question is on the legitimacy of variables. For most social scientists, theories must ultimately be translated into variables, and showing the relationship between variables is the way that truth is established. For many historians, the resort to variables is an objectionable simplification. Gaddis (2002) labels that practice "reductionism." He argues that the interdependencies between variables are such that it doesn't typically make sense to isolate any single variable as an independent influence on any other. We label the position "contextualism" in regard to its concern for the broader context around any phenomenon.

Management scholars may recognize the contextualist position against reduction to individual variables as a version of systems thinking, and we have some prominent examples of it in the field. For example Snook (2000) examines the strategic, organizational, leadership, decision making, and teamwork issues associated with a friendly fire incident where two US Army Black Hawk helicopters were shot down by two US Air Force F-15s over Northern Iraq in 1994, killing all 26 peacekeepers aboard the helicopters. The episode was associated with a cacophony of causal influences, involving the Black Hawks, the F-15s, the AWACs (flying radar) crew that monitored the no-fly zone, and broader factors.

The helicopters were in the no-fly zone before they should have been; they were not on the flight sheets the F-15 pilots had (because helicopters were not considered "aircraft" by the Air Force) and their pilots were tuned to the wrong codes on the friendly aircraft identification system. The F-15 pilots were not expecting to see anything at all in the no-fly zone when they entered it. They misidentified the Black Hawks as Iraqi hinds, perhaps because the helicopters were configured unusually with sponsons, perhaps because their training was insufficient with regard to identifying helicopters, based as it was on looking at slides of aircraft projected on a screen from a 35 mm projector where few of the slides were of helicopters, and most of those were taken from the ground looking up, perhaps because they struggled to control their own high-altitude aircraft as they descended to low altitudes over rugged terrain, perhaps simply because it is hard to visually identify any object when your speed relative to it is more than 300 miles per hour. They shot down the helicopters, which were no threat at that moment to anyone, despite the fact that in a few minutes two F-16s that were scheduled to enter the no-fly zone, which would have been better suited to deal with the low-flying helicopters. The quick action of the F-15 pilots occurred in a context of rivalry with other pilots, and in an era where a typical fighter pilot uses millions of dollars of training and equipment, but never gets an opportunity to fire a weapon in earnest. The AWACs crew that was meant to be monitoring the no-fly zone did not warn the F-15s. That crew was a poorly formed team, with new members, and an unusual configuration caused by the failure of a terminal. Members of the crew were uncertain as to who was responsible for the Black Hawk as it transitioned from outside to inside the no-fly zone, and members did not know the codename for the destination of the Black Hawks, a Kurdish town deep in no-fly zone. All of this is against a backdrop of interservice rivalry, a temporary Operation that had been going on for years, staffed by temporary participants from different basis that seldom train together, including an overstretched AWACs staff that was experiencing a morale crisis.

So just what is causing what in this episode? Snook (2000, p. 21) presents a causal map with some fifty interdependent causes. Some of these he identifies as "essential to the historical configuration as it 'actually' happened and a significant historical cause of what followed" (Griffin, 1993, p. 1101). But there are multiple essential causes, for example that the first F-15 pilot misidentified the Black Hawks as Hinds, and that the automatic system for identifying friendly aircraft also failed to recognize the Black Hawks. And each of these has a number of contributing causes, and so on. Snook is able to develop causal accounts that make sense at the level of the individual, group, organization and system, but none of those causal clusters are self-contained in the sense that changing something or even everything within any one of them would necessarily have produced a different result. Snook advocates looking at complex events "from a probabilistic perspective – one that emphasizes the importance of looking across levels of analysis and time – not in search of *the cause*, but rather in search of a broader set of conditions that increases the likelihood of such tragedies occurring" (p. 24, emphasis in original).

Of course, a multi-causal approach does not mean that that nobody is accountable, and it does not mean that historians view all causal influences as equal. Consider the treatment of historical causality by Bloch (1953), still one of the most influential statements of the historic method. Bloch considers a hiker who falls over a cliff:

> For this accident to happen, the combination of a great number of determining elements was necessary, such as, among others, the existence of gravity; a terrain resulting from protracted geological changes; the laying of a path … . It would be perfectly legitimate to say that, were the laws of celestial mechanics different, had the evolution of the earth been otherwise, were alpine economy not founded upon the seasonal migration of flocks, the fall would not have happened. Nevertheless, should we inquire to the cause, everyone would answer: "A misstep." It is not that this antecedent was most necessary to the occurrence of the event. Many others were just as necessary. But it was distinguished from all the rest by several very striking characteristics: it occurred last; it was the least permanent, the most exceptional in the general order of things; finally, by virtue of this great particularity, it seems the antecedent which could have been most easily avoided. (p. 191)

What this means is that historians must impose discipline on the counter-factuals they use to identify whether a given factor is causally essential (Griffin, 1993). Weber (1949, p. 164) said that posited historical alternatives must be "objective possibilities." Hawthorne (1991, p. 158) argues that the possible worlds of counterfactual scenarios should start with the real world as it was known before the counterfactual, should not require to "unwind the past," and should not disturb what we otherwise understand about the actors and their contexts.

Contextualism is not the same as multivariate analysis. That too recognizes a form of multi-causality, but it assumes independence, or some well-specified interdependence between the causal influences. For contextualists, that assumption is simply untenable in complex situations. This raises the question as to why social scientists use multivariate statistics while historians resist them. According to Gaddis (2002, p. 65) social scientists prefer reductionist over contextualist methods of inquiry because reductionalism facilitates efforts to forecast the future:

> That's why models depend on parsimony, for when systems become complex, variables proliferate and forecasting becomes impossible: systems themselves become entangled in events. Parsimony, therefore, is a life preserver for social scientists: it keeps them from drowning in complexity. Historians, who swim in that medium, have little need of it.

He goes on to argue that social scientists often oversimplify in the drive to produce "actionable" multivariate models:

> Too many social scientists, in their efforts to specify independent variables, have lost sight of a basic requirement of theory, which is to account for reality. They reduce complexity to simplicity in order to anticipate the future, but in doing so they oversimplify the past. (p. 70)

Others echo the position that historians don't forecast, for example, Collingwood (1956, p. 54) who noted "[t]he historian's business is to know the past, not to know the future, and whenever historians claim to be able to determine the future in advance of its happening we may know with certainty that something has gone wrong with their fundamental conception of history." Here again, alarm bells ring in the minds of management scholars. Ours is an applied field, and the ultimate goal of our research must be to improve practice *in the future*. So what good is history to us if it can't be used to forecast?

Fortunately, there is some wiggle room on the question of how the past can be used to predict the future. Understanding the past is of course relevant for understanding the future. Even Gaddis, who is so clear about the drive to prediction as the distinction between history and other social sciences, admits that "[w]e know the future only by the past we project into it. History, in this sense, is all we have" (p. 3). Part of the challenge for history or any other form of contextualism is that the "ceteris paribus" assumption of predictions from multivariate models often doesn't make sense. You cannot reasonably assert that "a one unit increase in X is associated with a .38 unit increase in Y" if you do not believe that X can be changed independent of a cluster of other influences, or if you fear that a change in X could have a systemic repercussion that produces not Y, but the Spanish Inquisition.

Nevertheless, historians use and contribute to theory, and history does generate insights about the future. Many historians would say that when a historian considers the future, she stops doing history (Fischer, 1970 calls historically informed prediction "pseudo-history") but most would agree that it can be done usefully. The concerns of the contextualist position put two constraints on historical views of the future. First, they tend to be limited and particular. The farther away from the context – temporally, specially, culturally – the greater the risk that their systemic insights won't apply. In other words, they carefully consider the scope conditions of their knowledge claims (Cohen, 1989). This is probably something that all social scientists, including strategy scholars, should be doing anyway, so it is not much of a constraint on the utility of history in our field. Second, contextualist understandings tend to generate more systemic predictions and prescriptions, suggesting a complex of interrelated changes rather than isolated mechanisms. For example, consider one of the great applications of systemic thinking in organizational theory, Diane Vaughan's (1996) *The Challenger Launch Decision*. Vaughan believes that understanding the Challenger disaster can help contemporary managers, and she derives multipart advice to them to target elite decisions, culture, structure and the normalization of deviance. But she would resist the attempt to translate the

Challenger episode into a single stand-alone manipulation that would be predicted to produce better organizational outcomes. Such a prescription would defy her systemic, multi-causal understanding.

The fact that history provides "complex prescriptions" may actually make it particularly useful for the field of strategic management, where simple prescriptions are less useful because if they were right, they would be done by all firms, and yield competitive advantage to none. The utility of history in this area is demonstrated by Bill Duggan's (2007) *Strategic Intuition*, which answers the billion-dollar question, "What can you do to get great strategic ideas?" The book uses history in two ways, as the source of understanding as to where great ideas come from, and as part of the recipe for strategic intuition. Duggan began by doing history, studying the origins of some great ideas. One instance he examines is Napoleon's breakthrough moment, the inspiration to break the siege of Toulon. Duggan attributes the big idea to the combination of four pieces of knowledge, about contour maps, light cannon, the British surrender at Yorktown, and the siege of Orleans:

> At Toulon these four elements came together in Napoleon's mind. The contour maps showed him l'Aiguillette, a small fort around the main fortress, as at Orleans. Light cannon hauled up there could command the harbor and cut off the British army from its navy, as at Boston and Yorktown. We can see from this example that a flash of insight for strategic intuition has the same basic structure as expert intuition, except that the elements that combine in the mind come from farther afield, usually from outside the strategist's direct experience. (2007, p. 57)

Part of Duggan's advice to strategists is to "take lessons from history" so they are prepared to do the creative combination that is part of strategic intuition. But importantly, combining lessons from history is only part of strategic intuition, and only part of Duggan's prescription. There are three other parts: presence of mind, flash of insight, and resolution. Without all of these, a strategist's lessons from history would not amount to anything.

Fig. 1 presents our answer to the "what is history" question. History is empirical research that uses remote sensing and a contextualist approach to explanation. This allows us to position it relative to other familiar forms of empirical research. Experimentalism uses direct observation of processes; it "reruns history" rather than making sense of its residue. It also uses reductionism to isolate single causes and effects. Multivariate statistics is like history in that it uses remote sensing, looking to the structures (archives, surveys, accounting records) in an attempt to understand the processes that produced them, and also uses the reductionist appeal to variables. Ethnography shares history's contextualism, and directly observes processes.

	Reductionism	Contextualism
Direct Observation	Experimentalism	Ethnography
Remote Sensing	Multivariate Statistics	History

Fig. 1. What is History and How Is It Different from Other Styles of Scholarship?

History is the form of empirical scholarship at the intersection of remote sensing and contextualism.

WHEN/WHY HISTORY?

Fischer (1970, pp. 315–316) lists five ways that history can be useful: (1) to understand the context of a contemporary problem; (2) through forecasting trends and prospects (he calls this process "quasi-historical"); (3) for refining theoretical knowledge; (4) to help us understand who we are; and (5) to help people think historically, which to him is the most important. The third item in this list is of obvious utility to strategy research, but the others are also relevant to strategy. Regarding the first item, the context of contemporary problems, we have ourselves argued that contention over Walmart's expansion, and the strategies of both the corporation and its opponents, should be understood against the backdrop of the anti-chain store movements of the early 20th century (Ingram & Rao, 2004; Ingram, Yue, & Rao, 2010). In the same spirit, Galambos (1975) provides context for understanding contemporary debates regarding the role of big business in society. Any of a host of studies of institutional change would illustrate the usefulness of "quasi-historical" forecasting for strategists and strategy scholars. Dobbin (1994) offers a fine example of a historical effort to help strategists understand "who they are." His comparative-historical examination of industrial policy in the railway age suggests that they are not rational economic actors, but rather products of culture and ideological path dependence. As for thinking historically, Duggan's (2007) compelling account of where great strategies come from would motivate any aspiring strategist to pay attention to history.

Below, we draw on two examples of ongoing work to describe how history can be particularly useful for the study of strategic and organizational phenomena. The first focuses on the utility of history as a source of exogenous variations and therefore an approach that allows for better causal inference. The second focuses on the utility of history to as a source of legacies and therefore an approach that easily supports analyses of path dependence.

History as a Source of Exogenous Variation

Rao and Dutta (2012) study how "free" spaces – that is, those far removed from surveillance by authorities – facilitate disobedience. As an example, Black churches can be conceived as free spaces which served as havens for activists and enabled them to organize the US civil rights movement. Specifically, Rao and Dutta explore the role of free spaces in enabling soldiers to overcome problems of pluralistic ignorance and organize mutinies. They begin by situating the study of mutiny in organization theory. Much of the literature on the firm treats shirking by *individuals* as the main organizational problem, and focuses on incentive and monitoring mechanisms as the solution. However, overt *collective* disobedience in hierarchies is also a problem – and mutinies aiming to overthrow authority are a particularly trenchant example.

Mutinies are interesting because "a military's ability to act decisively is founded upon the principle of discipline, and mutiny is the antithesis of discipline ... . It is more than a breach of regulations, and is the negation of the military essence" (Rose, 1982, pp. 562–563). More importantly, mutinies deserve scrutiny because soldiers lack power vis-à-vis their commanders and are subject to intensive socialization that does not allow them to question the status quo. Putative leaders face a very restricted political opportunity structure; they can neither frame grievances publicly to whip up emotion nor recruit followers due to surveillance by authorities and tough sanctions. Underground proselytizing is an option, but covert appeals and mobilization tactics put an upper bound on the scale of the rebellion – secrecy works only if the scale is small; otherwise, potential leaders can easily be detected.

Given these resource-mobilization constraints, soldiers in armies confront the problem of pluralistic ignorance – they may have incorrect beliefs about the beliefs of others, and may underestimate dissatisfaction. Moreover, when avenues of communication are constrained in a repressive regime, discontent may fail to emerge even when soldiers may be privately opposed to commanders because the public utterances of soldiers imply support for the regime (Kuran, 1989). Of course, it is possible that in an army, soldiers in a unit are more likely to mutiny once they observe mutinies of other units – however, this is an issue of interunit coordination, and begs the question of how people within a unit such as a regiment overcome coordination problems and mutiny. For soldiers within a unit to mobilize, their emotions need to be primed, a sense of shared identity has to made manifest, and common knowledge of the willingness of others to participate has to be created – each person must know the intentions of others to participate, and each person must know that each other person knows about it. A possible solution for soldiers is to exploit "free spaces" – social settings insulated from repression by authorities where people can organize.

There are a number of problems with extant research on free spaces. First, many studies chronicle successful movements but omit failures – thereby, selecting on the dependent variable. Second, even when a success and a failure are compared, it is unclear whether the free space is an antecedent of collective action or a consequence. Finally, it is also unclear as to whether capable activists were attracted to some settings and thereby, allowed the settings to have an effect on successful organizing. In other words, sorting of activists by quality than the character of free spaces may underlie effective organizing.

In order to explore whether free spaces matter, the best possible research design is to randomly assign free spaces to potential locations and then evaluate the results. Since this is unrealistic, the next best option is to exploit exogenous variation, where an act of nature or a system external to the dependent variable under the study allows for variation in the availability of free spaces. This is exactly where history comes in because the historical record can provide tantalizing examples of exogenous variation.

Rao and Dutta (2012) analyzed mutinies in the East India Company's Bengal Native Army's regiments in 1857. A number of writers trace the mutinies to administrative reforms that threatened the collective identities of Hindu and Moslem soldiers; changes in enlistment and pension of soldiers, the forced abdication of traditional rulers by the British in the previous few years, laws allowing remarriage of Hindu widows, and a rumor about contaminated cartridges. Rao and Dutta argued that religious festivals were free spaces that enabled soldiers to overcome problems of pluralistic ignorance. Religious festivals brought large numbers of people together, primed their emotions, stoked emotional contagion, and created common knowledge of the willingness of others to participate. Clearly, the timing of religious festivals in 1857 was fixed according to Hindu and Islamic religious calendars – fixed before the mutinies occurred – and hence, is "external" to the dependent variable of interest – in this case, the rate of mutiny.

They found that the rate of mutiny in the Bengal Army declines as time since a religious festival elapses – thus, mutinies are most likely to occur at or right after a religious festival. They also showed that religious festivals intensified moral solidarity when regiments had strong community ties – hence, regiments are more likely to mutiny at or right after a religious festival when they are physically close to the towns and villages they were recruited from. They also predict that exposure to an oppositional identity also magnified the solidarity enhancing effects of religious festivals – thus, mutinies would have occurred at or after a religious festival when regiments were located near a Christian mission.

We used the same strategy of resorting to a historical context as part of an identification strategy regarding an ongoing phenomenon in Silverman and Ingram (2012). In that chapter, described more fully below, we examined the efficacy of management ownership as a solution to the principal-agent problem by analyzing the success of commercial sea voyages in the 18th century. Specifically, we relied on the outbreak of war during long voyage to determine whether ships captained by owners had better results than others. This case, like that of the Bengal mutineers, shows the two particular advantages of history for exogenous variation. First, the perspective that history provides allows us more opportunity to understand what is connected to what, and what is independent. For example, we were able to resort to insurance records to confirm that the stakeholders of voyages did not anticipate the outbreak of war, a test that would probably not have been possible in a contemporary context, given that the records were private, and emerged only over time. Second, historical contexts may have the empirical advantage of being "pre-theoretical." One of the problems of examining the effect of owner management in contemporary contexts is that principal-agent theory is so well diffused that managers may operate according to it because they believe it, not because it reflects some independent behavioral reality. Sociologists of knowledge call this phenomenon "performativity." By going back in time, we create the opportunity to test a theory, instead of merely discovering a performance of the theory.

History as a Source of Legacies

We turn to a second study by Greve and Rao (2012) to illustrate how history matters as a source of institutional legacies. Their starting point is the idea that nonprofit organizations underlie civic capacity – nonprofits train activists, spin out other organizations, socialize members, and become a routine for how to solve collective-action problems. Greve and Rao ask why some communities have an abundance of nonprofit organizations over long periods of time while other communities suffer from a dearth of such organizations. This is a puzzle because the lengthy historical effects seem difficult to explain by the current presence of nonprofit organizations.

Unlike Stinchcombe who saw the organization as target and environment as the source of imprinting, Greve and Rao (2012) reverse the imagery and propose that nonprofit *founding events* imprint communities with a model for collective action and skills in building subsequent organizations. They build on the idea that communities that are early adopters of a specific organizational form solve a more difficult collective-action problem than the later adopters. Hence, early differences in mobilization amplify preexisting differences among communities in their capacity for collective action.

Greve and Rao (2012) rely on an empirical strategy in which the founding of one kind of nonprofit had positive spillovers on different forms of nonprofits at later points in time. They study whether solving the problem of collective risk pooling through mutual insurance and bank organizations in 19th century Norway can be related to the founding of cooperative retail stores in 20th century Norway. Their analysis demonstrates that the earlier a community in Norway created mutual insurance societies and banks to solve problems of risk-pooling insurance and finance in the 19th century, the more likely it was to create consumer cooperatives in the 20th century. Informal customs of aid giving became encoded into mutuals in the 19th century, and in turn, such institutions underlay the legacy. Greve and Rao found that the average treatment effect of having a mutual founded early increased in size over time, which is consistent with an institutional legacy creating a self-reinforcing cycle of organization building that eventually led to the founding of cooperative stores. Thus, an institutional legacy of mutualism in pioneering communities led to persistently high levels of mutualism 50 years later in a different domain.

This example illustrates most of Fischer's (1970) uses of history. It refines theory, it identifies the context of a contemporary question, it offers the potential for forecasting, and informs us as to who we are (or at least who the Norwegians are!). More generally, the phenomenon of institutional change is arguably the richest opportunity to use history in strategy research. Institutions are, of course, central to strategy making and organizational performance, as they define opportunities and constraints in the environments that organizations operate in (Ingram & Silverman,

2002). Institutions change over long periods of time, they are idiosyncratic, and represent complex interdependencies, so they are hard to analyze with ethnography, experimental or statistical methods. This leaves history, and it no coincidence that the classic examinations of institutional change are historical (e.g., North, 1990).

HOW HISTORY?

The first section of this chapter discussed "what is history" – how does historical research differ from, and complement, conventional strategy and organizations research. The second section discussed "when/why history" – in what circumstances might historical strategy and organizations research be particularly useful, and what are the benefits of such research. In this section, we discuss "how history" – if one is persuaded that such research is worth pursuing, how does one go about pursuing it? We describe an approach to historical strategy research and present "self-conscious" examples of the approach – that is, articles that seek to explicate the execution of such research as well as to contribute content-wise to the literature. We also discuss the execution of one of our own in-process studies to illuminate how we approached issues of inference, evaluation of data sources, revision of theory when confronted with data, etc. We hope that this discussion will provide a roadmap for other strategy and organizations scholars who are enthusiastic about historical research.[1]

At a broad level, historical research wrestles with the same challenges that beset conventional strategy research: how can we best explain a particular phenomenon, and what generalizable lessons can we draw for the explanation of related phenomena? Put most generally, how can we most effectively confront theoretical explanations/predictions with data so that we can draw reasonable inferences?

In addressing these challenges, historical research differs from conventional strategy research in least one conceptual and one empirical dimension. As noted above, historical research devotes more effort to the details of specific phenomena, trying to contextualize the phenomena. Also, historical research "thinks differently" about the use of variation in detailed data to draw inference and thus test theory. Whether in small-N or large-N settings, historical research devotes greater attention to "outlier" observations – that is, why didn't this event occur at a different point in time, or why is there a set of observations for whom the "average" cause–effect relationship does not appear to hold? The analytic narratives approach incorporates this perspective on details and inference into a methodological framework that is quite comfortable for most strategy scholars, as it continues to draw on conventional empirical tools (e.g., Bates, Greif, Levi, Rosenthal, & Weingast, 1998).

Analytic Narratives

The "analytic narratives" project is a methodological approach to integrate a systematic rational-choice lens with more traditional narrative explanations of historical phenomena. As Alexandrova (2009) notes, the pairing of models with narratives has a long and distinguished history. But the analytic narrative project, as initiated by Bates et al. (1998), is distinct in that it self-consciously attempts to simultaneously apply and exemplify this approach. Put most narrowly, studies adhering to this approach focus on confronting formal game-theoretic models with data from detailed narratives. We believe that the approach can be applied more generally within strategy research to confront a range of rigorous models, either formal or natural language, with detailed historical narratives.[2]

What is an analytic narrative? An analytic narrative is an approach to research that draws simultaneously on analytical tools commonly used in economics and on the narrative form that is commonly employed in history. In order to understand key phenomena – frequently, instances of institutional origin and change – analytic narrativists combine deep knowledge of the case and an explicit theoretical model. Compared to traditional historical efforts, analytic narratives make greater use of the types of theoretical models that bring comfort to strategy scholars. Compared to conventional strategy methods, analytic narratives make greater use of idiosyncratic details of the "case" or empirical context; in particular, analytic narratives seek to extract useful information from seemingly peripheral details that do not fit the basic theory, rather than dismissing them as "outliers." The key to an analytic narrative, then, is neither the data nor the theory, but rather the "interplay" between them – the way that a scholar iterates between model and data.

Consider, for example, Bates's (1998) examination of the International Coffee Organization (ICO), a cartel that regulated global coffee exports from 1962 until 1989. On the face of it, the ICO appears to have operated as a classic cartel, in which coffee-producing countries collaborated to restrict supply and keep prices high. But Bates notes several puzzles: Why did the ICO arise when it did? Why did it collapse when it did? Why was the United

States a member of the ICO when it is a coffee-importing nation and therefore should have preferred greater supply and lower prices?

As Bates describes, the ICO was born in response to mixed results of prior efforts at cartelization of the market. After Brazil became the dominant coffee producer in the late 19th century, its government attempted to set prices near the monopoly level. This effort attracted new entrants such as Colombia, and efforts to restrict output receded. By the mid-1920s, Brazil once again tried to restrict output, encouraging other exporters to cooperate and occasionally flooding the market if they did not. These efforts generally worked to restrict output by existing exporters and to prevent entry from new countries. But during World War II the European market was cut off from Latin American producers, and African countries took advantage of the opportunity to export coffee to Europe. In the 1950s, Brazil repeatedly threatened to flood the market if these recent entrants did not exit or restrict output, but never acted on those threats.

With the failure of the old arrangements, Brazil and other major Latin American countries moved to create the more formal ICO cartel. The big difference between the ICO and prior arrangements was the participation of the United States – the world's largest importer of coffee. This made it much easier to police output-restricting agreements and to ensure that non-ICO countries could not sell into the major import market. But why would the United States join an organization that would drive up the price of coffee for American consumers? Bates describes how Brazil and Colombia framed the ICO as a bulwark against Communism; by strengthening Latin American economies, higher coffee prices would help purchase national security for the United States. Bates describes the rather complex interaction among State Department officials, Congressional representatives, and large US coffee firms such as General Foods that led to the entry of United States into the ICO in 1962, concurrent with the Cuban Missile Crisis. The ICO's collapse in 1989 was concurrent with the fall of the Berlin Wall and the reduction in the perceived threat of Communism.

At various points during this narrative, Bates stops to consider the application of game-theoretic models to the story. He notes that the classic chain-store model of entry deterrence appears to explain behavior in the 1920s, but fails to explain it in the 1950s. This leads him to consider models of "third-party enforcement" to understand the role of the United States in the ICO. He first considers and discards the "Chicago school" view and the "realist view" of third-party enforcement; the former because it cannot explain why a consumer nation would take action that enhances producers at the expense of consumers, and the latter because it does not accurately reflect the complex disagreements among Congress, the Executive branch, and private firms before joining the ICO. Bates ultimately finds that the narrative of the ICO is best described by a combination of two models: a positive-political-theory model of domestic politics (Peltzman, 1976) and a model of raising rivals' costs (Salop & Scheffman, 1983; Williamson, 1968).

At the end of this study, then, we have a deeper understanding of the ICO than we would get from either a detailed narrative description or from a conventional application of economic/strategic models. And, while analytic narratives tend to emphasize explanation of a particular phenomenon over generalizable implications, we arguably have a richer sense of which combination of general models might be useful in explaining other cartel situations in the economy. We also have a sense of causality that is markedly similar to that invoked by Bloch (1953) and invoked above – just as the primary cause of the hiker's fall is a misstep, the primary cause of the ICO's success is the consensus among a variety of US entities that the ICO would simultaneously provide a bulwark against Communism and serve the economic interests of several politically connected firms, even though there were many other contributory causes in both instances.

Although the pioneers of the analytic narrative approach explicitly favor formal models, an alternative is to rely on rigorous yet nonformalized theory. For example, Hansen and Libecap (2004) generate new insight into the causes of the Dust Bowl – "one of the most severe environmental crises in North America in the twentieth century" (p. 666) – by combining detailed historical narrative with a collective-action lens. The Dust Bowl of the 1930s resulted from severe droughts and wind erosion that destroyed vast amounts of farmland in the American Midwest, causing severe health hazards and sparking a massive migration of desperate farmers to other parts of the country, notably California.

The conventional explanation for the Dust Bowl implicates "excessive cultivation" and the lack of investment in anti-erosion practices. But two anti-erosion techniques were well known at the time. Strip-fallow farming was a form of crop rotation based on alternating strips of planted crops with fallow strips (covered with wheat stubble) that reduced the amount of soil exposed to the wind. Alternatively, the planting of trees or bushes as windbreaks could protect downwind fields. This raises the question: why did farmers fail to engage in such erosion-enhancing practices, given the devastating outcomes associated with erosion?

Hansen and Libecap (2004) first describe the key features of the Dust Bowl. Chief among these is a description of precisely how wind erosion affected the soil. Specifically, when land has been extensively cultivated, the top layer of soil is exposed, dry, and broken up. Such soil could be swept up by the wind and transported for great distances. Tiny particles could be carried hundreds of miles away; heavier particles would travel shorter distances and, upon landing, could smother vegetation and/or destroy the soil on which it landed. Of particular interest, the main cost of erosion was therefore felt by downwind farms on whose property the heavier particles would land. Consequently, "a major externality in the 1930s occurred when sand from one farmer's unprotected fields drifted across the fallow strips and fields of his downwind neighbor, eliminating any of the productive benefits of those investments" (p. 672).

Reinterpreting the historical record through the lens of collective-action problems, Hansen and Libecap identify a key cause of underinvestment in anti-erosion: although a focal farmer would incur the costs of anti-erosion investments, most of the benefits would accrue to his downwind neighbor. In turn, a farmer whose upwind neighbor did not invest in anti-erosion practices would likely see his farmland ruined despite his efforts to stop erosion; therefore he had less incentive to invest in anti-erosion efforts himself. The authors generate testable implications from this: the above-described collective action will be worse the smaller the average farm size in an area.

Armed with this precise prediction, the authors then turn to the data. They collect county-level data on farm size, proportion of farmland that is lying fallow (a proxy for strip-fallow farming), average wind speed and rainfall, and extent of wind erosion. They demonstrate that counties with smaller farms have a lower proportion of farmland lying fallow. They further demonstrate that erosion is negatively associated with the proportion of fallow farmland.

Not content to stop there, Hansen and Libecap (2004) continue with a detailed narrative describing government efforts to encourage adoption of anti-erosion efforts in the late 1930s. By digging into the reports and internal communications of entities such as the Erosion Control Work Camp, the authors demonstrate that farms that agreed to cooperate with these government efforts were the larger farms within an area, while smaller farms dragged their feet. Indeed, the owners of larger farms encouraged government regulators to be more aggressive in their efforts to mandate anti-erosion efforts and thus compel small farms to join these efforts. Going further, the authors note that, although the US Midwest suffered droughts in the 1950s and 1970s that were more severe than the 1930s drought, erosion was minimal; while more proactive regulation receives some credit for this, the authors point out that average farm size expanded dramatically between the 1930s and later decades. Putting this all together, Hansen and Libecap make a compelling case that, while the conventional wisdom correctly identifies "excessive cultivation" and lack of investment in anti-erosion efforts as key factors driving the Dust Bowl of the 1930s, the underlying cause of these actions was a classic collective-action problem due to negative externalities.

How did Bates (1998) and Hansen and Libecap (2004) do these studies? Building on Levi (2002), we suggest that scholars must tackle five tasks in such a study: select a case, construct or adopt a model, collect and appraise source materials, engage iteratively in deduction and induction, and evaluate the results.

Select a Case
There are several distinct criteria that can be used to select cases for examination (Levi, 2002; Mahoney, 2004). In the analytic narrative approach, scholars typically start with a general theory and then find cases that actually test parts of that theory. The scholars sometimes bring to a study a deep knowledge about a particular historical setting, but often develop this deep knowledge after selecting the case. Thus, Bates started with a general interest in exploring the limits of game-theoretic models of collective action. Armed with this theoretical foundation, he searched for examples of collective action; in particular, he selected a case that exhibited both successful and failed attempts to act collectively over time. This variation over time is useful in analytic narratives because it can inject a comparative element into a "single-case" setting. Libecap has long studied the role of property rights in addressing the "tragedy of the commons." He and Hansen identified a case in which the commonly accepted explanation for a crisis – underinvestment in anti-erosion efforts during the 1930s Dust Bowl – appeared incomplete. Why should there be underinvestment in such efforts given the devastating results of erosion? Thus, their theoretical foundation enabled them to identify a case that would likely enable them to test parts of their theory.

Construct or Adopt a Model
Having selected a case with a general theory in mind, scholars then construct or adopt a specific model to (attempt to) explain the case. Analytic narratives tend to favor parsimonious models, in which a handful of key variables drive explanation. The choice of key variables is important to the narrative because it directs the scholar's attention toward these variables, and reduces the attention she devotes to other variables. Thus, as Levi

(2002) notes, "for Bates one sort of contingency was critical: movements in the price of coffee. Variations in US economic activity – however important they may be to the world economy – were much less salient." Put differently, Bates's adoption of specific models of collective action such as the chain-store model of entry deterrence, or the dominant-firm – as – cartel-disciplinarian model, privilege price and output as key variables by which to measure success of cartelization efforts. It is not surprising that much of his narrative then describes countries' reactions to changes in price and output.

Hansen and Libecap also construct and adopt a model, but the model is not a formal game. Rather, they draw on the basic model of the "common-pool problem," which privileges externality as the key variable by which to measure likelihood of underinvestment. This then contours their narrative, as they describe the dynamics of wind erosion in terms that make clear exactly when such erosion will or will not generate negative externalities.[3] Hansen and Libecap's case has variation both cross-sectionally and over time. Although the empirical estimations rely primarily on cross-sectional county variation in average farm size, the scholars also study the shift to active regulatory encouragement of collective action.

Collect and Appraise Source Materials
Historical sources may be either primary (original source documents, such as contracts, letters, diaries, strategic plans) or secondary (other histories). Historians take a skeptical approach to both kinds. For primary sources, these include an evaluation of who wrote the document, for what purposes, and for what audience. The key is not only what evidence it presents regarding some phenomenon of interest, but what values and interests it represents, and how these may be expected to affect its quality and character as evidence. Much the same critical screen is applied to secondary sources. Typical questions would be whether the facts they present are reliable or comprehensive and whether the interpretations they present of those facts are credible. The critical evaluation of both primary and secondary sources is aided by comparisons between documents, and as a result historians take comprehensive approaches, looking at almost everything they can get that may be relevant to the phenomenon. Good historians do not stop when they find evidence in line with their expectations.

Deduction and Induction: Engage Iteratively in Analysis and Narrative
Bates begins with an initial deduction that the ICO's behavior can be explained by a model of oligopoly behavior. He then confronts the deduction with data. Whereas a traditional strategy study will test the hypotheses

and then declare support (with some genuflection toward acknowledging outliers and the limited R^2) or rejection, after considering the narrative Bates revisits his theory to elaborate a better explanation of causal connections. He thus elaborates the theory inductively, by iterating between analysis and narrative, until he finds a theoretical model that appears to explain the salient features of the ICO's life: a model of political economy augmented with raising rivals' costs.

Bates's study, and the studies of his coauthors in Bates et al. (1998), go to great pains to lay out the iteration between analysis and narrative precisely because the book is designed to explicate the analytic narrative approach. It is likely that strategy journals will be less willing to devote extensive space for an article to lay out this iteration in great detail. Nevertheless, it is feasible for a scholar to engage in this process, and to streamline the presentation of the results in an article for a journal article (for examples in the analytic narrative approach in management journal articles see Ingram & Ingram, 1996 on institutional evolution at Niagara Falls, and Simons & Ingram, 2003 on the competition between the Israeli kibbutz and other organizational forms).

And not every study of this type will necessarily lead to extended iteration. Hansen and Libecap find evidence that is almost entirely consistent with their basic prediction that small farm size is correlated with underinvestment in anti-erosion efforts. If there are few items that raise questions about the initial deduction, then a scholar will end up engaging in relatively little iteration.

Evaluate the Results
Finally, a scholar must evaluate her interpretation, or at least must enable the reader to evaluate her interpretation. Levi (2002) suggests three criteria for evaluation: Is the interpretation logical, has the interpretation been confirmed by the data (and preferably, has it been confirmed more conclusively than alternative explanations), and does it generate any generalizable insight? In the course of considering and discarding models, Bates lays out the assumptions on which each model is based and thus makes it easy for the reader to assess whether these assumptions are plausible in the ICO setting. If one agrees that these assumptions are plausible, and if one accepts that each model logically generates its ascribed prediction given its assumptions, then one must accept the interpretation as logical. Bates explicitly discusses how some features of various models are confirmed by the data but other features are not, and he explains his conclusion that the political economy/raising rivals' costs model "wins" the

race for most features confirmed. Unless one can come up with an alternative explanation beyond those that he has already considered, one is likely to agree that his preferred interpretation has been confirmed more conclusively than alternate explanations. As for generalizability, although Bates does not dwell on this much, one can envision applying his preferred model to analyze other cases of cartel behavior, to discern the range of cases in which it is applicable, to identify its limits, and to seek to enhance the model iteratively to overcome those limits.

An In-Process Example

To further elucidate how to "do" history-infused strategy research, we briefly describe an in-process project in which we are dealing with these very issues. In a current project (Silverman & Ingram, 2012), two of us are studying the pattern of vessel ownership by Liverpool ship captains in the 18th century. Our general motivation for this study was a desire to contribute to the literature on incentive effects of asset ownership by employees (e.g., Baker & Hubbard, 2003; Nickerson & Silverman, 2003), particularly on the performance effects of providing stock ownership to top management (Bergstresser & Philippon, 2006; Core & Larcker, 2002). We were particularly intrigued by the idea of studying a historical example of this because contemporary instances of manager ownership are likely to be motivated by theories regarding the efficacy of the practice, and may even be effective because of those beliefs. With a historical approach we were able to examine a currently important theory in a context which is not itself tainted by the theory.

Selecting the Case

One of us has pursued research on the related industry of British shipbuilding (Ingram & Lifschitz, 2006; Ingram, Lifschitz, & Luo, 2010). But in all candor, the specific empirical setting for this project stemmed from Serendip: On a pleasure-related visit to Liverpool, one of us happened to wander into the archives library room while visiting the Mersey Maritime Museum. He quickly realized that there was a remarkable store of data about virtually every vessel that sailed across the Atlantic Ocean from Liverpool, going as far back as the 1740s. Among other items, the data included the names of all owners of each vessel, and the name of the vessel's captain. Roughly 20% of the time the vessel's captain was also a part owner of the vessel. Presto: given our general theoretical problem, we had what appeared to be a feasible empirical setting, with the necessary variation to explore the causes and consequences of asset ownership.[4]

Constructing/Adopting the Model

Organizational economics has generated strong predictions suggesting that asset ownership is often used to align incentives between principals and agents regarding protection of the asset. (Of course, although such asset ownership may successfully enhance the agent's incentive to protect the asset, it may distort incentives for other behavior, which explains why it is not universally used but rather employed in cases where the need for asset-protecting action is more likely.) Based on this general prediction, we developed the initial intuition that captains' vessel ownership would be more prevalent for voyages that were at high risk for damage to the vessel, and where the captain might not have an intrinsic interest in protecting the vessel. But what sort of voyages would these be? Clearly, owners don't want their vessel to sink in mid-ocean because they will lose their investment. But presumably a captain is quite motivated to prevent the vessel from sinking in mid-ocean, since he will likely lose his life in the process. To make progress on identification of voyages that carried high risk of vessel damage but not of harm to the captain, we needed to understand the setting more deeply.

Collect and Appraise Source Materials

Before this project, neither of us was a scholar of 18th-century transatlantic maritime trade; indeed, other than reading papers such as Peter Leeson's (2007) work on piracy and watching movies such as "Master and Commander," neither of us had ever thought much about this particular setting. So we began to learn the history, and we began to explore the data to understand the range of activity that was included.

To learn the history, we consulted original sources as well as books and articles by historians. We studied materials in three streams: general studies on Liverpool's history, studies of transatlantic maritime trade, and studies of the careers of sea captains. Our goal was to understand the general problems associated with this trade during the 18th century as well as the specific features of particular sea routes and of particular time periods during this century. Some studies presented detailed pictures of single voyages or of individual captains' excursions as exemplars of the opportunities associated with the trade and the challenges that had to be overcome (e.g., Behrendt, 2007; Schwartz, 1995). Others offered statistical information on the flows of transatlantic trade, the prices of transported goods over time, the effect of wars on maritime trade, the career paths of captains, and so on (e.g., Behrendt, 1991; Lovejoy & Richardson, 1995). Still others described the growth and social change within Liverpool throughout the 18th century (e.g., Brooke, 1853; Gore, 1766; and the town records of Liverpool).

There were a number of challenges to interpreting these sources. As is true in other forms of research, we had to consider carefully the processes that generating the data we relied on. For example, why and when did owners register ships, and to what extent could the residue of these processes be expected to represent the actual roster of owners? What is the original evidence regarding the incentives that ship captains faced, and can it support confidence as to the terms of employment that were generally present in the industry? Even more difficult was the fact that Liverpool was the capital of the British slave trade, and many of the voyages we examine were slave voyages. As the eighteenth century advanced, political and normative responses to slavery changed, and these forces must be considered when evaluating original sources. Similarly, with secondary sources, it is undeniable that cultural influences manifest themselves in the available histories. For example, historians' answers to questions such as "how profitable was the slave trade" have changed over time, and not merely in one direction as more evidence emerged, but oscillating like fashions in the width of ties or the lengths of skirts.

The need to approach sources with skepticism is evidenced by the forward to Gomer Williams' account of the Liverpool Slave trade (2010 [1897]):

> In dealing with the delicate subject of the Liverpool Slave Trade – a subject which, for reasons that may be guessed, has been lightly touched upon by most local writers – the author has endeavored to confine himself to a plain statement of facts – facts which need no comment or exposition. He has directed his indignation against the system, or national sin, rather than against individuals, for many of the slave-merchants and slave-captains of old Liverpool claim our regard as patriots and worthies of no common order. (p. x)

Williams begins by identifying a likely bias of Liverpool historians against examining the slave trade that would cause us to question whatever histories do exist, but which apparently doesn't apply to him. He claims to stick to the facts, and is indeed a unique source for many documents that he claims as original. But can we trust his representation of them, and what might he have seen but chosen not to report, given that he is indignant about slavery, but views many slavers as uncommon worthies? It is hard to imagine a more disconcerting claim of objectivity. Faced with these problems our approach was (1) to collect sources voraciously, going to original documents when we could (in one case we even recollected from original sources data that

appeared in summarized form in a recent historical journal article) and
(2) to triangulate between multiple sources asking "why was it written?",
"for whom?", "with what evidence?", and "representing what values?"

In addition to our collection and assessment of written materials, we
benefited tremendously from extensive discussions with historians of
Liverpool's maritime trade, notably Steven Behrendt. These historians gave
us insight into the variety of available source material, the nature of
shipowner–captain interactions during the 18th century, and the historical
debates about Liverpool shipping that had played out over the last 100 years
(which informed our assessment of biases in the sources).[5]

Deducing and Inducing: Engaging Iteratively in Analysis and Narrative
In the course of doing this research, we began to construct a narrative of the
Liverpool transatlantic trade. Given our theoretical intuition, we anchored
this narrative around features of voyages that might give captains divergent
incentives from those of shipowners, particularly around the issue of vessel
protection. Liverpool's 18th-century transatlantic trade consisted of two
distinct types: the direct trade, in which vessels carried manufactured goods
from England to the West Indies and returned with staples such as sugar
and rum, and, sadly, the "triangle" or slave trade, in which vessels carried
manufactured goods from England to the west coast of Africa, traded these
goods for slaves, transported the slaves to the West Indies, and then
returned to England with either staples or cash. On the triangle trade,
captain discretion and effort appeared to have a greater effect on voyage
success. Whereas captains simply sailed the vessel for direct-trade voyages, a
triangle-trade captain frequently negotiated with chieftains on the African
coast and with slave buyers in the West Indies. A triangle-trade captain also
had to spend time sailing along the Africa coast, where there was a high risk
of hitting underwater rocks. And a triangle-trade captain's actions could
significantly affect the value of cargo, since slave mortality was a common
occurrence on vessels. Our first narrative focused heavily on the need to
motivate triangle-trade captains more intensely in order to solve agency
problems.

We then confronted this model with the data. Specifically, we constructed
descriptive statistics that revealed the frequency of sinking, of capture, and
of captain ownership over time and for each of the two types of trade. The
data did indicate a modest difference between triangle-trade and direct-trade
voyages in terms of captain ownership across our entire sample period. But
they strongly indicated that this difference was accentuated during wartime.
This led us to reconsider our model – were shipowners able to manage

captains' incentives through other mechanisms, and, if so, then why did those other mechanisms not work for the triangle trade during wartime?

We returned to the historical treatises, and to our conversations with historians. But now our effort focused solely on two questions: (1) the compensation of 18th-century Liverpool captains and (2) the consequences of war for maritime trade. We also turned to the surviving records of a handful of Liverpool shipowners, including letters to captains and to co-owners. And we explored the many colorful histories of wartime shipping (e.g., Williams, 1897). Armed with our knowledge of the data, we revised our understanding of captains' incentives. Shipowners typically provided captains with sales commissions and other contract-based performance bonuses for the successful delivery of cargo. The commission rates and bonuses were steeper for triangle trade than for direct trade, reflecting the greater need to elicit effort from captains on the triangle trade. Since a captain needed to keep the vessel afloat to protect the cargo, the commission on the cargo would motivate the captain to protect the vessel in most cases.

But, during wartime, there existed a new hazard: enemy "privateers" would cruise the ocean trying to capture British merchant vessels. Whereas direct-trade vessels could sail far to the north to avoid this threat, triangle-trade vessels were particularly vulnerable to privateers. A captain who was approached by a privateer had two choices: (1) give up the ship, be treated reasonably well, get back to England after perhaps 6 months, or (2) try to fight off the privateer, and possibly succeed, but risk one's life in the effort. Suffice it to say that it is difficult to construct a bonus scheme that will efficiently motivate the captain to worry about saving the vessel. In this case, having the captain become a part owner of the vessel is an efficient way to encourage him to resist the privateer, at least on the margin.

We then revamped our narrative to devote more attention to the role of privateers, and returned to our data analysis. Our empirical estimation indicated that captain ownership is significantly more prevalent for triangle-trade voyages during wartime. Subsequent estimation indicated that captain-owned vessels are significantly less likely to be captured, after controlling for endogeneity.

This left us with one remaining source of perplexity. If vessel ownership provides an upside to shipowners by giving the captain an incentive to protect the ship, then what is the downside? Although the privateer threat is most significant on triangle routes during wartime, one could imagine various low-likelihood threats that would still imply benefits to vessel ownership by the captain, for example, the very small but ever-present threat of attack by pirates. If there is no cost to this incentive, then even with a tiny upside we should expect to see most or all vessels use it, rather than the 20% of our sample, mostly concentrated during wartime.

One variation of agency models, the multitask principal-agent model, notes that agents frequently must complete multiple tasks (Holmstrom & Milgrom, 1991). If a payment scheme heightens the incentive for one task, the agent is likely to shirk on other tasks in order to complete the highly incentivized one. Based on this model, we returned to the data and asked, "on what tasks might a captain shirk if he is unduly concerned about protecting his vessel?" Based on our historically grounded understanding of the setting, we hypothesized that a captain might (1) underemphasize the cargo and (2) sail particularly cautiously when part owner of the vessel, thus increasing the expense of the voyage and potentially missing the "market window" for the cargo. Returning to the data we found evidence of this: compared to vessels whose captains were not owners, captain-owned triangle-trade vessels carried fewer slaves than expected during wartime, and took significantly longer to get from Africa to the West Indies. These results both provide an answer to the "what's the downside?" question and provide evidence that shipowners were systematically working to solve a multitask principal-agent problem in 18th century transatlantic shipping.

Of course, this is not much different from understanding the empirical setting in conventional strategy research. When a scholar embarks on a new research project, she almost always must learn details of the setting. In our own work, this has entailed learning about competition in the American hotel industry, innovation in the laser printer industry, and French haute cuisine, to name just a few (the last of these was particularly onerous to study). So what is different in historical strategy research? Besides being the only option for studying some phenomena which are too big, too rare, and too slow to study with other methods, the primary advantage of history is perspective. It is because of perspective that we know that British shipping was a significant economic phenomenon, and a success, and that it is therefore a worthwhile place to look for effective organizational practices. It is because of perspective that we have been able to learn how these private companies were actually organized, which ones were successful, and what they believed about the risk of their endeavors.

Evaluating the Results
Does our interpretation make sense? That is really up to you. We attempted to be clear about the logical assumptions in the text and in a table that explicitly identifies features that create conflicting incentives between captain and owners, and that explicitly states whether the incentives can

be aligned through a contractual arrangement. We ultimately considered three alternative explanations for patterns of captain ownership, and found that while each of them explains some features of the data, each fails to correspond to other aspects of the data.

An Alternative Approach for Strategy: Comparative-Historical Analysis

The advantage of the analytic narratives approach over more typical historical narratives is that it facilitates a more explicit conversation between data and theory. The conscious use of theory makes analytic narratives more appropriate for social-scientific purposes, which emphasize generalizability to other cases over the maximally thorough understanding of one case. Yet another historical method that emphasizes theory is comparative-historical analysis, which uses an approach akin to grounded theorizing to refine theories by comparing cases (Mahoney & Rueschemeyer, 2003). Comparative-historical analysis goes further afield than analytic narratives in considering outliers and in using alternative methods to draw inference. It is more contextual/systemic and takes the idea of equifinality very seriously. Conceptually, the idea is to focus on causes-of-effects rather than average-effects-of-causes. Rather than relying on Gaussian insights and statistical assumptions, this approach focuses on necessary-and-sufficient conditions, Boolean algebra and Bayesian analysis. Kogut, MacDuffie, and Ragin (2004) detail the potential for the comparative-historical approach in strategy research.[6] For those interested in applying this method, Mahoney (2004, 2010) offers useful conceptual comparisons of this approach to statistical approaches, and Rihoux and Ragin (2009) offer a textbook for application of the approach. Finally, there now exist programs in STATA that will run qualitative comparative analysis, a common tool for comparative-historical analysis (Longest & Vaisey, 2008). We see the utility of comparative-historical analysis as being mainly for the development of theory, while the analytic narratives approach offers more potential for testing existing theory.

CONCLUSION

History can be understood relative to other research methods as occupying the intersection between a contextual approach to explanation and a remote sensing approach to evidencing. We recommend that history be pursued in strategy using a "theory conscious" approach, and detail the analytic narratives approach as one way to do history in strategy. Done this way, history offers a number of benefits to strategists and strategy scholars, most obviously as a source of exogenous variation to test theories, and as a method to understand path-dependent phenomena. For strategists, institutional change is perhaps the most important example of a phenomenon that lends itself to historical analysis. Ultimately, the advantage of history is perspective. As the Canadian novelist Margaret Atwood says of perspective, "[W]hen you are in the middle of a story it isn't a story at all, but only a confusion; a dark roaring, a blindness, a wreckage of shattered glass and splintered wood; like a house in a whirlwind, or else a boat crushed by the icebergs or swept over the rapids, and all aboard powerless to stop it. It's only afterwards that it becomes anything like a story after all. When you are telling it, to yourself or to someone else" (1997, p. 298). The same can be said for histories.

NOTES

1. Murmann (2012) provides a complementary view of the benefits of marrying history and strategy research, as well as an alternate roadmap to undertake such research.

2. In this volume, Kahl, Liegel, and Yates (2012) use analytic narrative methods to explore why the metaphor of computer as "giant brain" diffuses through one set of industries but not through another.

3. "All narratives have to have an anchor (or set of anchors). Analytic narratives make the theoretical anchor more explicit (and thereby easier to criticize) than in more configurative accounts" (Levi, 2002, p. 9).

4. Of course, "presto" does not mean that all of the necessary data were available in one place, or that they were available in an immediately usable form. This presto moment was followed by well over a year of tracking down and entering data in a variety of forms, and from a variety of sources.

5. We believe that these discussions also offered some value to historians, by raising the possibility that incentives played a role in captain compensation. Most historians have assumed that vessel ownership by the captain was simply an alternate way to raise the captain's income, without consideration of the incentive effects of asset ownership versus a higher salary (personal communication, various historians).

6. In this volume, Lampe and Moser (2012) offer a form of comparative history in their study of 20 patent pools organized during a time when regulators did not compel patent pools to license their patents to non-member firms. Similarly, Kipping and Westerhuis's (2012) comparative study of two Dutch banks that undergo multidivisionalization in the 1980s exhibits aspects of comparative-history methodology.

REFERENCES

Alexandrova, A. (2009). When analytic narratives explain. *Journal of the Philosophy of History*, *3*, 1–24.

Atwood, M. (1997). *Alias grace*. New York, NY: Doubleday.

Baker, G. P., & Hubbard, T. (2003). Make vs. buy in trucking: Asset ownership, job design and information. *American Economic Review*, *93*(3), 551–572.

Bates, R. H. (1998). The international coffee organization: An international institution. In R. H. Bates, A. Greif, M. Levi, J.-L. Rosenthal & B. R. Weingast (Eds.), *Analytic narratives*. Princeton, NJ: Princeton University Press.

Bates, R. H., Greif, A., Levi, M., Rosenthal, J.-L., & Weingast, B. R. (1998). *Analytic narratives*. Princeton, NJ: Princeton University Press.

Behrendt, S. D. (1991). The captains in the British slave trade from 1785 to 1807. *Transactions of the Historic Society of Lancashire and Cheshire*, *140*, 79–140.

Behrendt, S. D. (2007). Human capital in the British slave trade. In D. Richardson, S. Schwarz & A. Tibbles (Eds.), *Liverpool and transatlantic slavery*. Liverpool, UK: Liverpool University Press.

Bergstresser, D. B., & Philippon, T. (2006). CEO incentives and earnings management. *Journal of Financial Economics*, *80*(3), 511–529.

Bloch, M. (1953). *The historian's craft*. New York, NY: Vintage Books.

Brooke, R. (1853). *Liverpool as it was during the last quarter of the eighteenth century*. Liverpool, UK: J. Mawdsley & Son.

Cohen, B. P. (1989). *Developing sociological knowledge*. Chicago, IL: Nelson-Hall.

Collingwood, R. G. (1956). *The idea of history*. New York, NY: Oxford University Press.

Core, J. E., & Larcker, D. F. (2002). Performance consequences of mandatory increases in executive stock ownership. *Journal of Financial Economics*, *64*, 317–340.

Dobbin, F. (1994). *Forging industrial policy*. New York, NY: Cambridge University Press.

Duggan, W. (2007). *Strategic intuition*. New York, NY: Columbia Business School Press.

Fischer, D. H. (1970). *Historians' fallacies: Toward a logic of historical thought*. New York, NY: Harper Perennial.

Gaddis, J. L. (2002). *The landscape of history*. New York, NY: Oxford University Press.

Galambos, L. (1975). *The public image of big business in America, 1880–1940*. Baltimore, MD: Johns Hopkins University Press.

Gore, J. (1766). *The Liverpool directory for the year 1766: Containing an alphabetical list of the merchants, tradesmen, and principal inhabitants of the town of Liverpool with their respective addresses*. Liverpool, UK: W. Nevitt & Co.

Greve, H., & Rao, H. (2012). Echoes of the past: Organizational foundings as sources of an institutional legacy of mutualism. *American Journal of Sociology*. Forthcoming.

Griffin, L. J. (1993). Narrative, event-structure analysis, and causal interpretation in historical sociology. *American Journal of Sociology*, *98*(5), 1094–1133.

Hansen, Z. K., & Libecap, G. D. (2004). Small farms, externalities, and the Dust Bowl of the 1930s. *Journal of Political Economy*, *112*(3), 665–694.

Hawthorne, G. (1991). *Plausible worlds: Possibility and understanding in history and the social sciences*. Cambridge: Cambridge University Press.

Holmstrom, B., & Milgrom, P. (1991). Multitask principal-agent analyses: Incentive contracts, asset ownership, and job design. *Journal of Law, Economics and Organization*, *7*(SI), 24–52.

Ingram, P., & Inman, C. (1996). Institutions, intergroup rivalry, and the evolution of hotel populations around Niagara Falls. *Administrative Science Quarterly, 41*, 629–658.

Ingram, P., & Lifschitz, A. (2006). Kinship in the shadow of the corporation: The interbuilder network in Clyde River shipbuilding, 1711–1990. *American Sociological Review, 71*(2), 334–352.

Ingram, P., Lifschitz, A., & Luo, J. (2010). *Casting a net: Network leverage and relational exchange in Clyde river shipbuilding.* Unpublished Manuscript. Columbia University.

Ingram, P., & Rao, H. (2004). Store wars: The enactment and repeal of anti-chain legislation in the United States. *American Journal of Sociology, 110*, 446–487.

Ingram, P., & Silverman, B. S. (2002, June). Introduction: The new institutionalism in strategy. *Advances in Strategic Management, 19*(June), 1–32.

Ingram, P., Yue, L. Q., & Rao, H. (2010). Trouble in store: Probes, protests and store openings by Wal-Mart: 1998–2005. *American Journal of Sociology, 116*, 53–92.

Kahl, S. J., Liegel, G. J., & Yates, J. (2012). Audience structure and the failure of institutional entrepreneurship. In S. J. Kahl, B. S. Silverman & M. A. Cusumano (Eds.), *Advances in strategic management* (Vol. 29, pp. 275–313). Bingley, UK: Emerald Group.

Kennedy, R. F. (1969). *Thirteen days: A memoir of the Cuban missile Crises.* New York, NY: W. W. Norton & Company.

Kipping, M., & Westerhuis, G. (2012). Strategy, ideology, and structure: The political processes of introducing the M-form in two Dutch banks. In S. J. Kahl, B. S. Silverman & M. A. Cusumano (Eds.), *Advances in strategic management* (Vol. 29, pp. 187–237). Bingley, UK: Emerald Group.

Kogut, B., MacDuffie, J. P., & Ragin, C. C. (2004). Prototypes and strategy: Assigning causal credit using fuzzy sets. *European Management Review, 1*, 114–131.

Kuran, T. (1989). Sparks and prairie fires: A theory of unanticipated political revolution. *Public Choice, 6*(1), 41–74.

Lampe, R., & Moser, P. (2012). Patent pools: Licensing strategies in the absence of regulation. In S. J. Kahl, B. S. Silverman & M. A. Cusumano (Eds.), *Advances in strategic management* (Vol. 29, pp. 69–86). Bingley, UK: Emerald Group.

Leeson, P. T. (2007). An-arrgh-chy: The law and economics of pirate organization. *Journal of Political Economy, 115*(6), 1049–1094.

Levi, M. (2002). Mistorical processes wodeling complex hith analytic narratives. In R. Mayntz (Ed.), *Akteure, Mechanismen, Modelle: Zur Theoriefahigkeit makrosozialer Analysen.* Frankfurt: Campus Verlag.

Longest, K. C., & Vaisey, S. (2008). Fuzzy: A program for performing qualitative comparative analyses (QCA) in Stata. *The Stata Journal, 8*(1), 79–104.

Lovejoy, P., & Richardson, D. (1995). British abolition and its impact on slave prices along the Atlantic coast of Africa, 1783–1850. *Journal of Economic History, 55*(1), 98–119.

Mahoney, J. (2004). Comparative-historical methodology. *Annual Review of Sociology, 30*, 81–101.

Mahoney, J. (2010). After KKV: The new methodology of qualitative research. *World Politics, 62*(1), 120–147.

Mahoney, J., & Rueschemeyer, D. (2003). *Comparative historical analysis in the social sciences.* New York, NY: Cambridge University Press.

Murmann, J. P. (2012). Marrying history and social science in strategy research. In S. J. Kahl, B. S. Silverman & M. A. Cusumano (Eds.), *Advances in strategic management* (Vol. 29, pp. 89–115). Bingley, UK: Emerald Group.

Nickerson, J. A., & Silverman, B. S. (2003). Why firms want to organize efficiently and what keeps them from doing so: Inappropriate governance, performance, and adaptation in a deregulated industry. *Administrative Science Quarterly, 48*(3), 433–465.

North, D. (1990). *Institutions, institutional change and economic performance*. Cambridge, UK: Cambridge University Press.

Peltzman, S. (1976). Toward a more general theory of regulation. *Journal of Law and Economics, 19*(2), 211–240.

Rao, H., & Dutta, S. (2012). From spark to fire: Rumor and regimental mutinies in the 1857 Bengal native army. Unpublished Manuscript. Stanford University.

Rihoux, B., & Ragin, C. (2009). *Configurational comparative methods*. Los Angeles, CA: Sage.

Rose, E. (1982). Anatomy of a mutiny. *Armed Forces and Society, 8*(4), 561–574.

Salop, S. C., & Scheffman, D. T. (1983). Raising rivals' costs. *American Economic Review, 73*(2), 267–271.

Schwartz, S. (1995). *Slave captain: The career of James Irving in the Liverpool slave trade*. Wrexham, UK: Bridge Books.

Silverman, B.S., & Ingram, P. (2012). Managing agency problems in early shareholder capitalism: An exploration of Liverpool shipping in the 18th century. Social Sciences Research Network Working Paper. Available at http://papers.ssrn.com/sol3/papers.cfm?abstract_id=2070887

Simons, T., & Ingram, P. (2003). Enemies of the State: Interdependence between institutional forms and the ecology of the kibbutz, 1910–1997. *Administrative Science Quarterly, 44*, 562–592.

Snook, S. A. (2000). *Friendly fire*. Princeton, NJ: Princeton University Press.

Vaughan, D. (1996). *The challenger launch decision*. Chicago, IL: University of Chicago Press.

Weber, M. (1949 [1905]). *The methodology of the social sciences*. New York, NY: Free Press.

Williams, G. (2010 [1897]). *History of the Liverpool privateers and letters of marque, with an account of the Liverpool slave trade*. New York, NY: Augustus M. Kelley.

Williamson, O. E. (1968). Wage rates as barriers to entry: The Pennington case in perspective. *Quarterly Journal of Economics, 83*(1), 85–116.

AUDIENCE STRUCTURE AND THE FAILURE OF INSTITUTIONAL ENTREPRENEURSHIP

Steven J. Kahl, Gregory J. Liegel and JoAnne Yates

ABSTRACT

Purpose – *The broader aim of this research is twofold. First, we aim to better understand how the business computer was conceptualized and used within U.S. industry. Second, this research investigates the role of social factors such as relational structure, institutional entrepreneurs, and position in the formation of conceptualizations of new technologies.*

Design/methodological/approach – *This paper is theoretically motivated in the sense that it responds to the lack of attention to the failure of institutional entrepreneurs to change belief systems. Through detailed archival, network, and descriptive statistical analysis, the paper shows how the failed institutional entrepreneur fits conventional explanations for success. The paper then analyzes two matched cases, comparing the insurance industry's rejection of the institutional entrepreneur with manufacturing's acceptance, in order to identify what is missing in current explanations of institutional entrepreneurs.*

Findings – *Our analysis reveals that the role of the audience structure in interpreting the institutional entrepreneur's message influences the change*

History and Strategy
Advances in Strategic Management, Volume 29, 275–313
Copyright © 2012 by Emerald Group Publishing Limited

ISSN: 0742-3322/doi:10.1108/S0742-3322(2012)0000029013

outcome. In our case, the institutional entrepreneur's view of the computer as a brain that supported decision-oriented applications did not fit with views of the insurance groups who had centralized authority over interpreting the computer. Because manufacturing had less centralized control in its discourse around the computer, there were fewer constraints on assimilation, allowing the entrepreneur's views to resonate with some of the occupational groups.

Research limitations/implications – *This paper develops a theoretical approach to institutional entrepreneurship that situates the entrepreneurial efforts of individual actors within a system characterized by the structure of its audience and subject to distinct historical macro-structural processes that present significant obstacles to the realization of their entrepreneurial projects.*

Keywords: Institutional entrepreneurship; innovation; cognition; history of business computing

INTRODUCTION

Over the course of the last two decades, work on institutional change and agency has emerged as the dominant strain of research within institutional analysis (Battilana, Leca, & Boxenbaum, 2009). At the core of this line of inquiry is the concept of institutional entrepreneurship, which was proposed to characterize the strategic behavior of actors who mobilize their skills, knowledge, and other resources to create or transform institutions (DiMaggio, 1988). Across a wide variety of empirical settings, scholars have subsequently investigated how individuals and organizations are able to successfully generate new organizational forms (Greenwood, Suddaby, & Hinings, 2002), spread novel practices (Rao, Monin, & Durand, 2005), or de-institutionalize existing norms and beliefs (Oliver, 1992).

One of the central goals of research on institutional entrepreneurship has been to determine a common set of factors that enables entrepreneurs to successfully alter existing institutional arrangements or construct new ones altogether. And drawing on organizational, cultural, and social movement theory, scholars have identified key elements that characterize successful institutional entrepreneurship, such as recognizing opportunities for change (Leblebici, Salancik, Copay, & King, 1991), developing sufficient resource capacity (Ganz, 2000), framing the issue appropriately (McAdam, McCarthy, & Zald, 1996), and winning the support of key organizations and individuals (Maguire, Hardy, & Lawrence, 2004).

However, existing research on institutional entrepreneurship is limited in at least two ways. First, scholars have focused almost exclusively on cases in which entrepreneurs were able to accomplish their strategic objectives and effect institutional change. By contrast, little attention has been paid to those factors that cause entrepreneurs to fail. Yet in order to explain why and how institutional entrepreneurs succeed in some cases, we also must understand why they are unsuccessful in others. Second, much of the existing research focuses on characteristics and efforts of the entrepreneur at the cost of considering who or what they are trying to change (Aldrich, 2010). A full account of institutional change not only addresses who initiates the change, but also how it is received and processed by incumbents and other actors (Fligstein, 1997). Groups interpret and respond to the efforts of an institutional entrepreneur differently and their interactions can influence whether change occurs. Yet the audience perspective is largely absent in the institutional entrepreneurship literature.

The chapter addresses this research gap by examining the historical case of Edmund Berkeley's efforts to legitimize the notion of new business computers as "Giant Brains." As a pioneering evangelist from the insurance industry, prominent early computer expert, and leading advocate for the use of computer technology in insurance and more broadly, Berkeley seemingly possessed all of the necessary attributes to be a successful institutional entrepreneur. He occupied a central structural position and enjoyed high status within the insurance industry, was widely recognized as a leading expert on computers, and had strong, diverse connections to other actors both within the insurance industry and outside of it. Moreover, his position as one of the leading authorities in this nascent field provided him with access to considerable resources that he was able to wield to advance his strategic objectives. As an innovator in his field, he was able to perceive and articulate the transformative opportunity that computers represented, framing them as "Giant Brains" that could be leveraged to enhance decision-making capabilities within firms. While this conceptualization was well received by the popular press and in other industries, the insurance industry rejected the brain imagery in favor of a more conservative interpretation of the computer. Rather than viewing computers as Giant Brains, they conceived of the computer as a transaction-processing machine, an interpretation that characterized computers as an extension of existing tabulating machine technology.

The difference in these responses to Berkeley's framing allows us to investigate the role of the audience in institutional change. Our study demonstrates the critical role that audience structure may play in obstructing change even when actors perceive and attempt to act on opportunities for change (DiMaggio, 1988; Fligstein, 1997; Levy & Scully, 2007). In our case, we compare the insurance industry, which rejected the "Giant Brain" view of the computer, with the manufacturing industry, which partially supported that view. When it came to interpreting the computer, the insurance industry constituted itself as a relatively centralized structure of similar groups, while the manufacturing industry was more decentralized, allowing for different opinions to surface. More specifically, the three most relevant insurance associations formed committees to investigate what the computer was and how it could be used within insurance. These committees shaped the insurance industry's conceptualization, adoption, and use of the computer over the subsequent decade. Actuaries, accountants, administrators, and systems men – powerful occupations within insurance organizations – dominated these committees. Berkeley's "Giant Brain" image did not fit with these groups' interest in preserving their strong standing within the insurance industry. More generally, we build the argument that proposed institutional changes must more directly fit in with centralized audience structures; decentralized structures, on the other hand, place fewer constraints on assimilation.

Our analysis of Berkeley's inability to legitimize the idea of computers as "Giant Brains" in the insurance industry demonstrates why institutional change is frequently so difficult to achieve and why institutional entrepreneurs so often fail. Building on this empirical analysis, we develop a theoretical approach to institutional entrepreneurship that situates the entrepreneurial efforts of individual actors within a system characterized by the structure of its audience and subject to distinct historical macro-structural processes that present significant obstacles to the realization of their entrepreneurial projects.

In the rest of the chapter, we briefly synthesize the existing literature on institutional entrepreneurship, paying particular attention to those factors that are understood to be necessary ingredients for success and those that may contribute to failure. After some notes on data and methods, the empirical section is divided into two main parts. First, we map the early discourse around computing in the insurance and manufacturing industries. Second, we present Berkeley's proposed institutional change, and then look at the varied responses to it from the insurance and manufacturing industries. We examine explanations for this difference suggested by existing literature, and then propose an alternative framework that better explains why Berkeley was unable to realize his strategic objectives in spite of possessing all the necessary factors. In the conclusion, we discuss implications and extensions for institutional theory, as well as business and technology history.

INSTITUTIONAL ENTREPRENEURSHIP

The failure to articulate an endogenous explanation for institutional change represented a crucial limitation of early neo-institutional work (Christensen, Karnoe, Pedersen, & Dobbin, 1997). In order to rectify this shortcoming, DiMaggio (1988) proposed the concept of institutional entrepreneurship to characterize the behavior of actors who strategically mobilize their skills, knowledge, and other resources to create or transform institutions. Subsequently, work on institutional entrepreneurship has emerged as a central strain of research within institutional analysis (Leca, Battilana, & Boxenbaum, 2008). Scholars have expanded their initial focus beyond how institutional arrangements are created to examine how entrepreneurs transform or deinstitutionalize existing institutions (e.g., Ahmadjian & Robinson, 2001; Oliver, 1992; Scott, Ruef, Mendel, & Caronna, 2000). The primary focus of much of this work has been to discern the field conditions that foster entrepreneurship (Strang & Sine, 2002), to elaborate the characteristics and social position of effective entrepreneurs (Lawrence & Suddaby, 2006, p. 15), or to identify the different types of strategic behavior in which successful entrepreneurs engage.

Field Conditions

Scholars have identified a variety of field conditions that create space for entrepreneurs to act. In particular, researchers have pointed to different types of crises that enable actors to identify opportunities for change. These include political and economic uncertainty (Fligstein & Mara-Drita, 1996), regulatory changes (Edelman, 1992), resource scarcity (Durand & McGuire, 2005), social upheaval (Maguire et al., 2004), and technological innovation (Munir & Phillips, 2005). Maguire et al. (2004), for example, show how the emergence of HIV/AIDS during the 1980s empowered community organizations with strong ties to the HIV/AIDS community, leading to new practices of consultation and information exchange among pharmaceutical companies and community organizations. As in this example, change may be precipitated by shocks to the environment such as the emergence of HIV/AIDS. However, it may also surface from within the field itself (Durand & McGuire, 2005) or from friction at institutional interstices (Clemens & Cook, 1999, pp. 449–450). Overlap between competing institutions can create "contradictions" (Seo & Creed, 2002) that threaten the stability of existing institutional arrangements and introduce opportunities for change.

Consequently, one of the central challenges for institutional entrepreneurs revolves around problem or opportunity identification. Yet scholars disagree about whether fields that are turbulent or stable are more conducive to identifying problems or opportunities. Fligstein (1997, p. 404), for example, argues that when "the organizational field has no structure, the possibilities for strategic action are greatest." By contrast, Beckert (1999, p. 783) contends that stable environmental conditions create greater possibilities for institutional entrepreneurs to engage in strategic action precisely because they provide "the basis for actors to calculate the effects of their actions."

Social Position

In addition to the influence of field conditions on actors' ability to successfully identify change possibilities, scholars have also classified an entrepreneur's social position (Garud, Jain, & Kumaraswamy, 2002; Rao, Morrill, & Zald, 2000), or subject position (Maguire et al., 2004), as an important factor in shaping entrepreneurial success. Yet scholars also disagree about the consequences of an actor's position within the field on their ability to effect change. On the one hand, studies have found that actors located on the periphery of a network are more likely to engage in entrepreneurial activity than those located at the center (Battilana, 2006; Leblebici et al., 1991). On the other hand, others have found that change comes more often from the core (e.g., Rao, Monin, & Durand, 2005; Greenwood, & Suddaby, 2006), driven by actors with more diverse networks, higher status, and the clout to implement new things.

Whether in the core or in the periphery, an actor's position within the field may provide strong ties to other actors, facilitate the transfer of information and other key resources, and endow the actor with legitimacy and formal authority. Building on Aldrich (1999), Dorado (2005) maintains that entrepreneurs' links to other actors within their network shape their ability to identify and realize prospects for change. Likewise, Lawrence (1999) suggests that entrepreneurs' social position may help them mobilize resources.

Nevertheless, entrepreneurs must have the requisite social skill (Fligstein, 1997) to mobilize support for their actions. They must build alliances (Lawrence, Hardy, & Phillips, 2002), foster collaboration (Hardy & Phillips, 1998; Phillips, Lawrence, & Hardy, 2000), and incentivize key stakeholders. For example, experts may facilitate change by diffusing practices, creating standards and rules, and using their professional authority to validate entrepreneurs' claims (Hwang & Powell, 2005). Establishing linkages to other actors provides entrepreneurs with access to novel resources and information, thereby enhancing their strategic adaptability (McCammon et al., 2008) and capacity (Ganz, 2000).

Strategic Behavior

Research on institutional entrepreneurship has focused extensively on the conditions that promote problem/opportunity identification and on entrepreneurs' characteristics and position in a field. Yet it has paid less attention to the strategic behavior that entrepreneurs adopt to generate new institutions or transform existing ones. To the extent that it has, it has focused primarily on entrepreneurs' use of discursive strategies, particularly collective action framing (Benford & Snow, 2000; Snow & Benford, 1988), to specify existing institutional shortcomings and legitimate proposals for change (Seo & Creed, 2002; Tolbert & Zucker, 1996). Discursive strategies are important because the degree to which a frame resonates with its intended audience influences entrepreneurs' ability to mobilize resources upon which success often depends (Snow & Benford, 1988; Zuo & Benford, 1995). Rao et al. (2000, p. 244), for instance, maintain that "Institutional entrepreneurs can mobilize legitimacy, finances, and personnel only when they are able to frame the grievances and interests of aggrieved constituencies, diagnose causes, assign blames, provide solutions, and enable collective attribution processes to operate." In order to do so, entrepreneurs often transpose or recombine practices and forms that are perceived to be legitimate. As such, successful entrepreneurial projects are often the recombination of "existing materials and structures, rather than 'pure' novelty" (Hwang & Powell, 2005, p. 180).

METHODOLOGY

Given the general lack of research on institutional entrepreneurship failure, we combined theory elaboration (Lee, 1999) and theory generation (Eisenhardt, 1989; Eisenhardt & Graebner, 2007) in our analysis. Thus, we were aware of the existing literature on institutional entrepreneurship, and we used the relevant constructs to inform our historical analysis of computers in insurance and manufacturing. As such, we followed Ingram, Rao, and Silverman's (2012) call for more theoretically informed historical analysis. In particular, we developed a historically grounded understanding of conditions for change within insurance and manufacturing, and of Berkeley's structural position and strategic behavior. Since we are also interested in the differences in response among the insurance and manufacturing industries, we also analyzed the data from this perspective.

We chose to study the commercial introduction of the computer because the introduction of a radical innovation often creates opportunities for institutional change (Hargadon & Douglas, 2001). By computer, we mean the "business computer" – the technology used to process and manage mainstream corporate applications (as opposed to computational computers, which were originally used in the military). In studying Berkeley's attempt to effect institutional change, we chose the insurance and manufacturing industries as our sample, primarily for theoretical reasons (Eisenhardt & Graebner, 2007). These groups differ in how they responded to the new conceptualization of the computer, allowing us to assess the effects of the audience in the institutional entrepreneurship process. Berkeley came from the insurance industry, making it the obvious starting point. We chose manufacturing as the comparison group because it allows us to partially control for alternative explanations, which we address later in the chapter.

Since we are interested in institutional change, our data collection strategy focused primarily on the emerging discourse about the computer. Our assumption is that written discourse and exchange represented the belief systems and underlying cognitive understanding of the technology (this is a common approach in the management literature (see Barr, Stimpert, & Huff, 1992; Tsoukas, 2009). Thus, from a data perspective, we tracked the discourse about existing technology, Berkeley's and competing interpretations of the computer, as well as reactions and changes to existing conceptualizations of office technology. Since much of this discourse centered on how the computer should be used, we also collected data on actual computer usage as a confirmatory measure of actual institutional changes.

We concentrate our analysis on the mid-1940s to the late 1950s. A nice feature of the computer case for our analysis is that groups within insurance and manufacturing developed conceptualizations of the computer before they adopted the computer beginning in 1954. This allows us to partially isolate aspects of the institutionalization process from technical characteristics and from adoption and use processes. Thus, our time period captures early efforts to understand what the computer was before it was actually commercially available in 1954, as well as the initial period of use of the computer. We stop our analysis in the late 1950s, as technological changes and learning by using the computer may have altered these initial interpretations of the computer.

In the insurance industry, the discourse about the computer concentrated among certain occupational groups and trade associations (Yates, 2005): The Society of Actuaries (SOA), Life Office Management Association (LOMA), and Insurance Accounting and Statistical Association (IASA). We collected the discourse regarding office technology in general and specifically regarding the computer from the proceedings of these three associations. We also used the Edmund C. Berkeley papers at the Charles Babbage Institute of the University of Minnesota to document Berkeley's early interactions with the computer industry on behalf of Prudential Life Insurance Company (Yates, 1997). These papers identify different groups with whom Berkeley interacted, including computer vendors, academics, and other technical professions. Based on these interactions, we also collected data on these groups and their perspectives. We leverage Bingham and Kahl's (forthcoming) content analysis of this discourse to characterize Berkeley's proposed interpretation and show how it differs from existing conceptualizations. Unlike the insurance industry's discourse, the manufacturing industry's discourse was concentrated at the occupational and firm level. Similar to our data collection strategy in insurance, we collected proceedings and journal discourse about the computer from various occupational and trade associations, as well as firm-level data, particularly from General Electric.

Finally, we supplemented our primary archival data with secondary discussions about Berkeley and about occupational perspectives on computing. To capture how the computer was used, we turned to the Controllership Foundation, which conducted surveys of early computer usage from various industries from 1954 to mid-1958. We compiled the survey results for the insurance and manufacturing industries to capture early computer usage.

THE FIELD CONDITIONS FOR CHANGE AND BERKELEY'S STRUCTURAL POSITION

To present our analysis, we first consider the factors identified in the institutional entrepreneurship literature that are understood to be necessary for success. In this section, we focus on the enabling conditions for change within insurance and manufacturing and Berkeley's structural position. In the next section, we address Berkeley's strategic behavior. To determine Berkeley's structural position, we describe Berkeley's background and contacts and analyze the general connections between different groups involved in the discourse about the computer. We then present a stylized network map showing Berkeley's strong structural position.

Field Conditions for Change in both Insurance and Manufacturing

At the industry level, manufacturing and insurance were clearly different. Insurance was a heavily regulated industry that competed more on efficiency than through product differentiation. By contrast, manufacturing was less regulated and competed more on product differentiation. However, both industries faced significant growth challenges and uncertainty during this time period. From 1948 to 1953, the dollar value of life insurance in force grew 51%, and the total number of insurance policies (a better indicator of information processing volume) rose by more than 24% (Bureau of Labor Statistics, 1955). Growth in insurance employment was 12% during the same period, which was not enough to keep up with the increased data processing load. As a postwar life insurance boom exacerbated the wartime clerical labor shortage, insurance firms looked to technology as a possible solution to the need for increased efficiency. Manufacturing also faced significant growth, but of a different nature. Coming out of WWII, manufacturing was moving from mass production to providing customers with more product choice. The increase in product variation made the production process more complex, from sales forecasting through production planning and distribution. Thus, manufacturing viewed technology as a possible solution to deal with this increased complexity and uncertainty.

Berkeley's Interests and Contacts

Edmund Berkeley earned a BA in mathematics and logic from Harvard University in 1930.[1] After a brief time at Mutual Life Insurance of New York, Berkeley joined the actuarial department at Prudential Life Insurance Company in 1934. Although he excelled in actuarial work, becoming a Fellow of the Actuarial Society, he moved to the methods department in 1941. Within this group, Berkeley drew upon his educational training in symbolic logic to examine its potential application, in combination with new types of electromechanical machinery, to Prudential's methods and processes. In particular, Berkeley promoted the application of symbolic logic to improve punch-card tabulating operations. In a 1941 memo, Berkeley advocated an "Algebra of electric accounting [i.e., tabulating] punch-card operations: ... If a successful algebra is constructed, the most efficient and economical chain of machine operations to perform a given job will be able to be determined mathematically, and similar problems will be solved mathematically" (Yates, 1997, p. 25). Berkeley was quite prolific on this subject, writing many internal reports on it in the early 1940s (see Longo, 2004).

Through his early work, Berkeley became well-connected within the academic and practitioner community working on early computing issues. In December 1941, Berkeley helped form the New York Symbolic Logic Group, which included several professors from New York universities, several representatives from insurance, and Dr. Claude Shannon of Bell Labs, who would later be credited with founding information theory. He also attended the Numerical Computational Devices Symposium, a largely scholarly event sponsored by the Institute of Mathematical Statistics, the American Statistical Association, and the American Mathematical Society. In his report back to Prudential, Berkeley expressed interest in Wallace J. Eckert's paper on punch-card calculations in astronomy. Eckert would be hired by IBM after the war and become the first head of Watson Laboratory. Berkeley also met another IBM employee, John C. McPherson, and invited him to attend the newly formed New York Symbolic Logic Group. A paper presented by MIT's S.H. Caldwell on the differential analyzer, with comments by Norbert Wiener, also impressed Berkeley (Longo, 2004). Norbert Wiener would go on to be a major figure in the cybernetics movement, a field that was interested in the workings of the human mind and its relationship with computing. Wiener was a prominent member of the Macy Conferences (1946–1953) that helped establish the field of cybernetics, publishing two popular books on the subject in 1948 and

1950. Berkeley continued to interact with members of this group by attending mutual conferences such as the Symposium of Large Scale Digital Calculating Machinery at Harvard in January 1947.

Beyond embedding himself in emergent academic fields, Berkeley also interacted with early firms developing new computational devices through his role as a methods expert at Prudential. Before the war, he visited General Electric and Bell Labs. His internal Prudential reports reveal a developing interest in how computing devices could be used within insurance operations and what their potential limitations were. At the end of November 1942, Berkeley left Prudential to serve in the Naval Reserves for four years. He spent part of that time (August 1945 to April 1946) at Harvard, where he observed and worked with Howard Aiken on the Mark I automatic sequence controlled calculator and helped construct the Mark II. After his service ended in 1946, he intensified his vendor and developer contacts. Berkeley initiated a total of 60 visits with individuals and groups from August 1 to December 31, 1946. Most notably, he visited Wallace Eckert, now at IBM, at the Watson Laboratory at Columbia University. In addition, he met with another IBM employee, R.R. Seeber Jr., who was involved in the development of the Selective Sequence Electronic Calculator. And he also visited Bell Labs and RCA. Throughout these visits, Berkeley continued to identify specific potential uses of these devices in insurance, reporting his findings and recommendations to Prudential. His reports indicate that IBM, ERA, and Raytheon did not impress him as potential vendors of this new technology.

Rather, Berkeley was much more interested in the proposals of John W. Mauchly and J. Presper Eckert, Jr., who helped develop the ENIAC and founded the Electronic Control Company (ECC), which later became the Eckert-Mauchly Computer Company (EMCC). Berkeley worked closely with this group as they developed the UNIVAC, providing valuable information about Prudential's (and the insurance industry's) information processing and verification requirements. As a result of these interactions, EMCC (which was subsequently bought by Remington Rand in 1950) proposed a computing solution for Prudential, which Berkeley endorsed and for which Prudential eventually signed a contract (but which Prudential ultimately did not install).

In 1948, shortly after making his recommendation, Berkeley left Prudential to form an independent consulting and publishing company. During this time period, he reached out to two groups interested in the computer: interested members of the general public and a more technical group of computer enthusiasts. In 1949, Berkeley published the book, *Giant*

Brains, or, Machines that Think, which was aimed at the general public. This popular book (which sold an estimated 15,000 copies by 1959) represented his most detailed discussion of what a computer was and how it could be used, as will be described later in this chapter. Also during this period, Berkeley sought to develop an association that would enable engineers, academics, mathematicians, computer vendors, and anyone with a more focused and technical interest in computers to freely share ideas and information. This association engaged many of the technical people he had met throughout his experiences at academic laboratories and computer vendors (Akera, 2007; Longo, 2007). And by 1947, Berkeley had received letters of interest from 175 people representing 64 different organizations (Akera, 2007). In September 1947, Berkeley convened the first meeting of the Eastern Association for Computing Machinery at Columbia University. By the beginning of 1948, the association had 350 members and dropped Eastern from its name to become the ACM. Berkeley assumed the role of secretary and worked with the executive council to establish the association's by-laws and governance structure. The ACM would continue to grow, becoming a prominent association in the growing computing field, an association that is still active today.

Computer Discourse in the Insurance Industry

As a prominent member of the insurance community, Berkeley also interacted extensively with the three insurance professional and trade associations that were trying to learn about the computer during the immediate postwar era: the Society of Actuaries (SOA), the Life Office Management Association (LOMA), and the Insurance Accounting and Statistical Association (IASA).[2] SOA, the most prestigious, was a professional society formed in 1889, while LOMA and IASA were occupation-based trade associations. LOMA was formed in 1924 to provide a means for executives and managers to share ideas about systematic office management, including the use of office technologies such as tabulating equipment and eventually computers. IASA was formed in 1928 to focus on the use of office technology to support the accounting and statistical functions within the insurance industry. All three had yearly meetings (with published proceedings) at which members presented papers about relevant topics, including their use of pre-computer punch-card tabulating systems and their interpretations of the computer. IASA and LOMA also had technology committees that provided yearly progress reports on the latest developments in office technologies, and they sponsored exhibits at the meetings where members could interact with the manufacturers' sales forces about their latest machines. Berkeley frequently presented papers at the meetings of each of these societies. In fact, in 1947 he presented his early impressions of the computer to each society (Berkeley, 1947a, 1947b).

Around this time, each of these associations formed a committee to investigate what the computer was and how it could be used in insurance. In 1947, the Society of Actuaries established the "Committee on New Recording Means and Computing Devices," composed of actuaries from the 1st (Metropolitan Life), 4th (Equitable Life), and 14th (Connecticut Mutual) largest U.S. life insurance firms (Yates, 2005). Malvin Davis, the Chief Actuary of Metropolitan Life, acted as the chair. This small, centralized committee presented its initial findings and recommendations in an influential 1952 report that would become a blueprint for computer conceptualization, adoption, and use in the insurance industry for over a decade. This report was widely circulated in the insurance industry. In addition, committee chair Malvin Davis was frequently invited to present their findings about the computer at other academic and management conferences.

The committees in the other two associations were similarly small and centralized. Berkeley himself helped form the LOMA committee. Rather than produce reports, the IASA and LOMA committees sponsored conferences, jointly and individually, in the early 1950s. LOMA and IASA cooperated with Remington Rand to create the "Remington Rand Forum on the Use of Electronics in the Insurance Industry" in 1950, very shortly after that manufacturer's acquisition of the Eckert-Mauchly Computer Company, at which it presented its (still under development) UNIVAC. In 1953, IASA culminated its efforts by independently organizing a two-day conference entitled "Electronics and Its Future in the Insurance Industry," which included representatives from IBM and Remington Rand and considered applications of computers in insurance in more detail than the earlier Forum.

The generation of these reports and conferences built on pre-existing and deep relationships between these associations and IBM and Remington Rand, which were the two vendors of pre-computer tabulating technology; both firms were now moving into computers (Remington Rand by acquiring EMCC, and IBM by racing to develop internal capabilities in this area). Interaction of SOA, LOMA, and IASA committees with other potential vendors was limited or absent. Certainly, LOMA's and IASA's computer conferences only involved representatives from IBM and

Remington Rand. The SOA report mentioned no vendors, but clearly reflected knowledge about the UNIVAC, and the committee is known to have run tests of its recommended application on an IBM pre-computer punch-card system.

Thus, discourse about computers in the insurance industry centered on the report of a small, centralized committee of actuaries and two conferences run by committees of two other associations. It also focused on two vendors already well known to the industry.

Computer Discourse in the Manufacturing Industry

The manufacturing industry had a different pattern of discourse regarding the computer. Rather than concentrating discussion within select committees in just three occupational associations, manufacturing discourse was more broadly disseminated among various occupations and firms. Occupations varied in their interest and use of the computer. For example, accounting was primarily interested in how they could properly control and audit business processes that used computers, whereas production planning was interested in how they could leverage the computer to create new ways of managing production (Kahl, King, & Liegel, in preparation). As manufacturing firms assessed whether to invest in computing, they paid close attention to these different groups.

For example, consider General Electric, which implemented one of the first commercially available computers for business, the UNIVAC, at a new appliance division in Lexington, Kentucky, in 1954. In a *Harvard Business Review* article detailing the implementation, Roddy Osborn, a key manager involved in the project, argued that computer operations should not be considered the province of a single department, but as a "data processing center" that served different groups' needs. He argued that "The important concept here is that it [the computer] was not centralized accounting or centralized payroll, but rather centralization of the routine 'dog' work involved in each of these operations" (Osborn, 1954, p. 106).

One important emergent group in manufacturing was operations research. Operations research emerged from computer work done in WWII and sought to develop and apply management science and computation techniques to improve business practices. Many of their techniques were related to the broader cybernetics movement in that they leveraged computer techniques such as linear programming, queuing theory, and simulation to solve business problems. Operations research groups developed specific applications for manufacturing, including inventory analysis and sequencing of shop floor activities.

Another influential viewpoint also directly tied with manufacturing was the growing interest in office automation. John Diebold (1952) of Harvard Business School developed the concept of automation in his popular book in 1952. For Diebold, automation meant more than computerizing clerical work as described in the GE implementation. Rather, automation involved feedback that could help control and optimize the process, a concept which resonated with the cybernetic movement. In fact, Diebold even referenced cybernetics in a paper delivered at an automation conference. Automation became a hot topic in the 1950s, with several conferences and many papers written about the topic. Manufacturers frequently attended these conferences. Insurance firms were much less represented, although Malvin Davis of the SOA computer committee presented at an early conference in 1947.

Finally, unlike insurance firms, manufacturing firms relied on consultants to help purchase and implement computers. For example, GE used Arthur Anderson in their feasibility studies to determine whether to invest in the computer and to help with the programming of the computer itself (see Accenture, 2005; McKenna, 2006). Osborn explained, "we found it wise to employ an independent management consulting firm (Arthur Andersen & Co., Chicago), experienced in computer logic and developments. This firm has been particularly helpful in training personnel, arranging management orientation meetings, and planning conversion of initial applications" (Osborn, 1954, p. 106). In contrast, the data collected from the insurance community shows little engagement with consultants. Instead, insurance firms performed their own feasibility studies (Kahl & Yates, in preparation).

Berkeley was not in direct contact with manufacturing in the sense that his writing did not appear in manufacturing-related journals and proceedings. However, he was aware of manufacturing and did refer to manufacturing examples in his *Giant Brains* book. He also would have interacted with manufacturing firms at joint conferences, especially as it related to the ACM. So, while there is not a direct tie between Berkeley and manufacturing, his views as represented in the cybernetics movement and the ACM did enter the manufacturing realm.

Summary of Berkeley's Structural Position

Fig. 1 provides a stylized diagram of the network relations between the emerging computing community including Berkeley, on the one hand, and

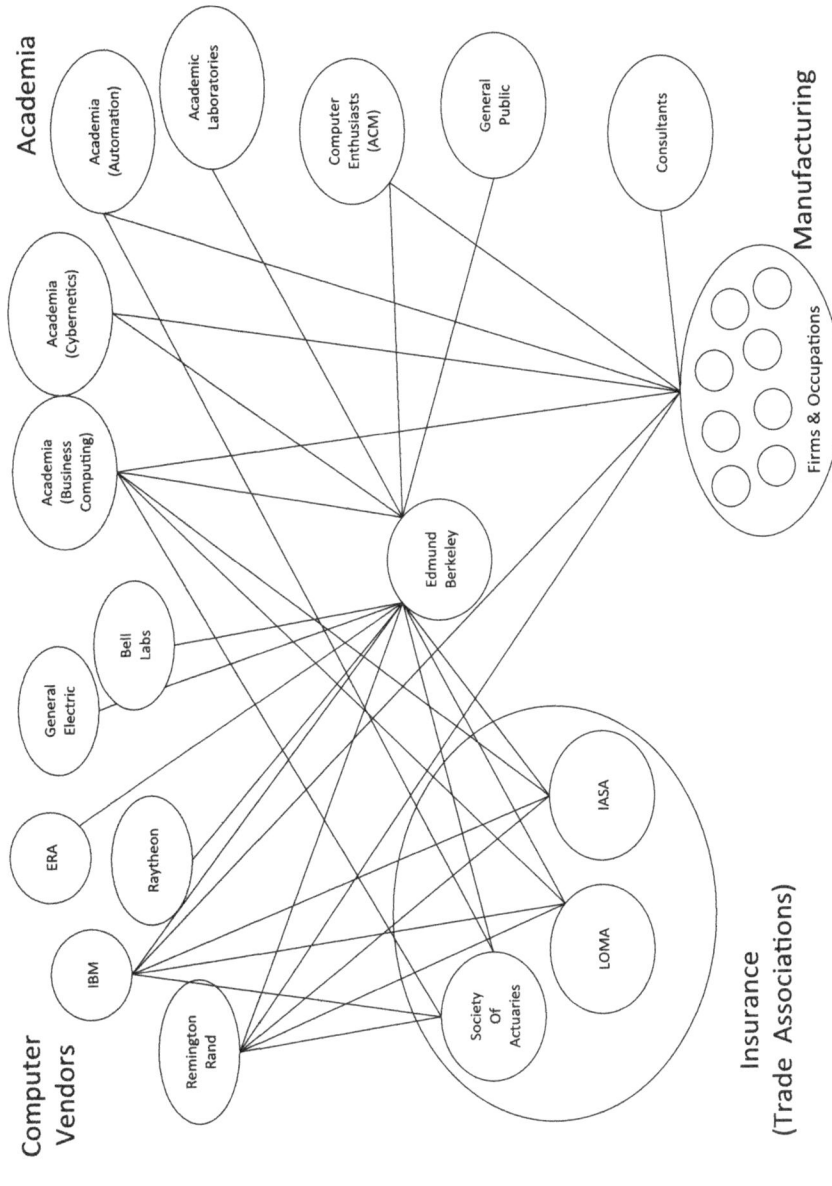

Fig. 1. Network of Early Discussion of the Computer, 1945–1954.

the insurance and manufacturing communities interested in computers, on the other, before the computer's adoption in 1954. To construct the map, we coded a tie between groups if they interacted, typically by direct visit as in the case of computer manufacturers, or through joint participation at a conference. Since we are primarily interested in Berkeley's position as an institutional entrepreneur, we first coded the groups that Berkeley interacted with and then, to build out the rest of the map, we considered the interactions of the primary groups within insurance (professional and trade associations) and manufacturing (occupational groups).

Fig. 1 highlights Berkeley's strong structural position within the emerging computing community. While both insurance and manufacturing had ties to computing vendors and other important groups, Berkeley's network was more extensive – reaching a greater variety of vendors and academics. In addition, he developed deeper ties in the sense that in some cases he actually worked with other groups or played a primary role in the governance of the association as in the ACM. This extensive network both broadened his exposure to different ideas and provided Berkeley the political clout to influence others' interpretation of the computer. The complexity and difficulty of understanding computing further solidified his position. In Latour's (2007) language, Berkeley was a "translator" – trying to convey the new technology in terms others, who lack such privileged access, could understand. Based on this position, the institutional literature predicts that Berkeley was well positioned to successfully effect institutional change, particularly in the insurance industry, but also in the manufacturing industry.

THE "GIANT BRAIN": BERKELEY'S PROPOSED INSTITUTIONAL CHANGE

In addition to identifying possibilities for change and leveraging the strengths of their structural position, successful institutional entrepreneurs seek to change belief systems, norms, and taken-for-granted cognitive perspectives through strategic behavior. In this case, the institutional change corresponds with the introduction of a radical new technology, the computer, and entails establishing interpretations about this new technology, as well as beliefs about office technology in general. To adequately measure the institutional change requires developing an understanding of existing beliefs toward technology and how Berkeley sought to change this perspective.

Berkeley was an early mover in that he presented some of the first reports about computers in the insurance associations in 1947. These papers provided at least two images of the computer, one as a machine similar to existing tabulating machines and one as a human brain. Berkeley's conceptualization of the computer as a thinking brain was influenced by his educational interest in symbolic logic and his ties with the cybernetic movement. Berkeley further developed this analogy in his *Giant Brains* book. The analogy links the relations associated with human thinking to the processes that the computer performs:

> These machines are similar to what a brain would be if it were made of hardware and wire instead of flesh and nerves. It is therefore natural to call these machines mechanical brains. Also, since their powers are like those of a giant, we may call them giant brains (Berkeley, 1949, p. 1).

Throughout the book, he develops the analogy to identify the functional and relational characteristics of the computer that correspond with how human brains think. He further defined thinking in terms of specific processes: "a process of storing information and then referring to it, by a process of learning and remembering" (Berkeley, 1949, p. 2). He categorized this process along three main functions: "Calculating: adding, subtracting, ...; Reasoning: comparing, selecting, ...; Referring: looking up information in lists, ..." (Berkeley, 1949, p. 181). For Berkeley, computers used symbolic languages and physical equipment to handle, transfer, remember, and reason with information just as the human brain used natural language and nerve cells.

By describing the computer as a thinking machine, Berkeley emphasized using the computer to help make business decisions. For example, the business example he provided in his *Giant Brains* book details how the computer can be used to help schedule and plan production within a factory:

> The machine takes in a description of each order received by the business and a description of its relative urgency. The machine knows (that is, has in its memory) how much each kind of raw material is needed to fill the order and what equipment and manpower are needed to produce it. The machine makes a schedule showing what particular men and what particular equipment are to be set to work to produce the order. The machine turns out the best possible production schedule, showing who should do what when, so that all the orders will be filled in the best sequence. What is the "best" sequence? We can decide what we think is the best sequence, and we can set the machine for making that kind of selection, in the same way we decide what is "warm" and set the thermostat to produce it! (Berkeley, 1949, p. 193).

Within insurance, Berkeley (1947a, 1947b) explained that a computer could be used to decide whether to underwrite an applicant for insurance.

Bingham and Kahl (forthcoming) analyze the content of Berkeley's conceptualization of the computer and show that it significantly departed from conventional thinking about office technology and its uses in insurance. They treat conceptualization in terms of a schema – the categories and their relations – and show the differences between Berkeley's brain analogy and the pre-existing schema. The existing schema concentrated around categories such as "clerk," "punch card," "policy," "tabulator," and "machine," and the relations between these categories centered on creating or inputting information on cards through the action of a "punch," processing the punch cards ("sort," "file," "merge," "matching"), and writing out the output ("print," "list," "post"). The brain analogy, in contrast, contained mainly new categories and relations associated with decision making: categories, such as "problem" and "operation"; and relations, such as "solve," "examine," and "think." In fact, their analysis reveals that the brain analogy only shared 12% of the pre-existing schema categories and 26% of the relations. Consequently, both in terms of the language used to describe the computer and the proposed uses of the computer, Berkeley's conceptualization of the computer as a human brain represented a significant departure from prevailing interpretations of office technology.

VARIED RESPONSES FROM INSURANCE AND MANUFACTURING

Despite Berkeley's strong structural position, his conceptualization of the computer as a brain met with mixed results. The insurance industry, in which his structural position was strongest, rejected Berkeley's view in favor of one that focused on efficient transaction processing. In fact, early respondents to Berkeley's paper on computing at the Society of Actuaries' 1947 annual meeting criticized the brain analogy. One respondent even mocked Berkeley, stating "I confess a certain apprehension that Mr. Berkeley may turn up next with automatic ears or atom-splitting digestive organs" (Wells, 1947, p. 1). E.F. Cooley, Berkeley's colleague from Prudential, argued: "I might use the term "giant brains" to tie in my subject with the more or less popular literature on this subject. But I hate to use that term since there are false implications in it, implications that these machines can think, reason and arrive at logical conclusions, and I don't agree that this is true" (Cooley, 1953, p. 355). In an internal employee magazine, *Metropolitan Life* (1956) directly asserted that computers were not like brains and could not replace people. Bingham and Kahl (forthcoming) note that of the 26 papers about computing presented in the insurance associations, only 5 portrayed the computer as a brain, 4 of which were authored by Berkeley. The remaining 21, including the SOA 1952 report, presented a more incremental interpretation of the computer as a machine that processes transactions similarly to, but more rapidly than, a tabulating machine. In contrast to the decision-making emphasis of the brain analogy, they show that the transaction view emphasized how computers can "sort," "merge," and "punch" information to process transactions. Their analysis reveals that the transactional view of the computer dominated thinking within insurance.[3]

Moreover, this view also dominated early uses of the computer. Table 1 shows the most popular applications initially developed on the computer within insurance from 1954 to mid-1958, coded by whether they were transaction-oriented or decision-oriented applications (bold). Eighty percent of the most frequent applications focused on transaction processes such as premiums – premium distribution, premium billing, premium collections, premium reserves[4] – or accounting functions – payroll and commission accounting. Only 20% were decision-oriented applications, such as planning/budgeting, and underwriting.

In contrast, the manufacturing industry supported both Berkeley's brain analogy and the more incremental transaction-oriented view of the computer. Osborn's description of the GE implementation showed support for both views. He explained that computers should be used to reduce the "dog work" of a department, which supports the transactional view. However, he also recognized that the computer can be a "management tool" that supports the decision-oriented view. Table 2 shows the most popular applications initially developed on the computer within manufacturing, with similar coding as Table 1. While transaction-oriented applications like payroll are the most popular, the material and production planning applications that Berkeley highlighted as an example of using the computer like a brain in his book are also well represented. In fact, GE tried to implement both payroll and production planning applications, recognizing that the planning applications represented "new information" and a new way of doing things. In general, the most popular applications initially developed were relatively evenly split between transaction-oriented (52%) and decision-oriented (48%).

Table 1. Early Uses of the Computer in the Insurance Industry, 1954–mid-1958.

Computer Application	Frequency
Commission calculations/accounting	26
Premium distribution	26
Premium billing	23
Actuarial studies	**23**
Valuation of reserves	18
Payroll	16
Premium collections	16
Loan accounting	16
Dividend procedures	15
Premium reserves	15
Policy issue	11
Claim distribution	11
Expense distribution	11
Automotive rating	10
Financial/operating reports	**10**
State book reports	**9**
Underwriting experience	**8**
General accounting	8
Sales or revenue accounting	7
Employee benefit plan accounting	7
Customer billing	6
Sales revenue analysis	**6**
Accounts receivable	5
Personnel records	5
Mortgage loan accounting	4
Labor distribution	4
Special analysis for planning/control	**4**
District agents records and production synopsis	**4**
Premium payment records	3
Planning/budgeting	**3**
ROI	**3**
Accounts payable	2
Selective underwriting	**2**
Cost accounting	2
Agency experience	2
Mortgage amortization	2
Total	343
% Transaction-oriented	80
% Decision-oriented	20

Decision-making applications are given in bold.

To code applications, we referred to descriptions of how firms used these applications. In cases where there were no descriptions, we coded applications with the words "report," "planning," or "budgeting" as decision-oriented applications since these words are associated with managerial decision making. Lastly, our default was transaction-oriented applications.

Table 2. Early Uses of the Computer in the Manufacturing Industry, 1954–mid-1958.

Computer Application	Frequency
Payroll	147
Labor distribution	102
Cost accounting	88
Engineering computations	**80**
Employee benefits	75
Material production requirements	**66**
Inventory control	**64**
Sales revenue analysis	**57**
Production/planning	**52**
Finished stock inventory	51
Sales or revenue accounting	50
Special analysis for planning and control	**48**
Design problems	**45**
Scientific research	**43**
Raw material and stores inventory	43
Customer billing	41
General accounting	38
Operations analysis	**38**
Planning/budgeting	**37**
Personnel records	37
Financial/operating reports	**35**
Purchase planning and control	**31**
Accounts payable	29
Sales forecasting	**24**
Machine load scheduling	**22**
Accounts receivable	20
Economic research	**19**
Salesman incentives	**9**
Process control	9
Work labor control	8
Total	1,408
% Transaction-oriented	52
% Decision-oriented	48

Decision-making applications are given in bold.

To code applications, we referred to descriptions of how firms used these applications. In cases where there were no descriptions, we coded applications with the words "report," "planning," or "budgeting" as decision-oriented applications since these words are associated with managerial decision making. Lastly, our default was transaction-oriented applications.

And the manufacturing industry was not alone in its acceptance of the brain analogy. It also permeated the popular imagination. One historian of the computer industry notes "By the early 1950s, through the reappearance of the term in many popular publications, 'giant brains' became the leading metaphor for early electronic digital computers" (Yost, 2005, p. 1).

POSSIBLE EXPLANATIONS

What explains the difference in the acceptance of the brain analogy by insurance and manufacturing? To answer this question, we first consider potential explanations prevalent in the literature and show that they are incomplete. We then develop the argument that a more comprehensive explanation must consider the structure of the audience groups interpreting the proposed changes of the institutional entrepreneur.

Industry Differences

The industry differences between insurance and manufacturing can potentially explain why manufacturing accepted the brain interpretation of the computer and insurance did not. For this argument to be successful, however, manufacturing operations and processes themselves or the industry conditions must be more likely to support decision-oriented applications than insurance operations or conditions. Yet closer examination of work practices in both industries reveals that both had a mix of transaction-oriented and decision-oriented processes, and that uses of earlier technology favored transaction-oriented processes. However, each industry faced different kinds of challenges that can help explain the differences in their responses.

First, both industries involve a combination of transaction and decision-oriented processes. In insurance, the activities associated with actuarial studies involved significant computations, and underwriting involved making decisions about whether to insure the potential customer. In fact, Berkeley even singled out underwriting as a brain-like use of the computer. Similarly, in manufacturing managing material requirements and production schedules also involved significant decision making, which Berkeley singled out in his book. By contrast, basic inventory control and customer order processing were more transaction-oriented.

Second, both insurance and manufacturing were early and important users of tabulating technology. By the 1940s, virtually all insurance firms used tabulating equipment. Indeed, IBM historians have noted that "Insurance companies were among the largest and most sophisticated business users of punched-card machines in the late 1940s and 1950s" (Bashe, Johnson, Palmer, & Pugh, 1986; pp. 176–177). Similarly, manufacturing was a heavy user of tabulating equipment and card-filing systems. Production-oriented textbooks during the 1940s and early 1950s highlight the use of tabulating equipment and Kardex card machines to manage inventory records and assist in production control. In both cases, much of the existing technology was used to process transactions as opposed to make business decisions. In the case of insurance, firms had generally divided and specialized insurance operations as they grew, and they used tabulating equipment in line with this approach. A typical insurance application performed a single, narrowly defined operation such as computing policy premiums or payroll. In manufacturing, the card systems were used to maintain control over inventory as opposed to make decisions about inventory levels and determine when new inventory needed to be ordered.

However, while both industries had both types of processes and were significant users of tabulating technology, they experienced different challenges during this time. As noted, insurance faced issues of increasing efficiency given the clerical labor shortage, even as manufacturing faced issues of growing complexity given the expansion of products after World War II. These differences certainly contributed to insurance's focus on improving transaction-processing and manufacturing's interest in improved decision making around the production planning process. However, these industry issues do not completely explain the responses. As noted, manufacturing was just as interested in transaction-processing applications (see Table 2). If we associate increased complexity with a focus on decision making, some additional factor must be considered to explain the mixed interpretations and uses within manufacturing.

Technological Differences

Hargadon and Douglas (2001) argue that design features of a new technology can influence how customers think about it. In particular, design features that invoke existing institutional scripts can make them more recognizable and spur adoption. In the case of the early computer, there essentially were two different designs – one that resembled existing tabulating machines and one that did not. Perhaps the differences in interpretation of the computer between insurance and manufacturing could be explained in terms of the two industries adopting different kinds of computers with different design features.

Both of the tabulating incumbents, IBM and Remington Rand, offered computers that were radically different from tabulators, as well as devices that were only incrementally different. Remington Rand, through its acquisition of EMCC, had taken an early lead in computers that by design were radically different from tabulating machines. The UNIVAC computer system filled a room with its large central processor, many Uniservo tape drives, and tape-to-card and card-to-tape converters. The room had to be specially prepared, with reinforced floors to support the weight and a powerful air conditioning system to reduce heat emitted from the many electronic tubes. This computer looked radically different from tabulators. Moreover, its selling price was around $1.25 million, a substantial capital investment. IBM was working to catch up with the UNIVAC technically, developing the large, tape-based 701 (available in 1953) for scientific and defense use and the 702 (available in 1955, but replaced by the more reliable 705 in 1956) for commercial use.

However, both firms also developed more incremental devices with designs that shared fundamental features of both tabulating and computer technology. IBM intended its 650 model, released in 1955, as an interim, small computer to keep its installed base of tabulator users from moving to other computer vendors as it completed development of bigger, magnetic-tape-based computers (Ceruzzi, 1998). The 650 shared some essential features of the larger, 700 series computers such as stored program capability, and some of tabulating machines, such as using cards rather than magnetic tape as its input, output, and long-term storage medium. Aside from technical differences, the 650 also closely resembled tabulating machines visually. The IBM 650 was housed in a cabinet of the same design and appearance as that of an IBM 604 tabulator, and it could be rolled into an existing tabulator installation to fit where the 604 had been (Yates, 2005). Remington Rand also recognized the need for an incremental hardware solution for customers not yet ready for the large UNIVAC, and it released two smaller, punch-card machines (the UNIVAC 60 and 120) in the mid-1950s. However, these machines, which lacked any internal storage capability, were technically closer to tabulators than to computers. Although the UNIVAC 60 and 120 were reasonably successful in the tabulator market, they did not really compete with the IBM 650. Several other early entrants into the computer market offered small and inexpensive drum-based computers during the early and mid-1950s, but they were slow, harder to program, less reliable, and tended to require IBM punch-card peripherals for customers desiring card input and output (thus diverting much of the revenue to IBM) (Ceruzzi, 1998, pp. 38–46).

If the technical design played a primary role in the emergent conceptualization of the computer, we would expect insurance companies to more readily adopt the smaller computers that resembled the tabulating machines as opposed to the larger, less tabulating-machine-like computers. Consistent with this argument, 68% of insurance implementations used the smaller IBM 650; whereas, only 23% adopted the larger UNIVAC or IBM 700 series (Foundation, 1958). However, manufacturing had similar adoption patterns: 65% bought the IBM 650 or comparable UNIVAC 60 or 120, and 27% adopted the larger UNIVAC or IBM 700 series. Moreover, this argument does not fit temporally. As described in the previous sections, both the insurance and manufacturing industries started to develop their conceptualization of the computer before it was commercially available. Therefore, while the technical design of the computer may have reinforced certain interpretations after 1954, it cannot fully explain the differences between these industries in accepting a particular conceptualization of the computer before commercial adoption in 1954.

Competition among Multiple Interpretations

Another possible explanation focuses on competing conceptualizations of the computer. Within insurance, Berkeley's brain analogy was not the only interpretation of the computer offered. As previously discussed, Bingham and Kahl (forthcoming) document a competing analogy that described the computer more as a tabulating machine. This interpretation emphasized the transaction-processing aspects of the computer over the decision-making orientation of the brain analogy. It was the view presented by the SOA 1952 report and it was much more consistent with the pre-existing schema of office technology.

However, not unlike insurance, manufacturing was also exposed to broader competing views about the computer. Through operations research and participation within academic and industry conferences, manufacturing firms were exposed to the brain analogy associated with Berkeley and the cybernetics movement. However, the automation movement's heavy emphasis on manufacturing also meant that they were exposed to the more transaction-processing emphasis of the computer as well. Osborn's description of the GE implementation showed support for both the transactional and decision-oriented view of computers. He explained that computers should be used to reduce clerical work, which supports the transactional view, but also recognized that the computer can be a "management tool," which supports the decision-oriented view. Consequently, since both groups experienced similar competing views, competition alone cannot explain the difference in acceptance of the brain analogy.

The Role of Audience Structure in Institutional Change

The previous explanations do not fully consider the audience who interprets the institutional entrepreneur's message. Sociologists have long connected the structure of social groups to their conceptual structure and how the groups respond to and integrate new information. Durkheim (1912 [2001]) argued that a group's conceptual structure reflects it social organization. Building off Durkheim, Mary Douglas (1966) showed that the social structure of various religious groups played an important role in whether they accepted or rejected anomalous concepts. More recently, Martin (2002) argued that conceptual structures that are highly interrelated and those that have strong consensus are harder to change. Such structures reflect groups that have cognitive authority and a clear power structure – more centralized social structures that reflect homogenous views. Collectively, this work reveals the importance of examining the role of the social structure of the audience interpreting the institutional entrepreneur's proposals in the overall outcome of the institutional change. Consequently, we analyzed the social structure of both the insurance and manufacturing industries to understand which groups did the work of interpreting the computer.

Our analysis revealed that the insurance industry differed significantly from manufacturing in terms of the structure of how the new conceptualizations of the computer were received and processed. In insurance, this structure was centralized among similar groups put in charge of figuring out the computer (committees within three occupational associations). Using a typical organizational chart for an insurance firm from the 1950s (see Life and Health Insurance Handbook, 1959), we identified the various occupational groups that worked in a life insurance firm. We then investigated at what level each of these groups engaged in discussing the computer. Our analysis revealed that initially not all groups within the insurance industry were interested in the computer. For example, underwriters, insurance agents, and legal professionals did not develop the same level of discourse as the SOA, IASA, and LOMA. The main groups represented in these associations included actuaries, administration, accounting, and *"Systems men"* (the group responsible for business forms development and process design, see Haigh, 2001). As a result, early discussion of the computer was centralized among only a few specific occupational groups within their associations.

In addition, as previously mentioned each of these associations formed committees to investigate the computer. For example, the SOA established The Committee on New Recording Means and Computing Devices for this express purpose. Such committees were a common organizational form within the insurance industry, used to govern and make risk decisions within the firm, as well (Life and Health Insurance Handbook, 1959). Kahl and Yates (in preparation) describe these committees as "cognitive authorities" (Martin, 2002) in the sense that others within the group deferred to these committees to interact with the computer vendors and develop an interpretation of the computer and how it can be used within insurance. They argue that these groups were initially interested in learning more about the computer because they were heavily involved in the application and management of partially existing office technology. For example, the bulk of clerical work to process billing and claims around policies occurred in the various subgroups of office administration, whereas accounting functions such as payroll and premium accounting resided within accounting. The administration group also contained the technical groups responsible for maintaining office technology.[5] For instance, "Systems men," who were responsible for designing the forms as well as the processes used by office equipment, were part of these technical groups (Haigh, 2001). Actuaries used office technology mostly for computational purposes, while the administrative and accounting groups used technology to process routine business information.

We characterize this audience structure as centralized in the sense that there was relatively little occupational variation in who investigated how the computer should be used and by whom. These efforts were further concentrated within the committee members who had centralized control. To the extent that actuaries, administrators, and accounting represented different tasks and interests, they were more aligned in that they were heavy users of the pre-existing technology primarily for clerical operations. The most computationally focused group, actuaries, interestingly, did not focus on this kind of work in their initial analysis of the computer. Indeed, the SOA report on computing rejected actuarial applications as insufficiently large to justify acquiring this expensive and powerful technology and emphasized using the computer for processing of policyholder premiums – a transaction-oriented process that they eventually called Consolidated Functions Ordinary (this corresponds to the Premium functions highlighted in Table 1).[6] In addition, Kahl and Yates trace how this conceptual discussion at the association-level transferred to the firm level. They show how the same occupational groups who dominated the early conceptual discussion prior to the release of the computer participated in the feasibility committees responsible for deciding whether the individual insurance firm would purchase a computer. Consequently, these groups had the authority to control how the computer was used inside the firm.

In contrast, the structure in the manufacturing industry was much more heterogeneous and lacked a centralized power structure. Unlike insurance, manufacturers did not develop cognitive authorities in the form of industry-wide committees that investigated what the computer was and how it could be used. Consequently, much of the early discussion about the computer occurred within different occupational groups – in particular, accounting, engineering, production planning (which was emerging as an occupational group during this time period – see Kahl et al., in preparation), and operations research. As previously mentioned, our investigation into the various journals and proceedings of these groups revealed that these groups varied in how they conceptualized the computer. Some, like accounting or industrial engineering, characterized the computer in Diebold's language of automation, focusing more on transaction processing aspects of the computer and how to control computer processes. Others, like production planners and operations researchers, emphasized the brain-like uses of the computer to help make managerial decisions.

At the firm level, similar to insurance firms, manufacturers formed groups to conduct feasibility studies on whether computing warranted investment (Haigh, 2001). But the feasibility studies in manufacturing differed from those in insurance in significant ways. First, manufacturing was more likely to bring in external consultants to help with the process. Roddy Osborn, the system manager in charge of the GE computer implementation, identified "Employ a competent consultant" as his number one recommendation for planning for a computer (Osborn, 1954, p. 107). Consulting external partners introduced different opinions. Second, whereas in insurance the feasibility committee exercised authority to which others within the organization deferred, in manufacturing these committees did not exercise this authority. Instead, they often sought input from different groups. For example, at GE Osborn was "Not content with presenting the opportunities as we saw them, we asked all managers and supervisors to review the areas of their respective operations and search for activities in which high-speed data processing would be helpful. We suggested that they report all possible applications, for us to consider until proved practicable or impracticable (Osborn, 1954, p. 102)." Part of this rationale of getting input from different groups was to develop broader support for the computer once implemented. Osborn explained that the " 'Selling' of computer applications involves offering initial applications to all management functions" (Osborn, 1954, p. 101). Finally, once the computer was implemented at GE, Osborn argued that computer operations should not be considered the province of a single department, but as a "data processing center" that served different groups' needs.

To summarize, through the use of committees with members of select occupations at the industry level and within the firm, the insurance industry developed a centralized structure of similar groups who exercised their authority over the computer. In contrast, manufacturing lacked the centralized structure and sought out more diverse opinions from the different occupational groups within the firm, as well as from external consultants. Table 3 illustrates the implications of these different audience structures. It aggregates the applications implemented from each industry from the Controllership surveys by the different occupational groups. For the insurance industry, close to 83% of all applications initially implemented were for the centralized groups – the administrative, accounting, and actuarial occupations. In contrast, a broader array of occupations

Table 3. Occupational Concentration of Early Computer Usage, 1954–mid-1958.

Insurance Industry (1954–Early 1958)		Manufacturing Industry (1954–Early 1958)	
Occupation	Percentage of all applications	Occupation	Percentage of all applications
Administrative	35.2	Manufacturing	27.5
Accounting	30.9	Accounting	27.4
Actuary	16.6	Human resources	14.9
Agent	5.6	Sales	12.8
Investment	5.6	Engineering	11.3
General management	3.3	Purchasing	2.1
Underwriting	2.6	General management	1.7
Legal	0.3	Shop floor	1.4
		Distribution	0.5
		Computer technicians	0.3
		Operations research	0.1

implemented applications within the manufacturing industry. In fact, linking Table 3 with Table 2 also shows that different occupations had different interpretations of the computer. That is, most accounting applications were transactional in nature, whereas, operations research was more decision-oriented and manufacturing applications mixed both transaction and decision-oriented applications.

More generally, examination of the different social structures of audiences interpreting and using the computer in insurance and manufacturing helps explain why Berkeley was unsuccessful in selling his conceptualization of the computer to insurance, but had partial success with manufacturing. Berkeley's view of the computer as a brain that supported decision-oriented applications did not fit with views of the groups who had centralized authority over interpreting the computer and who were interested in preserving the status quo. Because manufacturing had less centralized control in its discourse around the computer, there were fewer constraints on assimilation, allowing Berkeley's views to resonate with some of the occupational groups. The more heterogeneous groups given a voice in the manufacturing audience allowed for more variety of opinion.

CONCLUSION

By documenting the role that actors and agency play in processes of institutional change, the growing body of research on institutional entrepreneurship has rectified a crucial limitation of early neo-institutional analysis. To date, however, scholars have focused almost exclusively on cases in which entrepreneurs were able to successfully effect institutional change. From these studies, scholars have identified a set of factors common to entrepreneurial success. These elements include field conditions that allow for problem/opportunity recognition, sufficient resource capacity, framing that resonates with potential constituents, and the support of key organizations and individuals. While such studies provide valuable insights into why institutional entrepreneurs are occasionally successful, they do little to explain why efforts to create or change existing institutional arrangements so often fail. This suggests that in order to better understand why some entrepreneurs succeed, research on institutional entrepreneurship needs to pay greater attention to failure.

Consequently, our analysis of Berkeley's inability to legitimize the idea of computers as "Giant Brains" in the insurance industry contributes to the literature on institutional entrepreneurship by demonstrating why institutional change is frequently so difficult to achieve. Despite Berkeley's ability to recognize the transformative potential of the computer, his strong structural position within the insurance industry and nascent computer community more broadly, his access to resources, and strong ties to other prominent actors in this emerging field, he was unable to institutionalize his vision of the computer as a Giant Brain. In our historical case, neither technological differences, nor industry variation, nor a lack of competing interpretations about the computer can fully explain the failure of the Giant Brain analogy within the insurance industry. Rather, our analysis highlights the importance of the audience structure in shaping the success or failure of institutional entrepreneurship.

Because groups interpret and respond to the efforts of an institutional entrepreneur differently, a more comprehensive account of institutional change must address not only who initiates the change, but also how it is received and processed by incumbents and other actors within the field (Aldrich, 2010). Differences in how these actors perceive change initiatives may well determine whether or not an institutional entrepreneur is able to succeed. In our case, we have examined primarily customers who adopt the technology, but in this volume there are more complex technologies that act as platforms that mediate transactions between different audiences (see Cusumano, 2012; Leblebici, 2012). This work suggests that additional work could be done to investigate contexts in which there are multiple audience members and how this influences the institutionalization process.

In our case, we show that the key factor in determining whether or not the view of computers as Giant Brains was accepted was the specific audience structure present in each industry. Our study demonstrates the critical role that centralized audience structures may play in obstructing change even when actors perceive and attempt to act on opportunities for change. The insurance industry, through its committees dominated by actuaries, accountants, administrators, and systems men, was characterized by an audience structure composed of high status actors with clear centralization of control. By contrast, the manufacturing industry exhibited a decentralized audience structure in which a diverse range of groups without clear centralization of control and status provided input into how the computer was to be used and for what purpose. While some groups within manufacturing conceived of and indeed used the computer largely as a transaction-processing machine, other groups emphasized its decision-making capabilities. These latter groups were much more receptive of the Giant Brain analogy. This decentralized audience structure allowed for the partial support of the "Giant Brain" view of the computer within the manufacturing industry, in contrast to the insurance industry, where it was rejected.

Our findings have important implications for the strategy of institutional entrepreneurs. Since the audience structure represents a critical element in determining the success or failure of entrepreneurs' change projects, entrepreneurs must pay close attention to the social structure of the field they are trying to transform. To stand a chance of success with centralized audience structures, proposed changes must be perceived to be nonthreatening and even complementary to the established power hierarchy. In contrast, decentralized audience structures place fewer constraints on entrepreneurs and likely demand less in terms of assimilation. As a result, entrepreneurs have more leeway in proposing changes that are liable to be seen as radical.

Lastly, while this historical case shows how the politics and audience structure surrounding institutional entrepreneurship may lead to the failure of specific institutional projects in the short-term, such failures may lay the groundwork that leads to the transformation of the broader institutional environment over time. Even though Berkeley's conceptualization of the computer as a Giant Brain was initially rejected by the insurance industry, Bingham and Kahl (forthcoming) show that decision-oriented rhetoric gradually replaced the transactional view over the next 20 years. They attribute this shift to learning by using the computer, advances in computing technology in data management and processing, criticism from consultants, and the rise of the "systems movement" within insurance. They also show that this transition involved the re-integration of the decision-oriented perspective that dates back to Berkeley's "Giant Brain" metaphor. So, while Berkeley himself was not able to change beliefs and attitudes about office technology or about the computer in insurance during the 1950s, his ideas laid the groundwork for eventual institutional change. Future historical analysis should investigate the delay in this transformation as a means to better understand the temporal dynamics of institutional change.

NOTES

1. Except as otherwise indicated, this section on Berkeley is drawn from Yates (1997).

2. There were at least two dozen national insurance associations at around this time, but only these three devoted substantial attention to computing technology (Yates, 2005, pp. 18–19).

3. They also show that over time the decision-oriented view consistent with Berkeley's analogy prevailed. However, this transition cannot be attributed to Berkeley as much of the change occurred through learning by using, technological advancement, and criticism by consultants.

4. These applications reflect the Consolidated Functions Ordinary approach advocated in the SOA 1952 report.

5. Sometimes the methods group was under the control of accounting, specifically the controller, who also was interested in business process control. (For more information on these analysts, see Haigh, 2001.)

6. Because actuaries frequently became company presidents during this period, it is not surprising that they took a broader perspective than simply that of their department in the SOA report, looking at a range of possible applications and deciding that the policy-centered, transactional application was the best initial application for insurance companies.

REFERENCES

Accenture. (2005). Values-driven leadership. *The history of accenture*. Chantilly, VA: The History Factory.

Ahmadjian, C. L., & Robinson, P. (2001). Safety in numbers: Downsizing and the deinstitutionalization of permanent employment in Japan. *Administrative Science Quarterly, 46*, 622–654.

Akera, A. (2007). Edmund berkeley and the establishment of the ACM. *Communications of the ACM, 50*, 31–35.

Aldrich, H. A. (1999). *Organizations evolving*. London: Sage.

Aldrich, H. E. (2010). Beam me up, Scott(ie)! institutional theorists' struggles with the emergent nature of entrepreneurship. In W. D. Sine & R. J. David (Eds.), *Institutions and entrepreneurship: Research in the sociology of work* (pp. 329–342). Bingley, UK: Emerald.

Barr, P. S., Stimpert, J. L., & Huff, A. S. (1992). Cognitive change, strategic action, and organizational renewal. *Strategic Management Journal, 13*, 15–36.

Bashe, C. J., Johnson, L. R., Palmer, J. H., & Pugh, E. W. (1986). *IBM's early computers*. Cambridge: MIT Press.

Battilana, J. (2006). Agency and institutions: The enabling role of individuals' social position. *Organization, 13*(5), 653.

Battilana, J., Leca, B., & Boxenbaum, E. (2009). How actors change institutions: Towards a theory of institutional entrepreneurship. *The Academy of Management Annals, 3*(1), 65–107.

Beckert, J. (1999). Agency, entrepreneurs, and institutional change: The role of strategic choice and institutionalized practices in organizations. *Organization Studies, 20*(5), 777–799.

Benford, R. D., & Snow, D. A. (2000). Framing processes and social movements: An overview and assessment. *Annual Review of Sociology, 26*, 611–639.

Berkeley, E. C. (1947a). Electronic machinery for handling information, and its uses in insurance. *Transactions of the Actuarial Society of America*, 36–52.

Berkeley, E. C. (1947b). Electronic sequence controlled calculating machinery and applications in insurance. In *Proceedings of LOMA*.

Berkeley, E. C. (1949). *Giant brains; or, machines that think*. New York, NY: John Wiley and Sons.

Bingham, C., & Kahl, S. (forthcoming). The process of schema emergence: Assimilation, deconstruction, unitization and the plurality of analogies. *Academy of Management Journal*.

Bureau of Labor Statistics. (1955). *The introduction of an electronic computer in a large insurance company*. Washington, DC.

Ceruzzi, P. (1998). *A history of modern computing*. Cambridge: MIT Press.

Christensen, S., Karnoe, P., Pedersen, J. S., & Dobbin, F. R. (1997). Actors and institutions. *American Behavioral Scientist, 40*, 392–396.

Clemens, E. S., & Cook, J. M. (1999). Politics and institutionalism: Explaining durability and change. *Annual Review of Sociology, 25*, 441–466.

Cooley, E. F. (1953). Electronic machines – Their use by life companies. *Proceedings of the Life Office Management Association*, pp. 355–363.

Cusumano, M. A. (2012). Platforms versus products: observations from the literature and history. In S. J. Kahl, B. S. Silverman & M. A. Cusumano (Eds.), *Advances in strategic management* (Vol. 29, pp. 35–67). Bingley, UK: Emerald Group.

Diebold, J. (1952). *Automation: The advent of the automatic factory*. New York, NY: D. Van Nostrand Company, Inc.

DiMaggio, P. J. (1988). Interest and agency in institutional theory. In L. G. Zucker (Ed.), *Institutional patterns and organizations: Culture and environment* (pp. 3–22). Cambridge, MA: Ballinger Publ. Co.

Dorado, S. (2005). Institutional entrepreneurship, partaking, and convening. *Organization Studies, 26*(3), 385–414.

Douglas, M. (1966). *Purity and danger: An analysis of concepts of pollution and taboo*. Routledge.

Durand, R., & McGuire, J. (2005). Legitimating agencies in the face of selection: The case of AACSB. *Organization Studies, 26*(2), 165–196.

Durkheim, É. (1912 [2001]). *The elementary forms of religious life*. Oxford: Oxford University Press.

Edelman, L. B. (1992). Legal ambiguity and symbolic structures: Organizational mediation of civil rights. *American Journal of Sociology, 95*, 1401–1440.

Eisenhardt, K., & Graebner, M. (2007). Theory building from cases: Opportunities and challenges. *Academy of Management Journal, 50*(1), 25–32.

Eisenhardt, K. M. (1989). Building theories from case study research. *Academy of Management Review, 14*(4), 532–550.

Fligstein, N. (1997). Social skill and institutional theory. *American Behavioral Scientist, 40*(4), 397–405.

Fligstein, N., & Mara-Drita, I. (1996). How to make a market: Reflections on the attempt to create a single market in the European union. *The American Journal of Sociology, 102*(1), 1–33.

Foundation, Controllership. (1958). *Business electronics reference guide*. New York, NY: Controllership Foundation.

Ganz, M. (2000). Resources and resourcefulness: Strategic capacity in the unionization of california agriculture, 1959–1966. *American Journal of Sociology, 105*, 1003–1062.

Garud, R., Jain, S., & Kumaraswamy, A. (2002). Institutional entrepreneurship in the sponsorship of common technological standards: The case of Sun Microsystems and Java. *Academy of Management Journal, 45*(1), 196–214.

Greenwood, R., & Suddaby, R. (2006). Institutional entrepreneurship in mature fields: The big five accounting firms. *Academy of Management Journal, 49*(1), 27–48.

Greenwood, R., Suddaby, R., & Hinings, C. R. (2002). Theorizing change: The role of professional associations in the transformation of institutionalized fields. *Academy of Management Journal, 45*, 58–80.

Gregg, D. (Ed.). (1959). *Life and health insurance handbook*. Homewood, Il: R.D. Irwin.

Haigh, T. (2001). Inventing information systems: The systems men and the computer, 1950–1968. *Business History Review, 75*(1), 15–61.

Hardy, C., & Phillips, N. (1998). Strategies of engagement: Lessons from the critical examination of collaboration and conflict in an interorganizational domain. *Organization Science, 9*(2), 217–230.

Hargadon, A., & Douglas, Y. (2001). When innovations meet institutions: Edison and the design of the electric light. *Administrative Science Quarterly, 46*(3), 476–501.

Hwang, H., & Powell, W. W. (2005). Institutions and entrepreneurship. In S. A. Alvarez, R. Agarwal & O. Sorenson (Eds.), *Handbook of entrepreneurship research: Interdisciplinary perspectives* (pp. 210–232). New York, NY: Springer.

Ingram, P., Rao, H., & Silverman, B. S. (2012). History in strategy research: What, why, and how? In S. J. Kahl, B. S. Silverman & M. A. Cusumano (Eds.), *Advances in strategic management* (Vol. 29, pp. 241–273). Bingley, UK: Emerald Group.

Kahl, S., King, B., & Liegel, G. (in preparation). *Intraorganizational struggles for jurisdictional control: Technology innovation and occupational change in manufacturing firms, 1954–1980*. Working Paper.

Kahl, S., & Yates, J. (in preparation). *The hard-working obedient moron': The role of power and authority in computer use in insurance, 1947–1960*. Working Paper.

Latour, B. (2007). *Reassembling the social: An introduction to actor-network theory*. Oxford: Oxford University Press.

Lawrence, T. B. (1999). Institutional strategy. *Journal of Management, 25*, 161–187.

Lawrence, T. B., Hardy, C., & Phillips, N. (2002). Institutional effects of interorganizational collaboration: The emergence of proto-institutions. *The Academy of Management Journal, 45*(1), 281–290.

Lawrence, T. B., & Suddaby, R. (2006). Institutions and institutional work. In S. Clegg, C. Hardy, T. Lawrence & W. R. Nord (Eds.), *The Sage handbook of organization studies* (pp. 215–254). Thousand Oaks, CA: Sage Publications.

Leblebici, H. (2012). The evolution of alternative business models and the legitimization of universal credit card industry: Exploring the contested terrain where history and strategy meet. In S. J. Kahl, B. S. Silverman & M. A. Cusumano (Eds.), *Advances in strategic management* (Vol. 29, pp. 117–151). Bingley, UK: Emerald Group.

Leblebici, H., Salancik, G. R., Copay, A., & King, T. (1991). Institutional change and the transformation of interorganizational fields: An organizational history of the U.S. radio broadcasting industry. *Administrative Science Quarterly, 36*(3), 333–363.

Leca, B., Battilana, J., & Boxenbaum, E. (2008). Agency and institutions: A review of institutional entrepreneurship. *Harvard Business School Working Knowledge*. Working Paper Number 08-096.

Lee, T. W. (1999). *Using qualitative methods in organizational research*. Thousand Oaks, CA: Sage Publications, Inc.

Levy, D., & Scully, M. (2007). The institutional entrepreneur as modern prince: The strategic face of power in contested fields. *Organization Studies, 28*(7), 971–991.

Longo, B. (2004). Edmund Berkeley, computers, and modern methods of thinking. *IEEE Annals of the History of Computing, 26*(4), 4–18.

Longo, B. (2007). ACM established to develop communication about computing. *Communications of the ACM, 50,* 27–29.

Maguire, S., Hardy, C., & Lawrence, T. B. (2004). Institutional entrepreneurship in emerging fields: HIV/AIDS treatment advocacy in Canada. *The Academy of Management Journal, 47*(5), 657–679.

Martin, J. L. (2002). Power, authority, and the constraint of belief systems. *American Journal of Sociology, 107*(4), 861–904.

McAdam, D., McCarthy, J., & Zald, M. (1996). Introduction: Opportunities, mobilizing structures, and framing processes. In D. McAdam, J. McCarthy & M. Zald (Eds.), *Comparative perspectives on social movements* (pp. 1–22). Cambridge: Cambridge University Press.

McCammon, H. J., Chaudhuri, S., Hewitt, L., Muse, C. S., Newman, H. D., Smith, C. L., & Terrell, T. M. (2008). Becoming full citizens: The U.S. women's jury rights campaigns, the pace of reform, and strategic adaptation. *American Journal of Sociology, 113*(4), 1104–1147.

McKenna, C. D. (2006). *The world's newest profession: Management consulting in the twentieth century.* Cambridge: Cambridge University Press.

Munir, K. A., & Phillips, N. (2005). The birth of the 'Kodak Moment': Institutional entrepreneurship and the adoption of new technologies. *Organization Studies, 26*(11), 1665–1687.

Oliver, C. (1992). The antecedents of deinstitutionalization. *Organization Studies, 13*(4), 563–588.

Osborn, R. (1954). GE and UNIVAC: Harnessing the high-speed computer. *Harvard Business Review, 32*(4), 99–107.

Phillips, N., Lawrence, T. B., & Hardy, C. (2000). Inter-organizational collaboration and the dynamics of institutional fields. *Journal of Management Studies, 37*(1), 23–45.

Rao, H., Monin, P., & Durand, R. (2005). Border crossing: Bricolage and the erosion of categorical boundaries in french gastronomy. *American Sociological Review, 70*(6), 968–991.

Rao, H., Morrill, C., & Zald, M. (2000). Power plays: How social movements and collective action create new organizational form. *Research in Organizational Behavior, 22,* 237–281.

Scott, W. R., Ruef, M., Mendel, P. J., & Caronna, C. A. (2000). *Institutional change and healthcare organizations: From professional dominance to managed care.* Chicago, MA: University of Chicago Press.

Seo, M.-G., & Creed, W. E. D. (2002). Institutional contradictions, praxis, and institutional change: A dialectical perspective. *The Academy of Management Review, 27*(2), 222–247.

Snow, D. A., & Benford, R. D. (1988). Ideology, frame resonance, and participant mobilization. *International Social Movement Research, 1,* 197–218.

Strang, D., & Sine, W. D. (2002). Interorganizational institutions. In J. A. C. Baum (Ed.), *The blackwell companion to organizations* (pp. 497–519). Oxford: Blackwell.

Tolbert, P. S., & Zucker, L. G. (1996). The institutionalization of institutional theory. In S. Clegg, C. Hardy & W. R Nord (Eds.), *Handbook of organization studies* (pp. 175–190). London: Sage.

Tsoukas, H. (2009). A dialogical approach to the creation of new knowledge in organizations. *Organization Science, 20*(6), 941–957.

Wells, E. H. (1947). Discussion of berkeley's electronic machinery paper. In *Actuarial Society of America Proceedings* (pp. 1–2).

Yates, J. (1997). Early interactions between the life insurance and computing industries: The prudential's Edmund C. Berkeley. *Annals of the History of Computing, 19*(3), 60–73.

Yates, J. (2005). *Structuring the information age: Life insurance and technology in the 20th century*. Baltimore, MD: John Hopkins University Press.

Yost, J. (2005). *The computer industry*. Westport, CT: Greenwood Press.

Zuo, J., & Benford, R. D. (1995). Mobilization processes and the 1989 Chinese democracy movement. *Sociological Quarterly, 36*, 131–156.

ORPHANED JAZZ: SHORT-LIVED START-UPS AND THE LONG-RUN SUCCESS OF DEPRESSION-ERA CULTURAL PRODUCTS

Damon J. Phillips

ABSTRACT

Purpose – *This study is intended to extend scholarship on the management of organizations by examining the long-term performance of orphaned products.*

Design/methodology/approach – *This study uses the historical context of the 1929 stock market crash and the Great Depression to examine the long-run appeal (performance) of orphaned products – products from start-ups that fail soon after production. I use this setting to determine how factors within the purview of management, as well as the role of changing tastes, affect the appeal of music from short-lived start-ups founded in 1929 and 1933.*

Findings/originality/value – *I find that while the evolution of tastes has a substantial effect beyond the control of a firm's managers, a start-up's decision-makers were able to positively influence the long-run appeal of music when they (a) recorded tunes with new artists and (b) were able to*

History and Strategy
Advances in Strategic Management, Volume 29, 315–350
ISSN: 0742-3322/doi:10.1108/S0742-3322(2012)0000029014

create an early big hit with the tune. These results demonstrate how and why, even with cultural producers in one of the greatest economic disasters in U.S. history, managerial decisions were meaningful for product performance. Finally, I show that the effect of being a start-up on the long-run appeal of a tune is time-varying such that being a start-up in 1929 or 1933 does not harm a tune's appeal until after World War II. These final analyses point to further ways in which strategy, history, and sociology might combine to further scholarship on the management of organizations.

Keywords: Jazz; orphaned products; start-ups; post-failure product success

INTRODUCTION

Cultural markets are interesting contexts in which to examine the relationship between firm strategies and history. Not only is the identity of a cultural producer heavily influenced by the historical context, but cultural producers must contend with cultural and market forces that make a firm's performance complex and temporally dynamic (Hirsch, 1972). In particular, product performance is often driven by historically specific factors outside of the firm's control. Moreover, the appeal of the individual cultural product is often time-varying, even among the same sets of consumers (Babon, 2006; Phillips, 2011). These and other concerns constitute a daunting challenge for scholars and practitioners wishing to apply a strategic lens to cultural producers. These challenges can be offset by opportunities however. For example, one can use cultural markets to take advantage of dramatic social and economic upheavals as quasi-natural experiments. Moreover, this type of context can highlight the fruitfulness of historically informed studies on firm strategy and competitive positioning (see Murmann, 2012 in this volume).

In this chapter, I focus on particular components of cultural producers by emphasizing how a cultural product's success is a function of the context of production (including the identity of the producer) that consumers and other audience members use in their evaluations (Griswold, 1987; Kahl, Kim, & Phillips, 2010; Peterson, 1997; Phillips, 2011). From this perspective, a cultural producer's strategy involves the management of the context of production, in addition to actions and strategies that enhance the long-run success of products that have their own "social lives" beyond the moment of production (Carroll, Khessina, & McKendrick, 2010; Scott, 2004). And while cultural producers often have post-production influence on the success of their products, the greatest proportion of the influence occurs before and during the product's release (Sood & Dreze, 2006; Sorenson & Waguespack, 2006). This influence includes the construction of a cultural product's authenticity, which is key to its appeal and performance. As Peterson (1997) revealed in his study on the market for country music, firms and other commercial interests strategically created and cultivated social cues to "fabricate authenticity." Actions by organizations such as record companies and labels included everything from managing their organizational identities to selecting the clothing choices of artists to cultivating audiences, all of which ultimately converted the market for "hillbilly music" to "country music."

My goal in this study is to focus on the long-run appeal of products (recordings) from start-up cultural producers (record labels) in 1929 and 1933 to better understand three determinants of product appeal (performance) and their strategic implications. These three determinants are selected to reflect aspects of product performance that vary in the amount of control the firm's managers have over the performance. My question will be to better understand how factors under management's control, as well as factors outside of their control, affect the long-run appeal of their products.

Fig. 1 presents the annual number of jazz recordings produced per year worldwide (Lord 2005; Rust 1969). To get a sense of the demand for recordings over time, Fig. 2 shows the U.S. record sales (in millions of units) for a smaller window, from 1927 to 1938 (Gronow & Saunio, 1999, p. 38). Each helps to provide a context for this study. In Fig. 1, I segment the observation window into sections according to the type of era and record companies that were generally founded (Kenney, 1999; Phillips & Kim, 2009; Phillips & Owens, 2004). Firms founded before 1917 are called "Victorian-Era" firms after the cultural orientation and style of music (classical) that most of these firms recorded when they were first founded. Firms founded from 1920 to 1929 were "Jazz Era" firms, as they were founded during the Jazz Age (Fitzgerald, 1922) and were strongly associated with the dominant forms of jazz of that period. In particular, the mid- to late 1920s saw the increased appeal of symphonic jazz (Lopes, 2002), which by 1929 was a more dominant form of jazz than the music by currently recognized luminaries such as Duke Ellington and Louis Armstrong (Berrett, 2005; Phillips, 2012). I refer to the third period as the "Great Depression Era" to identify start-ups that were founded in this unique economic

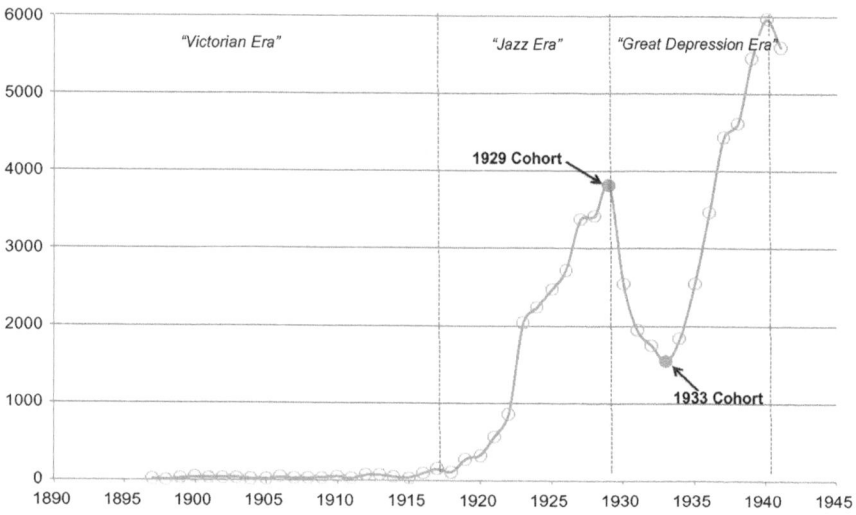

Fig. 1. Annual Number of Jazz Recordings Produced, 1897–1942.

circumstance but that also would have been heavily exposed to symphonic jazz even as the dominant style was transitioning from symphonic jazz to big band swing. This is certainly not to imply that symphonic was the only form of jazz, for multiple styles coexisted (Phillips & Kim, 2009). Indeed, the swing style of jazz arose in national popularity beginning in the mid-to-late 1930s as a form of jazz that was competing with symphonic jazz (Schuller, 1991). However, even with the success of swing, symphonic jazz was the commercially dominant form of jazz through 1933. Start-ups from 1929 and 1933 in my sample were founded when symphonic jazz was a dominant form of jazz, although the influence and association with symphonic jazz would have been stronger for the 1929 start-ups.[1]

My analysis offers an interesting and important twist in which the start-up firms that are the focus of this study were those founded in 1929 just before the stock market crash, or those founded in 1933 when the Great Depression in the United States was at its nadir, just before a dramatic rate of increase in recordings. The choice of these two cohorts is substantively important since the start-up record companies from 1929, founded before the crash, were subject to the crash as an exogenous shock, whereas the start-ups of 1933 were founded when economic conditions were clearly bleak, but just before the recovery began (see also Lampe & Moser's, 2012 examination of patent pools from 1930 to 1938 in this volume). The 1929

Fig. 2. U.S. Record Sales (Millions of Units Sold), 1927–1938 (Data Source: Gronow & Saunio, 1999, p. 38).

founders were likely unprepared for the stock market crash (the market for jazz recordings was consistently growing market up to the crash), whereas the 1933 founders would have had relatively more accurate information on the overall state of the market, but still may not have been privy to the market's direction, or otherwise might have been poor forecasters. In either case, essentially all of the start-ups for each of these two cohorts were short-lived, failing within a few years after their launch at a much higher rate than the start-ups in the 1920s that had taken advantage of the expanding market for recorded jazz.

Thus, to emphasize, I am not only focusing on the cultural products of start-ups, but of *short-lived start-ups*, to ensure that I observe and measure a firm's influence on the product solely around the time of production. For the products, coming from a short-lived start-up should have meaningful consequences. Only the decisions made by managers in the early years could affect the long-term appeal of these products. The normal post-production activities one might associate with record companies and labels would have been unavailable for these recordings (Caves, 2002; Scott, 2004; Sorenson & Waguespack, 2006). That is, to the extent that a recording's longevity would benefit from a marketing strategy or connections to distribution channels, many of these recordings would have been disadvantaged. They were, in a sense, the "orphaned" products of deceased producers (cf. Hoetker & Agarwal, 2007).[2]

The literature is understandably thin on understanding the dynamics and consequences of major economic crises for innovation-based markets since in the U.S. major crises are relatively infrequent. However, the advantage of taking a historical approach is that we can seek to understand how producers and their products in earlier innovation-based markets were affected, and then consider the generalizability of the findings. In this way, my study here is related to Hoetker and Agarwal's (2007) study of patent performance after the dissolution of focal firms in the disk drive industry. This similarity is especially salient since theirs is a technological innovation study where the key outcomes were patents and the citations to them. In my study of short-lived record labels, the indicator of a product's success is the extent to which it is "cited" by future musicians by re-recording the music of start-ups. In this way, the product's "citation rate" captures its appeal (or performance) akin to the way one would capture the performance of patents. For example, while most tunes have years where no one records them, "On the Sunny Side of the Street" (part of the 1929 cohort) was re-recorded 31 times in 1945. Tunes that are re-recorded the most often become part of the jazz canon and known as jazz standards (Phillips, 2011).

However, my study differs from Hoetker and Agarwal (2007) in that entire cohorts of start-ups were decimated, some (the 1929 cohort) through an environmental shock, others (the 1933 cohort) through the (apparently poor) choice of starting a new organization in perhaps the toughest economic time for recorded music markets in U.S. history.[3] While the 1933 cohort did get founded before an upswing, a big part of that upswing was in the form of radio broadcasts from more established labels, and their radio parent firms (Kenney, 1999).

In addition to my unique focus on short-lived firms, I draw attention to three factors. First, I examine how a recording's success was affected by one of the key early decisions that a start-up record label had a large degree of control over: whether to produce recordings by experienced or new artists. Second, I consider whether the early success of the tune – something that the firm would have had partial control over – affected the long-run appeal of the tune differently when the firm was a start-up. Creating an early big hit would have been something that a firm's managers could influence either through greater skill at selecting higher "quality" tunes or better initial marketing of tunes. Either way, my objective here is to understand whether and why early big hits from (short-lived) start-ups had different long-run appeal than early big hits from more established firms. Third, I examine the role of factors outside of the firm's purview: how the evolution of jazz over the course of the 20th century affected the long-run appeal of their products. Not only is it difficult for any record label to affect the long-run appeal of its recordings (Hirsch, 1972), but in my sample the start-ups were short-lived, which means that the producers did not even exist long enough to exert influence over the long-run appeal of the music. This third focus is intended to help to scholars better understand the "baseline" that a cultural producer may be compared against over time. Following past research which has found that a record company's identity is partially rooted in the time of their creation (Kenney, 1999; Phillips, 2012), record companies that were founded when a particular style of jazz dominated will produce recordings whose long-run success depends on the continued domination of that style of jazz over time.

This third factor pays close attention to how more macro changes in "tastes" (captured here as the legitimacy of one type of jazz compared to another type) have implications for product appeal long after the product is released and the start-up has gone out of business. Here I provide evidence that whenever the style of jazz associated with the period that my start-ups existed has had greater legitimacy over time, the recordings from those start-ups have greater appeal. In particular, the timing of record labels founded during the height of symphonic jazz in the late 1920s and early 1930s perpetually links the appeal of their recordings to the overall legitimacy of symphonic jazz. Thus, the more positively evaluated symphonic jazz was over time, the more appealing were the products from firms founded in this period.

Given the rather unprecedented goal of better understanding the fate of products of short-lived cultural producers, I proceed with predictions driven by past research and the historical context, but without the use of formal hypotheses. This begins with combining a brief theoretical development and discussion of the context with an empirical verification that music from short-lived record labels has lower appeal on average. I follow this by testing whether recordings from short-lived record labels improve when the artist or group for the recording was also new. One might expect that the combination of a new record label and new recording artists might be especially problematic for the appeal of the recording. However, there are both economic (e.g., adverse selection of talent) and sociological (e.g., the recording's authenticity and categorization) reasons to expect positive returns when the start-ups in my sample have new artists.[4] I also test whether start-ups benefit from producing early big hits more than established firms. In the context of economic crises, the motivation here speaks to long-standing discussions on the new entrants' strategy. That is, if returns from early success are disproportionately positive, managers of the start-ups would have done well in investing in creating an early big hit. Finally, I examine how the appeal of a short-lived producer's recording may vary over time. Ultimately, the question in these final analyses is whether and how might the changing legitimacy of jazz affect the products of short-lived start-ups from 1929 and 1933 differently than products of other firms that released labels in these same years. Following these analyses, I will conclude with considering the limitations, scope conditions, and strategic implications of the findings.

CONTEXT AND THEORY

The Market for Jazz Music in 1929 and 1933

Jazz scholars generally acknowledge that recorded jazz began in 1917, although jazz's roots in ragtime and blues extend back to the turn of the century (Gioia, 1998; Kenney, 1999; Peretti, 1997). Record production grew rapidly during the 1920s even with increasing competitive pressure by new entrants and radio interests that offered a new medium for commercialized music (Tschmuck, 2006). The year 1929 would serve to be a peak in record production before the market was heavily damaged by the market crash.

The period from 1929 to 1938 represented a transformation that ultimately restructured the entire market (Gronow & Saunio, 1999; Kenney, 1999; Tschmuck, 2006). Worldwide, the traditional leaders of the recording industry had become subsidiaries and subdivisions of larger firms.[5] Radio interests began acquiring record companies and labels – such that the previously dominant Victor Records would then be known as RCA Victor and Columbia Records would come under the ownership of CBS. Other major recording firms in the jazz market met similar fates. Smaller labels largely disappeared, especially the cohort of record companies and labels founded in 1929 right before the crash (Kenney, 1999). By 1938, only two of the six firms that dominated the industry were pure record companies. These two, Decca-U.S. and Decca-U.K., were founded after the crash and organized as separate entities (Gronow & Saunio, 1999). The other four companies were CBS and RCA Victor dominating from the United States, and EMI and Telefunken GmbH in Europe. CBS and RCA (which also controlled NBC) were broadcasting companies, whereas EMI and Telefunken were electric companies. This latter set of firms ensured that record production would no longer be driven by firms in the phonograph industry.

As Fig. 1 reveals, the year 1933 corresponds to an economic transition in the United States and a larger cultural transition in Europe that culminated in World War II. The period from 1929 to 1933 was the key period of the Great Depression, and with respect to GNP and unemployment statistics, recovery from the depression began in 1933 (Lucas & Rapping, 1972). The year 1933 also marks the last years of the symphonic style of jazz that dominated the market for recorded music until around 1935, when swing music would more clearly dominate (Peretti, 1997; Schuller, 1991). Swing would be associated with the improvement in the market for jazz after 1933, a rise that continued until World War II.

It is also important to note that the early market for commercialized music had important differences from more modern conceptualizations of cultural markets (Caves, 2002; Dowd, 2003; Hirsch, 1972, Peterson & Berger, 1975). The rise of jazz was synonymous with the rise of commercialized music. It was the popular music form that most drove the early rise and success of the mass production of popular recorded music (Kenney, 1999). By 1929, the market for recorded jazz was 12 years old and was an expanding market where firms' identities and relative market positions were beginning to stabilize in ways that would be familiar to more static conceptualization of markets. The stock market crash in 1929 would upend the market just when its structure was solidifying.

That said, the 1920s also featured the rise of radio, which continuously grabbed market share from the market for recordings. By 1929, radio was better positioned to survive the crash than the recording industry. Their improved position gave them the market power to acquire many of the large, but financially distressed record companies, reshaping the industry into multimedia firms that combined recordings, radio, and film. These firms, such as RCA, Warner Brothers, and CBS, would come to dominate their markets for decades.

Because of our emphasis on the long-run appeal of individual recordings, two additional features of our setting require elaboration. First, the early market for commercialized music was organized around singles rather than albums. In fact, albums did not exist at this point of the industry's evolution. Second, there was little variance in the price of recordings within the jazz genre. For example, when examining advertised prices from display ads in the *Chicago Defender*, *Chicago Tribune*, *New York Times*, *Wall Street Journal*, and the *Washington Post*, there was no evidence of variance in prices by type of jazz.

The Great Depression took a substantial toll on the recording industry as the purchasing power of consumers diminished. The U.S. unemployment rate sharply rose from around 3% in 1929 to 23% in 1933 (Steindl, 2008). As a consequence, the market for recorded music fell. For example, local markets (cities) produced an average of 136.15 original recordings in 1929, but that dropped to 96.43 in 1933.[6] That said, the change in production was geographically uneven. While the production in New York, Chicago, and Berlin dropped,[7] London and Paris saw little change in the number of original recordings produced from 1929 to 1933.

Furthermore, the markets in 1929 and 1933 also varied in global scope in other ways, with much more localized production in the 1933 market. Supplemental descriptive analysis provided evidence that the markets for jazz recordings in 1933 were less geographically diffuse than the markets for jazz in 1929: jazz was recorded in 20 cities in 1929, versus 14 in 1933; there were more local musicians and local labels that only recorded in the focal market in 1933 compared to 1929; and the long-run appeal of music from 1933 did not spread to as many cities as the long-run appeal of music from 1929, even when holding the total amount of appeal constant.

Finally, the proportion of start-up record labels participating in 1929 and 1933 was very similar (.11 versus .10), however, this too masks geographical variance. In the major markets (New York, London, Chicago), the proportion of start-ups increased as the larger firms of 1929 pulled back production or exited the market altogether (cf. Carroll 1985). In smaller markets the proportion of start-ups decreased or remained the same from 1929 to 1933. Thus, the increased founding rates in the major markets offset the reduced founding rates in smaller markets.

The Long-Run Appeal of Products from Short-Lived Start-ups in the Recording Industry

Independent of whether the start-ups began in 1929 or 1933, nearly all failed within a few years of their initial production. And while I draw attention to the role of the economic crisis, there is a long-standing observation and evidence that new organizations often fail. Indeed, among the most commonly observed findings in empirical studies of organizational performance is the low survival rate of new organizations. In fact, this "liability of newness" (Stinchcombe, 1965) is sufficiently familiar with organizational theory and strategy scholars alike that it no longer considered as a topic of novel research. The reasons for the liability of newness are many, but include insufficient financial and social resources, lack of entrepreneurial skills or vision, noisy or missing signals of the ventures success, or the lack of an organizational identity that prevents a favorable evaluation as a legitimate and capable organization (Hannan, Polos, & Carroll, 2007; Klepper, 2001; Sorensen & Phillips, 2011; Stuart, Hoang, & Hybels, 1999).

With respect to organizational identity, there is a long-standing emphasis on how the context of founding (the time and location) leads audiences to construct expectations and rules of behavior for firms (Selznick, 1957; Stinchcombe, 1965). Many of these rules, especially for newly founded firms, are those for which the firm's founders only have partial control (Freeman, Carroll, & Hannan, 1983; Singh, Tucker, & House, 1986). The liability of newness and its relationship to organizational identity is particularly important for cultural producers, whose identities are used by consumers and other audience members when evaluating their products (Phillips & Owens, 2004). Cultural producers often have a measurable advantage when they produce products that are seen as consistent with the identity of the producers, and face disapproval when their outputs defy their identities (Phillips & Kim, 2009). A record label launched during the rise of jazz, rock-and-roll, or hip-hop will not only struggle with the challenges of any start-up, but they also are more likely to be linked with the genre that dominates markets at the time of founding. Accordingly, their fates should rise and fall with their respective genres, even if the labels eventually produce a relatively diverse type of music (Carroll & Hannan, 2000).

I argue that the economic crisis is a special amplified case of the liability of newness. In the case of start-ups in 1929 and 1933, the conditions they faced around the time of founding increased the already high failure rates that any start-up would have had to encounter. That said, compared to the 1933 cohort, the 1929 cohort was founded before the crash, making the environment they faced at the moment of founding radically different than what they faced months later. My main interest is the performance of the original recordings of these firms given the overwhelming failure rate. These producers would have little time or resources to market, draw attention to, or otherwise facilitate the sale of their product after the point of production. Thus, *I expect that the long-run appeal of recordings will be lower for recordings from the short-lived start-ups, compared to more established record labels.*

I will also examine whether there is a difference in the appeal of the tunes from the 1929 and 1933 cohort. A priori it is difficult to ascertain which of the two cohorts would have products that were the most disadvantaged. On the one hand, tunes from 1929 start-ups are the products from the producers who faced an exogenous shock and with little latitude to adjust for the market upheaval. Indeed, it is likely that many of them would not have even produced the same tunes, produced the same tunes at the same cost (e.g., recording the same tune but with fewer musicians), or produced original tunes at all. These smaller 1929 start-ups would have also been especially disadvantaged with respect to the larger record companies who not only had more resources to promote their recordings, but also were eventually acquired by radio interests who would take the recordings from their newly acquired inventories and play those tunes on the air – increasing the tune's long-run appeal.

On the other hand, the 1933 cohort was founded at the lowest point in the Great Depression, which the literature on founding conditions suggests would be detrimental. Moreover, the 1933 cohort was competing with fewer, but much larger recording companies that had been acquired by radio interest. As a result, the 1933 cohort likely faced greater competition than the 1929 cohort. Finally, there are likely unobserved but real differences in the type of entrepreneur who founds a start-up in 1929 versus 1933. Like most studies in entrepreneurship, the motivation and opportunities that a potential entrepreneur recognizes are difficult to ascertain (Sorensen & Fassiotto, 2011). The only tool in my data is to make inferences from the results and supplemental analyses.

Does the Start-up Employ New or Experienced Talent?

One decision that is captured in my data is whether the start-up enters the market with a new musical artist or an experienced artist. The choice of a new or experienced artist is well represented in the data (detailed below) with 29% of the start-ups across the two cohorts releasing the original recordings with new talent. This allows one to examine the consequences of this managerial decision on the performance of the product. It is certainly logical to argue that new start-ups employing new artists would be doubly disadvantaged. After all, along with all of the liabilities that a new firm faces, if it also records a new artist who lacks skills in recording or an established set of consumers (a fan base), the subsequent success of the recordings might be adversely affected. However, there are economic and sociological reasons that I believe counteract those disadvantages.

First, start-ups run the risk of an adverse selection problem with experienced artists. Typically, successful artists either stay with their record label or experience upward mobility in terms of working with a record label that has greater (or broader) marketing power. This marketing power would provide more opportunities for the artist whose principal source of revenue during this period was live performances (rather than record sales or radio play). Thus, even though start-ups were known to allow greater musician autonomy (Phillips & Owens 2004), the type of experienced artist who became employed at a start-up is unlikely to be a "star." Rather, these artists would have been more likely to record with a start-up only if they were unattractive to other firms. Indeed, this adverse selection rationale should operate more strongly in 1929, when the market was robust and strengthening, versus in 1933, when the opportunities for musicians shrank independent of their quality.

Second, Phillips and colleagues (e.g., Kahl et al., 2010; Phillips, 2012) have shown that tunes that experience long-run appeal tend to have some congruence between the characteristics of the recordings and the characteristics of the firm that produced the recording. For example, certain early jazz recording by African-Americans have more appeal over time, but only if they come from less powerful record labels, which matches the lower status of the musicians with the lower status of the record label (Kahl et al., 2010). Future musicians and consumers find this combination more compelling, salient, and appealing than African-American musicians who recorded with market leaders, just as in contemporary contexts many might revere a rap artist from a smaller label as more authentic (and thus more appealing) than an artist with a major label.

These reasons suggest that while recordings from these short-lived start-ups on average have a disadvantage, tunes from start-ups with new artists had greater long-run appeal than tunes from start-ups with experienced artists.[8] Put another way, I expect that today we are more likely to be familiar with a 1929 or 1933 start-up's music if that music featured a new artist. Music from 1929 and 1933 start-ups that featured experienced artists are forgotten because they were either lower quality or incongruent. While not the focus of this study, I do expect that recordings from incumbent record labels do better when the artist was experienced, as a logic of selection and sorting would suggest. Therefore, *I expect that a product's long-run appeal was higher with a short-lived start-up that selected new artists.*

Do the Returns to Early Success Vary for Start-ups?

Cultural markets are among those settings in which firms make offerings that often fail soon after their introduction to the marketplace, but with exceptions that experience extraordinary success (e.g., "blockbusters"). The attempt to secure one of these big hits is thus a key goal of decision-makers in culture firms (Bielby & Bielby, 1994; Hennion, 1983; Hirsch, 1972; Perren, 2001; Whiteside, 1981). Typically, the firm takes one of two routes to increase the probability that a cultural product will be an overnight sensation – or what I refer to as disproportionate early success. First, the firm may invest in inputs that have high signaling value, such as writers or actors with widely recognized reputations (Bielby & Bielby, 1994; Sorenson & Waguespack, 2006). Indeed, this speaks to the first type of investment addressed in my previous discussion on whether start-ups produced tunes with experienced or new artists. Second, firms may invest in marketing, distribution, and other post-production activities (Perren, 2001; Sorenson & Waguespack, 2006; Whiteside, 1981). In either case, most scholars conclude that cultural products that dominate the attention of audiences increase the likelihood of experiencing disproportionate early success, which will in turn build positive momentum toward long-term appeal (Whiteside, 1981).

In this study, my question is whether this commonly observed long-run return to disproportionate early success is the same for all firms, or whether the long-run return systematically varies for the short-lived start-ups from 1929 and 1930. In particular, and especially for the 1929 cohort, their investment in making a song a early success could have been seen as misguided in hindsight, as all of their investments would have been disrupted by the stock market crash of 1929. However, I believe that a counterfactual is more compelling in this case: music from the short-lived start-ups that did not experience disproportionate early success would be completely forgotten due to the stock market crash, and thus faring very poorly with respect to long-term appeal. That is, the proper question is not so much whether investing in making a tune an early success helped, but whether *not* investing in that tune would have guaranteed its long-run failure. If this is true then the only tunes from the short-lived start-ups which survived the stock market crash and Great Depression would have been those that had disproportionate early success. Disproportionate early success of the product from any firm should have improved the tune's long-run appeal; early success from a short-lived start-up saves the tune from obscurity. Thus, *tunes from short-lived start-ups that experienced disproportionate early success have a relative advantage over tunes from short-lived start-ups that did not experience disproportionate early success.*

The Evolution of Jazz and the Long-Run Appeal of Early Recordings

In this chapter, I use the concept of imprinting (Selznick, 1957; Stinchcombe, 1965), which argues that the resources and capabilities of an organization influence the time and location of its founding. Here I draw attention to the fact that a cultural producers' role identity is linked to the time in which the firm was founded and persists in some form well beyond the early years of that organization. Thus, if a recording or a producer is associated with the dominant music in a particular period, then it stands to reason that the long-run appeal of that producer's recordings would be some function of how dominant the style of music it represents varies over time. In this way both the identity of the cultural producer and product is linked to the cultural context in which it is produced, where identity is captured by the expectations of consumers and other audience members.

Capturing imprinting and identity involves understanding the historical account of organizational foundings within a larger context in order to identify key capabilities and social cues that drive organizational and product appeal. The role of the founding context in understanding a new organization's capabilities and identity follows a rich tradition in sociology and organizational theory, usually under the rubric of imprinting, which includes studies on markets for experience and symbolic goods such as wine (Roberts & Sterling, 2011; Swaminathan, 2001), beer (Carroll & Swaminathan, 2000), opera (Johnson, 2007), and jazz (Kahl et al., 2010; Phillips & Kim, 2009; Phillips & Owens, 2004). For example, Phillips and Kim (2009) find that record companies imprinted with identities associated with classical music saw their 1920s jazz recordings receive lower appeal.

In this chapter, I wish to emphasize that the identity of a new cultural producer also affects the fate of its products as a time-varying function of the popularity of the music around the label's founding. All else equal, the longevity of music from record labels linked to a style of jazz will ebb and flow with the popularity and legitimacy of that style of jazz. Similarly, jazz music from labels associated with other styles will not be as exposed to the time-varying popularity of the focal style.

Part of my contribution here is the notion that products, as well as their producers, can be subject to similar social dynamics. Independent of the producer's contribution to products, products are influenced by the environmental context in which they have been produced. And while this may be true of all products to some degree, I expect that this is especially the case for cultural products, where an assortment of social cues is valuable for audiences to assess meaning and value. Information based on the context of production is one set of cues available.

To give a sense of variation in founding context, a broad overview of recording styles is helpful (Gioia, 1998; Peretti, 1997). Broadly speaking, beginning in 1917 the first jazz recordings typically featured a four to five piece, improvisational "Dixieland" style band (e.g., piano, banjo, trumpet/coronet, trombone, drums). While this type of band was recorded across my observation period, around 1923 more structured symphonic jazz orchestras began to dominate, and continued to dominate until 1935 (Phillips & Owens, 2004; Schuller, 1968, 1991). Thus, a firm entering the jazz market in early 1919 was associated with the Dixieland style (and typically recorded this type of group). Ten years later, in 1929, a start-up would have been associated more with the symphonic style and would have often produced music more similar to the symphonic style than either the "Dixieland" style or the "Swing" style that came to dominate in the mid-1930s.

Also significant is the fact that because these eras are well-known among the jazz community, audience members would look back to the record labels and tunes produced in each era when searching for a particular style of jazz. That is, if I wish to find an authentic "Dixieland" style early jazz recording, I might look for a recording from the earliest years of jazz (Brunn, 1960). If I was searching for an authentic symphonic style of jazz, I would search for music from the mid-1920s to the mid-1930s. Obviously, music released in those years has authenticity, but so would firms who were founded in those respective eras. Indeed, Phillips and Kim (2009) have demonstrated the role of founding period on the music's authenticity.

For firms and music that entered the market in 1929 and 1933, symphonic jazz was the dominant commercial representation of jazz. Given this association, my objective is to follow the legitimacy of this form of jazz over time by tracking the legitimacy of the most recognized symphonic jazz artist – Paul Whiteman – over time within the public discourse. My expectation would be that as symphonic jazz's legitimacy increased and fell, so would the appeal of music from 1929 and 1933 start-ups since these firms would have been most associated with this style of music. As an additional test, I will also track the legitimacy of two other jazz exemplars, Duke Ellington and Louis Armstrong, whose style of jazz competed with

Whiteman's. Fig. 3 compares the number of times "Paul Whiteman" is co-mentioned with "jazz" in the *New York Times* (solid line) to the times "Duke Ellington" is co-mentioned with "jazz" (dashed line) from 1920 to 1946. The graph shows that within the *New York Times*, Whiteman was the artist most associated with jazz until the late 1950s. He quickly became the name associated with jazz for the readers of the *Times*, and was often sought out as a spokesman and authority on jazz. In fact, the co-mentions of Duke Ellington and jazz do not experience a sharp rise until World War II. Indeed, Duke Ellington's position was sufficiently subordinate (among middle and upper class Anglo audiences) as he was advertised as the "Paul Whiteman of Colored Orchestras" in 1926 (Berrett, 2005, p. 150).

With respect to this study, my focus is on the relationship to the music of start-ups in 1929 and 1933, and the relationship between that music and the time-varying legitimacy of the popular music of their day (represented by the association of Whiteman and jazz in the *New York Times*). If I am correct, music from 1929 and 1933 start-ups is more sensitive to the evolution of symphonic jazz of Paul Whiteman and the competing styles of Duke Ellington and Louis Armstrong than the music of other older firms that also produced recordings in 1929 and 1933. Thus, *all things equal, I expect that the recordings of 1929 and 1933 start-ups were more likely to be affected by evolution of symphonic jazz than the 1929 and 1933 recordings from older firms.*

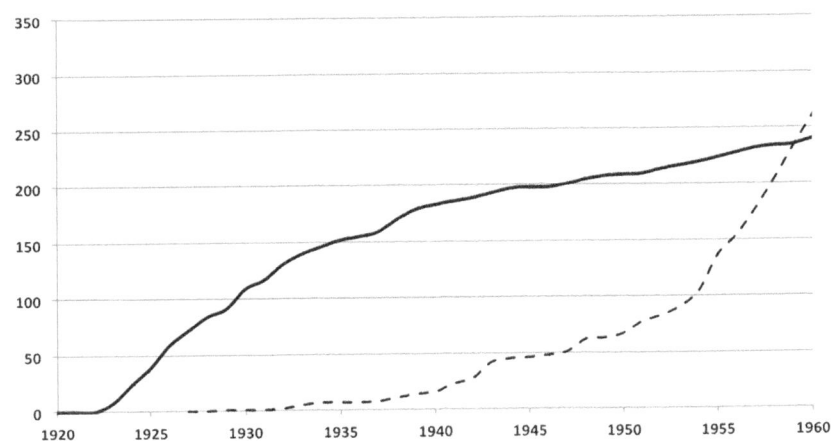

Fig. 3. The *New York Times* Cumulative Mentions of "Paul Whiteman + Jazz" (solid line) and "Duke Ellington + Jazz" (dashed line), 1920–1962.

DATA AND METHODS

Examining "orphaned" cultural products has some empirical advantages, as the short-lived producer's influence on the product's appeal does not extend very far beyond the original recording. For example, 5 or 10 years after production, the appeal of an orphaned product can be modeled as a function of conditions at the firm's founding, market conditions at the 5 or 10 year mark, and other controls for the time period, lagged dependent variable, etc.

I test my predictions using data on jazz discographies from the Lord (Lord, 2005) and Rust (1969) Jazz discographies. The discographies allow for a database that provides information on bandleaders, recording sessions, musician entries, and tune entries. Each of these databases is uniquely known for having very little missing data. As has been noted elsewhere (Phillips, 2011), the Lord discography builds upon the Rust discography, and the Rust discography is itself a well-established, reliable, and valid source of data according to musicologists (Crawford & Magee, 1992; Kernfeld & Rye, 1994, 1995). There is no other dataset of jazz recordings that approaches the Lord discography's global comprehensiveness. From this data, I analyze all of the tunes originally recorded in 1929 and 1933. I follow the tunes within each cohort until 2001. The final dataset for my analyses captures 189 tunes from 1929, followed over 73 years (for 13,797 tune-years), and 114 from 1933 followed over 69 years (for 7,866 tune-years). After two missing cases, the analyses reported here use 21,661 tune-years of data.[9]

Dependent Variable

My outcome variable of interest is a tune's annual appeal, measured as the annual count of re-recordings for every jazz recording originally recorded in 1929 or 1933. That is, in each year up to 2001, I count the number of times the tune was re-recorded by other musicians (in studio recordings and recordings of live broadcasts). The more a tune is re-recorded in a year, the greater the appeal among musicians, where the models capture the average annual appeal for a tune as a function of key independent variables and a host of controls detailed below. Similar to Phillips (2011), my assumption is that this appeal among jazz musicians is also associated with its appeal among other audiences such as consumers.

I run my analyses using zero-inflated Poisson regressions. The use of zero-inflated Poisson regressions is driven by the nature of the data and distribution of the dependent variable. I am estimating the annual appeal of a song over time, where annual appeal is captured by the number of times a recording that originated in 1929 and 1933 is re-recorded in year *t*. While this count variable suggests the use of a Poisson or negative binomial regression, the typical song experiences many years in which there are no re-recordings of a particular tune at all; in fact, these zeros make up the vast majority of cases. The subset of interest is the influential minority of tunes that became the most appealing. The zero-inflated Poisson regression allows one to model whether appeal is greater than zero in a given year (modeled as a logistic regression) separately from what the nonzero count of the appeal might be (modeled as a Poisson regression). In conducting the analyses I use the routine "zip" in Stata/SE 12.1. While I only report the second-stage regression that models the count of appeal, I will also note any statistically significant first-stage results.[10]

Independent Variables

The key independent variable is an indicator of whether the record label was new or not in 1929 or 1933. The variable equals one if the focal tune's record label was new, and zero otherwise. This distinction is consistent with the view that the imprinted resources and identity of the firm are captured at the birth or founding of the firm (Hannan & Freeman, 1984; Stinchcombe 1965). The results reported here hold consistently and have the strongest effect when age is captured as simply new (equaling one), or not new (equaling zero), rather than a continuous operationalization of age. Drawing upon research with similar data that revealed that lower performance of firms founded before 1917 compared to firms founded in the Jazz Age (1917–1929), my models include controls for whether the firm was founded in either one of these earlier periods.

To capture whether the artist (or group) was new, I coded a dummy variable for whether the individual identified as the bandleader was recording for the first time. To be clear, this variable captures whether the artist was a bandleader for the first time, but not whether they had ever recorded a tune before. As one might expect, many bandleaders began as "sidemen" in other groups, many of whom recorded often. Thus, being a new bandleader means that the artist was, for the first time, responsible for the selection of tunes recorded and was the focus of the firm's marketing for the recording. Much later in the history of jazz marketing, high-status sidemen would be promoted alongside the bandleader to boost a new bandleader's legitimacy. However, in this earlier period, the attention was almost always focused on the bandleader.

I coded for a tune's early success by capturing whether multiple recordings of the tune was released in this initial year. The existence of multiple recordings in the initial year is a supply-side indicator of immediate appeal. Music experiencing disproportionate early appeal was commonly re-recorded several times during its initial release to fully capture the early spike in the consumer demand for the music. The question I will examine is not whether early hits have greater long-run appeal (my models will show that they do) but whether early hits from start-ups have greater long-run appeal. Thus I coded a set of interaction terms using the dummy variable for multiple recordings in the first year, and the variable for whether the firm was a start-up. This allowed me to test whether tunes with disproportionate early success have different effects when the firm was a start-up.

To test for the difference in stylistic legitimacy, I examined each of our tunes to determine whether music from the 1929 and 1933 start-ups were more likely to be re-recorded (or have appeal) during periods of high legitimacy for symphonic jazz by capturing Paul Whiteman's annual popularity as a jazz artist in the public discourse. As suggested in Fig. 3, to capture Whiteman's legitimacy and salience as a representative of jazz, I calculated the annual proportion of the *New York Times* mentions of "jazz" that also included "Paul Whiteman." To test whether the tunes from 1929 and 1933 start-ups were positively associated with Whiteman's form of jazz, I created an interaction term between the dummy variable for the start-ups and the legitimacy of Paul Whiteman. To capture the effect of competing styles, I created similar variables and interaction terms for co-mentions of "Duke Ellington" and "Louis Armstrong" with "jazz."

Control Variables

Perhaps the most important controls are four variables that help to isolate the annual appeal of a recording over time. Each of the models include the lagged dependent variable (the number of re-recordings in the previous year), as well as the lagged cumulative number of previous mentions of the dependent variable. Accordingly, statistically significant effects are distinct from any momentum from the previous year or cumulative appeal. These controls also help to net out any aspect of the tune's appeal due to its inherent "quality" or other unobservable drivers of appeal. I also include the lagged total number of unique cities that the song has been re-recorded in to capture the geographic breadth of appeal as something distinct from the cumulative appeal or the appeal in the previous year. This third lagged variable controls for the possibility that even controlling for two tunes with the same previous appeal, that the tune with its previous appeal occurring in a limited number of cities, is not as influential as one with appeal in several cities, especially since the role of geography in explaining the long-term success of jazz recordings has been found to be very prominent in other research (Phillips, 2011). The fourth of these key control variables is an annual count of the appeal of all songs from the same cohort. This control helps to separate out time-varying cohort effects (such as years when all of the tunes from the 1929 were more or less appealing), which is especially critical in isolating the effects for the time-varying legitimacy of music from new labels.

Following past studies using these data (Kahl et al., 2010; Phillips, 2011), the models also control for indicators of the local market (city) where the recordings was produced. First, to ensure that my effects were not due to tunes originating in markets that were disproportionately competitive (enhancing the quality or visibility of the recording, as well as an indicator of how active the city was in the market for jazz), I coded the annual number of labels that recorded in the city, as well as the proportion of those labels that only recorded local artists. These indicators also help to ensure that the effect of the start-up label is not also capturing the level of local competition by generalist and local specialists. As an additional control, I also include a control for the number of years since the city last recorded jazz. It is likely that cities that produce jazz on a sporadic basis will also produce lower appealing jazz, and to the extent that this sporadic production is related to the prevalence of new record labels, this source of variance in appeal should be taken into account. Finally, I use a set of dummy variables for each city of the original recording to adjust for any city-level differences. For example, one may expect that any song from New York has a disproportionately annual appeal over time (which is in fact the case) for reasons that are not completely observable. The city-level dummies help to separate these effects when looking at the age of the record label and my other independent variables.

Given that I am modeling a global market, it is important to include proxies for the size of the global market. Thus, in addition to controls for the annual appeal for all tunes in each cohort, I also coded for the number of recordings produced in each year throughout the observation period.

This control helps to ensure that a particular tune's appeal is estimate net of the overall market size (using a supply-side indicator).

I also control for whether the recording had a title in a language that was not English, although the effects are unclear. While non-English titles suggest lower appeal from English-speaking audiences, other research has shown that uniqueness, especially when linked to geographic distances, is appealing (Phillips, 2012). Similarly, I coded for whether the tune had a geographical reference in its title, as this too has been found to affect the long-run appeal of a tune (Phillips, 2012) by influencing its salience to future musicians. Finally, in addition for a dummy variable for whether the song was in the 1929 or 1933 cohort, I control for the differences over time with dummy variables that capture three-year periods (e.g., 1942–1945, 1946–1949, and 1950–1953), as well as dummy variables for the record labels themselves, to separate fixed but unobserved firm characteristics (such as size) that may be confounded with the age.

RESULTS

Table 1 presents the means and standard deviations of the key variables.[11] Table 2 presents the results of the zero-inflated Poisson regressions. Model 1 demonstrates the main effects of whether the firm was a start-up in 1929 or 1933. Model 2 examines whether the tune's appeal was positively affected when the artist was also new. Model 3 includes interaction effects to estimates whether disproportionate early success had different implications for tunes from start-ups. Models 4–6 use interaction terms to examine the effect of the evolution of symphonic jazz and its competing styles of jazz on the favorability of recordings by 1929 and 1933 start-ups. Given the large number of cases (21,661), I not only found it important to examine the statistical significance of the effects, but also pay attention to differences in model fit using the model differences between log-likelihoods and the Akaike Information Criterion (AIC) (Burnham & Anderson, 2002).

Model 1 shows that start-ups in 1929 and 1933 produced original tunes that had lower annual appeal. This lower performance was somewhat greater in magnitude than "Victorian-Era" firms' tunes – where Victorian-Era firms had been noted in previous studies as having lower appealing recordings (Phillips & Kim, 2009). Thus, there is solid evidence that the liability of newness attributed to firms is also reflected in the performance of those firm's products. These models, however, do not help distinguish between start-ups in 1929 and start-ups in 1933. While the magnitude for the 1933

Table 1. Descriptive Statistics of Key Variables ($N = 21,661$ Recording-Years, from 303 Recordings).

	Mean	Std Dev	Min	Max
Dependent variable				
Annual number of re-recordings (appeal)	.11	.85	0	31
Main predictors				
Record label was start-up in 1929	.07	.25	0	1
Record label was start-up in 1933	.04	.18	0	1
Bandleader recording for the first time	.37	.48	0	1
Multiple recordings of the tune in its first year	.01	.12	0	1
Annual legitimacy of Paul Whiteman	.007	.010	0	.042
Annual legitimacy of Duke Ellington	.020	.011	0	.067
Annual legitimacy of Louis Armstrong	.015	.009	0	.049
Record label controls				
Record label was founded from 1917 to 1929	.16	.37	0	1
Record label was founded before 1917	.29	.45	0	1
Tune-level controls				
Cumulative count of appeal (lagged)	4.59	28.19	1	722
Geographic spread (lagged)	2.03	6.13	0	146
Tune was produced in 1933	.36	.48	0	1
Recording's title was non-English	.13	.34	0	1
Song title makes a geographical reference	.09	.29	0	1
Local market controls				
Number of years since jazz was recorded in the city	30.85	21.98	0	75
Total number of record labels in year of production	45.55	34.16	1	82
Properties of record labels focused on local market	.53	.25	0	1
Global market controls				
Annual appeal of entire cohort of tunes	19.04	23.03	0	228
Annual number of recordings worldwide	10463.24	4535.17	1542	20216

start-ups is greater, the statistical significance and subsequent improvement in model fit were driven much more by the 1929 start-ups. As a result, there is insufficient evidence from these main effects that any difference between these cohorts is meaningful for the product's performance.

Model 1 also brings to light control variables that have consistently significant effects across Table 2. As expected, recordings that began with early success captured by multiple recordings of the tune in its first year have long-run appeal. In the examination of various tunes, this effect is because these are the tunes that were the "big hits" in the focal year, and thus come

Table 2. The Poisson Component of Zero-Inflated Poisson Regression (Logit Inflation) of the annual Appeal of Recordings Produced in 1929 and 1933 (N = 21,661 Recording-Years, 303 Recordings).

	Model 1	Model 2	Model 3	Model 4	Model 5	Model 6
Main predictors						
Record label was	−.58**	−.76**	−1.26**	−1.23**	−.16	.09
start-up in 1929	(.18)	(.21)	(.25)	(.26)	(.23)	(.21)
Record label was	−.70*	−.79*	−1.24**	−1.29**	−.10	−.16
start-up in 1933	(.28)	(.30)	(.40)	(.42)	(.37)	(.32)
Bandleader recording	−.44**	−.48**	−.48**	−.44**	−.44**	−.44**
for the first time	(.08)	(.09)	(.09)	(.08)	(.08)	(.08)
Multiple recordings of	.74**	.73**	.66**	.76**	.70**	.69**
the tune in its first	(.20)	(.20)	(.20)	(.20)	(.20)	(.20)
year						
Annual legitimacy of	2.73	3.34	2.58	2.23	3.34	3.31
Paul Whiteman	(6.94)	(6.94)	(6.96)	(6.99)	(6.94)	(6.95)
Annual legitimacy of	−6.86*	−6.86*	−7.07*	−6.87*	−6.44*	−6.84*
Duke Ellington	(3.24)	(3.24)	(3.24)	(3.24)	(3.23)	(3.24)
Annual legitimacy of	15.07**	15.04**	14.69**	14.60**	14.59**	14.74**
Louis Armstrong	(4.78)	(4.78)	(4.78)	(4.78)	(4.78)	(4.77)
Start-up in 1929*		.74*				
group recording for		(.36)				
the first time						
Start-up in 1933*		.62				
group recording for		(.62)				
the first time						
Start-up in 1929*			1.47**			
multiple recordings			(.31)			
in the first year						
Start-up in 1933*			1.13*			
multiple recordings			(.49)			
in the first year						
Start-up in 1929*				76.28**		
annual legitimacy				(19.59)		
of Paul Whiteman						
Start-up in 1933*				27.91*		
annual legitimacy				(13.13)		
of Paul Whiteman						
Start-up in 1929*					−61.46**	
annual legitimacy					(15.88)	
of Duke Ellington						
Start-up in 1933*					−46.84*	
annual legitimacy					(22.74)	
of Duke Ellington						
						−66.24**

Table 2. (*Continued*)

	Model 1	Model 2	Model 3	Model 4	Model 5	Model 6
Start-up in 1929* annual legitimacy of Louis Armstrong						(15.04)
Start-up in 1933* annual legitimacy of Louis Armstrong						−57.05* (25.00)
Record label controls						
Record label was founded from 1917 to 1929	.08 (.15)	.09 (.15)	.08 (.16)	.07 (.16)	.08 (.16)	.08 (.15)
Record label was founded before 1917	−.48** (.13)	−.47** (.13)	−.48** (.13)	−.48** (.13)	−.48** (.13)	−.48** (.13)
Major record label dummies	Yes	Yes	Yes	Yes	Yes	Yes
Tune-level controls						
Previous year's appeal (lagged Dependent Variable)	.09** (.01)	.09** (.01)	.09** (.01)	.09** (.01)	.09** (.01)	.09** (.01)
Cumulative count of appeal (lagged)	.001 (.002)	.001 (.002)	.002 (.002)	.002 (.002)	.002 (.002)	.002 (.002)
Geographic spread (lagged)	.008 (.009)	.008 (.009)	.006 (.009)	.006 (.009)	.006 (.009)	.006 (.009)
Tune was produced in 1933	−.78** (.16)	−.79** (.16)	−.78** (.16)	−.76** (.16)	−.77** (.16)	−.77** (.16)
Recording's title was non-English	.52** (.15)	.56** (.15)	.57** (.15)	.57** (.15)	.55** (.15)	.56** (.15)
Song title makes a geographical reference	−.10 (.11)	−.11 (.11)	−.08 (.11)	−.07 (.11)	−.08 (.11)	−.07 (.11)
Local market controls						
Number of years since jazz was recorded in the city	−.07** (.02)	−.07** (.02)	−.07** (.02)	−.07** (.02)	−.07** (.02)	−.07** (.02)
Total number of record labels in the year of production	−.05** (.01)	−.05** (.01)	−.04** (.01)	−.04** (.01)	−.04** (.01)	−.04** (.01)
Properties of record labels focused on local market	−.04 (.29)	−.02 (.29)	−.08 (.29)	−.07 (.29)	−.07 (.29)	−.04 (.29)
City dummies	Yes	Yes	Yes	Yes	Yes	Yes

Table 2. (*Continued*)

	Model 1	Model 2	Model 3	Model 4	Model 5	Model 6
Global market controls						
Annual appeal of entire cohort of tunes	−.001 (.001)	−.001 (.001)	−.001 (.001)	−.002 (.001)	−.001 (.001)	−.001 (.001)
Annual number of recordings worldwide per 10,000	.62** (.15)	.63** (.15)	.65** (.15)	.65** (.15)	.66** (.15)	.66** (.15)
Time-varying legitimacy of jazz styles						
Period dummies	Yes	Yes	Yes	Yes	Yes	Yes
Constant	−.20 (.23)	−.20 (.23)	−.19 (.23)	−.20 (.24)	−.22 (.23)	−.23 (.23)
df (Poisson/Total)	46/81	48/85	48/85	48/85	48/85	48/85
Log-likelihood	−3056.24	−3053.51	−3042.96	−3047.88	−3046.21	−3043.84
Akaike Information Criterion (AIC)	6274.47	6277.03	6251.92	6265.75	6262.42	6257.69
Rank order of AIC	5	6	1	4	3	2

$^*p<.05$; $^{**}p<.01$ (two-sided t-tests).

to represent that year's music as the genre and market mature – just as the big hits of 2012 will be the songs that will come to represent 2012 when we revisit this year's music over the coming decades. This indicator is both an indicator of the music's "quality" and other factors such as marketing which increase its salience (cf. Sorenson & Waguespack, 2006). Another finding is that artists recording for the first time have recordings with lower annual appeal. The control variable for any song produced in 1933 is consistently negative, highlighting the fact that music produced during the nadir of the market (and overall economy) has had lower long-run appeal. Another interesting finding is that music with non-English titles experienced greater annual appeal. My intuition is that this is capturing the greater salience of the music. We are more likely to remember unusual titles that remind us of distinct and unique places (Phillips, 2011).[12] The local market controls were intuitive, showing that music from markets that infrequently produced jazz and those that were not too crowded produces songs that had lower long-run appeal. The global market variables were also unsurprising with the appeal of each tune being higher in years were the worldwide production of recordings was greater. Finally, as the jazz evolved, the overall appeal of

1929 and 1933 tunes increased when Louis Armstrong was a key representative of jazz in the public discourse, but decreased when Duke Ellington was a more common representative. Models 4–6 will examine whether these effects vary for start-ups whose identities and capabilities are more linked to the time of founding.

Model 2 shows the interactions with whether the bandleader (artist) was also new. Here the effect is positive for both cohorts, but only statistically significant for the 1929 cohort (the estimates are similar if the interactions are run separately). Summing the coefficients for the main and interaction terms indicates that for 1929 start-ups, the negative effect of being a start-up on its recordings is erased when the recording featured a new artist. This finding supports two possible arguments: that the congruence of the new label and new artist has more long-term appeal in the market for jazz (Phillips, 2011), and that start-ups at the peak of the market in 1929 were able to attract relatively high-quality new artists. Later in this chapter, I will reference supplementary evidence that suggests that the former explanation has greater explanatory power, but neither argument can be completely ruled out. The fact that the interaction is not statistically significant for music from 1933 start-ups that employed new artists does point to a difference in that music from 1933 start-ups was produced at a low point in the market that would have had real constraints on acquiring talent (compared to the established firms). For these firms, the long-run appeal was lower for start-ups independent of whether the artist was new.

Model 3 tests whether early big hits (disproportionate early success) have greater long-run appeal if the producer was a start-up, suggesting that the salience of the early big hit is more salient over time when the start-up was also new. The estimates for the interaction indeed suggest that short-lived start-ups with big hits have songs with greater long-run appeal (less than 2% of the cases were these bit hits). In fact, nearly all of the tunes from these start-ups that survived were also early hits. Tunes from the start-ups that were not early big hits – as evidenced by the main effects for the 1929 and 1933 cohorts – had very little long-run appeal. Also worthy of note is that Model 3 has the best model fit of all of the models, suggesting that start-up interactions with whether the tune as disproportionate early success explains the data better than any of the other models in Table 2.

Models 4–6 examine how the change in the legitimacy of various styles (captured by the legitimacy of Paul Whiteman, Duke Ellington, and Louis Armstrong) affects the recordings from start-ups in 1929 and 1933. Model 4 supports the argument that start-ups from 1929 and 1933 were more affiliated with the style exemplified by Paul Whiteman. The independent effect for the legitimacy of Paul Whiteman as a representative of jazz was positive but insignificant across all of the models in Table 2. However, the effect was positive and significant for tunes from 1929 and 1933 start-ups. For the sake of interpretation, in Model 4 the independent effects of being a tune from a start-up in 1929 and 1933 captures the appeal in a given year when Paul Whiteman had zero association with jazz in the *New York Times* (this occurred three times: 1946, 1962, and 1980). In years when Paul Whiteman's legitimacy was its greatest (1932, 1933, 1939), the appeal of tunes from the start-ups in those years was higher.

Here the difference between the effects for 1929 start-ups and 1933 start-ups was meaningful. A simple algebraic transformation shows that for the 1929 start-ups, Whiteman's legitimacy would improve the appeal sufficiently to offset the negative effect of being a start-up. For 1933 start-ups, the coefficients suggest that even in the peak years of Whiteman's legitimacy the appeal of the tunes did not completely offset the negative effect of being a start-up. In other words, 1929 start-ups benefitted more from the legitimacy of Paul Whiteman than 1933 start-ups.

Models 5 and 6 lead to a similar conclusion with models that respectively capture the legitimacy of Duke Ellington and Louis Armstrong, where each artist is an exemplar of styles that competed with symphonic jazz. In these cases, the long-run appeal of 1929 short-lived start-ups was diminished in the years that Duke Ellington or Louis Armstrong were more associated with jazz in the public discourse (again there are time controls in these models as well as the lagged dependent variable).[13] In fact, when these two artists were not key representatives of jazz, tunes from 1929 or 1933 start-ups had the same appeal as tunes from more established firms. The models also suggest that there is a more pronounced effect for the 1929 cohort than the 1933 cohort, but only for the Duke Ellington indicator. The Louis Armstrong indicator did not reveal any real differences between music from the two cohorts of start-ups. Rather, the most important result from the Louis Armstrong variable is that overall music from 1929 and 1933 had greater appeal, the more that Louis Armstrong was identified with jazz in the public discourse (the main effect) except for start-ups, which fared worse under these same conditions.

DISCUSSION AND CONCLUSION

Overall, the results point a strong and distinct effect for music from start-ups in 1929 and 1933 compared to music produced by more established firms during those same years. On average, music from start-up record labels had lower appeal even after a host of controls, including indicators that should address a tune's intrinsic "quality." While both cohorts of start-ups had lower appealing recordings, this disadvantage compared to more established firms disappeared for the 1929 cohort of start-ups when the musical artist was also new, suggesting that (a) new artists for the 1933 start-ups could not compensate or (b) new artists at start-ups in 1929 were "better" than the new artists at start-ups in 1933. The disadvantage for the 1933 start-ups was independent of whether the artist was new. The findings also suggest that early big hits from start-ups got a bigger return over early big hits from more established firms.

With respect to the time-varying legitimacy of different jazz styles, tunes from 1929 and 1933 had substantially different levels of annual appeal depending on whether the producer was a start-up. The tunes from start-ups were more intimately linked to the popular style of their time than comparable songs from more established firms. This implies that either start-ups were more often producing music that sounded like Paul Whiteman or that (independent of the style of music recorded) they were identified with a particular period and thus were less salient to future audiences when the style associated with that period waned. While this last effect occurred for both cohorts, it was stronger for the 1929 cohort. Moreover, overall there are clearer (more easily interpretable) and nuanced effects for the 1929 cohort. For the 1933 cohorts, it appears that the overall weight of the Great Depression on the supply and demand for music would have lasing effects for its music. That is, while managerial decisions made some differences, rarely did these differences offset the decimated market that 1933 start-ups were founded in. There is little prescriptively to glean from these firms.

Considering Sociological and Economic Explanations with Time-Varying Effects

With the models presented here, it is difficult to weight the strength or interplay of sociological explanations relative to economic ones, especially where the mechanisms predict the same observed effect. For example, the fact that tunes from 1929 start-ups have greater long-run appeal supports both sociological and economic explanations. That said, one can examine whether the effects for the two sets of start-ups varied over time and consider the type of arguments might provide the better explanation. Table 3 presents a set of supplemental analyses that rerun the Model 1 of Table 2 within four eras that broadly map unto societal and intra-genre jazz transitions (especially in the United States): 1929–1944 (from end of the jazz

Table 3. Poisson Regressions of the annual Appeal for Different
Time Periods.

	From 1929 to 1944	From 1945 to 1964	From 1965 to 1989	From 1990 to 2002
Record label variables				
Record label was new venture in 1929	−14 (.21)	−.98** (.32)	−.92** (.27)	−2.07** (.74)
Record label was new venture in 1933	−.09 (.33)	−.52 (.64)	−.16 (.83)	−1.74** (.84)
Record label was founded from 1917 to 1929	.09 (.20)	−.20 (.51)	1.28* (.61)	.27 (.44)
Record label was founded before 1917	−.07 (.16)	−1.54** (.36)	−.57** (.22)	−.70* (.35)
Controls from Table 2	Yes	Yes	Yes	Yes
N	4,390	6,060	7,575	4,242
df	35	38	39	34
Akaike Information Criterion (AIC)	1803.73	1448.38	1907.22	996.24
Rank order of AIC	3	2	4	1

*$p < .05$; **$p < .01$ (two-sided t-tests). All models use the controls from Table 2.

age to the beginnings of bebop); 1945–1965 (the transition to free, *Avant Garde*, and fusion); 1965–1989 (the transition to a neo-traditionalist movement led by Wynton Marsalis); 1990–2001 (the transition to modern jazz). The labels of each era matter little to this exercise, for the primary objective is to determine whether the appeal captured in Model 1 of Table 2 persisted across these time periods.

While not strong evidence for a sociological explanation per se, the pattern of results across the time periods casts doubt on a simple, ahistorical, argument that suggests that the products of start-ups are inherently and invariably inferior. If the products from these start-ups were inherently inferior, one would expect to see the effect in all time periods or at least see the negative effect greatest in the first period and then diminish over time. However, we see a pattern that is essentially the opposite. The appeal of music from the 1929 and 1933 start-ups had indistinguishable appeal before 1945, or the end of World War II. Put another way, if one had run an equivalent analysis during World War II, the conclusion would have been that the appeal of music is independent of whether the firm was a start-up or established. And even here, the post-war increase differs for the 1929 and 1933 cohorts. Tunes form 1929 start-ups have lower appeal from 1945 until the end of the observation period, whereas the effect for 1933 start-ups does not occur until after 1990. Fully exploring these explanation and implications of these analyses will likely require a combination of economics, history, and sociology to better appreciate, particularly if one's goal is to develop insights for strategy. I hope that future scholars can engage such topics to further demonstrate the value of combining history and strategy.

Table 3 points to the need for more focused research on understanding time-varying appeal, its relationship to characteristics of the firm and the decision its managers make, and when product performance is driven by factors exogenous to the firm.[14] I believe that it also points to both the value and need of strategy research that takes advantage of larger macroeconomic shocks such as the Great Depression (see Lampe & Moser, 2012). Ideally, this approach would enable strategy scholars to better articulate where and when strategy matters when studying innovation-based industries. Decisions on whether to employ new creative talent, such as new artists, might matter even when considering the long-run performance of the product. Indeed, it is quite interesting to find that this decision positively affected the appeal of a tune decades after the initial recording. The models also suggest that start-ups would have done well to invest heavily in a new big hit or at least be prepared to advertise their association with the big hit. Overall, the findings suggest that the best response during a crisis (conditional on having founded a firm such as a record label) is to invest in new talent and early products that had overwhelmingly immediate appeal. A more conservative approach for a start-up, either through hiring a trust source of talent or producing a product that had an immediate appeal that was merely typical, most likely meant that the tune would be largely forgotten over time. Early success and new artists increased the likelihood that the tune would be salient and appealing after World War II.

I expect that some of my sociological colleagues might be skeptical of the value of traditional strategic management in cultural markets, noting the limitations that managers face in forecasting the effect of strategic decisions (Hirsch, 1972). I agree that this challenge exists; however, it is also clear that strategic behavior is ever present among these firms, even if the ends are sometimes loosely coupled with the means (Phillips & Kim, 2009; Phillips & Owens, 2004). Indeed, I have selected a quasi-natural experiment that minimizes the firm's influence on its product and yet, especially for the 1929 cohort, managerial decisions matter greatly to the long-term performance of cultural products. My position is that strategy scholars can substantially add to the study of cultural industries, but any verdict on the effectiveness of strategic scholarship in these contexts is premature – researchers do not know enough about how these markets work yet. A greater understanding of historically embedded cultural markets will allow a better assessment of the scope conditions around traditional strategic approaches. It is an intellectual challenge that requires a synthesis of sociology, strategic management, and history.

NOTES

1. For a more detailed discussion of symphonic jazz, see Phillips and Owens (2004) and Phillips and Kim (2009).

2. When a firm failed, the fate of its inventory (its library of recordings) often hinged on whether its assets were purchased or acquired by other firms. This is a complex and poorly documented process that is worth study in and of itself, as one reason why a product would survive in the marketplace is that it would be acquired by a more powerful firm (with greater marketing resources). In this setting, however, there is more reliable data on the inventories of the failing larger recording companies being acquired than that of the short-lived start-ups. To the extent that the data is available, I could not uncover a link between whether a start-up's music was acquired and the music's forward citation rate by other musicians (my dependent variable).

3. My study also differs in that the rules for song licensing and patenting licensing vary. For Hoetker and Agarwal (2007), a focal firm A may be constrained from licensing the patents from another firm B before firm B fails. This might occur if firm B prohibits firm A from licensing firm B's innovations. In my recording industry context, this constraint is greatly reduced and more akin to a context where mechanical licensing is compulsory. That is, the constraint on firm A on re-recording a song that was originally recorded by firm B is substantially lower.

4. There is a long line of production of culture research within sociology that examines the inclusion of new artists on Billboard charts as an indicator of musical diversity. That is not my use of "new artist" in this study. That said, I am following the tradition of considering the recording of a new artist as an indicator of novelty, only in my case I will arguing that the appeal associated with any novelty of the artist depends on whether the record label is also new.

5. The set of major acquisitions began before 1929, but increased rapidly after the Crash as record producers became substantially cheaper assets to acquire (Gronow & Saunio, 1999; Tschmuck, 2006).

6. My data for this study use original recordings. That is, at the city level, I track recordings of tunes that have not been previously recorded, nor are they tunes that are simultaneously recorded in the same year across multiple cities; each of these tunes is selected out. The result is data of original music whose long-run appeal can be more credibly attributed to the founding conditions. This means that the statistics I report should be read with the understanding that I am undercounting the actual

production. If a startup record label entered the market by re-recording music that was already recorded (e.g., recording the "hits" from previous years), those data (or the strategy that they represent) are not included in my study.

7. The drop in production in Berlin was also a byproduct of the rise of the Nazi Party.

8. Here the artist is the performer, but not necessarily the composer of the music. This distinction is common when studying recorded jazz, where the musician performing the music often takes "cultural ownership" of the music even while the composer retains intellectual rights. For example, Body and Soul is known by many as a Coleman Hawkins tune, but he is neither the composer nor the first musician to record the tune. His 1939 recording is by far the most successful recording of that song, having influenced generations of musicians by the way he improvised using that song. Culturally, it is said that "he owns it."

9. A discography is a listing of recordings organized by the name of a band or artist. It contains data such as the musicians on the recording, the location of the recording, the date, instruments played, catalogue and matrix numbers, record label, other labels that the recording was reissued under, etc. (see http://www.lordisco.com; Kernfeld and Rye, 1994, 1995). For more details on these data, see Kahl et al. (2010) and Phillips (2011).

10. Each of the models presented here was also run with several different model specifications, including negative binomial, Heckman two-stage, etc., each with results similar to those reported here. In particular, all of the variables of interests maintained their level of statistical significance. Indeed, even a simple Poisson regression with the main variables and interactions effects (without any control variables) demonstrates the effects. The consistency of these effects speaks to their robustness.

11. Correlations can be made available upon request, but are omitted here to preserve space. Tests showed no concerns with multicollinearity, and the pairwise correlations ranged between -0.7 and 0.6.

12. Even thought the titles were foreign, listening to the actual recordings reveals that the music was often very similar to other recordings, at least for the recordings for which I was able to listen to. Unfortunately, not all recordings are available to me for listening, with the tunes using non-English titles missing at a much higher rate, so I cannot verify that the recordings I listened to were subject to a selection bias.

13. The strongest correlation between these three indicators is between the variable for Paul Whiteman and Louis Armstrong ($r = -.48$).

14. Note that, indeed, Kahl, Yates, and Liegel (2012) use variance in audience structure to capture variance in appeal in a way that also inform managerial decisions. The larger lesson is that sociological treatments of variance of the demand-side of emerging and young markets can be source of new insights.

REFERENCES

Babon, K. M. (2006). Composition, coherence, and attachment: The critical role of context in reception. *Poetics, 34*, 151–179.

Berrett, J. (2005). *Louis Armstrong and Paul Whiteman: Two kings of jazz.* New Haven, CT: Yale University Press.

Bielby, W. T., & Bielby, D. D. (1994). All hits are flukes: Institutionalized decision making and the rhetoric of network prime-time program development. *American Journal of Sociology*, *99*(5), 1287–1313.

Brunn, H. O. (1960). *The story of the original Dixieland jazz band*. Baton Rouge, LA: Louisiana State University Press.

Burnham, K. P., & Anderson, D. R. (2002). *Model selection and multimodel inference: A practical information – theoretic approach* (2nd ed.). New York, NY: Springer-Verlag.

Carroll, G. R. (1985). Concentration and specialization: Dynamics of niche width in populations of organizations. *American Journal of Sociology*, *90*(6), 1262–1283.

Carroll, G. R., & Hannan, M. T. (2000). *The demography of corporations and industries*. Princeton, NJ: Princeton University Press.

Carroll, G. R., Khessina, O. M., & McKendrick, D. G. (2010). The social lives of products: Analyzing product demography for management theory and practice. *Academy of Management Annals*, *4*, 157–203.

Carroll, G. R., & Swaminathan, A. (2000). Why the microbrewery movement? Organizational dynamics of resource partitioning in the U.S. brewing industry. *American Journal of Sociology*, *106*(3), 715–762.

Caves, R. (2002). *Creative industries: Contracts between art and commerce*. Cambridge: Harvard University Press.

Crawford, R., & Magee, J. (1992). *Jazz standards on record, 1900–1942: A core repertory (C B M R monographs)*. Center for Black Music Research Columbia College.

Dowd, T. J. (2003). Structural power and the construction of markets: The case of rhythm and blues. *Comparative Social Research*, *21*, 147–201.

Fitzgerald, F. S. (1922). *Tales of the jazz age*. New York, NY: Scribner's Songs.

Freeman, J., Carroll, G. R., & Hannan, M. T. (1983). The liability of newness: Age dependence in organizational death rates. *American Sociological Review*, *48*(5), 692–710.

Gioia, T. (1998). *The history of jazz*. New York and Oxford: Oxford University Press.

Griswold, W. (1987). The fabrication of meaning: Literary interpretation in the United States, Great Britain, and the West Indies. *American Journal of Sociology*, *92*(5), 1077–1117.

Gronow, P., & Saunio, I. (1999). *An international history of the recording industry*. London: Cassell.

Hannan, M. T., & Freeman, J. (1984). Structural inertia and organizational change. *American Sociological Review*, *49*(2), 149–164.

Hannan, M. T., Polos, L., & Carroll, G. R. (2007). *Logics of organization theory: Audiences, codes, and ecologies*. Princeton, NJ: Princeton University Press.

Hennion, A. (1983). The production of success: An anti-musicology of the pop song. *Popular Music*, *3*, 159–193.

Hirsch, P. M. (1972). Processing fads and fashions: An organization-set analysis of cultural industry systems. *American Journal of Sociology*, *77*(4), 639–659.

Hoetker, G., & Agarwal, R. (2007). Death hurts, but it isn't fatal: The post-exit diffusion of knowledge created by innovative companies. *Academy of Management Journal*, *50*(2), 446–467.

Johnson, V. (2007). What is organizational imprinting? Cultural entrepreneurship in the founding of the Paris opera. *American Journal of Sociology*, *113*(1), 97–127.

Kahl, S., Kim, Y. K., & Phillips, D. J. (2010). Identity sequences and the early adoption pattern of the Jazz Canon (1920–1929). *Research in the Sociology of Organizations*, *31*, 81–113.

Kahl, S. J., Liegel, G. J., & Yates, J. (2012). Audience structure and the failure of institutional entrepreneurship. In S. Kahl, B. S. Silverman & M.A. Cusumano (Eds.), *Advances in strategic management* (Vol. 29, pp. 275–313). Bingley, UK: Emerald Group.

Kenney, W. H. (1999). *Recorded music in American life: The phonograph and popular memory* (pp. 1890–1945). New York, NY: Oxford University Press.

Kernfeld, B., & Rye, H. (1994). Comprehensive discographies of Jazz, Blues, and Gospel (Part I). *Notes*, 2nd Series (Vol. 51, Issue 2, pp. 501–547).

Klepper, S. (2001). Employee startups in high-tech industries. *Industrial and Corporate Change*, *10*, 639–674.

Lampe, R., & Moser, P. (2012). Patent pools: Licensing strategies in the absence of regulation. In S. Kahl, B. S. Silverman & M. A. Cusumano (Eds.), *Advances in strategic management* (Vol. 29, pp. 69–86). Bingley, UK: Emerald Group.

Lopes, P. D. (2002). *The rise of a jazz art world*. Cambridge: Cambridge University Press.

Lord, T. (2005). The Jazz discography by Tom Lord, CD-ROM. Retrieved from http://www.lordisco.com

Lucas, R. E., Jr., & Rapping, L. A. (1972). Unemployment in the Great Depression: Is there a full explanation? *Journal of Political Economy*, *80*(1), 186–191.

Murmann, J. P. (2012). Marrying history and social science in strategy. In S. J. Kahl, B. S. Silverman & M.A. Cusumano (Eds.), *Advances in strategic management* (Vol. 29, pp. 89–115). Bingley, UK: Emerald Group.

Peretti, B. (1997). *Jazz in American culture*. Chicago: Ivan R. Dee

Perren, A. (2001). Sex, lies and marketing: Miramax and the development of the quality indie blockbuster. *Film Quarterly*, *55*(2), 30–39.

Peterson, R. A. (1997). *Creating country music*. Chicago, IL: University of Chicago Press.

Peterson, R. A., & Berger, D. G. (1975). Cycles in symbol production: The case of popular music. *American Sociological Review*, *40*(2), 158–173.

Phillips, D. J. (2011). Jazz and the disconnected: City structural disconnectedness and the emergence of the Jazz Canon (1897 to 1933). *American Journal of Sociology*, *117*(2), 420–483.

Phillips, D. J. (2012). *Shaping jazz: Cities, labels and the global emergence of a art form*. Book manuscript under contract with Princeton University Press, Princeton, NJ.

Phillips, D. J., & Kim, Y. K. (2009). Why pseudonyms? Deception as identity preservation among jazz record companies, 1920–1929. *Organization Science*, *20*(3), 481–499.

Phillips, D. J., & Owens, D. A. (2004). Incumbents, innovation, and competence: The emergence of recorded jazz, 1920 to 1929. *Poetics*, *32*, 281–295.

Roberts, P. W., & Sterling, A. D. (2011). Network progeny? Prefounding social ties and the success of new entrants. *Management Science: Articles in Advance*, *1*(1), 13. http://dx.doi.org/10.1287/mnsc.1110.1484

Rust, B. (1969). *Jazz records, 1897–1942* (Vols. 1 & 2). Essex, UK: Storyville.

Schuller, G. (1968). *Early jazz*. New York, NY: Oxford University Press.

Schuller, G. (1991). *The swing era: The development of jazz, 1930–1945*. New York, NY: Oxford University Press.

Scott, A. J. (2004). Hollywood and the World: The geography of motion-picture distribution and marketing. *Review of International Political Economy*, *11*(1), 33–61.

Selznick, P. (1957). *Leadership in administration*. New York, NY: Harper & Row.

Singh, J. V., Tucker, D. J., & House, R. J. (1986). Organizational legitimacy and the liability of newness. *Administrative Science Quarterly*, *31*(2), 171–193.

Sood, S., & Dreze, X. (2006). Brand extensions of experiential goods: Movie sequel evaluations. *Journal of Consumer Research, 33*(3), 352–360.

Sorensen, J., & Phillips, D. J. (2011). Competence and commitment: Employer size and entrepreneurial endurance. *Industrial and Corporate Change, 20*, 3.

Sorensen, J. B., & Fassiotto, M. (2011). Organizations as fonts of entrepreneurship. *Organization Science, 22*(5), 1322–1331.

Sorenson, O., & Waguespack, D. M. (2006). Social structure and exchange: Self-confirming dynamics in Hollywood. *Administrative Science Quarterly, 51*(4), 560–589.

Steindl, F. (2008). Economic recovery in the great depression, EH.Net encyclopedia. In R. Whaples (Ed.), March 16, 2008. Retrieved from http://eh.net/encyclopedia/article/Steindl.GD.Recovery. Accessed on January 9, 2012.

Stinchcombe, A. L. (1965). Social structure and organizations. In J. G. March (Ed.), *Handbook of organizations* (pp. 142–193). New York, NY: Rand McNally.

Stuart, T. E., Hoang, H., & Hybels, R. (1999). Interorganizational endorsements and the performance of entrepreneurial ventures. *Administrative Science Quarterly, 44*(2), 315–349.

Swaminathan, A. (2001). Resource-partitioning and the evolution of specialist organizations: The role of location and identity in the U.S. wine industry. *Academy of Management Journal, 44*, 1169–1185.

Tschmuck, P. (2006). *Creativity and innovation in the music industry.* Dordrecht, The Netherlands: Springer.

Whiteside, T. (1981). *The blockbuster complex: Conglomerates, show business, and book publishing.* Middletown, CT: Wesleyan University Press.